That Wonderful Mexican Band

A Memoir of The Great Depression

Thank you, Terry
Enjoy!
Thomas P. Ramirez

Thomas P. Ramirez

That Wonderful Mexican Band is a work of creative nonfiction. The events are portrayed to the best of the author's memory. Dialogue is not meant to represent word-for-word transcripts, but accurate representations of real conversations. While all of the stories in this book are true, some names and identifying details have been changed to protect the privacy of the people involved. Otherwise, the author endeavored to use factual information.

Copyright © 2017 Thomas P. Ramirez

All rights reserved. No part of this book may be reproduced, utilized, transmitted, or stored in an information retrieval system in any form or by any means, without prior written permission from the author.

Published by Thomas P. Ramirez, Fond du Lac, Wisconsin, USA

First printing, January 2017

ISBN 978-1540345745

Written by Thomas P. Ramirez

Cover art copyright © 2017 Thomas P. Ramirez

Cover design by Jason Ramirez (www.jasonramirez.rocks)

**This memoir is dedicated to Ma and Daddy,
who helped us survive the storm.**

With thanks to good friend David Williams
for assistance with proofing and publishing.

PREFACE

I began this memoir back in the late '60s, concentrating on what is now Chapter One. I sent this out as a short story myself—no agent at the time. Even though a major magazine sent an encouraging, personal rejection, I soon gave up on it. Life becoming busier and busier and other writing projects taking precedence, I buried the manuscript in a back drawer and almost completely forgot it.

In the late '80s, living on Social Security and investment income, I pretty much gave up writing. But then in July and August 2006, I happened to attend—just for the hell of it—a class called "Recreate Your Life" at the Fond du Lac Senior Center. The husband and wife instructors assigned appropriate topics and demanded a new article weekly.

And what do you know? "Look, Ma, I'm writing again."

The dialogue recorded in these pages is, of course, formulated. How could anyone remember exact conversations almost eighty years later? The substance, however, is painfully real; these things happened, and no mistake. All were neatly stored in another back drawer of my subconscious. Once jolted, the stories kept rolling out.

The task was arduous at times; other chapters almost wrote themselves. In the process, a grim era was re-explored, and a family history was revisited. And where I'd once considered my childhood prosaic (doesn't every nine-year-old squirt build and float a rickety boat?) I came to realize that my story was important in that my kid crazies took place during the Great Depression.

Here was family context, personal growing pains, and national history rolled into one.

How can the author explain the crazy liberties he was allowed, the blithe acceptance of trips away from home alone—camping, hitchhiking, tramping in the city's back alleys and nearby hobo jungles, peddling papers in near-blizzard conditions, running with juvenile hoods—all when he was nine, ten and thirteen years old? Such stunningly dangerous ventures would not sail today.

Another unexpected bonus: In writing this memoir, I rediscovered my childhood. I rediscovered my family. Most importantly, I rediscovered the depths of my love and appreciation for dreamer parents—total innocents—who valiantly fought their way through those tragic times. And emerged, their brood intact and thriving, with banners flying.

You will love Ma and Daddy. You will love Johnson Street. John Street will appall you. Just hang in. Things will improve. The Ramirez gang will prevail.

So here's to a wonderful, unique childhood and to a painful—yet rollicking—period in America's history. Here's to memory of a whacko time that will never come again.

Thomas P. Ramirez
Fond du Lac, Wisconsin
January 2017

CHAPTER ONE

That Wonderful Mexican Band

It was fifty-fifty with Daddy. Half music and half mechanics.

I remember the day it started. He'd spent Sunday afternoon at the movies and, upon returning, was all excited about a short he'd seen featuring the U.S. Marine Band.

"So wonderful it was," he said over supper, sighing and cramming his mouth with Ma's good Mexican cooking. "All different horns go at same time when conductor wave stick. Was hard believe. All notes, like directions…tell horn player, drum how to play."

He went on like this at great length, practically describing every member of the band. To his mind the band was like a machine. Ten, twenty, a hundred men tootling or pounding away. But what an end product! Such beautiful noise!

Like most Latinos, Daddy had music in his blood. Many Sunday afternoons he played his small collection of Spanish records, singing along in his soft, whispery voice when the spirit moved him. During those scratchy, shellac recitals, we kids either stopped breathing or cleared out of the house altogether.

Later he became involved in a secret project in the basement, working nights and weekends. What it turned out to be was a twelve-string Spanish guitar, a beautiful thing with cut glass jewels in the frets—diamonds and rubies in his proud eyes. Ma managed to temper her admiration; he'd dismantled her dime-store jewelry for its gaudy decorations.

Next, borrowing a guitar instruction book from the library, he taught himself to play it. How pleasant it was to hear him those lazy

Sunday afternoons, the guitar strumming, Daddy singing—sadly, it seemed—about *México Lindo*, his beautiful Mexico. He never lost his homesickness for the land of his childhood.

Anyway, none of us paid that much attention to the dreamy, faraway look in his eyes in the days following. *Wrong.* We should have been forewarned.

The next Wednesday, again at the supper table—his usual podium for earth-shaking pronouncements—it came out. A strained smile on his face, he talked faster than usual in his broken, comical accent. Comical today. But taken with deadly seriousness back then.

"I was think more about band," he said. "I was wonder why we can no have band of our own. *Our* band, a Mexican band. There are six: Tomás, Bernardo, David (pronounced dah-veed in *Español*), Ricardo, Mama, and me. When Martha is big, she play piano. I buy instruments second hand…pay installments."

At the time I was your original open slate. Anything Daddy said. *The Word.* If he bought a goat so the family could have fresh goat milk, would I help care for it? Yes.

Would I canvass the neighborhood for half-empty cans of paint nobody wanted and help paint the garage when I'd collected enough? Yes, yes!

And because I was the oldest son, my impressionable brothers—not overly gifted in the smarts department either—looked up to me; I became eternal Judas Sheep. Again and again they followed me to the slaughterhouse, bleating happily all the way.

What it was with Daddy was he was suffering from a terminal case of the American Dream. Ambition, hard work, and the red-white-and-blue. *Believe in it!* If you did, no doors would be closed to you and no aspirations would be insurmountable. Which, I suppose, was true in this case. Considering his impoverished, Mexican farm background, his childlike naiveté and limited education, he did achieve. He did make his rickety ideals come true. His life was—in finality—a true American success story.

One thing certain: He could have done a lot worse.

Bubblehead that I was, I hadn't the faintest idea of what I was letting myself—and my brothers—in for, what calamities would come of Daddy's starry-eyed plan.

THAT WONDERFUL MEXICAN BAND

"We can play at dances and earn money," I said, jumping aboard his dreamland express, already imagining our family band playing on Radio Station WLS, Chicago with Uncle Ezra and Lulu Belle and Scotty. Money always loomed large in my kid intellect.

Daddy was bowled over. He'd never dreamed we'd take it so well. "Will take much practice," he warned. "Lots nights boys want be outside play. But no, we have to practice. Mean lots and lots work."

We all chimed in: "What do we care? It'll be fun. We'll work hard, you'll see."

The Pied Piper was back in town.

The only skeptic was Ma, who sat with a dour expression, saying nothing. She knew Daddy was starting something he couldn't finish. Looking back, I wonder why in the world she ever consented. Perhaps she thought the band would be a wholesome, stabilizing influence on her live-wire sons.

We quickly saw that Ma held the deciding vote and began badgering her. "Can we, Ma?" we pleaded. "Can we have a band? C'mon, Ma. Please. We promise, honest...we'll practice every day."

"We'll see," she said, sidestepping. "Later...."

"Aw, Ma, we can earn lots of money," said David.

"We'll play in taverns Saturday nights," I added.

"No taverns!" Ma said, bristling.

"Oh, Ma..."

"That's enough! I said I'll think about it."

Right away we started fighting over who'd get which instrument. "I want the drums," I yelled. "No, I get the drums," Bernard piped in. "I get the sax." David said. "Anyway, I get the trumpet," Richard said resignedly. And Daddy, through all the racket: "*Cállate, cállate. Wait. We see. Mama must make up mind.*"

This all happened back in 1936. I was ten; Bernard, eight; David, seven; and Richard, six. Martha, the baby, was two. America (Fond du Lac, Wisconsin) was still in the depths of the Great Depression. Daddy worked at the tannery, earned twenty-five cents an hour, and was grateful to be working at all. Some days he got four, even five hours a day. Many days he got none.

Nevertheless. Daddy. His dreams.

We were all steamed up about the arrival of our instruments. But none appeared. Instead the mail man delivered a small bundle of Spanish music books for the various instruments. All the way from San Antonio, which was where Daddy bought his Mexican stuff, from *metates* to super-hot chili powder.

Along with the instruction books came the hated *Solfeo*, from which we would learn scales and timing. Each kid must master it before being issued an instrument. The *Solfeo* was the size of *Collier's* magazine, and even after all these years, I've never forgotten its detestable brown cover.

First came exercises with whole notes, which we must count—one-two-three-four—and sing. Next came half notes, until, finally, we progressed up through sixteenth notes.

We had a strict schedule and daily sat in a chair before a battered music stand, the hated *Solfeo* open upon it. Do-re, do-re, do-o-o. Mi, fa, mi, fa, mi-i-i-i. We sang the dreary progressions over and over in flat, listless voices. Daddy listened to our exercises nightly before supper. He would encourage us—sometimes gently, other times not so gently—always holding up vision of our shiny, new (secondhand) instruments, like a carrot before a stubborn donkey.

This began in late May, just before summer vacation. Imagine, kids our age spending sultry summer afternoons poring over the *Solfeo*, when by rights we should have been outside playing Tin Can Annie, swimming at Taylor Park, or fishing at Stinky Point.

But Daddy wouldn't budge. It was deadly business with him now. The dream had taken hold; it became more compelling with every passing day. He expected a lesson a day from each of us. Though we got a penny for each one we learned, that's not saying what we got if we didn't.

The clarinet was the first instrument to enter the house, this in mid-June. What excitement! We all took speculative toots on it, but it was finally awarded to Bernard because he had long, tapering fingers. Or so Daddy claimed. Those first times Daddy set him to playing were awful. Bernard couldn't stroke the reed right, and the resulting squawks curled our spines.

Nightly, those first weeks, after we went to bed, we could hear Daddy downstairs tooting on the clarinet. "How I can teach boys play if I no know myself?" he explained. He'd been told by Artie Laehn, of Laehn and Erickson Music Store on Forest Avenue, that the clarinet was basic to learning *any* instrument. Which drove him all the harder.

I was next, and I got the tuba instead of the dearly desired drums. Daddy awarded the drums to Richard and the trumpet to David, explaining that the tuba was the backbone of any band, and he needed someone older and more responsible—stronger was more like it—to handle the cumbersome beast. It was your standard snow job, and I was somewhat mollified, but down deep I never cuddled up to the tuba.

It was mid-July before all the instruments arrived. An example of how tough things were during the Depression: The weekly payments on all the instruments—tuba, clarinet, trumpet, bass and snare drums, alto and tenor saxes (which Ma and Daddy played)—came to one buck even. This with some music stands thrown in.

From a discarded sheet of hardboard I'd brought home from the alleys, Daddy rigged up a four-by-five blackboard—black after he painted it, that is. Using a straight-edge and an ice pick, he scored it with a series of staffs, and hung it over the kitchen sink. He'd write a string of notes on the board, and we'd attempt playing them. He helped each of us individually, for, by dint of sheer determination and hard work, he could now play each instrument himself. Later Daddy ordered a series of Ascher's band books, and we learned a gang of marches. He tried some simple arrangements of his own, but they were *muy* crude, and we quickly returned to Mr. Ascher.

The kitchen, the biggest room in the house, became our practice area. The sink was handy for draining spit valves. It was a real mess, and what with the blaring din of the instruments, the cramped quarters, the sticky summer heat, the room shortly became a torture chamber. The monotony of it all! Repeat and repeat and repeat.

Take the tuba for instance: It's oompah, oompah, over and over again. At least the trumpet and clarinet have a melody line. But the tuba? One-two, one-two, until, at times, I wanted to scream with boredom.

During those first few weeks, our practice sessions were exciting, and we knew a real sense of accomplishment as, night by night, we began bringing music out of chaos. But disillusionment set in fast. I recall the night that the first signs of rebellion surfaced.

It had been a dismal practice from the outset, and it seemed we'd been at it for hours. Everyone kept coming in wrong, hitting sour notes. It was Richard who triggered the explosion. He was continually off beat, and when daddy glanced up from his instrument—caught him watching a moth dive-bomb the lightbulb instead of his music—he promptly cracked him one on the head.

"Ouch!" Richard yipped, more surprised than hurt.

"Why you no watch music?" Daddy shouted.

"José," Ma cautioned. "Don't. He's so little, and it's late."

"I no care. He should watch music."

It was beastly hot in the kitchen. We were sweaty and tired, and the constrained sitting had made us all jumpy. My legs would dance themselves out of the room if I didn't escape this inferno soon. Poor Richard.

And just like that I lost it. "You call this music?" I snapped, Mr. Big Stuff all of a sudden.

"Yes. I call this music," Daddy said. "What you call it?"

"I call it noise." I was sorry the moment the words popped out. The hurt in Daddy's eyes was terrible to see. The band meant everything to him now, and to have his oldest son taunt him like this was a bitter blow. He turned away briefly, dropping his eyes, his mouth slack. My brothers stopped breathing, expecting I'd get a hand upside the head any second now. But Daddy did nothing.

"We play," he said, his voice husky. "We play until it sound like music." He sat, took up his sax. "From beginning. Everybody ready. Now, one-two…"

He kept us practicing until well after ten o'clock. It was pure misery. Richard, who was littlest, kept falling asleep, and Daddy was on him again and again. Finally Ma gathered courage enough to intercede.

"*Ya basta, José*," she said. "The boys are all worn out. It's too warm. It's way past their bedtime."

"All right," he said with a tired, exasperated sigh. "I just no know why they act like this. They think I no tired too?"

"*Si, José*," Ma said. "Everybody's tired. Let them go to bed now."

"All right, I s'pose." Then haltingly, pain in his voice: "Why? Why they no comporate?" He turned on us, his eyes fierce. "We gone to have band," he said, his words blurred with emotion. "Whether you boys like or not, *comprende*? We gone to have band. Now put instruments away, go to bed."

Clean slate the next day. Overnight we'd put the unpleasantness aside. Daddy's enthusiasms shot up accordingly; nobody in our family ever carried a grudge for long. We had more ups and downs, of course, but that angry session had cleared the air, and Daddy was careful about overlong practices after that.

So we went into the first days of August, the band improving remarkably now, until at night, the screen door open, our kid friends would camp on the front steps to listen. They got a bit rowdy at times, whistling and clapping after each number. Daddy would smile sheepishly, proud, almost as if he had a real audience. Some nights there might have been a half-dozen people standing on the sidewalk as well, taking it all in.

The Depression. Free entertainment.

It wasn't bad enough that Daddy got the family into the band business, but now he foolishly stirred up trouble in other quarters as well. Several times during our practices, some of his Mexican cronies and co-workers at the tannery—Señor Gonzalez, Señor Flores, Señor Ruiz—had visited, watching and listening carefully. Afterward they gathered in the living room, talking in excited Spanish far into the night. Coming downstairs for a drink of water one of those times, I found Ma in the kitchen making more coffee. She sent a glum smile and shook her head sadly.

The vulture of doom, the natural end to all Daddy's wild fancies, came home to roost two weeks later.

On this particular Saturday afternoon, he dressed up and mysteriously hurried off, an excited, glazed light in his eyes. An hour or so later, a taxicab pulled up before the house, and Daddy emerged, accompanied by a fat, little toad of a man who wore a rumpled, gray suit. Daddy hopped around like he was hatching eggs, taking the man's bags, paying the cabby.

A taxi, we all marveled. Such extravagance!

The man gave our trash-can neighborhood a harsh, appraising look. I couldn't help but notice the lingering look he bestowed upon the Tip-Top Tap, located across the street. He allowed Daddy to help him up the steps. We stood wide-eyed, mouths agape. Ma came from the kitchen, wiping her hands on her apron.

"*Muchachos*," Daddy said expansively, "I want you meet you new maestro, Señor Esteban. He really teach music to my boys."

Señor Esteban gave us the crooked, happy grin and the cheerful growl we'd all come to know so well in the months ahead. "Hi, kids," he said. "Is everybody happy?"

Then he extended a fat, liver-spotted paw to each of us. We all made awkward, wondering hellos, quickly warming to the clownish man. When Daddy took him upstairs to show him his quarters, I suddenly understood why I'd lost my room and was now bunking in with Bernard, David, and Richard.

Once the dust settled and the seventy-year-old man was comfortably established, Ma explained everything. Daddy had talked ten of his Mexican friends into starting a band, the nucleus of what would one day be an *important* Spanish orchestra. They'd hired Señor Esteban to direct them; from this income he'd supposedly pay Ma room and board.

"Señor Esteban is truly a great maestro," Ma told us. "He once directed the Los Angeles Civic Band."

We were awed upon seeing the large, framed photograph on his wall—the band, eighty strong, in full regalia. Down in front, in a white shako and a natty uniform stood *Directo*r Esteban. Early on, dim bulbs that we were, we couldn't quite grasp the reason for his present low estate. Why had he come to live in our ragbag house and teach music to unlettered laborers? Where had Daddy found him in the first place?

Soon we came to witness humorous, sometimes frightening incidents that explained his fall from grace. Esteban was—in plainest words—nothing more than a falling-down drunk.

The "New Spanish Orchestra" was launched with a flourish, and that first night, when the musicians gathered at our house, newly rented instruments in hand, we boys were tremendously excited. A real band in our kitchen and living room!

If Señor Esteban was pained by that first dissonant rehearsal, he didn't let on. Instead a happy, proud smile stretching his face, he directed with gusto. Perhaps he hoped for a second chance, a fresh start in a new world.

Just what we needed: another dreamer.

It was a picnic for us. On Tuesdays and Thursdays, when the orchestra met, we skipped our practices. Though Daddy ordered us to sit around the edges—and absorb the musical experience by some sort of osmosis. Mostly we sneaked outside to play after the first ten minutes. Some nights the band practiced until midnight. The crowds out front were larger now. Rumblings arose among those neighbors losing sleep, but Daddy remained blissfully oblivious. There was talk of renting a hall so the band could grow.

The rehearsals were to be held on a rotating basis, with members meeting in different homes. But here again Daddy's enthusiasms outran good sense, and he volunteered our house for *every* session. Plenty of wives all over the west side must have breathed long, grateful sighs. Ma, long-suffering saint, forced a smile, bore the burden.

Señor Esteban was supposed to instruct us boys during the day, but he never did more than listen to us sing the damnable *Solfeo* exercises. By this time he'd shown his true colors and spent most of his afternoons in Jake Solon's tavern across the street. He did write a few arrangements for our band, Mexican classics we loved to play, including *La Golondrina, La Paloma Blanca, Las Quatros Milpas, Besos y Cerezas*, and *Adios, mi Chaparrita*. These arrangements he charged for, so the money he paid for board went straight back into his pocket. And from there across the street.

Discontent soon arose among the members of the New Spanish Orchestra. Many nights Señor Esteban appeared at rehearsals too loaded to conduct. Other times he didn't show up at all. After a few such incidents, it became our job to watch him on practice days and to warn Ma when he started across the road. It was her job to coax him home. Even so, keeping a bottle stashed in his room, he rapidly went downhill.

The corker came the day he broke his leg. It was another of those quiet Sunday afternoons, with us boys sprawled on the front porch going through the funnies for the tenth time. We looked up to see him coming down the street, singing, weaving dangerously. Two Greek kids trailed him, mocking and pulling at his jacket. "*Amapola, lindísima Amapola,*" he sang.

"C'mon," said Bernard, always spoiling for a fight. "Let's get those skunks." We charged off the steps like four angry hornets. When the kids saw us coming, they tore off in twenty different directions. We triumphantly convoyed our blotto maestro home.

He was halfway up the steps when he lost his balance and fell backward, one leg twisting at sickening angle beneath him. Terrified, we circled him, tried to get him up. Señor Esteban let fly a string of Mexican obscenities, and we knew it was serious. Then, just as quickly, he began laughing—a harsh, high-pitched cackle—and he rolled around on the sidewalk, his left leg flopping. "*Amapola...*" he continued, "*...lindísima Amapola...*"

We couldn't help ourselves; we broke into giggles. That's when Ma came out. "Is everybody happy?" he croaked.

"José!" she screamed, her face turning white. "*Ven aquí!*"

Together they managed to pull him to one side, into the shade. Ma then raced next door to Steve's Bakery (open Sundays, of course) to call an ambulance.

The leg was broken in two places, and for the next two months, Señor Esteban gloried in his invalid role. Of course there was no money coming in, and again Daddy's brave schemes had backfired. By the time Señor Esteban was up and around again, all the orchestra members had headed for the high country. We were stuck.

Señor Esteban was a great guy, and we kids liked him a lot. It was hard to stay angry when he was around. Just the same, he became a terrible burden, and his drinking multiplied our family problems tenfold. A check arrived monthly from Los Angeles, a pension of some sort, but that went across the bar; Ma never saw a cent of it.

He blandly ignored Ma's broad hints about leaving now that the orchestra had disbanded. She told Daddy to give him the boot, but Daddy didn't have the heart to do it. Señor Esteban became a permanent fixture at 204 W. Johnson Street.

It was September now, and school had resumed. Practicing

became a double torment. The orchestra's failure had made Daddy even more determined that *our* band would succeed. He even allowed us a debut—non-remunerative of course. It was a Mexican feast day celebration, *Nuestra Señor de los Dolores*, held at a Mexican home on West Division Street. We played well enough, I suppose, and the people smilingly applauded every number. In between, one of the men slipped us beer when Daddy wasn't looking—their idea of a joke. By evening's end we were all woozy. Richard threw up behind the house.

I remember admiring a lovely Mexican girl—she couldn't have been more than sixteen—throughout the evening. I learned later she'd been shipped in from Mexico to be married to an old man of sixty. The times.

Our second public appearance was at the Retlaw Theater, where we competed in an intermission amateur hour. It was a gimmick the Thorpe brothers dreamed up in hopes of hyping attendance. Daddy had scrounged up some straw hats, and in attempt to capture true *campesino* flavor, Ma had sewn up some blue-checked shirts for each of us. It was Martha's first appearance; Daddy let her play the triangle.

The audience tittered when we trooped onto the stage from behind the screen, all of us desperately wishing we were somewhere else at that moment.

"Remember, all smile," Daddy urged as we started out.

"And now, folks," the emcee brayed, "here's Joe Ra...meer ...eez. Is that pronunciation correct, sir?" More laughter. Daddy nodded dumbly. They could have called him Joe Puppybreath just then; he wouldn't have cared. "Joe's brought his family band here to entertain us tonight. What's it gonna be, Joe?"

"Polka," Daddy stammered, his face frozen, quaking in his too-large, checked shirt, his straw hat sitting at a ridiculous angle on his head. "*Beer...Barrel...Polka.*"

"*The Beer Barrel Polka*, folks. Let 'er rip, Joe!"

It seemed the blasted number would never end. Daddy had us repeat it three times. The novelty of a family band got old in a big hurry; the audience got restless. Applause was light, despite Señor Esteban, our one-man claque, who'd scored a seat right down in front.

But no, we weren't done just yet. Trading on Martha's two-year-old cutes, Daddy announced that she would sing a solo, *Playmate*. We played softly in the background. She got a bigger hand than we did. Martha was ecstatic and ran back and forth across the stage three times. She'd never received so much attention before.

Later, the six acts reappeared onstage, and the audience applauded for its favorite performer. We won second prize—three dollars—thanks only to Señor Esteban's clamor. We lost the five-dollar first prize to a big-bosomed female vocalist who, besides murdering *The Isle of Capri*, was as scantily dressed as the law allowed. She knew how to gauge public taste; we didn't.

Contestants were invited to stay for the show afterwards. We set our instruments in the aisle, and people kept stumbling over them in the dark. "You were robbed," Señor Esteban consoled. "That girl was awful, no voice at all. It wasn't fair."

Daddy only nodded gloomily and tried watching the movie, a Barbara Stanwyck tear-jerker. We all felt blue, like we'd failed Daddy. Hadn't we smiled hard enough? But it wasn't us who'd failed him—it was his dream. The show was lousy. Martha fell asleep in Ma's arms. I felt like bawling.

That night the first crack appeared in Daddy's invincible confidence.

We went public once more, this fiasco taking place at the tannery Christmas party. Gratis again. *Jingle Bells* and *Silent Night*. Can you imagine the tuba part on *Silent Night*? It was a nothing performance, applause was merely polite, and once again we felt defeated, our dreams more out of reach than ever.

Then another performance, this time semi-public—the night the teachers came to supper.

As illustration of the sappy dream world we kids lived in back then: Here we were, wondering where our next nickel was coming from, living in this tumbledown shack next to the railroad tracks, surrounded by threadbare, second-hand furniture, located in one of the roughest parts of town. And yet we were oblivious to reality, happy, proud of ourselves, hopes high, contented with our hand-me-down existence.

So one can only imagine Ma's feelings the afternoon I triumphantly announced that I'd just invited Miss Stanford, my fifth-grade teacher at Washington School, and Miss Fahey, the principal, to a Mexican supper on the upcoming Monday.

"Good Lord, no," she wailed. "In this house? What in heaven's name will I serve them? Why did you do such a foolish thing without asking me?"

But, steadfast to the last, not even toying with idea of coming up with an alibi so she could cancel out—we'd moved to China or some such—she worked herself sick that week, cleaning and scrubbing, doing everything in her power to make our drab house presentable to visiting royalty. The thought of setting fire to the place surely must have crossed her mind.

When Daddy heard about it, he beamed. "Is good," he said. "Parent and teacher should get know each other. What better way than eat together...good Mexican food."

So the inevitable day arrived, and then the hour, and then—

The teachers.

But the dreaded, dull, forced conversation never materialized, for Daddy, broken English and all, charmed the gold right out of their teeth. Ma had fixed Spanish rice, *mole*, *tortillas*, and a cabbage-apple salad. And standing by, in case our guests didn't like Mexican: hamburger patties.

"I was tell my boys is good for parents to know teachers," Daddy said, a shy smile on his face. "You try *tortilla*?"

Miss Stanford and Miss Fahey each took one, and following Daddy's lead, graciously tore off a piece, tried forming a scoop to pick up their rice and *mole*, just as Daddy did. Bernard and I fought back giggles at their clumsiness.

"Please," Ma said, embarrassed for them, "use your fork."

"Oh, no," Miss Stanford said. "I wouldn't think of it. I want to try everything...savor this whole experience." She continued her grim struggle. We loved her for it.

While Ma cleared the table (we ate in the kitchen, of course), we boys entertained our company in the living room, showing them our model planes and stamp and rock collections. Richard had some bugs in bottles he *had* to drag in. Later, we moved back into the kitchen, assembled our instruments, and presented a half-hour performance of Ramirez oldies and not-so-goodies.

"Wonderful," Miss Fahey said afterwards, applauding vigorously, "I had no idea your family was so talented, Mr. Ramirez."

"Why, Tom," Miss Stanford added, "you never told me you could play an instrument, a tuba no less. Wonderful."

We were pleased with the compliments, also a bit puffed up because we'd played so well. Our recital had proved to be a bona fide smash.

Then Señor Esteban walked in.

Ma had taken special pains to arrange a supper invitation for him with another Mexican family, urging them to keep him as late as possible. Somehow he must have sensed that he was being excluded and had returned too early—and sloppy drunk.

"Is everybody happy?" he called in his raspy voice, his smile more askew than ever. He leaned against the wall to steady himself, sending our guests a sly leer. "Hel...hello...I am En...rique Esteban," he announced importantly.

Enrique? It was a first for us.

Ma sent Daddy an angry glance, and he rose quickly. Taking Señor Esteban in tow, he tried leading him past the teachers, upstairs to his room. "*Vente*," he said, pulling his arm roughly. Our maestro almost fell on his face when Daddy jerked the wall away from him.

"No," he said indignantly. "I want...stay and talk with...nice ladies." He sent them a roguish smile. "*Por favor, José?*"

Daddy was upstairs with him for a long time. We heard occasional angry outbursts, intermixed with pleading, carry down through the ceiling heat vent. Ma tried valiantly to make conversation, but it was useless; everything came out leaden. Though the teachers were gracious, pretending they hadn't seen anything amiss, it was obvious that theirs was a sheltered existence. They were definitely put off. Shortly they thanked Ma for the splendid meal, then excused themselves. They were gone by the time Daddy came down.

Ma was slumped at the kitchen table, her head cradled in her arms, sobbing brokenly. We all huddled around like frightened chicks, trying to comfort her. But it was no good. All we did was make ourselves feel worse.

We had a real scorcher of an Indian Summer that year, and even in late October, we were still able to practice with the doors and windows open. Daddy's back was up, and in blind stubbornness he insisted that we practice three nights a week, not two. Señor Esteban sat in some of those nights, directing (from a chair), walking us through new arrangements he'd prepared.

One of Daddy's proudest moments was the night that David and I picked out the notes of *Bicycle Built For Two*, he on his trumpet and I on the tuba. It was a simple arrangement we'd worked up ourselves.

It was on a Tuesday night when yet another crisis homed in on us. We were in process of fine-tuning *Sobre las Olas* (Over the Waves) when, suddenly, a large splintering crash cut through our playing and startled the livers out of us. We sat bolt upright, our instruments frozen in our hands. Shards of glass sprayed the living room. We looked up in time to see a rock bounce off Daddy's blackboard and fall into the sink, where it rolled with a brittle, grainy sound, then stopped dead.

Instantly Bernard was up. Eternal avenging angel, he called, "Let's go get 'em!"

Instruments clattered down. Richard ran with his drumsticks still in his hands.

"You boys stay right here," Ma ordered. "Don't go out. Do you hear me?"

Yes, we heard. But we ignored her just the same.

"There they go," Bernard yelled, already five yards ahead of us. "Down by Valley Coal! They're heading for the marsh!"

Big mistake. If there was anyplace on earth we knew, day or night, it was that marsh. We found the little sneaks in a gully along the railroad tracks, just this side of the bridge. It was Augie and Johnny Landgraf, two habitual troublemakers who lived two blocks south on Brooke Street. Instantly we piled on, punching right and left, Richard swatting with his drumsticks every opening he got.

They never had a chance; it was like a brick truck had tipped over on them.

"Why'd you throw that rock through our window?" Bernard snarled, driving a hard right to Augie's gut.

"We didn't throw no rocks," Augie blubbered, coming apart real fast.

Whammo! Pow! Two more shots. "Why'd you break our window?" David this time.

"We didn't, we didn't," Johnny wailed. "We don't know nothing about your damned window."

"You're lying," Bernard said, slamming him back onto the ground. "Tell the truth. If you know how." He punched him in the face again.

"All right, all right," Augie said, "We'll tell. Only don't hit us no more…" He struggled to stop his sobbing. "It was Old Man Callas. He put us up to it. He said he was tired of all the noise. He gave us a quarter to do it."

"We were just trying to earn some money," Johnny added lamely.

Bernard gave him another jolt to the face. "Next time earn it honest."

We twisted their arms behind them and marched them back down the street. Daddy and Ma were waiting on the steps when we reached the house, Señor Esteban silhouetted in the doorway. "Gus Callas put 'em up to it," I said, twisting Johnny's arm higher on his back, making him yip. "Go ahead, dummy, tell my Dad."

"He gave us a quarter to do it," Johnny blubbered, truly shaken. These Mexicans, his expression read. No telling what they might do next. They use knives, they—

In the dim light, we saw Daddy's face harden, his eyes glowing strangely. "Let them go," he said, a pained edge to his voice.

"But, Daddy, aren't you going to…?" I started.

"I say, let them go!" We released the Landgrafs, and they darted into the night. Daddy turned, and stalked back into the house.

"José?" Ma asked fearfully. "What are you going to do?"

He went to the sink, hefted the rock, and balanced it in his hand.

"José, no," Ma said as he started out of the house, a dark, determined fire in his eyes. "You'll only make more trouble…" But when he ignored her and just kept walking, she dropped her arms and backed away.

Gus Callas lived directly across the street, just west of the Tip-Top Tap. Even in the gloom, we saw curtains being drawn aside in an upstairs window. I could hardly breathe as I watched Daddy take a position before the house—short and squat against the light, testing his range—just before he wound up and let the rock fly.

There was a delicious, splintery crash, and one of the main windows shattered. Old man Callas came charging out like his drawers were on fire. Daddy stood waiting.

Callas was in his late fifties, and as best as I recall, he had perhaps four inches on Daddy and outweighed him by at least twenty pounds. He had hastily thrown on a pair of trousers; otherwise, he was bare-chested and barefoot. "You goddamn, dirty Mexican," he bellowed, storming down the walk. "What d'ya mean, breaking my window?"

"Watch you language," Daddy said levelly. "My boys listen. No need filthy talk. We catch Landgraf boys. They say you pay them throw stone. Tell me why."

"I don't know nothing about no stone. If they told you that, they're lying. I'm gonna call the police, tell 'em what you just did. That window's gonna cost you five bucks, mister."

"Go ahead," Daddy said, never backing down an inch. "Call police. We know where boys live. We see who start this thing. We see who pay for window."

Callas knew Daddy had him cold. He was silent for a moment, digesting things. "Oh, you…you…Mexicans!" he sputtered in tongue-tied exasperation, jittering in place. "Always making so much damned noise, keeping folks awake. I…." He caught himself, changed his tune. The lie again: "I didn't do no such thing, I didn't pay no kids to break your damn window." But the steam was gone; he'd hung himself, and he knew it.

He resorted to pure bluff. "I'm…I'm gonna knock your block off."

Daddy actually took two steps toward him, assumed a clumsy boxer's stance. "Try," he urged. "Come…try."

My brothers and I were hopping around almost as bad as Callas. This was high drama, real-life reenactment of the movies and nightly radio shows we ate up. "C'mon, try!" we mocked in unison. "See what you get!"

"*Cállate!*" Daddy ordered. Shut up. Instant silence.

Still Callas stalled, unable to gather his guts for that first swing. All bluster, nothing more. "I'll get you for this, mister," he kept repeating. "I'll get you. Just wait. You ain't heard the last of this."

"Come get me now," Daddy said, his voice even softer and deceivingly gentle. "Right now. I wait for you."

"You rotten Mexicans," Callas growled, turning away, "you're all alike. There's no dealing with you." He turned, started back toward his house.

"You ever send boys break window again," Daddy called after him, "I come break you neck." He turned, walked slowly back across the street, where Señor Esteban stood on the porch, laughing and hooting excitedly.

Talk about proud moments. We could have carried Daddy home on our shoulders. We kids didn't get to sleep until well after midnight; we kept rerunning the confrontation over and over with each other. Ma yelled and threatened to send Daddy up to shut us up.

But that was the real beginning of the end. The next night we practiced with one ear cocked. There was no rock. The night following, however, a brick hurtled through the front door screen and piled into the living room wall. Once more we charged out again, but there was no trace of anyone.

We looked toward Gus Callas' house. The windows were dark; nobody was home. There was no one to confront this time. Sullenly, we filed back inside.

"I told you, José," Ma said ruefully. "You were starting something you couldn't finish." Not a peep from him.

Daddy was truly driven now. Bullheaded was more like it. The following night we practiced again, the doors wide open. Around nine o'clock another rock came flying in, through the kitchen window this time, barely missing Ma where she sat close to the sink. We all jumped up, enraged, broke for the door.

"No!" Daddy howled at the top of his lungs, his voice a strange mixture of choking anger, despair, and hurt. His face twisted into an anguished mask. "No chase tonight." He blinked rapidly. Then, his tone weary, resigned: "Put instruments away. No more practice tonight. Get ready for bed."

And that was the end of Daddy's fanciful dream, the end of the wonderful Mexican band. The rocks had awakened Daddy, made him see what common sense could not. He finally realized that we were bumbling amateurs, being taught by another amateur. We'd never be more than that.

Afterwards things just generally petered out. We didn't practice for a week. When we did, Daddy's heart wasn't really in it; he had a sad, faraway look in his eyes. We didn't argue. Underneath we were glad to be off the hook. Let sleeping dogs lie and all that. Then it was a month, and we hadn't practiced. Finally came the night when, his voice wistful, Daddy said, "What you say get instruments out tonight? See how we sound?"

We grumblingly uncased our instruments, tootled a few warm up scales, played a few of our old favorites. But time had taken its toll, and without the frequent practices, we were rusty, very rusty. The music was pathetic. No timing, no pitch, no spark. Daddy forced a smile, but we could see that even he thought we were terrible. The last of his lingering hopes were now put to rest.

We never played together again.

We later discovered that Gus Callas wasn't responsible for the second and third rocks. Some neighborhood toughs, probably goaded on by the Landgraf tribe, had taken a turn. A boyish lark—the classic double dare. Unknowingly, they'd achieved an even deadlier result.

When it was time for junior high school, for some dumb reason or other, I actually joined the band. When David got to junior high, he did also. The director, Mr. Joe Schmitz, greeted me—and later David—with open arms. A modern-day miracle. An accomplished tuba player. There *was* a patron saint of band leaders after all.

David stayed in the band through junior and senior high school and acquitted himself well. Mr. Freeman, the high school director, even wanted to sponsor him for a college scholarship, but his blue-collar mindset served to nix the offer. However, David did become involved with a small polka band for a time.

As for me, I gave up after my first year, Mr. Schmitz's anguished pleadings to the contrary. Barely beginning to notice the fair sex, I took dim view of the not-so-dashing figure I cut walking to school (or riding my bike, for God's sake), with my tuba over my shoulder.

I remember the humiliation of slipping on the ice once while thus encumbered and falling on my prat as I rolled to protect my horn. The mishap drew shrieking laughter from a gaggle of girls clustered at the school entrance. As of that moment, a glittering tuba-virtuoso career went south.

As for Richard, taking one look at the hotshots competing for drum positions, he promptly passed. Bernard, eternal rebel, took a bye also. To his eyes the band kids were all "picky-pants"—his term for uppity, rich east-siders who actually wore wool trousers and suit-jackets to school. Which was a far cry from the well-worn jeans that became his standard "hell-no" statement. A lad ahead of his time. If creampuffs like that were in the band, he wanted no part of it. A crying shame because he played a mean clarinet.

Later I rigged myself up in a silly clown costume and marched in the Halloween parade. Prizes were awarded for best costumes, the city fathers hoping to forestall vandalism (remember soaping windows?) on that haunted night. As afterthought I took my tuba along, and booped it the length of Main Street to draw attention to my getup.

It was afterward, wandering home—no prize—that I was stopped by a couple drunks outside of Fond du Lac's infamous Schmitz Bar. "Play us a tune, kid," one said, his boozy breath making my eyes water, "and I'll give you a quarter."

I gladly gave them a free translation of my old standby, *Beer Barrel Polka*. Then they wanted an encore. And another. All in all I cleared seventy-five cents. That was the sum of any hard money I ever earned with my superb musical talent.

And Señor Esteban? Just after Christmas he simply disappeared. One morning we awoke to find he'd packed during the night, made his bed, and simply cut out. Months later we received a post card—no return address—from Florida of all places. Scrawled broadly across the back were these words: "Is everybody happy?"

We never heard from him again.

Whenever I have cause to think back, I ponder the way Señor Esteban so mysteriously entered our lives and just as mysteriously departed. Eternal question bothers: What became of him in Florida—or wherever he landed after that?

And at the very last, I can't help but wonder if, now and then, remembrance of the Ramirezes crossed his mind. In all of his ramblings, did he ever again come across the likes of our wonderful Mexican band?

CHAPTER TWO

Portrait of My Father

I have a photograph of my father taken when he'd been in the United States two short years. The shot is battered, faded, and stained, but Daddy's sad image still shines through. In the photo—frozen in a stilted pose, one hand balanced on a rickety wire chair—he wears a suit and hat and stares directly into the camera, his expression clearly deer-in-the-headlights.

The suit, shirt, hat, and tie might have been borrowed from a friend, but more than likely it was rented from the opportunistic Arkansas photographer himself. No matter, for the pose is universal, the stereotype of every immigrant photo ever taken.

The too-small hat—abbreviated stovepipe—perches precariously on the top of Daddy's head. The suit-jacket fits like a bag, the lapels curled, the white handkerchief drooping. There is a stain near the top button, and only the fingertips of his left hand protrude from the overlong sleeve. The trousers are what you would describe today as pipe-stem. The cuffs stop a full eight inches from the floor, exposing scuffed and wrinkled high-button shoes whose color appears to be a vile yellowish-brown. The shirt collar is floppy and curled, and the necktie resembles a knotted sock.

His shoulders are sloped slightly, as if momentarily expecting a blow from behind. Most prominent is the whipped-dog look in his eyes, mixture of naiveté and bewilderment. Even more touching: the sense of utter loneliness that pervades that smooth, brown, boyish face.

The overdone backdrop—a Moorish courtyard—only serves to

emphasize the reek of exploitation hanging about the photograph. The floor is unswept, littered with refuse. Definitely depressing. I can only wish that Daddy was still with us so I could ask, "How much did they rip you off for this monstrosity, *Padrecito*?"

Daddy came to the U.S. in 1915. Riding a train from Irapuato—the state of Guanajuato, located in central Mexico—for four days, with another train, crawling with government troops, sometimes running interference. He arrived in America on the eve of his sixteenth birthday. A bloody revolution in progress at the time—Carranza and Pancho Villa killing and pillaging in the name of liberty and tinhorn fame—his peasant father had scraped together enough money to ship his only son out of the country before he could be conscripted into that drunken, cutthroat rabble and, inevitably, killed.

It was the first train my father had ever seen. It was his first time away from home. Small wonder that so much loneliness pervades that awful photograph.

Entering at Laredo, Texas with an older uncle, he paid the guard a quarter and then crossed the Rio Grande on a narrow, rickety bridge. Old-time immigration—honest to God, that's how it happened back then.

Ahora soy Americano, he must have thought. Today I am an American.

War fever was virulent in the U.S. at the time, and laborers were scarce. So headhunters waited across the border to recruit ignorant greenhorns for jobs as field hands, mine workers, domestics, and railroad slaveys. A railroad front man fast-talked the two into signing on with the Missouri, Kansas and Texas Line at two dollars a day.

They soon learned they'd been conned. Assigned to a railroad crew laying a hundred miles of new track, they put in ten-hour days, lived in stifling boxcars on the job site, and ate rotten food for which they paid a dollar a day.

Guards patrolled at night to keep them from running off; they were roused at dawn by pistol-packing, cursing bosses who used fists and clubs to reinforce their commands. Daddy's uncle took sick and was allowed to return to Mexico. A newfound *compadre* escaped one night without him.

Four months later it was Daddy's turn. He and three others, having saved and planned carefully, jumped aboard a slow-moving passenger train that ran through the work site and hung on for dear life as it gained speed. They got off at the next town and hid in the woods for two days, while railroad goons beat the bushes looking for them. In Fort Worth they signed on with yet another railroad, hoping that here things would be different. But no, they'd merely exchanged one bully-boy section chief for another.

Various railroad jobs took him to Nebraska, Iowa, and Illinois, where his crew laid heavy rail for the Rock Island Line. In 1918, desperately homesick, having somehow saved three-hundred-dollars, he decided to return to his beloved Mexico. But when he fished his wallet from a clever hiding place inside his trousers, he found that his newfound friends had somehow managed to steal everything but sixty-dollars. *Adios a México.*

Next came pipelining in Oklahoma, where sympathetic bosses hid the pawky kid from army recruiters. Armistice Day found him digging gas pipeline trenches in Tulsa, Oklahoma. During the next two years, he worked deep in the shafts of various Oklahoma coal mines.

At Hickory Mines, on May 9, 1919, a twelve-pound can of black powder accidentally exploded. Daddy carried hideous scars on his back, neck, shoulders, and the backs of his arms to his grave. No such thing as worker's compensation back then, he depended on the kindness of a Mexican family who took him in and nursed him through a six-month recovery.

Then, despite the fact that the muscles in his left arm had tightened so he couldn't completely extend it, he returned to the shafts. However, oil and gas beginning to come into their own, many coal mines were closing. With work scarce, bloody union wars inevitably sprang up. Daddy leap-frogged from mine to mine all over Oklahoma for the next year or so, hard put to support the woman he'd married in January 1921. She was thirteen; he was twenty-one.

It was your typical boarding-house romance. She was white, Irish, the landlady's daughter, and Daddy, shy, knowing little English—yet seeming so worldly in her eyes—charmed her by bringing her cheese and oranges. The truth, I swear.

Eventually, realizing they had no future in the coal mines, my parents came north. They worked sugar beets in Minnesota for a time. The work grueling, the pay low, Daddy again returned to railroading, finding work with the Chicago & Northwestern. This move brought them to Fond du Lac, Wisconsin, where, in February 1926, I was born. My mother was eighteen.

Other Mexicans were finding good paying jobs at Fred Reuping Leather Company, and in due course Daddy joined them. However, the lime and acids used to clean the hides dissolved his fingernails, and the fumes peeled the skin off his shoulders, arms, and face. Time to move.

Once more it was the railroad, this time the Soo Line, where he worked as a mechanic's assistant in the roundhouse. Because the job was mainly standby, Daddy spent fifty percent of his time sleeping in convenient corners. As a result he became so fat—a definite first—that he couldn't even tie his own shoes; Ma had to do it for him.

The wages poor, it was back to the tannery, where this time, he managed to cope with the toxic conditions. His job: In the Beam House, hooking hides out of vats where they steeped in a salt-acid solution. Once out of this bath, they were sprayed with water, then thrown over tall wooden horses—a back-breaking job for a man as small as Daddy, who stood only five-three and weighed one-hundred-forty pounds most of his working life.

In time his arms became incredibly strong and muscular, his nails—with which he gripped the fifty-, sixty-pound hides—curved halfway over his fingertips and came to resemble deformed claws. His hands were perpetually pink and wrinkled from being immersed in liquids eight hours a day, and the sour tannery smell always clung faintly to his skin, even though he showered daily at the plant before heading home.

For a time, in the late 1920s, it seemed he and Ma were finally cozying up to the good life. At least they were nearing the head of the line. A few more years of steady work, and who knows? They could clean up all their bills.

We were constantly moving, each new house a tad nicer than the last. Granted, there were always train whistles in the background, and the house shook whenever the freights rolled past, but so what? The American Dream, right? We were chasing it, pennants flying.

The crash of 1929 and the ensuing Depression spiked that hopeful momentum. Where Daddy had been earning $25 a week, he now found his hours drastically reduced. Workers were being laid off in droves. Within six months he was lucky to draw a $12 paycheck every *two* weeks. By 1931 he lost out entirely.

Somewhere along the line, someone must have done a major brain-wipe on me, for I somehow managed to forget all the bad times yet remember the good ones. I was only five when Daddy got fired, so I can't be blamed if there was no traumatizing scar. If Daddy and Ma were living in a world of pain, I was blissfully unaware. Just so long as we were warm in winter and my kid brothers got a bottle shoved into their faces on schedule, all was well.

And who the hell was Hoover, anyway?

Even when I *was* old enough to notice our bleak situation, I was still "el blanko." So I only had three shirts, two pairs of overalls to my name, one set of Sunday duds, two pairs of shoes—an every-day pair and a church pair? Did I care? Almost everybody in our neighborhood was in the same fix.

So what if my dad was home most of the time, puttering in the garage and basement? Or was out pounding the bricks, searching for work that wasn't there? He got occasional pick-and-shovel jobs when FDR came on board; he worked as a field hand on a friend's farm—paid with produce—and helped a mover on rare occasions.

Once he even tried selling made-to-order suits door-to-door.

To this day I can still see the wool swatches, the little suitcase the company provided, and the phonograph record with the sales spiel on it, which he played ragged trying to psych himself up before making his calls.

Another photo from the family album: This time Daddy stands before our house on Division Street, just across from Verifine Dairy (again a half-block from the railroad tracks). It is winter, and bareheaded, wearing a suit and tie, no overcoat, sample case in hand, he stands in the snow, a determined, world-beater expression on his face.

"When you approach each prospect," I can still hear that tinny voice, "do not be intimidated. Remember, you represent one of the nation's finest manufacturers of tailored-to-measure men's wear. Minnesota Tailors offers the customer convenience, style, quality, and economy. Once you announce to your customer whom you represent, you will quickly be welcomed into the home..."

Can you imagine Daddy, short, painfully shy, speaking his mangled English, falling for such pie-in-the-sky nonsense? He never sold a single suit. But those were the times. People were desperate.

Even so, these setbacks didn't mess up *my* psyche. After all, didn't everyone's father sell suits door-to-door?

So 1934 gave way to 1935, and as Roosevelt's crazy alphabet—FERA, NRA, WPA, and all the other acronyms of the era—gained ground, and things improved little by little. Daddy was able to get back into the tannery. Even ten-, fifteen-hours a week were better than nothing. In 1936 he was working a thirty-hour week, bringing home $15 every two weeks.

I knew we were really making headway when, that year, on a late summer afternoon, he gathered his sons in the living room and proudly announced, "Today I begin give my boys allowance, every week, like other America boys. I give nickel on Friday if you be good, help you Mama. Maybe later, when things better, I give dime."

Well! Wrens could have nested in our mouths. We'd never heard of such a thing. An allowance? A nickel a week? Dear God, the earthly treasures a nickel could buy! And just for behaving, for helping around the house?

Yes, we conceded, things must be picking up. The Depression—whatever name you called it—was on its way out.

And this was when Daddy powered up his indefatigable dream machine. This was the time of the wonderful Mexican band, when this story began.

CHAPTER THREE

The Cheese Stands Alone

One lovely, brisk morning in early September, when I was five and living at the Five Points, Ma walked me the three blocks to Wilson School. It was located between First and Second Streets on Military Road, basically where the U.S. Post Office parking lot stands today. She had registered me that spring; now it was opening day.

Kindergarten. The bigtime at last.

"*Tomás*," she said as we walked, "*ahora y mañana te llevaré a la escuela. Después te vas solo. Comprende?*"

"*Sí, Mama*," I replied in perfectly enunciated Spanish. "*Comprendo. Es bueno.*"

Translation: "Thomas, today and tomorrow I will take you to school. After that you will go by yourself. Do you understand that?"

Moving right along: "Yes, Mama. I understand. It's okay."

What was Ma thinking? Sending number-one son to school with no English? At home we spoke only *Español*, why I'll never know. English was Ma's mother tongue. In the years since marrying Daddy, she'd learned to speak super-fluent Spanish. Why hadn't she brought *me* up bilingual as well?

So when I entered my classroom and was assigned to a chair, I was understandably terrified. I sat like a lump, uttered not a word to any of my classmates. Some mothers lingered in the back of the room in case their kid freaked out on their first day of school. Ma, however—with babies Bernard and David left alone for the scant five minutes it took us to reach Wilson School—had cleared out, but fast.

It didn't take long for racial clash to hit the fan. Miss Todd spoke no Spanish. Fair enough: I spoke no English. As she began her orientation lingo, I sat bewildered, understanding absolutely *nada*. What new corner of the universe had I just dropped into? When she smiled, the kids smiled back. When she said something funny, they all laughed. All of which went right over my pointy little head.

A little later she began calling names from a list in her hand. As she did, each kid stood, smiled, and responded to her questions. I panicked. *Qué pregunta?* What was she asking?

"Thomas Ramirez? Where are you? Please stand up." Natural-born copycat, I stood.

"How are you today, Thomas? And where do you live?"

Nada.

"Well, Thomas, please say something. Can't you talk? Do you understand me?"

A reply was certainly expected. I blurted out a frightened stream of Spanish.

"You can't speak English?" She burst out laughing. "How do you expect to learn anything then?"

Another desperate volley of totally indecipherable *Español*.

By then Miss Todd, the class, and the standby mothers were laughing. Such gibberish. Who'd had the audacity to drop this miserable misfit at Miss Todd's door?

I smiled self-consciously and went on with more of my rapid-fire Spanish. *I must make my teacher understand!*

More hilarious laughter, with the teacher scolding nonstop.

Finally, completely humiliated, I slumped into my chair and began to cry.

But there was no comfort, no sympathy tendered by Miss Todd; no kind classmate moved to hug and reassure me.

How could they when they were all laughing so hard?

Mercifully Miss Todd deserted me for the next pupil.

Today such a teacher would be summoned to the principal's office—possibly the superintendent's—and raked over the coals. Or run off. But back then, who cared about a dumb kid's feelings? Cruel sport. *Un Mexicano muy stupido*, what was one to expect?

Perhaps this flash-forward is pure fiction, but Ma later told me—

when I was ten and such details registered—that when I came home from school that noon, I simply stopped talking. Period. For six long weeks. No Spanish, no English. At the end of that time, I emerged from my cocoon speaking English.

Hard to believe? Ma's word. Gospel. Why would she concoct such a whopper?

As always, I was resilient, and as the school year progressed, I got used to the kids poking fun. Eventually they tired of it, and basically ignored me. Miss Todd made no effort to integrate little Tomás. I remained hardcore outsider. Racism was alive and well at Wilson School.

Then one fine October morning, I arrived at school understanding—and speaking—English. I can imagine Miss Todd dropped a few teeth at that. And how had that happened? Never underestimate a kid's blotter brain. I suppose I listened extra hard in class and on the playground; I sucked in *Inglés* like sand drinks rain. I tuned in to my playmates' gabble at the Watson Apartments, I listened to the radio—and to Ma whenever she lapsed into English.

Y, ahora, soy Americano!

So kindergarten wasn't a total loss after all.

We played with blocks, we cut paper, we sang, we marched around the room while teacher pounded on the piano. We played games.

My favorite was *Farmer in the Dell*.

Surely we all remember that one. The class joins hands and circles one kid, who is the farmer. "The farmer in the dell, the farmer in the dell, heigh-ho the derry-o, the farmer in the dell."

Remember it now?

"The farmer takes a wife, the farmer takes a wife, heigh-ho, the derry-o, the farmer takes a wife."

The wife takes a child, the child takes a nurse, the nurse takes a cow. A cow? C'mon!

The cow takes a dog, the dog takes a cat, the cat takes a rat, the rat takes the cheese, and at long last—the cheese stands alone. One by one the kids stepped into the middle, while the others rejoined hands and continued circling. Miss Todd added appropriate verses so as to include every kindergartener.

Oh, yes, "The cheese stands alone." And which cheese was that?

Queso Mexicano. The Mexican cheese, of course.

But I didn't really mind being called cheese. A basically amiable (dumb) kid, I was thrilled to have someone pay attention to me.

Then there was "Oats, peas, beans and barley grow, open the ring and choose one in, oats, peas, beans and barley grow." Remember the drill? The farmer stands erect, takes his ease, stamps his foot, claps his hands, hoes his lands, and turns around to view his lands. Around and around we went, then paused, dropped hands, and mimicked the farmer's every action. At the end, the farmer chose another kid, and he became the farmer. Over and over.

Another totally stupid childhood game.

I loved it.

One injustice rankles to this day: Teacher passed out little waxed cardboard containers of milk every morning along with a straw and a little packet of graham crackers. But only to those kids whose parents had money. The milk only cost two cents, but Ma couldn't raise that. *Los pobres* just sat watching.

On the playground the girls skipped rope, played hop-scotch and jacks, while the boys worked the monkey bars, the slides (we brought waxed bread wrappers from home to slick them up), did the teeter-totters, and raced around the yard playing cowboys and Indians.

Even more compelling: Cops and Robbers.

The Prohibition years were rife with such names as John Dillinger, Pretty Boy Floyd, Al Capone, Bonnie and Clyde, Baby Face Nelson. Ma Barker. Impressionable kids, we soaked it up. Capone and Dillinger even camped out in Wisconsin for a time. These thugs, perversely enough, became kid heroes, and we fought over who would play Dillinger or Capone at recess and who would get stuck with being the cop. Elliot Ness, Melvin Purvis, J. Edgar Hoover—the names still resonate.

The Lindberg kidnapping was front page news. Accounts of the ladder at the window, the baby's death, the capture and electrocution of Bruno Hauptmann—very little of it got past us kids. We definitely got chills at bedtime. When I offhandedly mentioned this to Daddy one night, he sent me one of his shy smiles and said, "Who gonn' kidnap you, Tomás? We got no money."

During my gangster period—newly moved to Johnson Street—Daddy made me a Tommy gun. He carved a beautiful stock from some wood scrap, then drilled a hole in the front end, and imbedded a piece of pipe for the gun barrel. He even sawed a thick wheel of wood to simulate the machine gun's cartridge drum. The hand grip and trigger section were especially lifelike. Talk about authenticity!

Laid off at the time, he sawed, filed, and sanded on it for a week, then painted it all black before surprising me with it. In my mind's eye that crude work of art still dazzles—dear God, what a treasured keepsake it would be today! I was so proud of it that I popped buttons all the way to North Fond du Lac. Daddy had gone to all that work for *me*?

That gun became the envy of every kid on the block. I constantly fought off Bernard and David. They wanted one just like it. But Daddy was all Tommy-gunned out; he never made another. I felt so smug calling it a "Chicago typewriter."

Ah, radio crime shows!

Ah, kids!

CHAPTER FOUR

Life at the Five Points

We were living on W. Division Street—directly across the street from the Verifine Dairy—when I was born. I have a photo of Ma standing coatless in front of the house in mid-winter. That's about as close as I'll ever come to recalling that place. And yes, still on the wrong side of the tracks. Still hard on the Fond du Lac River. Still looking for the bluebird.

It seems to me that we moved a lot. I have vaguest remembrance of two other houses—one on Lincoln Avenue, another on Seymour Street—before we landed at 204 W. Johnson Street. Why all these moves? I can only imagine that Daddy couldn't scrape up the rent, so off we went to a cheaper place. We might have even skipped out on the landlord. I can't imagine Daddy doing something that underhanded, but those were the times. I certainly don't have any recollection of the Ramirez family stealing away in the dead of night, the sum total of our meager possessions loaded onto a borrowed trailer.

From Division Street we moved to the Five Points, where five streets intersected on one corner—cagey name. Our new address was 190 S. Military Road. We occupied a lower flat at the sumptuous Watson Apartments. The rent was eight dollars a month, pretty much the going rate for slums at the time.

It was a fairly busy area. A couple of taverns stood kitty-corner from our building—also a drugstore, a bakery, a second-hand store, all at varied tangents. Behind Watson's, to the west, stood Helmer Milling Company. The Combination Door Company bounded the property to the north. There weren't that many cars in 1931, but there were enough that I must be extremely careful crossing Military to get to the Bluebird Bakery to buy day-old bread. Week-old sometimes. The Ramirez family only dreamed of fresh.

Daddy had lost his roundhouse job at the Soo Line Railroad and had only recently begun working (again) at Fred Reuping Leather Company. Located five blocks north on Doty Street, it was close enough so that Daddy could walk to work. (Didn't everyone leg it to work back then?)

Exactly what Daddy earned at Reuping Leather, I have no way of knowing, but I expect it was close to twenty-five cents an hour for a forty-hour week. And as the Depression tightened its grip, forty hours shrank to thirty, then to twenty. During the darkest days, Daddy became a standby employee, sometimes going in for only five or ten hours a week. And sometimes no hours at all for dreary week after dreary week. Belt tightening time. I was blissfully unaware.

The Watson Apartments stand out because that's where my memories begin; I pretty much draw a blank on kid things before that time. Also, even though I didn't realize it then, that was when things started going downhill fast—for the nation and the Ramirez family as well. My two brothers, Bernard and David (Richard and Martha not yet born) barely survived diphtheria and pneumonia while living there. As result, most of the few dollars Daddy earned went to doctors and to the drug store.

There were times when Ma and Daddy were forced to simply wait out some of these crises; they had no other choice. Being a perpetual worry-wart, I can only imagine the desperation Ma suffered during those long, scary nights.

I often find myself asking how come I still recall so many details from those just-out-of-the-egg years. Imbedded miles deep in my subconscious, one memory triggers another, and out they tumble. A gift, I suppose.

For example, the Christmas that almost never came.

I recall one early December and how my neighborhood playmates bubbled over with talk of Christmas, of Santa Claus, and of the presents they were expecting. Santa Claus? Gifts? It was a splendor I couldn't even begin to imagine.

THAT WONDERFUL MEXICAN BAND

All this must've been gleaned through osmosis, because at the time, I was not bilingual—Spanish was pretty much it. No matter. The message somehow managed to break through.

When I asked Ma about Santa Claus, she turned evasive and told me she didn't think he'd be coming to our house this year. This with a straight face. How did she keep from bawling?

One night, with Christmas days off, we were sitting in our grubby, ground floor apartment. Bernard and David—three and two, respectively—had already been put to bed. We sat in near darkness, our only light a kerosene lamp. Yes, a kerosene lamp. There was a woven wick and a little wheel that raised the wick when it burned down. The glass base held the kerosene; a long, glass hood shielded the flame and had to be cleaned whenever the wick smoked it up.

Yes, electricity had been invented by then. But Wisconsin Power and Light declined to provide it for free. So kerosene lamps. Lamps that had to be lit in various rooms. Or carried from room to room.

The stale smell of kerosene hung in the air 24/7.

Crummy as the apartment was, we had—would you believe?—a fake fireplace on the south wall. And there we sat, Daddy working at a week-old newspaper he'd scrounged somewhere, Ma darning socks, while I played on the floor. We were enjoying, I can only suppose, our meager Christmas decorations, which consisted of some green and red crepe-paper ribbons draped over the mantle and three red votive candles carefully placed lest they start a fire.

And Merry Christmas to you, too.

Abruptly there came a loud knocking on our door. Eternally curious, I jumped up and made a dash, but Ma yanked me back. It was seven o'clock, dark outside; we lived in a tough neighborhood. She opened the door. No one. She stepped out onto the stoop and looked around. Then she froze in her tracks.

"*José*," she called excitedly, "*ven aquí!*"

"*Qué pasa?*" Daddy said, hurrying outside.

A mystery, just outside our door? Gangway! I was on it like a flash.

There, sitting a little to the left of the door: a bushel basket brimming with cans of food, bags of flour and sugar, even a cellophane-wrapped turkey. And tucked around the edges? A half dozen, small, gift-wrapped packages.

But what thrilled me most was the beautiful, five-foot balsam that lay right next to the overflowing basket.

There was no sign of anyone; no jolly ho-ho-hos or Merry Christmases rang in our ears. Nothing but footprints in the snow. Ma could only assume that it was someone from St. Patrick's, the Roman Catholic Church we attended at the time. But how did they know we were a needy family? Could it possibly be the raggedy-ass clothes we wore to church?

Daddy just stood there, a crooked, dumb smile on his face. While Ma turned to him, her eyes glazed with tears. "Oh, José," she said.

Well, in came the basket of goodies, in came the gorgeous tree. And while Ma sorted through the stuff and fought me away from the presents, Daddy stood looking at the tree. If we had no ornaments, we certainly didn't have a Christmas tree stand. He'd have to figure something out.

Well. I went to bed that night all excited, visions of sugar plums and such—the whole nine yards.

Next day, a short shift at the tannery, Daddy came home early. Grubbing around on our back porch, he chose some short scraps of wood he'd salvaged from Combination Door Company discards. Out came his hammer, a saw, and some nails. Then and there he constructed a Rube Goldberg Christmas tree stand. Ma scrounged up a large coffee can to hold water. We were in business.

Bernard and I were hopping around like we had live coals in our shoes as Daddy lowered the tree into it. The balsam teetered, then began to fall. But Ma caught it and held it up, while Daddy hurried out back for more slats. He jerry-rigged additional struts by pounding nails into the tree trunk itself.

Even so, it still leaned slightly to the left. If truth were known, it was a pretty mangy tree. But to us kids? Heaven.

Ma had been working all afternoon—between riding herd on us ruffians—making popcorn, then building a mile of garlands with needle and thread. She let us help drape it on the tree. From somewhere—God only knows—she'd scrounged up eight or ten shiny ornaments.

And when all were hung, wasn't that about the most beautiful

Christmas tree any kid could ask for?

So what if the wrapped gifts amounted to very little (coloring books and a box of crayons)? We were satisfied with bare bones. Ma instructed us to put our stockings under the tree just in case Santa happened to look in. In the morning there was an apple and an orange in the toe of each, with unshelled peanuts on top. But no matter. Santa had remembered us. We weren't total unknowns, woebegone victims of Hoover's chicken-in-every-pot blather.

I also remember the following Christmas and more Santa lore. There *was* money for a tree that year and for a precious few more ornaments that Ma scattered widely among the popcorn strings. But not *that* much money!

I still see the Santa chair where we left cookies and milk on Christmas Eve. Once varnished, it had a curved maple back, spindles carried down to the chair seat itself. It was light blue, badly scarred; ragged patches of paint hung on for dear life. The seat was a wild tangle of lines where Ma's inept paint job had crazed.

It was on that battered seat that we placed our wish lists for Santa. My list, of course, was the longest. My brothers, still babies, didn't have a clue.

On Christmas Eve, just before bedtime, Ma drew me to the chair, sat me down, and took up my list. "*Ahora, Tomás,*" she said in Spanish, her voice deadly serious, "let's tell Santa *exactly* what you want for Christmas. You have too many things here…the other little girls and boys won't get anything if Santa brings you all these toys."

And down the list she went, item by item, carefully weeding out those she and Daddy hadn't been able to afford. "You don't really need this football, do you? You're too little to play football. This nice truck…maybe you'd have more fun with that."

Before she finished my ten items had dwindled to three. And sure, I was a bit put out because I wasn't going to get all the loot I most certainly deserved, but Ma's logic was irrefutable. I was happy that I wasn't such a selfish little boy

But not all *that* happy!

On Christmas morning, when we opened our presents, sure

enough, there was the little red truck and the pop gun and the bow and arrow—exactly what I'd asked for. How had Santa found out on such short notice?

And weren't we just as happy with our pitifully few toys? After all, what did we know of the bounteous goodies other kids all across America might be receiving that Christmas morning? Or of the goodies that other kids—even poorer than we—*wouldn't* be getting?

But for the Ramirez tribe, all things considered, it was Christmas enough, resplendent with happy laughing and yelling, with the safety of family, with love unending.

The Watson Apartments, what a glorified dump! I remember the Johnson, Edkins, Dietz, and Chavez families. I played with all those kids; a couple remained close friends all my life.

Then there were the Blocks—sigh!—who lived in the apartment directly above ours. Both were belligerent drunks, whom no one at the complex had anything to do with. Where they got the money to go out drinking or to bring bottles home, I don't know. Mr. Block must have been a banker or some such.

Just kidding.

The worst was when they fought. You could hear them screaming and swearing at each other night after night. Other times—high society functions—they brought home tavern cronies and caroused into the wee hours. I remember being awakened more than once by loud noise. When I wandered into the living room I found Ma standing there, scowling angrily, banging on the ceiling with a broom handle. More noise.

"Shut up!" she'd shout. "We're trying to sleep down here. Quiet down up there! Do you hear me?"

She might as well have howled at the moon. They paid absolutely no attention. We'd hear them good-nighting their falling-down-drunk guests at four and five in the morning. Once Ma met Mrs. Block in the yard and asked her to cease and desist. A total waste of time; all she got was an earful of extremely blue language, with a lot of "dirty Mexicans" thrown in for good measure. Complaints to Mr. Watson, ditto. Who were we to expect peace and quiet in this falling-down rat cage?

I have to give Ma credit; she had guts. None of the other neighbors ever dared confront the Blocks.

It was at the Five Points that I first met Simon Legree. I must have been five or six when, rummaging around in Ma's books, I came upon a battered copy of *Uncle Tom's Cabin*. I was immediately enchanted by the ink sketches of all those darkies—Eva, Topsy, and Eliza. And, of course, Uncle Tom. Naturally I was curious, and one illustration—of Legree viciously lashing poor old Tom—especially rocked me. What was that all about?

I begged Ma to read it to me, a request she ignored. "That book's too old for you." But when I kept begging, when I kept putting the book into her lap night after night just before bedtime, she finally relented. And as she read, I came to learn the realest meaning of tear-jerker.

What in the world could Ma have been thinking? Was there an object lesson here? How come she always picked the ugliest parts? Did she intend pointing up a connection between this racial abuse and that which we Mexican kids often encountered? Poor Uncle Tom was always getting whipped; Eliza was always jumping ice cakes, wild dogs chasing her. Oh, how I wept.

"Why are they so mean to Uncle Tom?" I asked. "Why did they treat those people so bad?" And even though I knew it was just a story, I was, just the same, overcome by a crushing sadness. Those poor slaves! And where did slaves come from in the first place?

Then, when I'd cried enough, Ma closed the book and shuffled me off to bed. The terrible dreams I had some of those nights!

But the next evening, there I was, at it again. "Please, Ma, please, I want to hear more about Uncle Tom." Ma shook her head wonderingly and let me have it. This night Simon was starving his slaves, and I sobbed all over her.

Again she put the book away. The next time I begged, she said, "Why should I read it, Thomas? You always cry."

"I promise not to cry, Mama. Honest." She read a few more pages—the ones in which Simon Legree beats Uncle Tom to death. I howled worse than ever.

No more *Uncle Tom's Cabin*. He simply escaped the plantation one day and was never seen again. But our talks about slavery afterward opened my eyes to the evil that exists in the world, and perhaps I became a better person for it. I always treated my African-American friend, Louie Williams, with the utmost of kid respect. I defended him whenever anyone made racial slurs.

If there was a lesson, Ma, I learned it well.

To this day—though I own a copy—I have yet to read *Uncle Tom's Cabin.*

Another Watson Apartments adventure had to do with a large, ornate veranda located at the building's south end. Thirty or so steps—perhaps twelve feet wide—led to that porch (reminder of better days at the Five Points), and they became an irresistible playground. We loved running up and down those stairs and playing tag or hide-and-seek on the wide landing.

But most vivid memory of all: the afternoon we trashed those steps.

Where the old automobile bench seat came from no one knew. But there it was—five-feet long, upholstered with gray velour. Shielding steel springs, wooden slats lined its underside. Someone came up with the idea of sliding that impromptu sled—kids aboard—down those steps. There were at least eight of us, and we all took turns riding that car seat to the bottom over and over again. Then we'd carry the improvised sled back up the stairs.

Then, alone or with a companion, we'd sit on it. Other kids would teeter the seat, until it overbalanced, and they'd give it a good shove. And down the incline we'd go, screaming at the top of our voices.

We could have been killed. Or maimed at the very least.

Someone—not the landlord—finally put a stop to our fun. Too late. By then the stairs were shredded beyond repair and would have to be totally replaced. But not in our lifetime. Mr. Watson, eternal tightwad, never bothered.

When he canvassed his tenants, demanding to know whose kids had desecrated his stairs, every adult lapsed into three-monkey-mode. Hear no evil, see no evil, and speak no evil.

Must've been the gypsies.

The Combination Door Company, to the north of our complex, provided other forbidden adventures. A large pile of cutoffs stood back there—residue from the sashes and doors the company manufactured—which we kids often pillaged during noon hour while the employees ate their lunch out front.

Scrap wood—of course—must be used for building. Building calls for nails or screws. So, back to the mother lode. Bernard and I, the more daring of our neighborhood gang, would sneak into the buildings themselves and charge out with pockets full of nails of all sizes. And so to work!

We got chased only once and half-heartedly at that. What sport!

Another Mexican couple, Florentino and Timotea Chavez, lived at the Watson Apartments. They were family friends, and Timotea was in and out of our flat almost daily. She was always weeping and wailing because her husband slid his paycheck across the bar instead of bringing it home for her and Jorgé, their seven-year-old son.

Witless kids that we were, it became constant joke to watch Florentino weave his way across the street, singing *La Cucaracha* at the top of his voice. We envied Jorgé big time because whenever his mother sent him to Wenzell's Tavern to bring his father home, Florentino paid him no heed. Instead, to shut him up, he plied him with pop and candy bars.

Timotea, afraid to invade the bar herself (she had once, only to have her husband attack her), was forced to rely on Jorgé to plead for him to come home—or to, at the very least, beg some household money from him. Often Jorgé and father wouldn't drag in until ten o'clock at night, Florentino falling-down drunk, Jorgé queasy from all the candy bars he'd put down.

Bernard and I used to hover at Wenzell's side door—ladies' entrances back then—and wait for Jorgé to sneak out and drop surplus Baby Ruths or Butterfingers into our greedy little palms. The tragedy of the situation didn't register. To our eyes, Jorgé was the luckiest kid in the world. Sometimes, unfeeling little beasts that we were, we wished Daddy was a drunk too so we'd have our own chocolate windfall.

It was at the Watson Apartments that I had my first and last encounter with fairies. Ridiculously gullible as I was, older kids told me that little, winged creatures lived out in the yard. An old, rotten tree stump near the sidewalk was their favorite hangout. I must go out after dark and stand watch until they showed up.

So there I sat, night after night, just before bedtime, perched hopefully near the fairy ballroom, angry at passing cars for scaring them off. I never once wondered why these same kids weren't out there standing vigil with me. And guess what? No fairies. Even after my playmates admitted their spoof, I was still convinced that they would appear—if only I was patient enough, if only I would believe.

All this happened long before Peter Pan and Tinkerbell appeared on the scene! I swear, some kids should be locked away.

The Five Points location was also where I began my love affair with radio serials—*Dick Daring* and *Jack Armstrong* among the first. I raced home from school to be at the radio by 4:30 PM, when kiddy hour kicked off.

And how about *Billy the Brownie*, who was beamed from WTMJ Milwaukee and hit the afternoon airwaves between Thanksgiving and Christmas? His squeaky-voiced leadup to Christmas Eve was a *must* listen. Santa had us in an absolute lather that last week. Would he and his reindeer make it from the North Pole in time? Tune in tomorrow.

And if all these fantasies weren't enough to kick-start my overactive imagination, the Watson Apartments offered one final, enchanting delight:

Underneath those same stairs that we kids had mangled was a pass-through walkway leading to the backyard. A retaining wall—perhaps six-by-eight feet—stood to the left, and somewhere along the line someone had pasted a wealth of circus memorabilia upon it. An unemployed signboard professional? A circus worker who'd been run off? The display had to be years old.

Gaudy circus posters, newspaper ads, dismembered circus programs, even photographs were pasted to the wall, and—dazzling, kaleidoscopic display—became near shrine to me! The alcove open on both ends, the art brightly illuminated—especially at mid afternoon—I never tired of sitting in my hideaway, all but memorizing every square foot of the display. I returned there time and time again.

Talk about beautiful! How my baby mind raced!

Though I often asked, I never found out how that exciting panorama came to be. Why had it survived, why hadn't an army of brats passing through those apartments over the years torn down, defaced, or applied kid graffiti to that magic wall? Had the wrecking crews who eventually demolished the Watson Apartments given their vandalism slightest thought? Had they even noticed that splendid splash of living color?

When we moved, it was a thing I remembered most vividly from our short time at the Five Points.

I can see it now. And wow! Wasn't that something!

CHAPTER FIVE

Meet Me at the Food Bank

"Aw, Ma, not this garbage again."

Ma bristled. "Are you telling me I feed my children garbage?"

"But we had it yesterday…and the day before."

"And you'll probably have it again tomorrow," Ma replied, a mix of irritation and resignation on her face. "I'm sorry, but that's all there is."

"But why can't we have something different once in a while?"

"Because your dad's out of work, that's why. When you start bringing home a paycheck, Mr. Big Shot, maybe then we'll eat steak every day. Kids all over America are starving out there, and you're complaining."

"But it doesn't taste good."

Ma came back with one of her favorite—and most tiresome—taglines: "It isn't what you want that makes you fat," she droned. "It's what you get. Now eat your dinner. Be thankful you've got *something* to eat."

The objectional "garbage" was Ma's version of *tomato au gratin* —soggy bread pieces floating in a sea of tomato sauce, salt and pepper optional. The bread she baked; the tomatoes came from our garden. And no, we didn't have the messy concoction *every* day, but it sure seemed like it.

Sometimes we got anemic sandwiches with a mayo picnic spread, seldom lunch meat. Other times we had just plain tomato or chicken-noodle soup, very watery. There might even be soda crackers to dunk.

We all perked up when she served a more robust soup made from the "bones for the dog" we cadged at the butcher shop—those rare times we visited those sanctified grounds. When cooked, small shreds of meat might be found clinging to the bone. There was lots of macaroni without cheese. If we were really up against it, we spread lard on our bread and sprinkled sugar for flavor. Yum!

Plenty of times we went back to school still hungry.

Ma was right: I had no business griping. Dad was out of work most of the time. If he was lucky, he might earn a few bucks when Old Man Osborn—his backyard butted onto ours—had a moving job. Heavy work for super-light pay. Otherwise he was out pounding the pavement looking for work that simply wasn't to be found.

And kids *were* starving all over the country. Or so I kept getting told. No skin off my nose. So long as I had mine. Wearisome and unappetizing as it was.

Breakfast was usually oatmeal or farina—more relief staples. On rarest of occasions, real store-bought cereals like Wheaties or Post Toasties. Milk was a given, but even then—with five kids gulping it down—portions were skimpy. No seconds.

Supper was the big meal because Daddy was home. We ate tortillas, fried potatoes, garden vegetables in season, and the eternal pinto beans. According to Daddy it wasn't a meal if we didn't have beans.

A long string of small, dark red chili peppers hung in the kitchen. These were Mexican specials—tongue blistering—and Daddy shredded them on almost anything he ate. Ma also made a molten chili sauce, grinding the red hots in a small *metate* with a *mano*, then stirring in onion and tomato. Ma's eyes watered when she ground them. Daddy dumped it on his food like raspberry syrup.

On Sundays there were skimpy portions of chicken—fifteen cents a pound—and on rare occasions real meat. Hamburger cost eighteen cents a pound; veal, twelve cents. Eggs came in at a quarter a dozen. Butter was twenty cents a pound. A head of lettuce cost four cents or three for a dime. Coffee ranged from seventeen to thirty cents a pound. And last but not least, premium beer was a quarter for four bottles, and cigarettes were ten cents a pack. These, of course, never made *our* shopping list.

Low prices? You bet. But not when day laborers earned a quarter an hour—*if* they could find work. One day there was money, the next there was none.

Oddball remembrance: Meat was sold in meat markets, and you dealt face-to-face with a butcher. Shopping carts didn't appear until 1938. Before that customers took a bag when they walked in and went around filling it. Later wire baskets were provided. In neighborhood stores you gave the grocer your shopping list, and he bustled about gathering your groceries while you waited. However shopping carts didn't catch on quickly. Real he-men would carry their own purchases; they weren't sissies. Women also took affront. They found pushing a cart unfashionable.

Once Daddy and two Mexican buddies chipped in to buy a live pig. How much? Who knows? But it had to be dirt cheap, or the pig would've stayed home. They set up an improvised slaughter house on the vacant lot to the south of the Tip Top Tap, and they killed, skinned, and sectioned out the unfortunate oinker on the spot. There was a huge kettle of boiling water on a tripod over an open fire; they must have boiled off something or other. Memory fails.

We kids stood around watching excitedly—a big event in our humdrum lives. Some of it was for mature audiences only. Like the way the poor animal squealed when they slit its throat.

What I do recall clearly was that we were able to gorge ourselves on pork for a week after. As always there is downside. Ma canned most of our share in Mason jars, stored it in the basement, and we had pork for months. Sad to tell, even as hungry as we were, canned pork loses something in translation, and we were pretty well sick of it before it was all gone.

After that, starvation alley again.

No more porkers? Nope, no more money.

Welfare as we know it today simply didn't exist in the early days of the Depression. If you didn't have a job, tough. Brother, can you spare a dime? In 1933, the country verging on revolution, Congress (read FDR) created the Federal Emergency Relief Act (FERA), which allotted state funds for the unemployed. The program later became the NRA (National Recovery Act). Those little blue eagles were everywhere.

These funds were commonly known as relief, and food was doled out locally by what was then called the Food Bank. ("On the dole" remains byword to this day.) FERA, NRA, who cares? What loomed large to the Ramirez tribe was the free food.

Thanks, Franklin. Hoover sure's hell didn't help. A chicken in every pot, indeed!

Daddy hated Hoover. He once told me, "Hoover say America worker lazy, become freeload if gov'ment give relief. He say we no work." He scowled, let fly with a rare bad word. "*Caca!* What work?"

Ma agreed. She was no great shakes when it came to politics, but she sure knew how to hate Republicans. "Can you believe," she once told me, "that when Roosevelt tried to change the child labor laws, the Republicans fought him tooth and nail? Kid sweat shops are just fine with those crooks. They have no shame."

Then came the CCC camps, where young men lived in barracks, got paid $20 a month, and did forestry, built bridges, or worked on highways. It sure sounded romantic to me; I could hardly wait to be eighteen.

To most of the great unwashed, "going on relief" became a mortifying stigma. Many families held out as long as possible—they'd die before accepting relief—until, finally, pride must be swallowed, and you applied, hat in hand.

That was us. *Proud* was not in our dictionary.

Our food bank was located on the corner of Brooke and Second Streets, just south of the Chicago and Northwestern depot, in a building leased from Helmer Milling. As the oldest son, it was my honor to present the relief slips and bring home the goodies. They filled my little red wagon with bags of prunes, dried apples and apricots, elbow macaroni, flour, cornmeal, oatmeal, and beans, beans, beans.

No shame attached. I was Daniel Boone, heading home, triumphant after the day's hunt. Food around the corner!

There is vague remembrance of script to the tune of four or five dollars a month, which was presented at a grocery store, a pharmacy, whatever, for necessaries unavailable at the food bank. I recall Ma's rant at being subjected to three pages of humiliating questions when we applied. You couldn't own anything, not even a car. If you did—

tough luck.

Mostly we got those farm products glutting the market because most Americans couldn't afford to buy them. The government paid farmers not to plant crops and became the main broker when there was surplus. They actually bought pigs, killed, and burned them in the fields for some whacko reason or another. People were starving, and the government did things like that? Direct me to the nearest loony bin.

We got lots of oddball stuff while on relief, items that sell for outrageous prices today. Dried apricots, dried apples, and prunes for example. Now and then canned produce became available. Hominy was a drug on the market. (Does anyone today know what hominy is?) If you wanted bread, mostly you baked it yourself. Though little fresh produce was offered (spoilage), we did get potatoes, onions, turnips, parsnips, rutabagas (ugh!), even apples and oranges on rare occasion. All depending on which truck came in on time.

Sometimes oleomargarine was available. But in deference to Wisconsin's dairy farmers, it couldn't be yellow like real butter. Each pale, anemic pound came with a little packet of yellow dye. It became my job—this first son stuff gets old fast—to break the cellophane and stir, stir, stir until—abracadabra!—we now had butter. Stow the O word.

We also received clothing—baggy and gray mostly, some brown and black, and shoes, all looking like prison issue. These garments—sweaters, jeans, skirts, shirts, and stockings—were so distinctive that you were marked as a "relief kid" the minute you wore any of it to school. This was particularly mortifying to girls, but we boys didn't care. We could poke our detractors in the snoot; girls were above such rowdyism. But it did happen. Some wild schoolyard hissing and hair-pulling went on now and then.

Mostly all this national travail was lost on us. The Depression, Bub. Enjoy it. Because so many other families in our neighborhood were furiously bailing out the same boat, it all seemed normal. But the stress and worry did get Ma down now and then. I recall busting in more than once to find her, head in hands, weeping at the kitchen table. When she saw me, she'd jump up, wipe away her tears, and say it was nothing.

Poverty *du jour.*

We never got real haircuts; our barbershop was the basement. Here Daddy did honors with a set of scissors, combs, and clippers, most likely second-hand. He didn't exactly use a bowl, but there were times it sure looked that way. God love him, he did the best he could. I was thirteen and selling papers on Main Street before I could afford a *real* haircut—thirty-five cents. Ouch!

Daddy also operated a basement shoe repair shop. Again, where did he find his equipment? He had this black, steel cobbler's leg bolted to a piece of tree stump. He attached different sized lasts, and our shoes got repaired *ad infinitum*. He put on heels and soles, sewed torn uppers until little of the original shoe was left. Many nights we'd fall asleep to the sound of his basement poundings. He never quite got the handle on the right sized nails, and he'd hammer the points flat if they poked through the insole. Even so, we must layer cardboard (Hoover leather) inside to keep our stockings from getting torn up. Cardboard also served—holes in our soles—before Daddy got to performing his basement magic.

Tears in the leather? No problem. Daddy had a glue that would hold leather patches in place until doomsday. It would've stabilized the Tower of Pisa!

And yes, I *did* say stockings. They were tan, ribbed, and came up over our knees. More relief issue. It was what kids—boys as well as girls—wore back then. In the winter we wore long johns. What a job to keep our stockings from looking lumpy! We welcomed spring, when long underwear went back into the drawer for another year.

We wore garters. Otherwise thick rubber bands served, and Ma eternally darned the stockings. But when it came to point of no return, she simply cut off the feet, and stitched a straight line (not even an angle) across. Now we had shorter stockings. Which got shorter and shorter as spring approached.

Knickers were a big deal then, and most of the rich boys had them. Plaid-patterned stockings were, of course, *de rigueur*—they were transformed into pint-sized Ben Hogans. It was just as well that we couldn't afford them; our amputee stockings would've looked awful with knickers. I remember wearing bib overalls—no style sense—until eighth grade. They covered a multitude of sins.

I never, until I was grown and married, lived in a house that didn't have linoleum flooring throughout. It became state occasion when we could afford to put down new linoleum! Tablecloths? Get real. We used oilcloth, which was always flaking at the folds.

No Medicare in those days, of course. When Daddy was working, we had privileges at the tannery clinic. One doctor there, a sadist named Whitman, was on hand two days a week. Ma always insisted he was deliberately rough with us because we were Mexicans. Paranoia? Sounds reasonable. Earaches, colds, fevers, flu, inflamed tonsils, diphtheria, rickets, several cases of pneumonia—all were common thread to us.

I can still envision myself sitting in the clinic waiting room, endlessly studying a gruesome poster that hung on the wall opposite. ATTENTION, it read. IGNORING INFECTIONS CAN LEAD TO THIS:

There, beneath the banner line, were three pictures of a worker's hand during stages of mortification because the man hadn't managed a simple cut. Hideous shots of early stages of infection, with the hand swollen grotesquely as the infection progressed. The last photo showed the same hand with three fingers amputated. To this day I am Mr. Speedy when it comes to splashing on the iodine.

If there were emergencies, Dr. Whitman (and other Fond du Lac doctors) did make house calls—a dollar a visit, prescriptions extra. I'm sure they charged *rico* households more, but that bargain rate still registers. Even so, with Bernard, David, and Richard sick so much of the time, and Daddy bringing home *poco dinero*, raising a buck was hard. Lots of times Ma just waited the illness out and let nature take its course.

We dreaded telling her we weren't feeling well (as if she didn't already know) because we knew castor oil was her main cure-all. She'd give us a tablespoonful and hold our noses until we swallowed. Then she'd stuff an orange slice into our face to quell our gaggings.

However, if the illness defied castor oil's curative powers, then it was off to the tannery doctor, like him or not.

Dental arts were primitive at best. Most of us sport crooked teeth to this day. If the dentist was working on credit, niceties were mostly forgotten. Braces? Ha, ha. There was pain, there was blood. Take it or leave it.

Remember the tooth fairy? Where kids today find a dollar under the pillow the next morning, the fickle wench never quite made it to the Ramirez bedrooms. When she did show—in later years—she left a penny, a nickel, maybe even a dime. Piker!

What did the family do for fun? For certain, we never ate out. I recall skimpy picnics at Taylor Park, visits to other Mexican homes, and tannery Christmas parties, where a woebegone Santa passed out candy canes—one to a customer. That was our recreation.

A summer gathering at an Oakfield farm comes to focus. Here we kids discovered a cask of homemade wine wedged between some rocks in a small creek. Primitive refrigeration. After watching the men bring a pitcher to the creek, attach their mouths to the hose at one end, and siphon wine into it, we took a whack at it. The minute the coast was clear, we were on our bellies sucking that hose.

Whammo! We became silly geese in minutes.

When someone alerted Daddy, he found us giggling and rolling on the ground. He swatted us good and made us sit where he could keep an eye on us.

Early to bed that night. I threw up three times.

Now and then we heard kid friends talking about allowances. It seemed their parents gave them a dime or fifteen cents every week. They told of chores performed. Others got it just for "being good." C'mon!

To the Ramirez scrubs, such largesse was unheard of. Any money we got we worked for or wheedled from our parents. Or Grandma Eva. If we whimpered long enough about other kids' parents, Daddy might break down and give us a penny or two. Which sent us racing to the store. The candy a penny would buy back then!

When we could afford it or had lucked out with a relief order, a Valley Coal Company truck pulled into our yard. A chute went through a basement window, and down the beautiful black stuff came—into a make-shift coal bin next to the furnace. Ma hung a sheet to keep the coal dust where it belonged.

Every night and morning, Daddy would descend to the basement and go at the furnace. At night he'd add a little coal, then adjust the damper so the fire burned lower—and kept burning—as we slept. In the morning we'd hear him clanking down there as he revived the fire for the day. Lullaby by night, reveille by day.

Then came the wearisome chore of hauling ashes—shoveled into five gallon pails—to the curb every few days. I'd carry them up the steps, then traipse through the living room, out the front door, down the steps, and to the curb. What a mess!

Most houses had cisterns back then. There was a spigot at the base of the concrete enclosure (some held two-hundred gallons) where you filled a pail and carried it upstairs. Ma always washed our hair with rain water. Many people kept a barrel under the eavesspout. No Culligan Man back then.

Home entertainment centers? Unheard of. We'd simply gathered in our cramped living room on a winter evening, played games, read, did homework, or listened to the radio. The mere presence of seven closely packed bodies generated modest heat, and we were almost comfortable. Sweaters and jackets were mandatory. There was just one furnace register in the *entire* house. It was located in the floor between the kitchen and living room, and we'd huddle as close as possible. A single ceiling register allowed vagrant heat to meander upstairs. It was all that kept our bedrooms from turning into meat lockers in winter.

No bathtub or shower. Just a toilet and a wash basin. One. Downstairs, just off the kitchen. To serve a family of six. How many tangos we boys learned while waiting outside that bathroom door some mornings is beyond counting. School mornings—pure madhouse. We washed our faces and brushed our teeth at the kitchen sink. In *cold* water. Many mornings we left for school without washing at all. Maybe our hands before we ate, but that was it.

Saturday nights Ma set a big washtub in the middle of the kitchen floor. She heated water in a copper boiler on the kitchen stove (kerosene) right after supper. We'd take turns in the tub, Ma pouring in hot, then tempering it with cold. In we'd go—never more than six inches of water in the tub—one by one, two kids to a fill. In between she'd empty the tub into the sink. As for a final rinse—we should live so long.

Clean underwear. Lay out our good clothes for church. And off to bed.

No stigma. Half the houses in America were without bathtubs. Showers? Still in the distant future, like space travel.

No wonder some of those school rooms smelled ripe.

No refrigerators either. We had insulated ice boxes made of white-enameled zinc or varnished wood, depending on your financial status. Here were shelves for foodstuffs, with a bin to hold the ice on the right side. The melt water drip-drip-dripped into a squat galvanized tub beneath. I swear I can still hear Ma screaming, "Thomas, did you forget to empty the pail again?" Mop up time.

We placed an oblong card—bearing numerals 25, 50, or 100—in the front window. Only rich people could afford a hundred pounds; fifty was our limit. We could make that last for three or four days, depending on the weather. The ice man rolled up in a horse-drawn wagon, scanned our sign, then scurried to the back of the wagon. Out came his trusty ice pick, and he expertly sectioned off a twenty-five- or fifty-pound block of ice. In would go the tongs, and up the front steps he'd come, hurrying so as not to drip. Ma would grumblingly lay a nickel on him, and he was gone.

If truth were known, nothing came out of that ice box really cold. Milk, which we virtually inhaled, never had a chance to spoil. It came in glass bottles, which the milkman placed on your porch. In winter it might freeze, and a cylinder of cream would rise three inches above the neck. Those rare times we had meat, Ma cooked it quickly. Meat going bad called for a national day of mourning.

In summer, when the ice man arrived, we'd charge out to gather scraps of ice from the wagon floor and chomp them down. In winter he could work in solitude. It never crossed our kid minds that the ice came from the same lake—Winnebago—that Reuping Leather and other Fond du Lac factories used for a sewer.

I, for one, should've known better. I'd watched crews saw ice chunks at the mouth of the Fond du Lac River. The chunks were sectioned and then stored in a huge warehouse on the river's west bank. In summer Bob and I sometimes walked in on our way to go fishing. It was dark, dank, forbidding—definitely chilly—and squares of ice, layered in thick beds of sawdust, were piled all the way to the ceiling.

Other privations beyond our threadbare Christmases:

I recall Ma making patches out of patches in effort to keep her kids halfway presentable. And of course there were hand-me-downs. Bernard got my remainders, and David got his. By the time it was Richard's turn, there was precious little to hand down.

There are no photographs of the Johnson Street house or garage. And later, no pics of life on Doty Street. Only after we moved to John Street and I bought a cheapie camera, did random photos surface. Daddy owned a battered Brownie, but the price of film and developing prohibitive, he took but two or three photos a year.

So. A prized shot of the five of us kids, dressed in our Sunday best, taken in the back yard at the edge of Ma's garden—Steve's Bakery providing baroque backdrop. Another of the band in our stage costumes. Then to John Street for some trick photos of David holding Martha in his hand, along with ones of the house and the backyard. A photo of our dog, Snoopy. Bernard sitting in the lake at church camp. That's all, folks.

No washing machine. Not to fret. Sixty percent of American housewives were in the same boat. Only *los ricos* had washing machines *and* hot water. Every Monday morning Ma filled her copper boiler, turned on the kitchen stove, and waited for the water to bubble. Two large wash tubs went on a wooden bench—one for washing, one for rinsing. She transferred water from the boiler with a cooking pan. A scrub board, a box of Oxydol, a bottle of bleach, and two water-reddened hands—these were total extent of her cleaning gear. Plus a large, economy-size jar of elbow grease.

It was an all-day job. First she washed the delicates, and then came our shirts, jeans, socks. Then to the rinse tub. As for a clothes wringer—what were hands made for? I suspect that's where Ma developed her kid-whopping muscles. Into the clothes basket and then outside, weather favorable, to hang them on wire clotheslines. (Would people today even recognize a clothespin?) In winter the stuff got hung inside, some in the kitchen, the rest in the basement. It was my Monday job, just before school, to wipe the wire lines with a damp cloth.

And didn't those clothes smell fresh when we brought them in!

Laundering took the best part of the day, and by late afternoon she might get a head start on Tuesday's ironing. No electric iron, of course. Ma heated flat-irons on the stove lids. There was a clamp-on handle to pick up the hot iron; the cold one went back onto the stove grate. Back and forth the heavy sled went, smoothing out the wrinkles on our dress-up clothes. The rest went into the "wrinkled" drawer.

Daddy never helped. *Muy macho.* Women's work. But that didn't apply to his macho sons. We pitched in or else. Even so, kid helpers or not, Ma was really dragging come supper time.

Looking back, I find it hard to believe things were that tough. Did everyone live that close to the line? But as the song goes: "Those were the days, my friend..."

It seems that wherever we lived—except at the Five Points—there was a garden.

I have phantom recall of a large garden on Lincoln Avenue, where Ma grew everything under the sun, even corn. Another picture surfaces, and here I am, pulling a wagon—I had to be four at the time—with little bunches of scallions, radishes, and carrots arranged in the bed. I knocked on doors all around the block. "Would you like to buy some vegetables? Fresh...my mother picked them just this morning."

Either the price was right, or the ladies were charmed to see a little tyke in the produce business. I usually sold out. One of those mornings, as I worked my way down Gould Street, a bigger boy, perhaps seven or eight—Jack Boukaris, I'll never forget his name—appeared and gave me a hard push.

"I'll take some radishes," he said, sneering. He grabbed a bunch and immediately started eating one.

"Those cost three cents," I protested.

He knocked me down this time. "Go home and tell your mother she wants you," he taunted as he walked off.

Crazy. I remembered Jack to the day he died. I saw him occasionally during my adult years. And I wondered: Do they sell radishes in hell?

On Johnson Street Ma carved out a sixteen-by-sixteen plot in our back lot. Carved is the word because the yard was composed of mostly cinders. Daddy found money enough to order a load of black dirt, and she managed to coax up a few veggies in that section. Whenever we went fishing, we brought home *every* single fish we caught. Some we ate, but the carp and sheepshead she buried. Organic fertilizer.

Marie, Marie, how does your garden grow?

Our garden on John Street garden was pretty much a bust because the kids next door—all seven of them—kept sneaking in and pulling carrots, radishes, and tomatoes. We chased them out constantly, but—brain-shy brats—they always weaseled back.

There was a token garden on Doty Street, but when we moved to Tompkins Street, things got big in a hurry. Here the garden took up much of a vacant lot next door, a patch that belonged to an obliging neighbor. Ma and Daddy worked out there constantly, digging, planting, weeding. Each son inherited a section. Daddy inspected our plots regularly and came down hard if he caught us shirking.

Even with a garden, Ma never let *anything* go to waste. In spring she sent us out to gather dandelion greens, lamb's quarters and pigweed. She'd boil them, add butter, cook eggs into them sometimes, and onto our plate they'd go—a welcome change from relief fare. Dandelions were a bit bitter, but lamb's quarters and pigweed were delicious. I gather and eat pigweed to this day.

Another ethnic delicacy: Daddy bought cracklings at the meat market in ten-pound lots—three cents a pound—and would patiently fry them down until they puffed up and became crisp. He called them *chicharrónes*.

Today they've become Piggy Puffs. Not three cents a pound either.

Daddy encouraged us to eat the fat off whatever meat was served. That, and the cracklings, usually came with this misguided recommendation: "They grease you joints. You be able run fast."

Which brings up the "Night of the Flying Tortilla." Time marches on here.

* * *

THAT WONDERFUL MEXICAN BAND

So many nights, all of us crowded around the kitchen table, Daddy was prone to reminisce. Either he told us stories of his Mexican boyhood—the sheep and goat thing—or he lapsed into Bible stories, most of which he mangled. To Daddy's mind these wearisome tales were decidedly educational. "You listen...pay attention," he'd scold.

Bored to tears, we'd fidget, anxious to be off and running. Heaven help us if we interrupted or tried cutting his monologues short. Salvador Vega, a Mexican crony who had palsy and was basically a welfare case, would stop in, always just in time for supper. He was very fat, I recall, and his bald head was usually shiny with sweat.

This particular night, living on Tompkins Street then, Daddy was in fine form, and the oft-told tales poured out nonstop, with Salvador joining in. It was *"sí, José"* this and *"sí, José"* that. We became resigned. We'd be there until Christmas!

Fifteen at the time, I'd finished eating and was being as patient as possible. While they kept chewing up the old days, I toyed with a small scrap of tortilla on my plate, idly flicking it with one finger. Not good. For I flicked once too often—and too hard. The tortilla chip took wing and climbed with incredible speed.

Ka-ping! It caromed off the top of Salvador's bald head and sailed off into the wild blue yonder, finally bounced off a kitchen cabinet.

The perplexed, stupefied expression on his face, the sight of the flying tortilla—Bernard and David saw it happen—was just too much. I covered my mouth and fought to suppress my giggles, but it was no good. The three of us laughed like ninnies.

Total family embarrassment. Daddy glared. If looks could kill! *"Tomás,"* he ordered. "Leave table. Now!"

Immediately the others chimed in: "Can we be excused too?"

We all scrambled out the front door. We lay on the lawn laughing, almost busting a gut. Why we didn't get a strapping that night I'll never know.

Humiliated, Salvador stayed away for three whole weeks. But then he was back—suppertime, of course. However it became mixed blessing. For now, whenever he ate with us, we kids were excused the minute we cleared our plates.

Even today, whenever the story comes up, it never fails to send my sibs and me into fits of laughter. Dear God, the expression on poor Salvador's face!

Summer, 1941. By then Daddy was working fairly steady; little by little our quality of life had improved. A stellar incident pops back:

One day he brought home a second-hand ice cream maker. A gift from a friend? A curbside discard? No matter, we kids went into paroxysms of excitement.

Ice cream, ice cream, we all scream for ice cream!

Ma would stir up the ingredients and then pour them into the long, cylindrical container. Daddy would lower it into the narrow, wooden tub and insert the paddle unit. Down went the cover. He'd carefully place the cranking hub, lock the gears, and clamp the clips on each side of the churn. Next he'd cram crushed ice all around the edges. He spread a thick layer of rock salt on top. The salt—don't ask why—made the ice colder. He'd keep adding ice and salt as needed.

Daddy would set the unit on a rickety bench, and we'd all take turns cranking. The whole procedure usually took twenty minutes. At first, the mixture still liquid, the work was easy. Little by little, as the milk froze, cranking became harder and harder. First Richard would drop off, then David. Finally, only Daddy, Bernard, and I were strong enough to man the crank. Slower and slower, harder and harder. Daddy was last, and then, perhaps three minutes later, even he couldn't budge it.

The ice cream was ready. Ma wedged out the wood paddle and scraped it down. Back went the cover.

Those special Sundays Ma would kill one of her backyard chickens, and we ate chicken until we cackled. Finally, the table cleared, she'd open the canister and ladle out overflowing bowls of ice cream. Hard, so cold it made our teeth ache. Always plain vanilla, sometimes with shreds of pineapple.

Finally, two quarts down, we simply couldn't swallow another spoonful. Ma would scrape out the rest, put it into a big bowl, and set it in the freezer—no ice box anymore. There would be a last small bowlful for all come suppertime.

Simple pleasures, indeed.

Little did we know that ice cream would never, but never, taste so good again!

CHAPTER SIX

Big Backyard

I hate to admit it, but early on, I really liked to play hopscotch. Such a sissy! I often challenged Dorothy Radtke, who was my age and lived next door. I beat her time and time again. She could have spit nails. Imagine, a boy beating a girl at hopscotch!

Later the games became somewhat more complicated.

No computers, no Game Boys, no iPods back then. *There was no television.* Our entertainments were, of necessity, homemade.

Our Johnson Street house didn't amount to much size-wise. Downstairs was a cramped living room, then a combined kitchen/dining area. The far end was where the band practiced. There were two bedrooms upstairs where we boys camped out; Ma and Daddy's bedroom was just off the kitchen. When Martha arrived, she slept there.

Ma strung up hollyhocks and morning glories on the front porch. The lush overgrowth provided welcome summer shade.

But if our house was small, our backyard ran a hundred feet deep by eighty feet wide, huge in our eyes. This was our playground

At the south end of the yard stood a long shed that could have housed three cars—if we'd had three cars. Or even *one* car. Daddy used it mostly for storage. It was here I built *The Tar Baby*. (More on that later…)

Steve's Bakery bounded our property to the east. To the west was a vacant lot, where a contractor had dug a basement excavation for a house that—thanks to the Depression—never got built.

Just beyond this depression lived Art and Mabel Radtke and

daughter, Dorothy. To the south, behind our garage, loomed a two-story storage barn, property of Gilbert Osborn, who ran a small moving and hauling business. Going west, beside the Soo Line tracks, the Valley Coal Company swallowed up two, three acres.

Often eight to a dozen kids would be playing in our back yard. During the day, and most especially after supper until just before dark, it was the site of endless games of Red Rover, Pom-Pom-Pullaway, Stoplight, Kick the Can, and Capture the Flag.

Most of these were line games, but when push came to shove, we played with as few as four kids on a side. It was decidedly more fun when there were more players. Sometimes a few tomboy girls invited themselves in. We played until our moms called us home to bed. Then came the familiar "Olly olly oxen free," and everyone came running in.

See you tomorrow, Billy.

I suppose it all sounds dumb, but fun is where you find it. None of us being the brightest light in the harbor, we thought we had life by the tail.

I recall one summer night—totally zany—we were somehow allowed to build a fire in the backyard. Mob psychology proved more than a myth that night as, for some idiotic reason, we started running around the fire in a wide circle, hands to our mouths, whooping like demented Indians. We must have circled the blaze for five minutes straight before the noise brought Ma out to halt the mass hysteria. Who knows, had she not intervened, we'd still be out there whooping.

In summer the basement excavation was wild with weeds and grass, and it became a great place for hide-and-seek. But in winter, with this thaw and that, water collected. When it froze, we'd shovel it clear and—whoopee—our own hockey rink. No skates, just street shoes. Broomsticks became hockey sticks; we used a stomped-down condensed-milk can for a puck. If there weren't enough bodies, we'd basically play keep-away.

The Ramirez Rangers are now taking the ice, folks.

Poor David. He was born under an unlucky star. Rickets, diphtheria, pneumonia, constant colds, earaches, toothaches—he seemingly had the corner on every ailment known to man. The same with our hockey games. Many times, when our tin-can puck took flight, it was David who got hit in the eye, in the nose, or in the forehead, the shot sometimes drawing blood. He'd run home howling. Game called on account of pain. If it wasn't a head shot, he often got a broomstick across the ankles. Bad Luck was David's middle name.

When more kids appeared, we had a goalie, and it almost became hockey. Cold as it was, we'd be sweating bullets before darkness closed in.

And when there were no games to be played, we kids entertained ourselves with myriad junk-box toys.

Roller-skate scooters, rubber guns, kites, bullroarers, willow whistles, whizzers, paddle boats, whirligigs, stilts, hoops—the list is endless, all made from everyday detritus. A man came around to the schools and taught us how to work yo-yos. If you could afford one. A whole dime.

Rubber guns were a big number among Depression kids. You took a foot-long length of half-inch-thick wood, sawed it into a gun shape (the longer the barrel, the greater the range), and stretched a heavy rubber band between the nose and the back of the gun. Did I say rubber bands? Nope. Ours were cut from discarded inner tubes—plentiful back then, '30s tires being what they were. Once stretched, we'd pinch the end of the rubber ring together and clamp it between the jaws of a spring clothespin taped to the gun's back end.

Then we'd aim, depress the clothespin, and whammo! Off the rubber band flew to smack Black Bart in the puss. Or in the chest. Wherever. I never heard of any kid getting an eye put out during our rubber-gun wars.

Really tough hombres had two and three shooters. These smarties affixed two and three clothespins to the side of the gun stock, and loaded two or three inner-tube rings. When the outlaw got in range, fire one. Fire two. Fire three. The rubber really flew!

Come spring and the March winds blew, every boy in the neighborhood flew kites. Kits sold for a nickel or a dime at every dime store in town. Another nickel got you a ball of string. Usually, by adding this to last year's leftover string, we'd get those kites up to a hundred feet or more.

Now and then the wood cross-pieces might snap, or the cheap

tissue would tear. Kites with holes don't fly, so I'd go down to Molagaines' Grocery Store or Buehler's Meat Market downtown, where I'd beg a large square of butcher paper—or a skinny roll should the butcher be in a good mood. This was cut to shape, then carefully folded and glued over the framing strings. Butcher-paper kites took a stronger wind to launch, but they were ten times more durable when they crash landed.

I remember little sister Martha nagging me to launch her kite.

"But, Thomas, I can't run fast enough to get my kite up," she coaxed. When I got it to fly, I'd hand her the ball of string. Her smile could've lit candles.

Oh yes, roller-skate scooters. Take two yard-long two-by-fours. Nail them together at one end, forming a ninety-degree angle. Saw a triangle-shaped plywood brace and nail it to each side of the corner. A piece of two-by-two at the top became the steering handle. We'd separate a roller skate and nail a set of wheels at each end of the horizontal member. Then off we'd go, lickety-cut, down the sidewalk. A solitary ride mostly, but now and then we raced neighborhood kids.

Fun? You had to be there.

Some kids built fancy handles; others nailed a peach crate to the upright for racy effect. A tin can got nailed on to resemble a headlight. Variations were endless. If a girl built one, it could be hilarious—dolls and flowers got shelved inside the peach crate.

It seems to me we used a lot of condensed milk back then. The empty cans got put to good use. We placed them sideways on the sidewalk and stomp, stomp, stomp—right foot, left foot—until they collapsed. The ends curled and clinched onto our heels. A few more stomps to seat them solidly, and down the sidewalk we'd go, merrily clack-clacking all the way. Such simps! So easily amused!

Cap guns were universal, one of the few must-have toys we'd buy. You bought rolls of caps and threaded them into the gun. Pop, pop, pop. Big sellers on the Fourth of July, but they were available year-round.

On the Fourth of July, stores sold lady fingers—strings of miniature firecrackers—as good as cap guns anytime. Tight-fisted as I was at the time, real firecrackers were a wasteful extravagance. And to fire off a whole pack at a time as the richies did—total folly! For some crazy reason, we took our lady fingers (one package only) out to Wilson's Woods and fired them off one at a time. At dusk the family would walk to Lakeside Park to see the fireworks—nothing very special back then. That was our pitiful Fourth of July.

Then there was the summer I got my first pair of roller skates. Daddy had brought them home—partly rusted, dirty—a curbside find. I was ecstatic.

I sanded the wheels to a dull shine; I oiled them until the ball bearings spun with a soothing hum. Then I clamped them onto the soles of my shoes as tightly as possible. (Daddy always yelled when they got pulled off.) A skate-key hanging from a string around my neck, I set off down the walk.

I was floating! I was flying! I had never moved so fast before! And yes, I was clumsy at first and got some nasty skinned knees. But, quickly back on my feet, I sent the skates into a longer, wider thrust, working up even more speed.

I must have skated for an hour that first time. I was amazed to find myself so quickly at Johnson and Main. By then I was moving with gliding ease, and I turned and headed back.

But when I got home, I didn't stop; I wanted to keep skating forever. I went past the house, skated west, all the way to Hickory Street, the city's outskirts. Here, drenched in sweat, I did a snappy about face and made one last, record-breaking dash for home.

Now my strokes were long and even, the clash of the skates on the concrete a lulling, hypnotizing song. I became, most certainly, the best skater in the world. Upon reaching home, I fell onto the porch steps with an exhausted, delighted sigh.

And how could such a simple thing as roller skates make a kid so supremely happy?

Then there was the winter I built some skis. Bob Keller had let me try his, and I'd skied down some mild slopes east of the Chicago and Northwestern tracks. No real challenge, but I loved it, and this skimpy sample convinced me that I must own some skis. My imagination working overtime, I pictured myself sweeping down the hills at Sun Valley, swerving to a graceful, snow-swooshing stop at the bottom.

Buying skis was out of the question. So I set out to build my own. My how-to-do-it book—the library, eternal road to perdition—said that barrel stave skis were pig-easy to make and were just the thing for novice skiers. (A big fat lie.)

Barrels weren't designer items during the Depression and were easy to come by. I scrounged the alleys for a week before I found one big enough.

In Daddy's basement workshop, I broke out two barrel staves—oak, roughly three-and-a-half feet long—and spent hours sanding the gliding edges to silky smoothness. Scraps of Daddy's tannery leather became bindings. As final touch, the manual strongly recommended ski wax. So I melted some candles and dripped the wax on the sliding surface, quickly smoothing it out with a putty knife before it congealed.

Come the next heavy snow, I was eager to try out my little gems. I walked to the vacant lot next door, put them on, and proceeded to slide down the gentle slope.

Only I didn't slide.

The blasted barrel-stave skis were seemingly glued in place. I almost fell on my face every time I tried moving them. Not enough wax, I decided.

Back to the basement. More candle wax.

Back to the slope.

Lean forward, Tom. Prepare to fly.

But no fly.

Naughty words. Other naughty words.

Furious at my gullibility, bemoaning the hours I'd worked on the skis, I yanked the ugly, smirking imposters from my feet and made for home.

They ended up in Daddy's kindling bin. The "ski wax" made them burn merrily.

Sad. Truly sad. A tragedy of stunning proportion.

For I knew, in my heart of hearts, that the U.S. had just lost one of its greatest future Olympic ski champs.

CHAPTER SEVEN

Old Man River

The Fond du Lac River featured prominently in my childhood; it was a strong, formative influence. It was also a lifeline of sorts.

"Thomas," Ma would say when relief issue ran low, "could you go down to the river and see if you can catch some fish for supper?"

Which made me feel like Mr. Big Stuff. I was helping feed my family. I began fishing when I was eight. I was ten before I got the real hang of it and could most always come up with something—bullheads at least.

My earliest memories of the Fond du Lac River begin with the Watson Apartments at the Five Points, where it ran no more than two short blocks to the west, just past where Tobin Tool and Die once stood. On Division Street it ran a short block to the east. On Johnson Street, it was a block to the south. Our subsequent move to Doty Street put the river half a mile away—no impact at all. Upon moving to John Street, the river—a half block to the north—rolled back into our lives. At our last address, 361 Tompkins Street, right next to Galloway-West, the river was closer than ever, not more than three-hundred feet behind our house.

We lived at the Five Points during Prohibition. Going out to play one morning, I became aware of a strange odor. Older playmates excitedly told of a government raid that had taken place on Ruggles Street, a block behind the Watson Apartments. Someone had rigged up some stills in a deserted factory building right across from Tobin Tool and Die; illicit hooch fermented around the clock.

One of my friends, Milton Dietz, reported being awakened that morning by a big commotion. Looking out, he saw a dozen men rolling big wooden barrels toward the Fond du Lac River. Others followed, carrying axes.

Prohibition? Whiskey? The Feds? The words meant nothing to me. Even when I asked Ma and she explained, it didn't make sense. I do recall that I later ran down to the river where it dead-ended on Ruggles and found the water was a different color—a brownish yellow. Again that sharp, alien smell. Dead fish floated.

Large red signs were stapled to the building's doors for months after.

Another Prohibition story: The famed Brickles Tavern wasn't always located on the corner of Fourth and Main. Back in the '30s and '40s, a ramshackle two-story building on the southeast corner of Fourth and Macy served.

The Brickles seemingly ignored Prohibition. Whiskey, brandy, and gin were openly dispensed from beneath the bar. This winter night an inside contact provided advance warning of an impending raid. The Feds are coming! The owners frantically carried all the bottles out behind the tavern and buried them in a convenient snowbank. Upon storming in, the Feds found only near beer and soft drinks. And who'd given them that bum steer?

However, during the wee hours, a warm front moved through east-central Wisconsin. In the morning, arriving early, the Brickles found the bottles openly exposed, victims of a quick thaw. A frantic back-and-forth to rescue them immediately ensued.

Apocryphal? Perhaps. But all part of the Depression/Prohibition era just the same. A Fond du Lac fable to this day.

Division Street brings no recall. Only the photo of Daddy standing outside this house—ready to make his suit-salesman calls—remains.

But on Johnson Street, when I was nine, ten and eleven, the river hammered us good.

During the '30s the Fond du Lac River was always a city headache, especially during spring thaws. Today Fond du Lac's emergency crews are Johnny-on-the-spot when the ice goes out; they immediately launch vigorous attack on the huge floes that clog the mouth of the river where it hits Lake Winnebago. Dynamite charges are set off to pull the plug on any killer backup.

During the '30s there were no such safeguards. Once the ice started to go, it simply backed up—and fast.

Come March and the worst of the spring thaw, the runoff from the melting snow covered the river to a depth of five to eight feet. The ice beneath would crack and heave, piling up in ten-, fifteen-foot crags, and slowly begin moving toward Lake Winnebago. When that happened every house along the river—and many located one or two blocks away—would find their yards underwater, their basements converted into holding tanks overnight. No basement? The living rooms became indoor swimming pools.

The onslaught of ice and drain-off sometimes damaged the bridges the entire length of the river—from Western Avenue to Brush Street, to Scott Street, and all points in between. Huge cakes of ice buried the railroad tracks alongside the tannery. More than once the wood-covered railroad bridge near our hobo jungle got badly torn up.

Of course, as the breakup and flooding commenced, there were always idiot kids who would ride the ice cakes as they floated downriver. Macho derring-do? Pig stupid is more like it. Reckless bravado was definitely not my thing. I was, then and now, content to hug the sidelines. During the thaws, before the ice broke, I might oh-so-daringly test the river's rubbery surface. When my footprints almost immediately filled with water, I was gone.

No Polar Bear Club for me.

Back then we didn't have the wimpy winters we do today. Our winters were real bears, with annual snowfall in the seven- to eight-foot range. So, come spring, there was a helluva lot more water for the river to handle than today.

Also it was wicked cold in those days, and the snow hung around longer and built into truly serious drifts by spring. I remember my brothers and I happily trooping home atop the plowed drifts. When we used the walks, the snow walls loomed so high we'd have to look straight up to see the sky.

Often, after supper, we went down to the Mobil filling station at the corner of Rees and Main, where the snow piles stood ten to twelve feet high. Because it was against local ordinance to haul snow to the river, the Konens would pile it as high as they could. At midnight they might fill a pick-up truck and make some furtive river runs. They certainly weren't alone—another reason the west side got flooded so often.

We'd play King of the Hill until we were exhausted and soaking wet with sweat under our winter gear. Always—imaginations sparked—the snow piles became Rocky Mountain peaks, and we were reborn as Buck Jones, Tom Mix, or The Lone Ranger. Always fighting off renegade bandits.

Take that, you crook! We need some help over here, Tonto.

Snow clearing in those days was primitive; snow couldn't be plowed, loaded, and hauled away within twenty-four hours as happens today. I have photos of Fond du Lac's Main Street that show eight-foot walls of snow on each side, with only a single lane for those drivers intrepid enough to venture out. A narrow tunnel, barely four feet wide, runs between the store front and the towering drifts. Business came to dead standstill when a blizzard blew in from the plains.

In another picture, my wife's father—an engineer with the Chicago and Northwestern Railroad—stands beside a stalled locomotive, where a spectacular drift dwarfs the engine itself. Rugged winters? You bet.

In my mind's eye, I still bring up spring-thaw image of a man and woman, two kids and a dog, sitting in a boat and rowing down Johnson Street as calm as you please. Yeah, we row out here every spring, their broad smiles proclaim.

Our basement always flooded. We had a dog, a copper-colored bull terrier named Penny, who was relegated to the basement at night. One morning, looking out to discover the world underwater, we hurried to rescue Penny. Opening the basement door, we edged down three steps, and found the basement flooded almost to the ceiling. And there, floating atop an old mattress, a very doleful look on her face, sat poor Penny.

Then, when spring truly arrived, the river was clear, and the sun stayed up longer with each passing day, the fishing would start. Early on we fished for bullheads and carp. The bullheads were gutted, skinned and fried. Some were smoked. Sometimes we hooked carp, but mostly we waded in Supple's Marsh—barefoot, no boots—and speared them. Some got smoked also, but they weren't as tasty as bullheads.

When we moved to Tompkins Street—I was fifteen then—*real fishing* entered our lives. Daddy was working steadily at long last, I had my paper route, and my brothers were earning small change here and there. Finally we could afford real fishing equipment—rods, reels, and lures.

The northerns and stray walleyes swam upstream as the river warmed. Walleyes were elusive; we concentrated on northern pike, which spawned in greater numbers in our part of the river. The northerns were mostly speared, mainly by brothers Bernard, David, and Richard—this late at night, when game wardens were scarce. Illegal for sure, but so what? Food on the table. Case closed.

Earlier I mentioned that Bernard, two years younger, was pretty much a loner. He didn't play with the kids we ran with; he was a secretive, sometimes sullen kid—a ticking time bomb. He had a mean streak a mile long. When he was angry, watch out! He backed off for no one.

It was a strange, in a way, how Ma gave us kids so much free rein. We had hours of course. "Be home by nine o'clock," Ma would warn, "or else." When I recall my reckless, sometimes near-criminal comings and goings during my teens, how I hitch-hiked as far as Milwaukee and Chicago and was gone for two, three, even four nights, I wonder about this scary freedom.

Was the world really that much safer back then? Or was she—perhaps unwittingly—putting us to the test? Hard questions.

Back to Bernard: He was eternal outsider, living on the edge of things. One of those dangerous boys, the kind ninny girls went for back then. Nowadays as well.

He made a fish spear from an old barn rake, sawing off the two outside tines and leaving only the two middle ones. I used it when I speared carp in the marsh. But on some of those early spring nights—again on Tompkins Street—right after dark, he and his spear would disappear. He always went alone. Usually he didn't return until after nine. And usually with one or two northern pike on his stringer.

A feeder stream led west near Tompkins and Hickory—where the west branch of the Fond du Lac River began—with an abundance of low spots, mini inlets, and such. Some parts were wide and marshy; others, no more than a brook. The water was relatively shallow, and Bernard scouted the banks, flashlight in hand, seeking spawning fish. It was cold, treacherous work, and if you had no boots (he didn't), you came home with soakers.

This particular night, working the north bank of the creek, he'd speared two good-sized northerns and was heading home. Preoccupied, perhaps worried about getting home late, he wasn't as alert as he should have been. It was as he reached an area known as Hattie's Hill—a prime spot for sledding and tobogganing back then—that trouble came looking.

Suddenly a figure loomed out of the undergrowth to his right. "What have you got there, kid?" the man—a game warden and no mistake—challenged. "Don't you know it's against the law to spear game fish?"

Instantly Bernard spun in his tracks, and charged down from the base of the hill, making for the marshy area on his side of the creek, with the game warden—hardly as nimble as a thirteen-year-old kid—in full pursuit. Bernard never let loose of his spear or the fish. Reaching the overflowing creek, Bernard gradually out-distanced the game warden, who was swearing up a storm.

"Stop, you thieving little bastard. You can't get away from me. I know who you are."

Like hell he did.

He reached a barbed-wire fence that ran along the creek. Using his spear for balance, he hopped over, and plunged into the water, at least twenty feet wide at this point. Without second thought, he waded in, his feet sinking into deep mud. The game warden, who wore hip boots, was gaining on him.

Again, driving the spear into the mud, he lunged and pulled his feet out of the clinging mud. The creek deepened; he was now in up to hips. Toward the center, he encountered rocks, slippery and uneven. Somehow he made it across without falling.

The warden, bogged down in the mud—no spear for balance—

was having a terrible time pulling himself free. Then, hitting a low spot, he slid and fell face down. His cursing reached tournament level.

How Bernard managed to keep moving and not freeze in place in the bone-chilling water, I'll never know. But he did. Finally, fighting more mud as he reached the south shore, his shoes totally ruined, he scrambled out and ran east at full speed toward the Hickory Street bridge. Looking back, he saw the game warden still stuck in the mud.

Crossing Hickory at a slow trot, alongside Rossey's Filling Station, he followed the railroad tracks toward Galloway-West. Here, plunging down the gravel roadbed, he came in behind our house and headed for our back door. Opening it stealthily, he made straight for the basement, leaving a trail of water and mud with every step.

Bernard hoped to keep Ma from catching him in muddy disgrace. But she'd been waiting for him, and when she heard him come in, she immediately followed him down.

"*Dios mío*," she cried. "Bernard, what happened? You're soaking wet...mud all over."

"Arnie Klosterman...the game warden...he almost caught me," he explained, fighting for breath. "But I got away...waded...across the creek."

"Did he follow you? Did he see where you came in?"

Bernard laughed. "No, he got stuck in the mud. For all I know he's still sloshing around out there." He reached down, dragged up the pike, each over twenty-five inches long.

That changed Ma's mood in one big hurry. If her son was safe, if the law wasn't hot on his trail—things suddenly took on a brighter light. She quickly became solicitous. "Did you hurt yourself, Bernard? It looks like you've cut your arm."

"Yeah, I got tangled up in some barbed wire."

"We'll have to take care of that right away. That dirty water...full of germs. You get your pants off before you catch pneumonia. Yes, right here. Get upstairs and get into some dry clothes. I'll get some iodine."

There was no trace of anger in her voice now. Free food. Peace in the valley.

Another game-warden story, another night, another year, recalled by brother David, this one featuring Arnie and Ryan Gillard, neighborhood toughs who also got caught illegally spearing. One was eighteen and the other seventeen. *Big* brutes, high-school football varsity.

When Klosterman came out of hiding, and threatened them with arrest, they both froze. Caught in the act. He was digging out his warrant pad when, just like that—almost as if pre-planned—they dropped their spears and rushed him. Each taking an elbow, they simply lifted him off the ground and walked him back to the river bank. Where they calmly threw him in. Laughing like loons, they gathered their fish and spears and faded into the night.

Afterward, changing at home, Klosterman perhaps considered changing careers.

Come late May the white bass swarmed up from Lake Winnebago by the thousands. They headed into every branch of the Fond du Lac River, spawning on their fishy minds. They came in so thick that you could seemingly cross the river on their backs. Gross exaggeration of course, but when there was a constant boil on the surface as far as the eye could see, when you saw a sliding screen of myriad flashing, silvery fish in the murky water—their fins cutting the surface—you'd swear it was so.

Just before Memorial Day, the lilacs in full bloom, then the main run began. You could bet the ranch on it. Around the twentieth of May, we boys, along with other eager-beaver anglers, began testing the waters, determined to be the first to welcome the white bass. We'd roam the river banks, testing our prize spots. Shortly we'd give up. Too soon, we'd grumble. Maybe tomorrow.

Then, when they arrived in earnest and the early birds began catching them—ten, twenty fish an hour—the word went out: The white bass are running!

Every year the *Commonwealth Reporter* ran a front-page story alerting the city. "Fishermen report that white bass are being caught in good numbers in the Fond du Lac River. Prime fishing spots are…"

Overnight the river would be lined with fishermen on both

sides—men, women, and kids standing almost shoulder to shoulder. Everyone hauling in white bass one after another. Not everywhere along the river, to be sure, but at certain hot spots we kids knew well. There the white bass really caught hell!

Mostly we soaked minnows, but there were times when they'd hit crank lures—daredevils, spinners—or even suck in streamers. What a thrill to see your bobber plunge down and begin to run underwater. Or to feel the jolt of a hard strike on your casting rod. And then, setting the hook, reeling furiously, the fish fought you every foot of the way. Onto the stringer they'd go.

We'd get twenty, thirty white bass in an hour, sometimes so many that we gave them away to non-fishing families on our street. White bass abounded in Lake Winnebago year-round, but in summer the meat was soft and not as tasty as those taken in the spring or through the ice in winter. How did I know? Because Daddy's fisher friends often dumped their summer white bass on our doorstep, which Daddy would dutifully clean. And we would dutifully eat, soft or not. Food was food.

Happy days indeed. As little kids, living on Johnson Street, the river was always an irresistible magnet. As summer arrived, fish were few and far between—sluggish, sullen-mouthed bullheads mostly. Otherwise we'd roam the riverbanks, gathering tadpoles, catching minnows in window-screen nets, cutting pussy willows, finding fallen bird nests. Aimless wanderings, but so much fun.

Once David and I headed off a big snapping turtle, grabbing him before he made the river. We put him into our wagon and took him down Johnson to the Tip-Top Tap, where they served turtle soup—when they had a turtle.

"Wanna buy a turtle, mister?" I asked, walking into the smelly, gloomy tavern.

"Let's see what you got, kid," the bartender said. When he came out and looked the monster over, he said, "How about a quarter?"

For the first time in my life I refused the first offer thrown my way. Sure a quarter would be nice; it would buy two plane kits. But David had dibs. That turtle was worth more than a quarter.

"Nope," I said, putting on my best business face. "Not enough."

The man scowled. "Okay, how about fifty cents?"

"Deal," I said. "You got yourself a turtle."

Now David and I could both have two plane kits.

Other times we'd climb the tall willows across from the hobo jungle and go up, hand over hand, from one branch to another—as high as possible—until the branch began to bend. Then we'd shimmy out that one extra super-critical foot and wait for the branch to give way. And down we'd go, whooping wildly, a thrill ride beyond compare.

Our weight minimal, the branch wouldn't bend all the way, so we'd dangle four or five feet from the ground before dropping off, laughing in sheer delight as the branch whooshed back up. We could have broken our necks, I suppose. But we never did. Safety was for girls. Simple joys. Go for it!

While I was no Lord of the Ice Cakes and backed off from danger at every turn, there came a time when the river—and near death—came to call in a most unexpected manner.

It was a gloomy, cloudy Sunday in March, and Lord knows why, I'd neglected to change from my church clothes upon returning home—a definite no-no where Ma was concerned. Waiting for the noon meal, I killed time by wandering around outside.

There had been a quick thaw, and the Fond du Lac River had overflowed its banks here and there. "There," that day, came pretty darn close to Johnson Street.

The Valley Coal Company's coal piles were confined by a ten-foot-high wooden fence, which ran two-hundred feet along a gully that led toward the river. Already the river was encroaching, the water at least three feet deep.

Why I ventured into that treacherous area—especially in my Sunday clothes—I can't say. Perhaps I was lured by Jimmy Fletcher, twelve to my ten at the time and who—wearing hip boots—intended to wade the icy stream all the way to the river. Not wanting to be called chicken, I followed him, walking warily on the gully's edge, keeping to the grass so I wouldn't muddy my Sunday shoes. It was a coolish day, the temperature flirting with fifty degrees.

Anyway, there was Jimmy down in the water, with me on the east bank, when all hell broke loose. He was splashing along, balancing with a stick he'd found along the way.

We'd walked perhaps halfway to the river—houses on our left, the Valley Coal yards on our right—when Jimmy got a too close to the fence. And then, definite freak of nature, that section—approximately ten feet high, twelve feet wide—suddenly let loose and came crashing down on top of Jimmy, driving him, face down, into three feet of water.

He tried to duck, but he wasn't fast enough and got whacked just the same.

Who knows why the fence gave way just then? Apparently it was badly rotted at the base; perhaps, over time, enough coal had backed up against it to further stress the uprights. Had Jimmy's waves been the tipping factor?

There was no warning. Jimmy made no outcry. One moment he was blithely splashing and poking, the next he was drowning, pinned under the fence.

Momentarily I turned to stone, not knowing which way to turn. I thought to run for help. No good. It would be too late before we got back; Jimmy would be gone by then. Where the decision—where the bravado—came from, I'll never know, but all at once I was sliding down the grade into the icy-cold water, good shoes, white shirt, dress trousers, and all. Somehow, suddenly blessed with extraordinary powers—it was Sunday after all—I managed to wrestle up the corner of fence trapping Jimmy. I lifted it high enough for him—gasping, screaming, spitting water—to fight his way free. He looked like a muddy, brown salamander as he oozed up the bank.

I felt my feet sinking into the mud, and the minute Jimmy was out, I fell backwards into the water, kicking to stay free of the fence as I let loose. Upon righting myself, I turned back toward Jimmy.

But he wasn't there. Instead, bawling like crazy, he was hotfooting it for home, his boots going glunk, glunk, glunk as he ran. And how about that? No thank you for saving his life, no go to hell, no go kiss a pig—nothing.

Well. There I was, soaked to the skin and mud everywhere—on my face, in my hair, my shoes squishing as I walked—a total mess. Suddenly I got the shakes, part aftermath, part paralyzing cold. And what would Ma say when she saw me?

By the time I finally staggered out from behind Old Man Osborn's barn, headed for the house, I'd devised a plan of sorts. I'd ditch my shoes, then sneak in the back door, make for the stairs leading to our bedrooms, where, hopefully, I could change and cover my tracks as best I could. I'd clean up the floor later. And how was I ever going to get those clothes dry, let alone clean?

Wrong move, mister.

Somehow—my natural born affinity to bad luck—Ma had spotted me coming across the backyard. She was waiting for me at the door, fire in her eyes.

"Don't you dare come tracking in here like that, Thomas," she stormed. "Take off your clothes right there."

She swatted me behind the head with all her strength, and I saw Technicolored stars. "How many times have I told you to change your clothes before going out to play?"

"I can explain, Ma," I said, dodging another lethal right. "Really, I can—"

"I don't want to hear anymore. Move. Get out of those clothes. What were you doing, *rolling* in the mud?"

"Yes, Ma, I *was* rolling in the mud. But there was a good reason—"

Whap, whap. "I told you already, none of your excuses. Throw those clothes on the back steps."

I dodged her slaps as I shed my clothes. Not fun. "Jimmy Fletcher and I were walking down to the river…and—"

"Walking down to the river? When it's flooding over? I can see the water from here. What kind of foolishness is that?"

"I was walking…on the bank…and he was walking…in the water—"

"Walking in the water? Why would he do that? Nobody's that stupid. Don't go starting with one of your stories…"

"He had boots on…that's how come he was in the water. And then the fence fell on him—"

"What fence?"

"The fence between us and Valley Coal. He got too close, and it fell right on top of him."

Ma's anger boiled over about then. She was apparently having a bad day and had no time for my foolishness. Falling fences, indeed. "That's nonsense. You're making all this up. Well, your lies won't help you this time."

"He was *drowning*, Ma. Honest to God!" I was blubbering by then. And why wouldn't she believe me? "If I hadn't jumped in and lifted that fence off him, he would've drowned. He was face down in the water…there was no way he could get out from under the fence. I saved his life!"

Another slap. "No more, Thomas. I don't believe a word of it."

One last try. "Let me take you down there, Ma. Once I get some clothes on. I can prove it." And in my most anguished voice: "If I hadn't been there, Jimmy would be dead now. I saved his life."

"Enough!" She grabbed me by the ear and dragged me, naked as a jaybird, through the back entry into the kitchen. She shoved me toward the sink. "Grab that washcloth," she ordered. "Get yourself cleaned up."

Then, cold water and all, Ma took the rag at last and swabbed my back. She threw a towel at me. "Get yourself dried off, go upstairs, and get some clothes on. No more of your crazy stories. You're lucky your dad isn't home. He'd give you a good whipping for sure. Just be thankful I'm not telling him." She raised her hand again. "Get!"

As I headed for the stairs I saw her gathering the sodden mass of clothes, carrying them toward the sink. "I'll never get these clean again," she was muttering. She saw me standing at the stairs. "And stay up there too. Don't you dare come down, hear? No dinner for you."

So I didn't get any dinner. But I did get supper. In the meantime I'd got into some dry clothes and crawled into bed, crazy desperate to get warm. I slept the afternoon away.

When I was summoned to supper, she was still steaming. My brothers all stared, puzzlement in their eyes, wondering about the doomsday expression on my face. I ate like a starving castaway. Daddy regarded me solemnly, shooting a questioning look at Ma. But she remained poker-faced and said nothing. I was plenty grateful for that.

The next morning, before school, I went at it again, I begged Ma to let me show her the fence. But she wouldn't listen. "You'll be late for school, big liar. Get going."

As I started down the front steps with brother Bernard, heading toward Washington School, I was awash with self-pity. And why wouldn't she listen? She'd be really proud of me if she knew the truth.

When I got home from school late that afternoon, I took yet another shot. "Ma, *please* let me show you the fence and explain just how it happened."

Ma raised her hand menacingly. "Don't start, Thomas."

And that was the end of it. I finally gave up. There was absolutely no way to change Ma's mind once it was made up. A granite vault for sure.

So much for being a hero.

CHAPTER EIGHT

Adventures with *The Tar Baby*

I was nine when I built *The Tar Baby*. The word "built" is used loosely. And where in the world did I get the idea that I—all by my lonesome—could build a boat?

Easy answer. The chips never fall far from the tree. Right, Daddy?

I'd had the fishing bug ever since I was old enough to know a fish from a fender. At age six—despite Ma's constant warnings to stay away from the river—I followed the older boys down and watched them fish for minnows. A slim willow branch, a strand of black thread, a bent pin, and a matchstick bobber was all it took. I got my branch, my thread and pin; I got myself some garden worms. But I got no minnows.

No aptitude.

Daddy's friends would go out on Lake Winnebago or drive to any of numerous, nearby lakes on a Saturday or Sunday morning and return with stringers of silvery walleyes; squat, rose-bellied sunfish; or green-striped perch. Too full of whiskey and beer by then to bother cleaning them, they often dumped them on Daddy. Never having learned to swim, he had a deathly fear of water; they couldn't have coaxed him into their boat for a hundred dollars. But free fish, for the cleaning? *Gracias, sí!*

We'd all pitch in, already salivating at the prospect of eating fresh-caught fish; Ma would be breading them, dropping them into the sizzling lard before we finished scaling the last one. And good! Fish will never again taste so delicious.

I longed to go out on the water; I dreamed of the day when Luiz Landeros or Pedro Calzado might invite me to go along. But no, fishing on a lake, in a boat, was strictly man stuff. I could wait until I was grown, with a boat of my own.

Later I came by a castoff bamboo pole—the alleys again—complete with fishing line, some spare hooks, and a cork bobber. One or another of my brothers—mostly Bernard, patient, stoic, a perfect fishing mate—accompanying me, we'd spend long hours sitting on the riverbank or fishing off a railroad trestle (definite no-no—don't tell Ma) because the big ones always lurked in deeper water. Our perseverance might net us a sullen bullhead or two, an undersized carp or a sheepshead. Bullheads were okay to eat, but the rest? Forget it.

A guy named Larry Mansky had erected a dip net two hundred feet to the right of the bridge, and we used to hang around—at safe distance, Larry being a surly specimen—and watch him fish. In those days a person could build a mini pier on the river and mount a twenty-five-foot-long pole on a pivot post driven into the river bed. (You saw dozens along the Fond du Lac River, all the way out to Lake Winnebago.)

Larry had probably dropped and trimmed a tall willow on the spot. The barrel end of the pole was weighted with railroad steel or chunks of concrete to make the pull easier. A five-foot square net dangled from the far end.

At that time it was legal to net rough fish—carp, sheepshead, redhorse—you either pitched them or sold them to area mink farmers. But game fish were to be thrown back. Which regulation was largely ignored. During spring and early summer, when the white bass, walleyes, and northerns swarmed upstream to spawn, the game fish toll could be deadly. They were hidden in cleverly-camouflaged live boxes or in the depths of the marsh itself. Game fish were eaten or sold to friends, meat markets, and taverns for Friday night fish fries. Dip-net violators could bring up anywhere from one to twenty fish per pull—especially when the white bass spawned in late May.

We'd always check out Mansky's net when he wasn't around. Usually he'd collapse it when he was done; it went home with him. But often he'd disappear for an hour or so (beer break) and just leave it hooked up. Daring stuff for us to strain for all we were worth, swing the net out, and drop it into the river. We'd wait a few minutes, and then—Bernard, David, and I hanging on for dear life—up it came. If there was anything in the net, we'd swing it to shore, drop it onto Larry's platform, and run to see.

Usually we caught carp or sheepshead, and back they'd go. One day I brought home a three-pound walleye. "Honest, Ma, Mr. Mansky gave it to me." Once or twice Larry caught us fooling with his net and ran us off. His language wasn't nice. Mostly it had to do with dirty, thieving Mexicans.

Other times we hiked two miles to Lakeside Park and fished at Stinky Point. We'd sit on jagged chunks of concrete lining the shore near the sewage disposal plant (thus the vile soubriquet) and soak a worm. We'd catch bullheads, sheepsheads, sometimes a random white bass. While the rich kids, with their fancy rods, cast their spinners or spoons far out into the lake and brought in walleyes and northerns. At the Big Hole, boats docked with bags full of perch, white bass, and enormous walleyes. Disgusting.

I was just a natural-born masochist, I guess.

So, in retrospect, it's not hard to see where the word *boat* became synonymous with fish. Many fish. Many, many *big* fish.

When I was eight, I took up with a kid named Bob Keller. His dad ran a candy and peanut route, and though he was no Rockefeller by any stretch of the imagination, he at least had a job. Bob was one of your natural-born consumers, veritable backbone of American free enterprise. If he wanted something, he went after it. A bike? Get it. An air rifle? Get it. Fishing equipment? For damned sure.

His wanton philosophy carved insidious inroads. I'd been brought up in a family where the concept of just up and buying something bordered on heresy. In our deprived, passive lifestyle, the key word was *wait*. If God intended that you have a bike, you'd find one hanging from a tree one fine morning.

Our family went without—without knowing it was going without.

And yet, even Bob heard the call of eternal Lorelei. *If we just had a boat...*

Thus, when the boat-building fever hit—harking back to Bob's go-for-the-gusto credo—I pounced on it.

Waking up that mid-July morning, I found my head buzzing. By 10:30 AM, after hurrying through my chores, I was at the Fond du Lac Public Library, frantically laying waste to the boy-builder shelves. How do authors get away with such stuff? Would you believe, right here in plain sight: *Ten Boats Any Boy Can Build*, by "Whittling Ben" Wilson. Such stuff should've been hidden beneath Miss Kraemer's desk, right beside the birth manuals.

I checked the book out so fast the floor was still hot when I hit the front steps. The project, of course, had to be a deep, dark secret. If Ma got slightest inkle of this new zany, she'd chain me to the bed. I would build it on the sly, and only when my boat was done—a *fait accompli* too dazzling to reject—would I go public. I was always building something; Ma paid scant attention to my bangings and sawings. As for talking her into letting me float it—we'd cross that bridge when we got to it.

All afternoon, sitting in the shade beside the garage, I pored over the book, narrowing down possibilities. After all, fifteen-foot dories were out of my league. I finally settled on an eight-foot punt. This I could handle, muscle-wise and material-wise.

And brain-wise.

The plans specified "Prime, seasoned, number one pine, three-fourths inch thick, for side-boards and decking." I found nothing like that in Daddy's various scrap piles.

I did a quick reconnaissance of the immediate neighborhood. The Valley Coal Company was replacing a fence. Any scrap there? There was, but all so badly rotted that it wouldn't hold a nail. I checked behind Fond du Lac Burial Vaults. Nothing. I scouted Wadham's bulk station, Molagaines' Grocery, and Steve's Bakery. Net results: one orange crate, one peach crate. Hardly an auspicious start.

More drastic measures were called for. Tomorrow! To the alleys!

David was awake, so I invited him along. I never mentioned my boat project. As far as he was concerned, ours was just a routine junking expedition.

We explored the west side of Main Street first, starting with Gambles, then moving on down to Sears-Roebuck, Fond du Lac School Supply, Woolworth's, and Grant's five-and-dime in the next block. There were random finds of paper and rags, a torn lampshade, a used-up hammer, which we indifferently gathered. "No trow tings away," Daddy was fond of saying. "Never will tell when find use for them."

The oracle. Into the wagon the oddball items went.

But I was just going through the motions. What I sought was lumber—anything vaguely resembling "prime, seasoned, number one pine." I broke down a couple apple boxes; I found a six-foot length of one-by-six. But alas, no neatly stacked pile of precut, eight-foot by eight-inch by three-fourths-inch boards. We trudged on.

We lucked out behind Miller Appliances. Here, partially broken down, stood a crate that had, only yesterday, housed a shiny new Norge refrigerator. And while its longest members were only six feet long, its slatting a mere three-eighths inch thick, it became the most promising find so far.

"What do you want that for?" David grumbled. "Nobody's gonna pay anything for wood."

"Good lumber," I said. "We just might want to build something someday."

"Like what?"

"Oh," I said, forcing a smile, "a doghouse maybe."

"But we don't have a dog," David said. Such a pragmatic kid.

"Well, we might get one. Won't hurt to be prepared."

He let that one hang, and we pushed on, coming up with more rags behind Dana and Worm, a rusted eggbeater, some Mason jar lids (zinc) in a box of trash at City Liquor. We crossed Main and headed toward home. I became antsier by the minute.

Wood. Show me the wood!

And what was that beautiful, big crate was doing behind The Fond du Lac Store? I almost broke into a run. Three feet high, three feet long, made of half-inch stock with two-by-four framing—it would make ideal bracing members and decking.

"Another box?" David protested. "The wagon's all loaded the way it is."

"Never mind. We're taking it. Here, help me rearrange the load."

It was 7:30 when we got home. Daddy was long gone, and Bernard and Richard were stuffing their faces with corn flakes—Martha mushing her Pablum—as we walked in. Ma never questioned our junk runs; it was how we earned our spending money. Nor did she show any interest in the day's finds. Had we found a melon, perhaps some over-ripe apples she might trim?

"Proud" was not found in the Ramirez family dictionary.

David and I went out to the garage, split the scrap metal, and threw it into our respective holding bins to wait upon the junk man's visit. I didn't protest when David grabbed the best junk. *The wood. The boat.* That was the only thing buzzing in my pea brain at the time.

I grabbed a hammer and began dismantling the biggest crate. "Wanna help me, David?" I asked, knowing full well he'd duck out.

"I helped you bring that crap home," he said. "That's enough. I gotta go over to Elmer's house." He was gone in a flash.

Bernard tagged along with David, Richard took off to play ball with Hermie Scott. Ma, watching Martha and keeping ahead of the housework, had her hands full. I was all alone. *Muy bien.*

Our backyard was composed of mostly cinders, acquired free from the city gas plant by our cheapskate landlord. Daddy had paid for a load of black dirt—one whole dollar—which he spread in back. Our garden. The cinder driveway and backyard were perpetual affront to Ma's plainswoman mentality, and she came out there so seldom as to make it a cultural event.

This to stress the sanctity of my garage lair. It was a good eighty feet from the house; a hootenanny could be held there, and Ma wouldn't hear. It was more warehouse than garage—fifty feet wide by twenty feet deep, three doors.

The storage area overflowed with your usual household detritus—castoff furniture, boxes of magazines, old clothes, Daddy's tannery junk. Even so, it was sufficient space for the launching of my shipbuilding empire. Even when I opened the garage door for air, I could labor totally unseen from the house.

So, to work. First I broke down the crates and pulled (and straightened) all the nails. I put different sized stock into separate piles, just as any master boatwright might do. This done, I returned to my manual and immediately ran into a brick wall.

A punt is a simple watercraft, flat-bottomed with a square,

snubbed prow and stern. Even so, there were just so many liberties I could take with those specifications. First off, the plans called for an eight-foot length and forty-inch width. But my biggest crate was a mere six feet, with one end of each slat shattered by careless dockmen. My punt magically shrank to five and a half feet. The second crate was only thirty inches long, and suffered a bad case of split-ends also. New width: twenty-eight inches.

No big deal. I wasn't all that big—fifty-eight inches, eighty pounds, and none of my brothers or buddies any bigger—who needed such a big boat in the first place? Just so there was enough room for all the fish. Heh-heh.

"What are you building, Thomas?" Ma asked as I came in for the third time, lugging out Daddy's saw, his square, and any extra nails I could find.

"A little bookcase, Ma," I fibbed, a strained smile on my face.

"That's nice," she said, "be careful. Don't cut yourself with that saw."

By noon the sides were cut, the cross members in place. Anyone stumbling in would easily have recognized the boat skeleton. One of the sideboards had split, stenciled THIS SIDE UP was visible here and there, but all in all, a creditable job for a novice. "Whittling Ben" would have been aghast, but then it never pays to be too particular.

I'd closed the garage door by the time my brothers dribbled home for lunch; nobody was the wiser.

The afternoon passed in a swarmy, excited fog. By three o'clock the side bracings were in and the floor firmly hammered in place.

A minor roadblock with the deck slats: The last slat to butt to the end of the bow—the stern? Hard telling on a punt—just wouldn't fit. It was always either a fraction of an inch too short or a fraction too long. As my frustration built, I nattered nonstop; more than one "hell" or "Goddamn" popping out. But that was okay; all boatbuilders talked like that.

My pile of "half-inch" stock sank lower and lower. By the time I finally achieved that near-perfect fit, I'd used my last piece. Which left the punt with its ends wide open. Not so good. Reasoning that the ends would bear no weight, I finally resorted to using orange crate slats—a scant quarter-inch thick.

It was almost four o'clock; I knew I must close down before Daddy came home. Even so, I couldn't drag myself away. Standing back, admiring my splendid craftmanship, I almost popped my buttons. So what if it was made of dumb scrap wood? So what if it had no seat? I'd kneel on the floor, like in Eskimo kayaks.

Lost in my happy, proud daze, I didn't see Richard, a motor-mouth twerp of six, as he drifted into the garage. Only when he loosed a long, drawn-out, "Wo-o-ow!" did I come to. By then he was already sailing out the door.

"Richard," I called, making a desperate grab but missing. "C'mon back here! It's a secret! Don't go telling anybody. Don't..."

Too late. He was hotfooting it toward the house. "A boat!" he yelled at the top of his lungs. "Thomas built a boat! Ma, come see the boat Thomas built!"

Well. The fat was in the fire for fair then. He was just a little kid; I couldn't really blame him. His big brother had built a boat, and he wanted to share the news with the whole world.

"Can we ride in it?" he yammered. "When're we gonna take it down to the river?" Worse and worse. "Can we take it out on the lake? What a beautiful boat!"

Just about then David ankled in and stood staring, raw skepticism in his eyes. "Some doghouse," was all he said.

I froze, waited for the worst as Ma came storming in.

"Shut up," she said to Richard. "That's enough. Nobody's taking any boat on any river." She turned on me. "A bookcase, huh? You had to lie to me besides."

"I was gonna tell you, Ma," I said, grabbing at any straw. "I really was. I just built it to see if I could. That's all, Ma. Honest. I thought maybe when I'm older...you...ah...might let me...try it in the...river. I—"

"More of your lies!" she said, her eyes all but smoking. I knew I'd best draw back fast, or I'd be down in the basement with Daddy again. "If I ever catch you putting that boat into the river, you'll be in big trouble, do you hear!" She took a feeble swing at me, but I ducked. "Now get in the house before I really lose my temper."

When Daddy got home, Ma cornered him, bent his ear good. He

got a perplexed look on his face but said nothing. Shortly he went out to the garage to see for himself. He was gone quite a while. When he returned, his expression was more bemused than angry. I could tell he was proud of my handiwork but that he was caught in the middle and couldn't let on. He shot me a dirty look, but there was no real steam behind it.

Suppertime was a morgue. My brothers, sensing I was in the soup, zipped up but good. Ma wouldn't look at me, let along talk. Except when she sent me to bed early.

It was stifling hot in my bedroom. Stripped down to my BVDs, I lay as close to the window as possible. Even as I drifted into a fitful sleep, I was figuring angles to get around Ma. In my dream I was in my beautiful boat, rowing out onto Winnebago, heading for a spot where the big ones were waiting. Now I dropped anchor and began setting out my lines…

Ma kept me in the house all the next day. I sat in the living room and read, listened to the Chicago Cubs game on the radio. Every time I tried explaining to her, she gave me a rap on the head and told me to shut up. It was torture. I wanted to go see my boat; my fingers were aching to put finishing touches on her.

Double murder: When I looked out the window, I saw my brothers and the neighborhood kids, hanging around the garage. I saw Richard climb into the boat and pretend he was rowing. I leaned out of the back door and yelled, "Hey, you jerks, get outta there!"

Ma rapped me. "I told you to shut up. Get back in your chair."

The next day she'd cooled off a little, and I got her to at least listen. "I just built it for something to do," I said. "To keep busy. You know I wouldn't put it into the water without your permission."

"Busy? You want busy? When you finish the dishes, you can weed the garden…dig up around the corn. After that you can cut the grass. But I'm warning you. Stay away from that blasted boat."

Just the same, I managed to steal a few moments in the garage. The boat was okay; my dumb brothers hadn't wrecked anything. Lord, I sighed, but wasn't she a beauty? If I could just get back to work on it.

"Ma," I said, commencing my good-graces campaign after finishing the assigned chores, "please let me finish my boat. I can't just leave it half built. Let me get it done, and then I'll put it away, leave it alone until...I'm...older. It's not doing any good standing in the way like that."

"You promise, Thomas?" she said, relenting slightly. "You mean that? You won't take it to the river? Maybe when you're fourteen, when you can swim better..."

"I promise, Ma. Cross my heart."

"What still needs to be done?"

"I have to caulk it, build some seats. It'll need a couple coats of paint."

Her expression was dubious. "You know how to do all that?"

"Sure thing. It's all in the book."

But the next morning, back in the garage again, I wasn't quite so sure. "Caulking tools," my boat bible specified, "caulking fibre and self-hardening caulking compound." But when it came to explaining how to caulk a boat, things got skimpy in a hurry.

"So," said brother Bernard, self-appointed helper now, "what're you gonna do? You got any money for this caulking stuff?"

"Maybe just some thick paint would work," David chimed in.

"Let me think." I sat on a peach basket and sank into a minor trance. And just like that: "Hey, I know. We'll tar it."

"You mean like they tar the roads?" David said.

"Right! Tar will plug up those cracks faster than anything. Make the floor stronger too, I'll bet."

"And just where," Bernard said, "are you gonna get any tar?"

My junking safaris to the rescue. "There's some down by the old Demountable Typewriter factory. A roofing company took over after they shut down."

Bob Keller had showed up about then. "Great! Get your wagon. Let's go."

Five minutes later, tossing a couple cardboard boxes into the wagon, we hurried down Brooke Street. The Demountable was located a half mile south, between West Ice Storage and Tobin Tool and Die. In one corner of the yard, against a concrete wall that backed up to the river—just as I remembered it—was this pile of trash. Sure enough, scattered amongst the refuse: chunks of tar, some as big as your fist, the rest gravel-sized residue from the big, cylindrical blocks the roofers used.

We filled one box quicker than scat. But then the mother lode petered out fast, and it took another hour to fill the second box. At the end we crisscrossed the yard like hungry sparrows, poking in the ground with sticks to bring up every last shard of black gold. We finally threw in the towel at noon and went home to eat.

After lunch we filled an old tub with water and washed the tar chips. They came out like gleaming, black obsidian. We'd watched the city crews as they patched the street—even stealing tar shards and using them for chewing gum—so we knew what came next. We dumped the chips into one of Daddy's junk pails from the tannery.

Next we set up some concrete blocks beside the garage and laid steel rods across them. We set the pail of tar chips onto this grid work. Then we dragged the boat out, horses and all, and built a fire. As the tar melted, we took turns stirring with a piece of broom handle. All this, of course, without a word to Ma.

A half hour later, the tar was bubbling merrily. But, as it melted, we saw the kettle was only half full, hardly enough to do the whole boat. We lifted the pail off the fire, and sat down to think. Another brainstorm. Ten minutes later, armed with two of Daddy's putty knives and a hatchet, we charged out onto Johnson Street. Dodging cars, watching for police cruisers, we peeled city tar off every crack in sight.

We then dumped our collection of tar into the melt pail. Not the cleanest of tar, but so what? We restoked the fire, set the pail back in place. Shortly the reassuring plop-plop-plop began anew.

Then all hell broke loose. Later nobody could recall how it happened, but suddenly the blasted tar caught fire. Flames roared from the pail, sending up clouds of dense, black smoke. Panic time. I vainly swatted at it with the broom. Nobody thought to simply drop a cover on the pail. Next thing we knew, here came David with a dishpan full of water from the outside spigot.

"Don't throw that in there," I yelled. "You'll ruin the tar."

But David had momentum. In went the water. And up went the tar. Luckily he'd jumped back as it exploded. There was a big *whoosh*, and everybody scattered. But not in time. Hot tar was falling all around us. We hopped around, yipping with pain. What a mess! It was on our clothes, on our arms and faces, in our hair, all over the boat.

But even worse than that, we now had the only polka-dotted garage in town.

Even though the explosion had extinguished the fire, the remaining tar began bubbling away again as if nothing had happened. By this time Ma had come out the back door. Stunned by the sight of five tar-spattered boys and a ruined garage, she simply stood there with dismay, anger, and concern playing across her face.

It was last straw.

After a few minutes, saying absolutely nothing, she slowly turned and, shoulders slumped, went back inside. Those quiet times of hers were the worst. We knew, then and there, that we were really in for it when Daddy got home.

Always one to look for silver linings, I temporized that we hadn't exactly been ordered to stop tarring the boat. Surely Ma would agree that the wisest course would be to finish the job at hand. All this good tar shouldn't go to waste, should it? The garage—we kids—could be cleaned up later. But for now: back to business.

Taking up the broom, I scrubbed at the runny spots, evened them out as best I could. Then, dipping sparingly into the pail, I began painting the sides and the bottom, working it on as smoothly as my crude brush allowed. When the outside was totally covered—the tar set fast—we turned the boat over and began "caulking" the inside.

Surprise, surprise. The tar spread easier and covered more square feet than expected. Before we were done, we had two full coats, inside and out. And, oh, but didn't she look pretty? Black was a great color. The way it shone! Then and there—burst of sheerest inspiration—we named her *The Tar Baby*. Later we tried to print the name in white paint, but it wouldn't adhere to the tar. So we lettered it onto two pieces of tin and tacked one on each side.

Despite the hovering vulture of doom, we felt pretty good about our day's work. We kept walking around *The Tar Baby*, appraising her from all directions. And if that wasn't the smartest, jauntiest little boat we'd ever seen...

THAT WONDERFUL MEXICAN BAND

When Daddy came home and saw the garage—some tar had even shot to the east, spattering Steve's Bakery—his face went very dark, but he said nothing.

But finally: "*Ándale, muchachos.* In the basement. Tomás go first." And where he usually delayed his razor strap drills until after supper, that day he waived the genteel formalities.

So I went first. He was waiting, that solemn, regretful look in his eyes. He didn't truly enjoy whipping his sons, I knew. Anyway, he always said so.

"This gon' hurt me more than hurt you..." he always began.

His father had whipped him; wasn't that how kids learned to mind? And when number one son keeps getting into one scrape after another and keeps splashing tar on his garage? What's a father to do?

I got the worst of it. Because I was the oldest, Daddy patiently explained. I should know better. Who could argue with logic like that?

Oh, I danced! A regular Fred Astaire. We had a full ballet troupe before he finished. But no hard feelings. We had it coming, for sure.

The four of us spent the next day on ladders with putty knives, a paint scraper, a wood chisel in hand. We scraped tar off the garage for hours. We scrubbed with gasoline-soaked rags, until every offending smudge was gone. We scrubbed part of Steve's Bakery too. Even so, memory of our disgrace would haunt for over a year— the cleaned spots stood out like a sore thumb. Ma simply washed our clothes and let us wear them, tar spots and all.

Daddy stood *Tar Baby* on end, then hung it over a nail that was hammered into the roof plate. Under no circumstances were we to touch it, *comprende*?

The truce lasted for exactly three days. And finally, on a particularly bright, clear Wednesday, putting Martha into the buggy, Ma headed for the tannery doctor's office. Afterward, some downtown shopping. She'd be gone for two hours at least.

We had it all planned; each knew his designated role. Ma was barely down the block when Bernard and I lifted *The Tar Baby* off its nail. David pushed our wagon underneath. Richard put the crude oars we'd built on the sly into her gleaming black depths. Wagons, roll!

Across the back yard and down Johnson Street we went. We hit the Soo Line tracks, turned left. Then almost to the bridge, where we turned right.

We stopped short of Larry Mansky's pier (deserted in mid-summer). Here, in a shallow, reedy swale, we eagerly lifted the punt (it weighed seventy pounds if it weighed an ounce—mostly tar) and slid her into the tepid, muddy water. What a thrill, to see the boat bob and turn in the current—*to see it float!* We stood for long moments, saying nothing, sappy, proud grins on our faces.

"Well," I said finally, "don't just stand there. Let's take a ride." Three of us gingerly climbed in, hunkered down on our heels. *The Tar Baby* promptly sank. We clambered out, oozed into mud up to our knees.

We pulled the boat up on shore, tipped her over, then put her back into the river. "Too much weight," I said. "We'll take turns. Bernard and I go first."

We got in, and David and Richard pushed us out. Excitement! We were actually afloat; we were drifting out onto the river. I got the whim-whams when I saw we were riding only six inches out of the water. Whenever we both dipped oars, *The Tar Baby* rocked, and water poured in over the sides.

"Sit still," I ordered. "Let me row." I took slow, experimental strokes, barely daring to breathe for fear we'd capsize. How we made it across the river—a distance of perhaps sixty feet—was sheer luck. Then as we headed back, when I was just beginning to get the hang of it—more trouble.

Somehow, in the hauling and the loading in and out, we must have sprung one of the floor boards; water was seeping in. A trickle at first. At mid-river the crack really opened; we could see the water fountain up, spread across the bottom. No bailing can, of course. Stupid cluck! I paddled as fast as I dared, hoping to reach shore before we went under. By the time we landed we'd shipped four inches; the river was almost smack-dab even with the top rail.

Right away we sent Richard to scout up a tin can. We tipped and drained *The Tar Baby* over yet another time. I hammered the loose slat down with a piece of brick. Then it was David's turn to ride. Getting in, he lost his balance, and his foot came down hard, breaking the seal on yet another slat. By the time we were halfway across the river, he was bailing like crazy. I put her into reverse and headed back to shore. *The Tar Baby* went down ten feet out. We jumped over the side and found ourselves in water up to our waists.

With Richard and Bernard pulling on the bow, David and I pushing and lifting the stern, we managed to get close to shore. Then it hit bottom and wedged solid. We bailed forever before we got it on land this time.

Sitting on the overturned craft, we stared glumly at the river. "Some boat," David—ever the pessimist—said.

"It needs work," I defended, verging on disappointed tears. "It's the first boat I ever built. What do you expect? I'll put a cleat down the middle…right here…that'll keep those slats rigid. Don't worry. She'll float. You'll see."

Back to the house we went, wet, muddy, totally demoralized. *The Tar Baby* went back up on its nail. We spent what remained of the morning cleaning our tennies, drying out our clothes. Quick, before Ma gets home!

Well, it never did turn out to be much of a boat. Picking a time when Ma was away, I nailed a three-inch-wide cleat on the bottom. Completely on my own now—my brothers washing their hands of the whole deal—I went down to the Demountable, where I scrabbled up more tar scraps. Back home, I gave it another complete coat—this when Ma and Daddy were away most of the day.

By myself I wheeled the boat down to the river. I launched and paddled it across again and again, fighting hard to convince myself that I was still proud of my handiwork, that I was having the time of my life. The cleat and the extra tar helped, but the punt was never leak-proof.

I took it down to the river twice more—Bob Keller with me one time—but the spark was gone. It was a Jonah, and I knew it.

Eventually Daddy tired of having it cluttering the garage and threw it out beside the garage. Weeks passed without anyone even looking at it.

*   *   *

Well, that should have been the end of the story. But no, late in August, just before school took up again: the final chapter. Bob got this swiss-cheese idea of going over to Montello (forty miles away) for a fishing expedition—a goodbye-to-summer sort of thing.

And why couldn't we take *The Tar Baby* and go out onto the Fox, where the big walleyes waited?

Ma thought nothing of our hitchhiking jaunts by then, so it wasn't hard to get her to agree to another. I made no mention of the boat, of course. The day we left I yelled goodbye to her down the basement steps (she was doing the washing). Bob and I hoisted *The Tar Baby* onto the wagon and headed out as fast as we could. Richard tagged along to bring the wagon back.

We set up two blocks away across the tracks, a thick stand of marsh to our backs. We'd head west on Highway 23, Rosendale, Ripon and Princeton standing between us and Montello. There we stood, two grubby, sawed-off kids, our thumbs waggling, this black, ugly boat full of camping and fishing gear beside us. We'd figured that someone in a pickup would stop, and we'd dump all our stuff in back. No pickup trucks. So we did a thumbs-up for any vehicle that went by.

Dumb, dumb.

We kept shop there for an hour, our thumbs getting sunburned, without a single vehicle slowing down.

Just before noon a farm truck finally stopped. "I can take you as far as Ripon," the hayseed said. He even helped us load our junk—and *The Tar Baby*. Today I can't help but think that he must have been a confirmed sadist—his idea of a joke. He certainly must have known what sort of a dead-end trap we were heading into.

The twenty-three miles to Ripon passed amiably, the farmer joshing us about the boat and talking fishing all the way. His turnoff was on the outskirts of the city, and he dumped us there. We could see the Rippin' Good Cookie Company in the distance. So we were really stuck. Who in hell would pick us up—heading *into* Ripon?

Now, finally—too late—we came to. We were really in a pickle now!

Even if we'd wanted to hide the boat, there was no place. There it stood in plain sight, scaring away car after car, truck after truck.

Desperation grew. At long last, realizing that we'd be stuck on the outskirts of Ripon until Christmas, Bob took the other side of the road. Now we tried for a ride in either direction—to Montello or Fond du Lac. We ate the bag lunch we'd made; we pumped our thumbs at anything that moved.

We kept trying all through that hot, eternal afternoon. It wasn't bad enough that we'd blindly walked into such a stupid fix, but we had to endure the smirks that the people sent our way as they whizzed by. How could anybody be *that* dumb? Now and then Bob would stop a car. I'd see him talking to the occupants, pointing across the road at *The Tar Baby*. End of story. They'd zoom off in a cloud of dust.

By five o'clock we knew we'd had it. Drastic measures were called for. Like maybe setting fire to *The Tar Baby* on the spot.

Seeing a gang of five farm kids coming in our direction, I got a wild idea. When they reached me, I said, "How would you kids like to have a nice boat?"

They were all about Richard's age, six and seven. They looked at *The Tar Baby* with big, wide eyes.

"Sure," the biggest kid said. "You giving it away?"

"Not exactly. You got any money? Anything to trade? Maybe some fishing stuff? Something to eat?" It *was* late; we were hungry. We'd expected to be eating crisp, fried bluegills by now.

"Not with us," another boy said. "But we'll go home and get something."

Even as young as the little weasels were, they knew they had us at their mercy.

A half hour later they came back with the biggest collection of nothing you ever saw. A bag of green apples, a broken casting reel, a couple comic books, a squirrel tail, a nickel. They had us but good.

A minute later they had the boat too.

They acted like a swarm of ants scoping out a sugar lump, excited, hopping around, not knowing what to do first. Finally they got arranged, and with all kinds of grunts and groans, they lifted the black hulk and began carrying *The Tar Baby* down the road.

We watched for a while, me with a heavy, defeated feeling in the pit of my stomach. I didn't have a whole lot of time to feel sorry for myself, for just about then a car stopped. We were heading home.

We threw our gear into the Chevy's trunk. We climbed in.

I sent a final glance out the back window. I saw the boys, black specks in the distance, all sitting—resting—on the overturned boat.

The car gained speed. The specks became smaller, then faded completely.

That was the last I saw of *The Tar Baby*.

CHAPTER NINE

Kind Lady Lives Here

Ma was a suspicious woman. Neighbors, the grocer, the baker, bank tellers, the government, the milk man, the doctor, even some of our playmates—almost anyone she dealt with was out to get her. Or her kids.

"They're up to no good," should have been engraved on her tombstone.

She counted her change two or three times, she tested every apple or orange that went into her grocery basket, she challenged the iceman.

"Are you sure that's a twenty-five-pound block? Looks small to me." Eternal pessimist, she was certain that any venture she started would invariably turn sour before running its course.

There were roving bands of gypsies then. They would knock at the door and offer "free" palm readings. We'd heard stories of one gypsy telling fortunes while her companion would sneak about the house looking for things to steal.

Ma ran them off before they even started their spiel.

But I never saw her turn away a tramp. Whenever one of those unfortunates appeared at the door, her abiding distrust instantly went south. Bum, hobo, rail-bird, vagabond, king-of-the-road—pick a term. Living near the tracks, as we did, tramp encounters were daily fare. Time and time again, coming home from somewhere, I'd find a hobo sitting on our back steps wolfing down a sandwich or chomping leftover beans and tortillas. Often they sent me a whipped-dog look, as if expecting to be run off.

Now and then they would ask if there was work they could do to pay for some food. More often than not, they ignored even this lame offer. They knew there weren't any chores; it was simply a face-saving way to beg a free lunch.

Other times the vagrants would come knocking, attempting to sell cleverly woven baskets made from willow twigs they'd cut in the nearby marsh. Ma had a half dozen of those too.

"We don't got so much food," Daddy would protest upon discovering Ma's latest largesse. "Why you always feed them?"

Ma's face would harden, warn Daddy off. "Because they're hungry. And they don't have anywhere else to go."

And that was the end of that.

The nation gasping for air during the Great Depression, thousands of desperate men took to the road, mostly via the U.S railroad system. Living near the tracks, the sight of these wanderers—perched in boxcar doors, feet dangling as trains drifted past, some jumping down with their bindle and branching out through the neighborhood—was commonplace.

And how did they know Ma was a sucker for their plaintive, "Can you spare a little food?"

"They've got a code or something," she once told me. "There must be a way they mark a house where they can get a free meal."

Upon hearing this, I checked out front for chalk marks on the edge of the sidewalk, crossed sticks, arcane arrangements of pebbles or gravel—anything to label Ma as "Kind Lady Lives Here." I found nothing.

And if they weren't dropping from boxcars on the Chicago and Northwestern tracks, they were—one block west—arriving via Soo Line rolling stock. Sometimes they just jumped to the ground; other times they turned sideways on their hip, held onto the car door, lowered their legs and ran along with the train, retrieving their duffle at the last possible moment. From there they spread out, many turning directly south, heading toward our "hobo jungle."

A rusty railroad trestle spanned the Fond du Lac River there. Once across, it was a short trudge along the tracks before veering off into a marshy area—a willow-covered spit of land between the east and west branches—right behind Verifine Dairy. There were always twenty or so hobos hanging out there. You saw skeins of smoke by day, glowing fires by night. And how did they know a camp was nearby? Again, the hobo telegraph, an underground traffic known to only the hobos themselves.

When we lived on Johnson Street and later on John Street, the jungle was never very far away. We thought nothing of walking among them. It was a different age back then; kids weren't taught to fear strangers.

Ma explained the reasons for their constant wanderings across the American landscape. "Most are looking for work," she told me, making a face. "Fat chance they have of finding anything. Others are ashamed, in disgrace, because they can't support their families. And so they run away, some actually hoping to find work somewhere. Others run because they can't stand seeing their wife and children hungry. They feel like they've failed their family."

When she told me about the suicides, it really got grim. "I keep hearing," she said, her eyes sad, "that hundreds of these men simply commit suicide."

A shiver went down my back. "Why would they do that?"

"Because some of them are just too proud, and they simply can't go on…they can't bear the disgrace of being out of work. So they kill themselves."

"How?" I asked, my sense of the ghoulish piqued. Ma sent me an angry glare. "Never you mind."

"What about all those whiskey bottles I see out in the marsh?"

"Well, some start drinking to forget things. Some just don't know when to quit." Even here, though Ma was dead-set against drinking, her sympathy never wavered.

Taken in that context, we kids felt sorry for them and came to pity them instead of poking fun. Sometimes, when we ventured into the hobo jungle, we talked with the bums. Sure, there were those who'd scowl, cuss us out, and tell us to get lost. One even tried kicking me once. But these hard-nose types were few and far between.

How they survived out there when the weather turned bad—snow, rain, summer heat—I couldn't imagine. As I wandered the hard-clay pathways the bums had carved into the marsh, I saw shelters made of woven brush, short sticks supporting a cardboard roof, even cardboard boxes, some occupied, others simply flattened to form a roof over a shallow trench they'd hollowed into the ground. And always the campfires, with the dirty, ragged bums—sitting on wooden crates or rocks—hunched over the flames.

Now and then, in the summer, we'd see some of them perched on the river bank to the west, fishing with tree branches. They caught bullheads, sheepshead, carp, white bass, and sometimes even a lost-his-way northern.

Then there was the time I got a free hobo lunch.

I'd paused to watch a man cutting up potatoes and carrots (probably stolen from somebody's garden) and dropping them into a kettle he held between his knees. No water spigots in the marsh, but no problem. He simply went to the river bank, sank a coffee can into the murky water, brought it back, and poured it into the kettle.

"Hungry, kid?" he said, smiling. "Hang around, I'll give you some."

Hungry was a state of being with me then; it was mid-afternoon, and supper was still a long ways off. So I planked myself down beside him and waited for chow time. I couldn't help but notice that he didn't look as scruffy as most bums. His face and hands were clean, and he wore what had once been dress pants. His shirt looked fairly fresh underneath his battered but neat suit jacket. His scuffed black wingtips had seen better days.

Shortly he asked my name, where I lived, my grade in school, stuff like that. This opened up things for me as well. I learned his name was Albert Harper.

"Where are you from, Mr. Harper?" I asked.

"Hey, Tom, just call me Al."

"Can't. My folks tell me I gotta call grownups Mr. or Mrs. Or ma'am."

He laughed. "All right, have it your way. I'm from Fargo, North Dakota."

"North Dakota? Wow, that's a long way off." It seemed like the end of the world to me. "Why'd you come to Wisconsin?"

"Looking for work. I need to send some money to the wife and kids."

"How many kids you got?

"Two.' His expression turned wistful. "A little girl and a boy about your age. How old are you?"

"Nine."

"Yeah, my Ben is nine too. He's a bit bigger than you. Smart little kid."

"What kind of work did you do back in North Dakota?"

"Insurance man." He struck the ground sharply with his stick. "I *was* anyway. Hell, nobody buys insurance these days. They had to let me go."

"That's too bad, Mr. Harper. What kind of work are you looking for?"

"Anything I can find. Maybe I can get some farm work. I was brought up on a farm. I can still throw hay with the best of 'em. Or maybe..." his voice trailed off "... I'll find something at one of the canneries. They might need some help."

"How about your wife? Is she doing okay?"

"I figure by this time she's drawing relief. They give stuff to the families when the husband's...run..." He paused a beat. "...are gone away. I sure hope she's doing well. I sent her a letter a few weeks ago, told her I was holding up. But there's no way in hell she can get in touch with me. That's hard...and...." He broke off.

"How long you been away?"

"I've been on the road for three months now."

"You must miss them a lot."

"Yeah, Tom, I sure do." He looked away and poked the fire with his stick.

So the time passed, and before we knew it, we were like buddies. I kept asking questions, but after a bit he went quiet and didn't answer.

"Let's talk about something else, son," he said. "What does *your* daddy do?"

And how come he had a kettle and cooking utensils—spoons, forks, even salt and pepper shakers, in his knap-sack? Most bums traveled pretty light. As we sat talking and waiting for the stew, the aroma carried up and made my mouth water. Finally, after much stirring, he said, "About ready, Tom. Let's see what we can use for a bowl."

From somewhere in his duffle, he produced a shallow tin can. Which he rinsed in the river before filling it with steaming stew. He handed me a spoon, and I dug in.

When I got home and told Ma about Mr. Harper, she sent me a reproachful look. "How could you take his food? That's probably all he's had in days."

No comeback from me. I knew I was treading on dangerous ground.

Later, as the Depression dragged to a close and work was to be found, tramps gradually faded from the scene. When we finally moved from John Street, it became a novelty to see one at all. Sure, random bums—they call them homeless today—can still be found, but not by the hundreds like when I was a kid.

And why do I still remember that brief, innocent kinship I shared with one Mr. Albert Harper that day? And how good—river water and all—that open-air stew tasted?

A kid adventure, no more than that?

Or was it perhaps because the carrots and potatoes were so generously seasoned with human kindness? Generosity seized from despair?

One can only suppose.

CHAPTER TEN

Out at the Fairgrounds

When the circus rolled into town in early August, it was a major event in our humdrum lives. We waited anxiously for the big day, having been forewarned by the publicity crew that came through two weeks before the actual date, plastering huge, garish signs on billboards and smaller ones on telephone poles, also in obliging storefronts all up and down Main Street.

We kids would take in the snarling lions and tigers, elephants, trapeze artists, and men being shot from cannons and practically vibrate with excitement.

And though we knew there wasn't the chance of a snowball in hell that we'd ever see the inside of a circus tent, we contented ourselves with idle dreamings.

These were Ringling Bros., Barnum & Bailey, and Coles Bros.—really big circus names back then. When they rolled in, always on Chicago and Northwestern track, the line of cars—fifty or sixty at least—stretched down the line as far as you could see. Our house stood no more than two-hundred feet from the tracks themselves.

Location, location!

The circus train rumbled in at three or four in the morning, the locomotive overshooting the depot, the line of freight and passenger cars blocked traffic a half mile each way.

We had the date of arrival branded upon our tiny brains—the event assuming status of Second Coming—and the night before, we'd lay out our clothes for easy access. Our bedroom windows up, we slept with one eye open. And if we weren't awakened by the clack-clack of the rolling stock, the squeal and boom of the braking cars, or the loud, strident shouts of the roustabouts as they began unloading, there was always the magic shuff-shuff-shuff of the elephants' feet as they came down their ramps and moved toward the railhead, where they began dragging down the tack wagons.

That got us out of bed, but fast.

"C'mon, guys, wake up. The circus is here!" I'd hiss, shaking my sleepy brothers awake. We crept downstairs in the dark, pulling on our clothes as we went, closing the front door an inch at a time, lest Ma and Daddy hear us. Then we raced south on Brooke Street toward the depot, where the main action took place.

Some of those mornings were rainy. Others were clear; still others, damp and chill with fog. We'd stand there in just shirts and jeans, more than likely barefoot, teeth chattering, shuddering, yawning, totally lost in the grubby enchantment of the moment. The walking stock—camels, giraffes, alpaca, show horses and ponies—would head east and trudge almost three miles across the city until they reached the Fond du Lac County Fairgrounds. The dray horses were hitched to the wagons as the elephants dragged them down, one by one. Finally the elephants were harnessed to their last load, and they headed out. The performers' coaches, now side-tracked, remained dark.

By this time the sun would be coming up, painting the dawn sky red, then orange, silhouetting the huge beasts—big as a moving house to us—as they lumbered down Brooke Street. What a thrill to walk beside them, all the while yearning to at least reach up and touch one. But we never did. First we were afraid, and second we thought we'd most likely get whopped by one of the elephant guys if we tried.

That—and the parade—was the extent of our circus. These rubberneck sessions were the closest we ever got to the glamour of the Big Top. It was enough, we supposed. Beggars can't be choosers, as Ma always said—another of her tiresome adages.

At 10:00 that same morning, Ma took us kids downtown to secure a good spot to view the circus parade, which started at 11:00. It was a surefire gimmick—the circus honchos hoping to lure the rubes into parting with a buck-fifty for a ticket to the afternoon or evening performances.

It was here my lifelong love affair with bands began; the eye-popping pageantry knocked me out. The crowds; the noise; the cages containing lions, tigers, and gorillas; the capering clowns, some on darting unicycles; the gaudily costumed jugglers; the elegant ladies astride prancing Arabians—all announced by the thunderous blare of a twenty-piece circus band perched atop a large gilded, ornately embossed wagon. They pounded out stirring Sousa marches, and I was transported. I became one with them. I should be up there playing that enormous tuba.

And there we'd stand, the smell of the clowns' funny car exhaust, the smell of popcorn, the smell of the animals, the smell of fresh manure, all floating on the air in heady redolence. And as the trumpets and trombones and tubas blasted, the snare drums tore at our ears, and the bass drums boomed away (was the ground actually shaking?), it seemed my heart would pound itself from my chest.

Bliss. That's how it was when the circus came to town.

We had minor encore on Memorial Day and the Fourth of July, when the Fond du Lac Military Band (Daddy playing cornet) and a gang of high-school bands strutted their stuff. Thus I remain today total sucker for a military band. As for the legions of floats and immense balloon figures in Macy's Thanksgiving parade or those floral extravaganzas rolling past the Rose Bowl grandstands—who needs them? *The bands.* Just let me hear them, let me jitter to the jarring beat of the drums, the growl of the horns. Show me the band members marching in perfect cadence. Even via TV's synthetic sound, the thrill remains; I am bowled over.

That love affair was, most probably, why I became such easy prey when Daddy first proposed our family band—that wonderful Mexican band!

Then the parade was over, and we were left with a strong sense of loss and sadness. Done so soon? And even though we'd scarfed down a couple boxes of popcorn Ma had been nagged into buying from a strolling vendor, it was small consolation. We let the glitter settle in our brains as we trudged home, back to our bleak, real world.

And boo-hoo to you!

* * *

One time Bob Keller came up with the goofy idea of following the wagons out to the fairgrounds in hope of finding something we could do to earn a free pass. And I, eternal patsy, went along with his dumb idea.

When we arrived at the fairgrounds, we were stunned by the chaotic scene. We couldn't believe there was that much canvas in the whole world. It seemingly blanketed acres of landscape. And when the elephants and tractors and tent crews began pulling from all directions and the monstrous poles slowly rose, the canvas top flapping and flowering as it was snugged to hundreds of ropes and cables, we stood amazed, breathless.

Next the ground loops were dropped over gigantic wooden stakes. The roustabouts—white, black, and all colors in between, torrents of sweat streaming from naked torsos—sledge-hammered them deeper into the ground. Little by little the slack was taken up, and the center post shuddered, stood tall and firm, gaily colored pennants already waving from each spar. Now the side posts staggered upright, the flapping canvas walls fell into place like immense drapery.

The Big Top was barely up, the tent gangs still pounding stakes, tightening ropes, when more trucks, loaded with endless miles of steel superstructure, rolled into the vast hippodrome. Moving like an army of ants, hammers driving bolts, wrenches flashing, the bleacher framework went up, section by section, on the east and west sides of the tent.

No sooner was the framework placed than other trucks arrived, carrying the seating planks. Again, precise clockwork, going from riser to riser, the crews bolted these with amazing speed. As they left, sweepers and wipers attacked, to clean the seating.

Each man had a specialty and did his job expertly, swiftly. They had to give it all they had, for there were thousands of men out there desperate for work; slackers didn't last. More trucks entered, and crews began spreading sawdust in the three main rings that had seemingly sprung, full grown, from the fairground turf itself. The audience skirts fell into place yard by yard.

Watching the back-breaking labor—from a good distance, lest we be trampled by the elephants or swatted by the workers—we marveled at the teamwork, the master plan that brought all this magic to life. And we'd thought there might be circus work mere kids could handle?

The sideshow tents went up next, the menagerie area roped off, and the animal cages—the tigers and lions, hippos and rhinos roaring to be fed—were strung in semi-circle behind the roped off viewing area.

And even though the novelty eventually wore off, we still continued to gawk, our tonsils getting sunburned in the bargain.

By this time it was mid-morning, and the parade wagons and the performers were assembling to move into town for the parade. Seeing a large, open cookhouse tent where the crews were drifting in for a late breakfast, we suddenly found ourselves ravenously hungry also.

And hadn't Bob—always Mr. Practical—brought a bag lunch? Which necessity had never occurred to beautiful dreamer here.

Now what? Go hungry, and watch my buddy eat in front of me while my stomach curled around my spine?

We huddled in the shade of a small tree, and Bob, goodhearted to the last, tore off half of his sandwich for me. Which was—of all things—made with limburger cheese. I was momentarily repulsed—that smell! And honest, even as famished as I was, it was all I could do to bring it to my mouth, to force myself to take that first bite. But hunger is a cruel taskmaster. I finally chomped down. I chewed. I swallowed.

And, dear Lord, but didn't it taste good! Whether it was my famished state or the flavor of the limburger itself, I found it delicious beyond belief. I took my own sweet time eating my scrap of sandwich, savoring every bite. When I finished, I fervently wished for more. Bob had brought an apple, which he halved with his pocket knife; it served as dessert.

Yet, as good as the cheese tasted that day, I have never eaten limburger again. To this day I can't smell it without my stomach tilting. Strange, strange.

But my fairgrounds saga doesn't end here. I was to revisit the place again and again in my young life, often with bizarre results.

* * *

Every year, in early August, the *Fond du Lac Commonwealth Reporter* sponsored "Newsboy Night" at the County Fair. Bona-fide carriers got free admission plus a dozen coupons good for free rides and snacks.

I was selling *The Reporter* on Main Street at the time—no route—so I wasn't exactly legit. But my benevolent boss, Bill Bredlaw, saw to it that I got the freebies just the same.

At 6:30 that night we all met outside the main gate, got our coupons and were admitted en masse. Knowing none of the accredited carriers, I was on my own. Which was just fine with me; I could explore the grounds without second-party interference. First stop was the cotton candy stand. After that I rode the Ferris wheel, the Tilt-a-Whirl, and the bang-'em-up cars. Some popcorn and a soda came next.

Somewhere along the line, I got suckered in by the contest stands, eternal carnie fare. You could shoot .22s at moving steel bunnies, throw baseballs at milk bottles or cloth dolls, or test your strength with a big mallet and win a gang of utterly useless prizes. Always close with a dollar, I stood back and watched a few young bucks throw baseballs at milk bottles, hoping to win a plaster doll for the girlfriend.

I studied the action for ten minutes or so, trying to figure an angle before plunking my ticket down. My final strategy? Hit 'em as hard as possible—and close to the neck of the bottle.

Finally, my heart pounding—definitely a first for me; a whole dime ticket at stake—I moved up to the line and handed one over. Three balls for a dime.

"Good luck, son," the genial carnie encouraged.

Wham, I hit the center bottle dead on. It wobbled, but refused to fall. My second ball hit close to the base of the pyramid. *Nada* again. I paused, drew a deep breath, and wound up with my last ball. I put all the steam I had into it. The ball hit dead center, and for a second there, I thought the pile would fall. A definite teeter. Close, but no cigar.

Manic bravado seized me, and angered, sure I could do this, I handed over another ticket. Three more times I wound up and let fly, throwing even harder this time. But again the bottles laughed at me. If I hadn't seen those other guys topple them, I'd have sworn they were glued down.

Another ticket. Same result. And boy, was I steamed. This had to be an A-1 swindle!

Semi-clear heads finally prevailing, I forced myself to walk away, a sullen, hangdog expression on my face. Only four tickets left. I'd be darned if I'd waste them on a rip-off like this. I bought an ice cream cone, then rode the Tilt-A-Whirl—my favorite—again.

But the challenge of the stubborn milk bottles lingered, and still smoking, I returned to the scene of the crime.

"Gonna try again, kid?" the carnie asked. "Good for you."

I had two tickets left. There was a big plaster cowboy on the rack that I really wanted. I threw three balls. Nothing. I threw three more. Again nothing. Now I really lost my head, and a stubborn streak closed in on me, but hard.

I'd brought along fifty cents of my own for extra treats, but I was so ticked at my failures that I ended up handing over all of it, one dime after another. Still the bottles refused to go down. Afterward I became so furious with the smirking carnie—and with myself—that I came close to blubbering.

All that money wasted! For what? Oh, but I was mad!

So there I stood—it was only eight o'clock, still light—with no tickets, no money. Just because I'd been so pig-headed, so sure I could win that damned cowboy. What a dope! I walked the midway, watched the kids on the rides and the kids eating popcorn and cotton candy, feeling sorrier for myself by the minute. Finally, around 8:30, I checked out. Retrieving my bike at the main gate, I headed home, angrier and angrier at myself with every passing block. That was real money, you mutt! I scolded. You don't waste money! Where's your stupid head, anyway?

Never again, I vowed. I'd certainly learned my lesson.

But had I?

Our John Street backyard—the barn an ideal backstop—inspired a plan. Next year, just wait and see, I'd get even with those conniving crooks.

Winter passed, and it was summer again. In early July, reminded of last year's disgrace, I began implementing my holy vow. It was time to go to work.

I had no oversized milk bottles like those at the carnival booth—they'd been specially built, cast of solid lead, no doubt—so I must improvise. I sawed some rough replicas from two-by-six scraps and nailed them to double thickness. Next I rasped the hard edges to form rough approximation of those at the fair. It took hours.

Then I placed them on a box, roughly the same height as the fairgrounds set-up—three on the bottom, two on the second tier, and one at the top. I dug out my tattered softball.

I was in business.

I spent at least four hours a week throwing that ball at the fake bottles. Standing twenty-five feet back, I tried throwing full strength. I tried soft pitches. I threw at the bottom of my target. I threw at the top. Before long I was knocking them down almost every try. Next I moved back fifty feet, and again I became master of the midway.

The week before the county fair, I practiced relentlessly, spending at least an hour a day out there, knocking bottles over one-two-three, seldom missing. Brother, was I ready! I'd need a wagon to bring home all those prizes.

Newsboy night again, and the minute I had my coupons in hand, I made quick beeline for that rip-off concession stand.

But then, when I arrived—hard to believe—I froze. I got the shock of my life. I let loose with a few colorful words, cussing myself all over the fairgrounds and back. Talk about stupid stunts! You dummy, I trash-mouthed. How could you be so stupid?

Watching a man throwing at the bottles, it was like someone slapped me in the face. And where I'd been throwing from twenty, twenty-five, even fifty feet—

Those blasted milk bottles were only twelve feet from the pitching line!

It had to be some kind of trick. They'd moved the bottles since last year! The earth suddenly spun off its axis. And why hadn't I thought to practice at short distances?

Instantly my braggart confidence flew out the window. I was positive I'd miss from that silly range. All my hard work, all those hours of wheeling that dumb softball at my phony-baloney milk bottles—for what?

I stood there for perhaps ten minutes, head spinning, as two more suckers took a whack at the demonic milk bottles. And whiffed. The carnie operator kept looking my way, puzzled I suppose, by the stricken look on my face. When was I going to step up to the plate? Maybe he thought I'd gone *loco*, filled my pants or something.

But his sly smile didn't work. *No*, I stormed inwardly, not this time. *I won't pour good money down that same rat-hole again!*

My stomach churned. I felt like I'd swallowed a pound of buckshot. Abruptly I wheeled and walked away. I headed for the cotton candy stand. After that I ate my first hot dog of the evening.

A learning experience? Hard to tell. Unless I'd come to realize that life isn't always fair. And that some boys are simply born dumb. Really dumb?

In the days following I repeatedly scolded myself. Why hadn't I at least tried? Just one time, for crying out loud! Who knows, my hours of practice might have won the day. I might have knocked down bottles all night.

But then, counter argument, and I convinced myself that I'd done the right thing. I'd have only made a fool of myself again, just like last year.

And who needed that dippy plaster cowboy anyway?

Another fairgrounds turnabout, one that blindsided me a few years later: Contrary to all my wimpy whinings about never getting inside the Big Top, it did happen.

As best as I can recall, I was fourteen and in ninth grade at Roosevelt Junior High. And what do you know, from out of the blue, some charitable group—the Masonics, Elks, Eagles (one of those funny-hat outfits)—had presented Ma and Daddy with circus tickets for their deprived brood. Again August, again Ringling Brothers, Barnum & Bailey, again the Fond du Lac Fairgrounds.

And who got put in charge?

Big brother is watching.

We walked to the fairgrounds that afternoon, arriving a half hour before the 2:30 show. Bernard and David were okay with the whole thing, but Richard, ten, and Martha, only seven at the time, were dubious. Scared silly is more like it. The crowds, the noise, the nonstop commotion, the lions and tigers in their cages—they were truly spooked.

Not only did I have to reassure my sibs nonstop, I had to find our seats and get them settled. I was no circus savant; this was all new to me too.

Our seats were up in the two-hundredth row—it seemed that way anyhow. Martha was crying, and Richard was darned close to it. Ma had insisted that, for this stellar event, her kids would have some treats during the show. Where she scrounged up the buck, I don't know, but before we started up, I bought bags of popcorn all around.

No railings, open air between the risers. I ended up carrying Martha; David and Bernard helped Richard. And so, balancing her—my popcorn and her popcorn—we headed up. By the time we reached our level, she was terrified. "I wanna go home," she whimpered, "I don't like this."

So there we were, finally in our places, wishing for oxygen masks, waiting for the performance to start. I'd finally stuffed enough popcorn into Martha's face to shut her up, but I was still nervous about Bernard and David, who kept bouncing all over the place, not watching Richard at all.

The circus! We're finally here! Heaven can wait.

Only, to me, it wasn't all that great. I was plenty nervous too—all that open air behind me and beneath me. It was at least forty feet to the ground.

You kids, sit still and eat your popcorn. Don't look down.

Big brother be damned, I was frustrated, seething inside. It just wasn't fair. I'd dreamed of one day seeing the circus, and loving every minute of it. Now it had come to pass. And, damn it all to hell, here I was, saddled with the galling, restricting responsibility of riding herd on these kids. What if something awful happened? This wasn't the way it was supposed to be—not on this so special of days!

Well, here came 2:30, and whammo, all hell broke loose!

The band blasted a fanfare, and down at on end of the Big Top, the circus parade began. Gorgeously costumed women mounted on horses, caged lions and tigers, the lion tamers and trapeze artists strutting and waving, the clowns (that crazy car again) cart-wheeling and squirting seltzer at each other, flirting with the women in the front rows. Motorcycles roaring, elephants trumpeting, the audience cheering and clapping—everything going round and round the outer ring.

And carrying over that, the ear-splitting ringmaster's patter. Altogether too much for greenhorn kids to take in. Our eyes kept darting from one ring to the other, up and down, back and forth.

Martha was petrified. Richard wasn't far behind. She sat stiff as a picket-pin, her hand frozen in the depths of her popcorn bag, not the slightest trace of a smile on her face. She crowded closer to me, and I put my arm around her.

"I don't like this," she wailed. "I'm scared. What if I fall?"

Once the show began, things got no better. And yes, we were seated on the fifty-yard line and had excellent view of all three rings. Which, basically, was the problem. For when the motorcyclists were climbing the walls in their steel cage at the far end, the elephants doing stunts in the next, and the trapeze artists swinging in yet another, it drove me bananas.

Why couldn't they just slow down, why couldn't they perform in one ring at a time and allow us to concentrate on each act?

So it went for the next two hours. The lion tamers, the dancing stallions, the acrobats, and the trapeze artists all came in rapid flow, generating more dismay than joy. Even the clowns became a bore. If this is the circus, I fumed, you can keep it! Not fun at all.

Marta and Richard eventually calmed down. Bernard and David laughed and yelled and clapped nonstop. But for me it was a hundred-carat bummer. When the show *finally* ended and we worked our way down the risers—more treacherous than climbing up—I found myself comparing the dismal afternoon to the excitement I'd felt years back while watching the circus trains unload and, after, to the joy I knew as the parade passed by.

Final score: no contest.

Memory of that sad letdown has always bothered. I've never been back.

Is there a moral here? If so, it can best be summed up by the well-frayed refrain: Be careful—be *very* careful—of what you wish for.

Works for me.

CHAPTER ELEVEN

Movie Daze

Remember Bob Keller? That eternal fountain of go-get-it optimism? I swear, nothing daunted that guy. Well, here we were, on a hot, lazy July morning, sitting on his back steps, tossing gravel into a coffee can and mostly missing.

Out of the blue, nothing we were talking about triggering it, he said, "Wanna go to the show this afternoon, Tom?"

"Can't."

"Why not?"

"No money."

"We don't need money," Bob assured in his usual, grandiose nothing-to-it manner. "We'll sneak in."

Sneak-in I knew. "Yeah?" I challenged. "Got a new angle?"

"Yep."

"What?"

"Meet me here after dinner," he said. (We called lunch dinner in those days, while supper was the evening meal.) "And you'll see. Errol Flynn. In *Captain Blood*. You sure wanna see that one, don't you?"

I sure did.

So. At 12:30 sharp there I was, on Bob's doorstep, waiting for him to finish eating.

When he came out, we trip-trapped our way four blocks downtown to the Fond du Lac Theater, my mouth already watering to see the movie of the year.

But instead of going to the theater entrance itself, Bob led me around to the back, on Portland Street, then into the alley running along the north side of the building. Alleys I knew; they were my bread and butter.

"What's the plan, Bob?" I asked.

The plan? We'd simply pry one of the fire exit doors open and barge in.

So much for detailed strategy.

Bob reminded that there was a heavy velvet screen that covered each door on the inside; nobody would notice the momentary burst of daylight as we eased in. Also the movie newsreel would drown out our noise.

Now, for the first time, I noticed the oversized screwdriver jutting from Bob's back pocket. And as Bob drew it out, began working on the door: "Keep your eyes open, Tom. Yell if anyone comes around the corner."

Bravado was definitely not one of my strong suits. In my book this was out-and-out breaking and entering. Right away my shoes filled with ice. "Bob," I said, "I don't wanna do this. We'll get caught. They'll send us to reform school."

"Don't be such a scaredy-cat," Bob reassured. "I tell you nobody will hear, and if you keep your eyes open, nobody's gonna catch us. During matinees they only have two people on duty, the usher and the ticket lady. They're miles away."

My heart lodged in my throat, nervous as a cat at a dog show, I played lookout, while Bob "delicately" worked at the door.

His idea of "no noise" was a far cry from mine. For, as the door stubbornly resisted, he became more and more determined and wrenched the screwdriver more and more savagely.

"Damn it, damn it!" he fumed. "Why won't this thing give?"

And how could the theater patrons, sitting no more than four feet from the door, not hear all that commotion and alert the usher?

I expected the door to burst open at any moment, to be confronted by one of the Thorpe boys or an usher at least. Even as I stood guard, I adjusted my tennies into fast-running mode.

Eventually he'd give up, and we'd head for home. No movie today. Or so I thought. But no, Bob was nothing if not determined. He simply moved to the second door, the one closest to the stage and the screen, started prying there. Again, gently at first, then angrily as the door refused to yield.

After about five minutes of effort and God knows how much noise inside, he finally jammed the screwdriver back into his pocket and growled in exasperation. "Well, I'll be damned."

Now? Home?

Nope. Bob had another idea.

He headed back into the depths of the alley with me tagging along behind, already picturing myself in prison gray. Definitely not my color.

He stopped beneath the heavy, steel fire-escape stairs and looked up. "More than one way to skin a cat," he muttered. "Damn, I *wanna* see that show!"

The next thing I knew, Bob was crouching down, his hands against the brick wall. "Here, climb up on my shoulders. We'll pull that fire escape down."

"No, Bob," I protested. "C'mon, let's get outta here. Someone's bound to show up, catch us for sure."

"Don't be such a sissy," he snapped. "Climb up, you hear?"

So I raised one leg, placed my right foot on his shoulders, hoisted myself up. Now the left foot.

"Lean against the wall," Bob ordered. "Now try standing up."

We did that three or four times, with me losing my balance and hopping backward, landing on my heels. Finally I was able to straighten up, hold my position.

"Can you reach the stairs?" he said.

"Oh, Lord," I wailed as he slowly straightened up, hoisting me into the air, "I don't like this one bit, Bob." His hands grasped my knees firmly, helped brace me. Up, up I went.

The fire escape was perhaps nine feet off the ground. Take my five feet and Bob's five-two, I was able to get my hands on a steel rail and hang on for dear life.

"Hold on," Bob said. "I'm gonna let go."

Before I could scream in protest, he was gone. And I was dangling in midair, my feet waving wildly. But if we thought my weight was going to bring it down, we were gravely mistaken. So there I hung, five feet off the ground.

Good old resourceful Bob. "Grab on!" he ordered. "Tight as you can."

Oh, yes. I grabbed on!

Next thing I knew Bob began pulling on my legs. And little by little, with much incredibly loud squeaking, the fire escape stairs came down and hit the ground with a loud crunch. We ran up them in a flash.

When we reached the platform supporting the stairs, they, of course, slowly rose again. Trapped! I thought. We'll be here until Thanksgiving. What now?

What now—if Bob Keller had anything to say about it—was that we were going to see ourselves a movie. Out came the screwdriver, and—seasoned pro by now—he once more pried the door for all he was worth. Noise be damned!

Then, for a wonder, the door finally gave, and Bob pulled it open inch by slow inch. We darted inside.

When the door was snugly back in place, we waited for our eyes to adjust to the gloom. "We can sit in the balcony," Bob said. "Nobody'll be the wiser."

We scooted quietly down the carpeted hallway, entered the first door we came to. Oblivious to everything else, flush with a decided sense of victory, we crept down two landings, flung ourselves into the first seat we came to, then sat back to enjoy the movie to the fullest. Free, of all things! Why hadn't we thought of this before?

But then—disaster! What the hell?

For as we stared down at the screen—we saw absolutely nothing.

The screen was dark, completely blank.

The theater was as empty as our ditzy heads!

If brains were leather, between us we couldn't have saddled a flea!

Now I realized why nobody came running when all the commotion began downstairs or when the fire escape had screamed to high heaven.

Had we bothered to check show times, we'd have discovered that the Fond du Lac Theater had matinees only on Friday, Saturday, and Sunday. Wouldn't you think—consummate movie fans that we were—that the light would have come on sooner than it did?

"Well, wouldn't that frost you?" Bob muttered, using one of his favorite nonplussed tag lines. "What a bunch of dopes. Let's get outta here."

Up the stairs we went, turned right, opened the door, peeked out to see if anything moved in the alley. Then, the coast clear, we darted out into the daylight. "What do we do now?" I said. "How do we get down?"

"The same way we got up," Bob said. "On the stairs. C'mon, we've both gotta walk out on that thing until it drops down."

Which was exactly what we did, stepping carefully—almost halfway—along the treacherous framework, before our combined weight finally counterbalanced, and the fire escape, again screeching in agony, haltingly descended. The stairs opened, and down we scooted, jumping before it even landed, hitting the ground running.

Then, back out onto Portland Avenue, heading for home, laughing all the way.

"Wouldn't that frost you?" Bob kept saying over and over again. "Wouldn't that just frost you?"

Dumb, dumb, dumb! How could anybody be so incredibly stupid?

At this time in my life I was stark, raving, movie mad.

If I wasn't in the movie house, seated way down front every Saturday at 1:00 PM sharp, the world would certainly tilt off its axis.

And when the weekly dime was in jeopardy—came the old battle cry—back to the alleys!

Though it was sheer misery prying myself from my cozy bed those mornings, I was nothing if not resolute. Willpower was always one of my strong suits. Moaning and groaning, I'd yank myself out. Onto the floor, into my clothes. Then downstairs, out to the garage to grab my wagon, and off to the alleys by 6:00 AM, summer, spring and fall—seldom in winter—two or three days a week.

Junking! What an all-American ring to the word!

Dragging my American Flyer, I trudged the five blocks to downtown—past the tannery, along the Fond du Lac River, up Merrill to Main Street. No dumpsters back then, trash was put into barrels, bins, boxes. Often people just piled scrambled refuse at their back door. A garbage collector's worst nightmare.

Starting at Gibson Chevrolet, I headed south, scouring the alleys behind the stores for perhaps six long city blocks. Reaching the Fond du Lac County Court House (where Main Street turned residential). I crossed the main drag and headed back, hitting shops on the east side. I hit perhaps sixty businesses in all, which took maybe ninety minutes, depending on how many goodies I found.

Gibson's, Gambles, Sears Roebuck, Ford Hopkins, Grant's, Woolworth and Kresge's dime stores, Smith Produce, J.C. Penney, Walgreens, Haber Printing, Hill's Department Store, Dana and Worm, Brauer's, O'Brien's, Fond du Lac Department Store—these stand out. I sought paper, steel, metals, rags—anything I could sell to Dick the Junkman to afford my weekly movie fix.

Once in awhile I budged brother David—"C'mon, Dave, get up…let's go junking!"—or, less often, Bernard, to tag along. Those mornings, someone to breeze with, time passed quickly. Also there was help should I need to lift heavier stuff.

I'd stumble onto discarded auto parts behind Gibson Chevrolet. Gambles was a hardware store; no telling what you'd encounter. Copper and aluminum (no beer cans then) were real finds. I'd stomp glass light bulbs, then hammer the zinc base to pulp. I'd strip copper wire. I'd peel tinfoil from cigarette wrappers and transform layer upon layer into a baseball-sized lump.

Ahern's was usually good for a few mangled copper elbows, Y joints, or random pieces of pipe. Should I happen upon a discarded auto battery—fifty whole cents right there!

Rags and metal brought a half-cent a pound. It took a big bale of paper to make a nickel's worth. Copper was two cents. Hard work to earn a dime. I rescued scrap from the streets. I rambled the railroad tracks looking for spikes, tie plates, any Soo Line and Chicago-Northwestern junk I might stumble upon. When oil or paint concealed the metal's real nature, out came my pocket magnet. If it didn't cling, it was worth more money.

Dick the Junkman worked the whole west side and reached our area on Thursdays. In summer we'd wait all afternoon for him to show up. School in session, Ma would watch while he weighed. You could hear his horse, Helen—pulling a dilapidated four-wheel wagon—clop-clop-clopping a half block away. He'd lead her right into our driveway. What fun to pet Helen's nose and feed her grass and alfalfa from the vacant lot next door!

Dick used a hand scale with a hook on the end. He'd throw my scrap into a square of burlap, hook it on, and weigh. And when our business was completed: "Aw, Dick, only eight cents. C'mon, weigh it again."

Dick was gentle and patient; times were tough for him too. Even so, friendly or not, I often felt he was cheating me. His dumb scale wasn't reading honest weight.

Sure, I could haul my stuff four blocks north to Sam Manus' junkyard. But Sam wouldn't even leave his shed if I didn't have a wagonload. "Go home, keed," he'd yell, "come beck ven you got some-ting to zell." Anyway, how was I to know *he* wasn't ripping me off too?

And since I needed cash fast—Dick the Junkman.

Those weeks when the mother lode ran out, I'd have to fall back on Plan B: badgering Ma out of a dime.

The typical song-and-dance—Ming the Merciless about to destroy the universe—found Ma stonily unmoved.

"But, Ma," I'd plead, squinching my face up to signal impending tears, "I just gotta see what happens this week. Flash Gordon's rocket ship was just about to crash into Saturn. I *have* to see this episode. Gee, it's only a dime. Please, Ma…"

She'd keep peeling potatoes like I wasn't even there. "If wishes were horses, all beggars would ride" was her favorite comeback. Or else: "You won't die if you don't see Flash Gordon."

Poor Ma. No imagination whatsoever.

Then came Plan C: Daddy paid us a penny a bushel for coal. We pulled our wagon a block west to the Valley Coal Company and scrounged scraps off the tracks where the coal cars unloaded. It was tedious, wearisome work; it took us forever to fill a bushel basket with dribs and drabs of coal.

I remember once a Soo Line freight rolled slowly past, and the fireman, seeing us grubbing away, kicked out two or three huge chunks of coal. Did we chase! Two baskets right there.

Then, one morning, the sun just peeking over the horizon, inspiration struck. Dummy! Why hadn't I thought of this before?

Another block and a half to the west—on ten acres of nothing—sat the Wisconsin Power and Light plant. And right beside it stood this pile—at least fifty-feet high, two-hundred-feet long—of coke. Surely they'd never miss a few bushels every now and then.

Yes, it was a longer haul. But Lordy, didn't those baskets fill up fast!

New axiom: Go west, young man!

We'd scoot through a stretch of marsh, cross a big field, and then come upon Coke Mountain. We dug in. At least two mornings a week, David and I became coal runners. Getting home, the coal bin window open and waiting, we'd dump two bushels, then hurry back. With some real hustle we could make a dime a morning. Which dime I was obliged to split with David, but so what? It sure beat combing the railroad tracks.

Dad, proud of our industriousness, never questioning the change from bituminous to coke, happily paid the pennies.

This was okay during spring, summer, and fall, but during the winter, no way. Ever try dragging a wagon through three feet of snow?

And when push came to shove, and I couldn't go junking or steal coal:

Plan D involved going downtown and climbing some dirty, rickety stairs to Grandma Eva's creepy Second Street apartment. It was situated right over the Black Hawk Tavern, and at night you could hear the trade laughing and arguing, the dice boxes slamming on the bar, the jukebox blasting.

Grandma was half crazy most of the time. She worked as a dishwasher at the Retlaw Hotel. The other kitchen workers poked fun, played tricks on her, and taunted her at every turn. She constantly muttered and grumbled about how everyone took advantage of her. And so? Here comes number one grandson to—

Take advantage, what else?

There were no curtains on the grimy windows, no electricity; she cooked her meals on a tiny gas stove. At night she'd sit beside a kerosene lamp, studying her Bible, muttering, and copying verses on scraps of paper far into the night.

There was a kitchen, sitting room, and bedroom—all in one ratty twenty-five-foot square room. At her kitchen table sat four unfinished chairs (Sears Roebuck) she'd put together herself. She'd attached the legs every which way, and once the glue set, there was no turning back. Not one of them set straight. We'd teeter-totter back and forth on them when we sat. She should have handed out seat belts.

Later she borrowed a handsaw and sawed here, sawed there, to no avail. The chair seats just got that much closer to the floor. Level was not in her vocabulary.

Grandma always wanted me to sit down and eat something. But I'd seen the inside of her ice box—not even the mice would touch its contents. Why she didn't die of ptomaine poisoning, I'll never know. I had to talk fast so as not to hurt her feelings. "Thanks, Grandma, I just ate. I'm not the least bit hungry."

She always seemed glad to see me, but I never felt quite comfortable around her. So we'd briefly pass the time of day, and shortly I'd commence my song-and-dance.

"Hey, Grandma, there's this wonderful Tarzan movie that I'm just dying to see, but I don't have enough money and…"

Whine, whine.

Without a moment's hesitation, she'd reach down the front of her dress and drag out a small leather change purse.

"Well, Thomas," she'd say, like I was doing her a favor by cadging money, "I can help with that. What does the movie cost?"

Mostly I'd settle for a dime, but sometimes (devious little sneak), I'd angle for a quarter. "It's a special feature, and the admission's a little higher than usual…"

Weasel—my middle name.

And plop, plop, the coins would fall into my greedy little palm. "Oh, thanks so much, Grandma. I'll pay you back the next time I go junking." (I had no intention whatsoever of repaying her.) "Honest I will."

"Never mind paying me back. I'm glad to help. You come see me anytime you need something."

I felt guilty as hell. I hated myself every time I pulled my Pitiful Paul number on her. Grandma was being grossly underpaid at the

Retlaw—a quarter an hour tops—doing work nobody else wanted to do, just barely hanging on. And here I was sticking it to her again.

If Ma learned I'd gone begging to Grandma, she'd have skinned me good.

But Grandma never told. As I said, her receiver was off the hook most of the time; the minute I was gone, she'd forget I'd ever been there. Back to The Bible.

And who, exactly, were some of my favorite movie stars back then? For starters, the cowboys: Gene Autry, Hoot Gibson, Johnny Mack Brown, Buck Jones, Tom Mix, Ken Maynard, and Harry Carey. How that gang of bow-legged bozos made our innocent little hearts race! And sure, these oaters were pure formula, the same in every picture—cowboy meets girl, cowboy rescues girl, cowboy kisses horse—but we'd have it no other way.

The theater, jam-packed with kids, would erupt in frenzied yelling, all of us on our feet, as Buck or Gene raced down the canyon on Trigger or Champion, arriving just in time to thwart the baddies. Curses, foiled again! They scooped up the pretty little lady (always dressed in immaculate gingham) and yank her away from danger at the last minute. Or, better still, here came the U.S. Cavalry, thundering across the prairie, to run off those pesky redskins!

What else twanged our banjos? *Tarzan of the Apes* was the reddest of meat to us; we didn't dare miss a one. Johnny Weissmuller was a hero to remember. And Maureen O'Sullivan, as Jane, was just right—some mush, but not a lot.

Then those movies about the Foreign Legion, *Beau Geste*, the India epics, *Gunga Din*, *Wee Willie Winkie*, and *Lives of a Bengal Lancer*. In one battle scene (bloodless back then) in *Bengal Lancer*, a little Indian boy lay dead. I sat through that one twice just to see the kid's toes wiggle.

Freddie Bartholomew and Spencer Tracy in *Captains Courageous* became an all-time favorite. I bawled like a baby every time the Portuguese fisherman died, sawed in half by a steel cable. Manuel became instant surrogate dad for every kid in America. It was dark, after 7:30 PM, when I came out of the theater. I'd watched three whole shows. Did I catch it from Ma when I finally got home.

Who can forget seeing Errol Flynn swing out of the trees in *Robin Hood* or the sublime joy when he dueled nasty, sneering Basil Rathbone to the death.

This is The Life, with Jane Withers, is burned in my memory forever. As are Shirley Temple in *Heidi* and Spanky McFarland in *Trail of the Lonesome Pine*.

Then came *Treasure Island*, starring Jackie Cooper and Wallace Beery. When hideous "Blind Pew" tottered into sight, I cringed in terror. Long John Silver was such a rat fink, but Beery brought him across so well that I felt total devotion at the end as he conned Jim Hawkins into letting him escape.

"Honest we will," he told Jim, vowing they'd be shipmates again.

Aye, Long John, I sighed happily. I'll be waiting.

The Wizard of Oz with Judy Garland was, I suppose, the most memorable movie of my boyhood. Judy was incredible; I was madly in love. Those ruby slippers! My first sexual awakenings—although I had no idea what those tinglings meant at the time. One thing certain: Shirley and Jane never worked me up that way.

Movies *were* the opiate of the masses during the Great Depression. Once in the theater, all the travail of our deprived, humdrum days was—for that brief interval—whisked away.

And if the Depression cramped our national style, it posed even greater disaster for the Thorpe brothers, owners of The Fond du Lac, Retlaw, and Garrick theaters. Those seats *must* be filled if they were to stay open. So they came up with gimmick after gimmick to lure the masses into their fantasy dens.

"Dish Night" was not original with the Thorpes; it was a theater drawing card across the nation. Every Wednesday evening each adult ticket got you a free dish—the famous Weeping Willow pattern. Everyone would want the complete set, wouldn't they? And how many movies would that take? Those who could afford weekly escape to Hollywood Nirvana flocked in, and attendance shot up.

The amateur hour (the same one where our Mexican band got scuttled) was another draw. Ads in the local paper announced fab prizes for the contestants—five-dollars for first place, three-dollars second, and free movie tickets after that.

Mostly the Thorpes managed to round up five or six suckers, and the show went on. This worked okay, but after they ran out of contestants and the same no-talent turkeys kept showing up, the audiences began to boo—no hook necessary.

"We want the show!" they thundered.

Special matinees at Easter, Thanksgiving, and Christmas featured free prizes—hang onto your ticket stub, kids—like plush bunnies, candy baskets, pilgrim and Santa dolls, toy guns, and baseballs for the boys. Santa *in person* stood behind the ticket taker to hand out schlock bags of candy kisses as we entered. Heart, be still!

Then the Merchant Matinees. These promotions offered free tickets (with minimum purchase) from participating businesses. Other times it took bread wrappers, paint can labels, store-imprint bags, cash register receipts. There were also canned food for the poor shows.

Hey, front and center—we *were* the poor.

One such matinee called for Great Western Paint labels. Just by chance I'd stumbled upon a mountain of empty paint cans behind Fond du Lac Concrete Products, mostly Great Western. I waded in and peeled labels like crazy. That Saturday my brothers—plus virtually every kid in the neighborhood—became my guests. The ticket taker rolled his eyes when he saw the long line of Johnson Street ruffians—at least a dozen of us—all waving paint labels.

Other tickets obtained from choice merchants were two-for-ones. With each purchase you got a coupon to present at the box office, which allowed a second person—wife, child, girlfriend—to get in free. Many were the times I worked the line, coupon in hand. Spotting a lone man or woman, I'd flash it and go into my lingo: "Please, sir, would you pretend I'm your little boy so I can go in to see the show?"

Mostly they laughed and herded me in beside them. The women were easy; I'd put on my Tiny Tim face, and they'd melt.

Piece of cake.

Another gimmick involved putting on my most raggedy clothes and hanging around the theater lobby for hours on a Sunday afternoon. I'd look at the posters longingly until the usher/ticket taker took pity and said, "Go on in, kid." But this only worked once or twice. Unless they hired a new ticket taker.

To hype the concession trade, there was usually an intermission between features, and a gang of patrons would step out for snacks or for a smoke. Bob and I, or one of my brothers, would place ourselves strategically at the outside door, then zip in when the usher got distracted. We'd melt into the crowd and from there casually walk in. We only saw the last feature, but what the heck—beggars can't be choosers!

Once or twice I actually resorted to outright begging. "Please, mister, would you be kind enough to give me a dime so I can see this movie?" This in my most woeful voice. "I wanna see this show so bad..."

Do the Calypso! How low can you go?

Strange sidelight: My wife actually recalls seeing me swing into my act on a Sunday afternoon way back when. Her dad was the nice guy who laughed and planked down an extra dime for that pitiful "urchin."

But far and away, the best gimmick theater owners foisted on America's small-fry were the Saturday afternoon serials. There was rigid order to be sure: First came the coming attractions, then several cartoons or maybe short-reel stuff. Remember *The March of Time*, *Pete Smith Specialties*, or *The Passing Parade*? After that came the week's serial. Then the main feature. By the time the lights came up again, it was 4:00 PM.

Back to the real world.

The most popular cliff-hangers were *New Adventures of Tarzan* or shoot-'em-up westerns. Buster Crabbe, fresh from Olympics competition, starred in *Flash Gordon*. The ridiculous special effects they foisted upon us when rocket ships supposedly zipped between planets! They looked like tin cans with fins. But to shrimps like us they were the real McCoy—dazzling! And wasn't Dale Arden, in her skimpy outfits, about the sexiest thing we kids had ever seen?

We also grooved on *The Phantom Empire*, *Zorro Rides Again*, *Dick Tracy*, *Jungle Jim*—the list goes on. The serials ran twelve to fifteen episodes. But never fear, a new series was always waiting in the wings.

No *Rebecca of Sunnybrook Farm*. These serials *were* geared strictly for boys; girls didn't rate. Like it or lump it. It was a macho world.

Those movie serials became theater salvation. Get those little brats hooked; keep 'em coming back every Saturday. So we got fifteen minutes of incredible action, with the hero going off the cliff at the last minute. Then that hated "CONTINUED NEXT WEEK" banner-line flashed across the screen. The collective groans and cries of protest would shrivel your ears. But if we were in agony, the theater owners stood in the lobby rubbing their hands. How could kids be so dumb?

Worth mention is the fact that air conditioning never came along until the late '30s. In summer you could almost see steam rising from all the bodies in the theater. *Dante's Inferno*. When AC did arrive, the Thorpes were quick to hang big banners—icicles and all—along the marquee to announce "Refrigeration Inside."

Another of our movie venues was the local YMCA. On Friday nights we saw three shorts in a row featuring *Our Gang* or *Laurel and Hardy*, priced at three cents. One or more of my brothers along for the ride, we'd howl our heads off!

During Lent, Fr. Dunnigan, our much loved St. Paul's Cathedral priest, started "Kid's Night" in the Parish Hall. Again, more *Our Gang* and *Laurel and Hardy*. But there was a catch. We must sit through a Biblical film beforehand—small enough price to pay for an hour of belly-busting laughter.

I guess, even back then, I was fated to become a writer. Town Talk Bakery, located on North Macy just off Division Street, ran a contest offering theater tickets for the five best essays on why we little monsters liked Town Talk bread. I sank into my bread prose trance and wrote stuff to wrench a mother's heart. I took second prize, which got me five sets of movie tickets, two to a set. I felt like Father Christmas when I took one or another of my brothers or buddy Bob Keller along.

Yet another whacko movie house adventure lingers:

This particular summer afternoon, David, Richard, and I, plus a neighborhood kid named Billy Simon, were at loose ends and wandered up and down Main Street, mainly killing time. We entered the library, spent an hour with the stereopticons. Then we were on the move again.

As we walked west on Sheboygan Street, we passed a cul-de-sac housing the Retlaw Theater's fire exit and found the door was halfway open.

"At least we can catch the end of the show," I told my gullible minions. "Let's go."

Experience tends to lead one astray at times. Wise brother indeed!

This time we had warning from the get-go. Big letdown: The theater was dark and empty; the afternoon matinee, long over. It was cleanup time, and preparation for the evening show was underway. Why bother going in at all? Did we intend to hide out inside until the evening feature began?

The logic evades me. Mainly because there wasn't any.

Anyway, instead of backing off, we eased our way down the side aisle and headed for the stage, the blank screen mocking us all the way.

"C'mon, let's go up and see what's back there," I whispered.

We mounted some stairs and felt our way carefully into the gloom. We made our way behind the screen and stumbled around in the dark.

Shortly our eyes became accustomed to the half-light, and we saw a mishmash of boxes, film canisters, rolls of cable, pails and brooms, and even a couple of standup microphones scattered helter-skelter. And to the extreme right, a grand piano.

Just then one of the ushers, whistling as he came, headed down the main aisle toward the stage.

"Hide," I hissed. "Don't let him see us."

Mostly we slid behind a bank of back curtains and hoped he wouldn't come all the way onstage. As usual, our luck was bad; he *did* come up, perhaps to put his mop away—who knows? There was a click, and suddenly a dozen spotlights exploded around us. Poor David didn't duck fast enough and the usher, a pawky seventeen-year-old, spotted him.

"Hey, what are you doing back here, kid?"

David was caught flat-footed and was at definite loss for words.

"I came in to…see…the movie," he said, his face panicky.

"Some helluva place to see a movie," the usher said. "Anyway, the show was over an hour ago. Now beat it before I call the police."

In retrospect I suppose the usher was as surprised as David. But to us kids, he was a man, full blown, a force to be reckoned with; we never thought to question his authority.

Next I emerged from behind my curtain. Richard followed, adding to the guy's chagrin. He actually looked scared. There is such a thing as strength in numbers; I suppose we could have charged him or some such foolishness. But just as quickly his bravado roared back; he became Mr. Boss Man again.

"You oughta know better than to sneak into a theater," he grumbled. "Now, all you little shits get outta here! Vamoose, or I *will* call the cops."

We were fresh out of snappy comebacks. And hunched down, shame-faced, we headed for the stairs.

Just then Billy Simons, the smallest of the gang, popped out from under the piano. "You want me too?" he asked.

The usher whirled around. And just how many little sawed-offs were there? he must have wondered. They're coming out of the walls!

"All of you!" he shouted. "Get your little asses outta here. *Now!*"

We were out and onto Sheboygan Street, but fast! Faltering momentarily as our eyes adjusted to the late afternoon light, we bolted toward Main. The people on the street looked around as we fled but with no great concern. *Kids. There was no telling what they'd get into next.*

We were a block and a half down Main, almost to Division Street, before we eased off and settled into a fast walk, satisfied that the guy wasn't on our tail.

When we arrived in time for supper, neither Ma nor Daddy asked where we'd been. And we certainly weren't about to volunteer any explanations.

But then, when Bernard began giving David the old fish eye…

"We were downtown looking in the stores," David falteringly began to explain.

I wanted to sock him one. Sleeping dogs and all that. Richard and

I said nothing but nodded like wise little owls. Seeing our glares, David abruptly veered off.

"It would sure be nice to have some money," he gabbled, "so...ah...so we could...buy some...candy or something...once in a while."

"Money, huh?" Ma said, giving us the look as she clanked beans onto our plates. "Candy? Just be thankful you've got food on the table. I haven't seen any of you losing any weight lately."

We all grabbed a hot tortilla and dug into our *frijoles*; we ate like it was work.

Not another word from any of us.

Yes, those were the days!

Movie daze!

CHAPTER TWELVE

How about a Walnetto?

Today's TV viewers might remember Martin & Rowan's wild and whacky TV show *Laugh In*, which aired from 1968 to 1972. And in particular, Arte Johnson, "the dirty old man" who harassed spinster-stereotype Ruth Buzzi nonstop. He usually appeared in a baggy coat and bowler hat, riding a kiddy tricycle. He'd squeeze in beside the disdainful, hair-netted Buzzi on a park bench.

Then he'd ask, in a low growl, "How about a Walnetto?"

There were those who read lewd overtone into the phrase, little knowing that those naughty Walnettos actually referred to a tasty brand of caramels containing walnut shreds, a very popular confection during the '30s. There were, I think, six caramels to the package—each thin, wrapped in wax paper, and hard as a rock. I bought mine at a tiny grocery store located around the corner from our John Street house. Two cents, cheap.

I was Mr. Big Stuff then, flush with paper route earnings, and could usually afford my Walnetto fix. I'd plunk my pennies onto the counter, and the lady would smile and shove the caramels over. I'd grab them, hop on my bike, and race madly for Roosevelt Junior High. No, Tom, not tardy again!

I never dug into the package right away but saved the yummy suckings and chewings for class. Miss Edna Ford's fourth-hour science class was usually where the crime took place. Back then eating candy or chewing gum in class took on proportions of a felony and drew after-school detention. I couldn't be late reaching the Main Street corner where I hawked the *Fond du Lac Common-*

wealth Reporter. We boys would bomb out of school at closing bell, grab our bikes, and race to be first in line at *The Reporter* dispatcher's cage.

Even so, I refused to let this threat deter me. The daring and suspense of fooling the teacher was a definite part of the game; it made my Walnettos all the tastier.

Stealthy unwrapping of each caramel without detection became extra triumph. Then—supreme audacity—assuming innocent, studious expression, I'd stare Miss Ford directly in the eye. She never suspecting that heaven was melting in my mouth.

Jimmy Cagney would've been proud.

I became devilishly adept at sneaking each candy into my mouth when she wasn't looking, soaking it there, letting the delicious syrup slide down my throat. Or in total recklessness—actually chewing one. I can taste it now!

But Walnettos were only tip of the iceberg when it came to the vast array of penny and nickel candies available during the Great Depression. We kids became the bane of the storekeeper's existence as we dawdled at the candy counter for five minutes at a time, agonizing over which treat to squander our penny on.

Would you believe, some stores actually provided a step stool before the candy counter to help small fry view the array of sweet delights?

"C'mon, kid, make up your mind; I ain't got all day." The words could have easily become a line in our National Anthem.

Chewing gums of infinite variety, tiny wax bottles containing sweet colored water, Ju-Ju Babies, Necco Wafers, nonpareils we called "chocolate pennies," Snaps, Goo Goo Clusters, Tootsie Rolls, jumbo gum drops, Milk Duds, licorice whips, candy cigarettes—mostly selling for a penny apiece or by the tiny scoopful. I remember twelve-inch strips of paper embedded with myriad candy buttons that we chewed off one by one. Ecstasy!

Wax mustaches and lips were a gag item. After you placed them in your mouth and made faces at all your friends, you crunched them like regular chewing gum. Salted pumpkin seeds were a real steal. A penny a box, they lasted for hours.

Popsicles and Eskimo Pies were five-cent staples. We also bought small cups of ice cream—Dixie Cups, three cents—with photos of movie stars on the back of the cap. We saved Eskimo Pie wrappers and took them to Verifine Dairy on W. Division Street to trade for prizes—jackknives, marbles, and cap guns for the boys; play dishware sets, dolls, fancy skip-ropes for the girls.

Years later, moving to Tompkins Street, we discovered a small shop around the corner on Hickory Street, where they sold off-brand popsicles for two for a nickel. Best of all, we had inside track; the east-side kids never homed in on this bonanza.

Around Valentine's Day came the tiny candy hearts, same as today, printed with sassy slogans. "OH, YOU KID," "BE MY VALENTINE," "HI BABY," "BE MINE," "SWEET ONE,"—they ran the gamut of sappy affection.

Power House and Baby Ruth candy bars went for a nickel and weighed a quarter pound. Four whole ounces, folks—a far cry from today's micro bars costing a half-dollar or more. We could make a nickel Holloway sucker last for hours. Often we re-wrapped what was left to savor the next day. Money's worth? You bet!

Jaw-breakers, big as golf-balls cost two cents—multi-layered with different colors of candy that lasted a whole afternoon. You could break your jaw, or at least chip a tooth, if you got careless. A dentist's delight.

Fleer's bubble gum for a penny. A pink gob, big as a small walnut—you chewed it for hours. Some show-offs who were more flush than I crammed two or three into their mouth at the same time and chewed like hippos. Ugh and double ugh! We saved the wrappers, flattened them with a warm iron, the better to read (and preserve) the miniature comic strips printed on each. Fleer Funnies, they were called.

And yes, Cracker Jacks, but they were expensive for the times. Five cents a box. But so delicious! However, the prizes seldom lived up to expectation.

Fond du Lac had its own factory, Bonita Candy, located on the corner of First and Marr Streets. Their big seller was a bar called Leaping Lena. The Bragg School kids would scoot over at noon hour and beg free samples from the employees eating lunch on the shipping dock. Sometimes they were rewarded; mostly they were not.

THAT WONDERFUL MEXICAN BAND

Don't start something you can't finish.

When I was six and living at the Five Points, I spent many a penny on Indian Chewing Gum. It came in a wax wrapper that contained a thin piece of gum, playing-card size. Each pane of gum came with a card picturing a famous Indian chief—Geronimo, Black Wolf, Tecumseh, Pontiac, White Cloud. A brief history of each Indian was printed on the back. A beginning reader at the time, the bios got short shrift.

I collected at least fifty of them and kept them secured with a heavy rubber band. Often, sorting through my collection—the cards still redolent of chewing gum—the aroma would trigger overwhelming need, and off I'd scurry for a fresh pack. There were baseball cards and football cards as well. But these didn't light my fires. Indians! Give me Indians!

Later on, when I sold papers on Walgreens' corner, I often interrupted commerce to run down to Newberry's five-and-ten for a half pound of Spanish peanuts or chocolate drops—five cents. Candy corn, bulk potato chips, orange slices, vanilla wafers, lemon drops, marshmallow peanuts—all ten cents a pound. I'd wedge the bag of peanuts or whatever into one corner of my paper sack and nibble while taking care of business.

Then the peanut butter kisses. Sometimes I'd save some for our dog, Snoopy. When the candy got caught in his teeth, he'd roll around on the floor whining, fighting to pry the gob free. We'd laugh our heads off. Immediately, upon dislodging and swallowing the last morsel, he'd come tail-wagging for seconds.

I had a newsboy buddy, Ray Baum, who was the original big spender. He sold *The Milwaukee Journal* on the same corner, and we chewed up a lot of schoolboy politics—he was for Wendell Willkie; I loved FDR—while awaiting customers. Often, as our day ended, he'd say, "C'mon, Tom, let's go down to Fairmont's and grab a sundae."

A real moocher, I'd tag along and let him spend his dimes. But did I ever buy back? Hell no! Mini-Scrooge, I hoarded every penny. Such sporty gestures were lightyears beyond my stingy comprehension.

Odd, the memories that drift back. In those days every store on

Main Street had an awning that stretched halfway across the sidewalk. Every night around five, someone had to roll them up with a noisy crank. Gone today. How come? The sun still shines.

Later, a surplus candy store opened on the east side of Main Street, directly south of the Retlaw Theater. They sold off-brand, outdated, and damaged sweets—mangled gum drops and chocolates, odd cuts of licorice, stale malted-milk balls—for five and six cents a pound.

Double-dip ice cream cones went for a nickel. Jelly beans, red-hots, jaw-breakers, candy corn, coffee beans, coconut squares, chocolate clusters, nigger babies (sorry, that's what they were called then), and more—the candy parade stretched to the farthest depths of the store.

Here also, I'd chip in with one of my brothers to buy a pint of ice cream for ten cents. We'd ask the lady clerk to slice the carton in half and throw in an extra ice-cream paddle. Then we'd sit on the curb before the store—colorful, free advertising—and eat ice-cream till we burst.

They sold twenty-eight-ounce bottles of root-beer, ginger-ale, cola, orange, and grape for seven cents. So cold it would jar your teeth. We'd request two straws. Perched on the curb, we'd slurp it down, racing each other to get more than our share.

Someone should have taken a photograph.

Sometimes we just fell into unexpected bonanzas. We had a super-polite African-American buddy (we called them "colored" or "darkies"—Ma swatted us if we used the N-word) named Louie Williams, who, for some reason forever unknown to me, became a sort of mascot at Hope's Candies, the city's elite candy shop on the corner of Sheboygan and Main.

Louie was gifted with a pound of stale chocolates whenever he appeared at their back door. "Let's go down to Hope's," we'd wheedle whenever Louie was along, and off we'd go. But not every time. Even as a kid, Louie knew his limits—best not to kill the golden goose by showing up too often.

Same thing with brother Bernard. He got on a charity list at the Caramel Crisp Shop, located one door south of the Retlaw Theater. Here they sold crispy, caramel-coated popcorn and did a good movie business. (You could bring in your own snacks back then.) The husband and wife, both gray-heads, fawned on Bernard, and he never left the store without a big sack of the mouth-watering treat. These times we shadowed him relentlessly, hoping for dibs.

At Christmas they gave him a five-pound tin to share with his family. Our cup runneth over!

Mrs. Mable Wetzler, a kind widow who lived on Linden Street just off Western Avenue, sort of adopted me. Now and then, when I delivered her paper, she'd meet me at the door and give me a small bag of home-baked cookies, her thanks for faithfully placing *The Reporter* between the doors. When I made my monthly collections, there'd be warm and loving conversation—and a *bigger* bag of cookies.

Often, at supper, when Ma saw me picking at my food, she'd scold: "What's the matter, Thomas? You usually have such a good appetite. Why aren't you hungry?"

Yeah. Why, indeed?

CHAPTER THIRTEEN

Flying Down to Rio with Jenny

Then there was strange turnabout wherein I actually had to be bribed to watch a movie. It was called *Flying Down To Rio*, and it was a loser from the word go.

This wild departure took place when I was seven, living on Johnson Street. I came in from playing that particular Sunday morning and found two strangers in the kitchen drinking coffee with my parents.

"Thomas," Ma said, "this is Jenny and Francisco."

I acknowledged them and went about my business. Those were "children seen and not heard" days, remember?

It seemed to me that the couple (they were only sixteen and eighteen I later learned—grownups in my eyes) was very secretive, and definitely on edge. Francisco kept walking back and forth, looking out the window. Daddy took him outside. They stood in the yard, their heads together for a long time, Francisco paying close attention.

They were with us the rest of the morning and ate an early dinner (lunch) with us. Shortly after, Francisco gave Jenny a hasty kiss and then hurried out the back door, his expression even darker than before.

Wonder of wonders, Jenny approached me shortly afterward and said, "Tomás, would you like to go to the movies with me? There's a good show on. I'll pay your way."

Well. How would I like a pocket full of silver dollars? I was ready in an instant. Ma and Daddy had secret business; neither could accompany Jenny to the movies. Since she was from Milwaukee, someone must lead her downtown. I could walk to any of Fondy's three theaters in my sleep.

The matinee started at one o'clock; we were in our seats in plenty of time. As I said—seven—I wasn't ready for a sophisticated movie like *Flying Down To Rio*. Unbeknownst to me then, it was Ginger Rogers and Fred Astaire's first team-up. I remember that, beyond their dancing, there were a million chorus girls hanging on ropes from airplanes, dancing on the wings, waving and singing. Which I thought was pretty sharp.

In between: endless dance production numbers that bored me silly.

The only really clear memory I have was of some guy standing in the jungle when a golf ball came flying through the palm trees and hit him square in the head. Down he went. Now *that* was funny. I laughed like a loony.

But Jenny never laughed once—not then or through the entire show. It was like she wasn't even seeing the screen. Glancing over at her now and then, I saw her face was tense, her eyes sometimes glistening with tears.

But, hey, no cowboys, no Indians, no horses, no action that I could really get into. When the movie ended, I'd had enough. It was time to go.

But Jenny didn't budge. "Let's stay and watch it again, okay?"

I balked. "Why? It's a dumb show."

"But you liked that part where the man got hit by the golf ball, didn't you?"

"Yeah, but not enough to sit through another whole show for."

"Please?"

"No. It's almost supper time. I'm hungry."

"If I buy you some popcorn? Maybe a candy bar? Would you stay then?"

An offer no red-blooded American boy could refuse. And when she pressed a whole quarter into my greedy little palm and said, "Go buy what you want, Tomás," I became instant bought man. I spun up the aisle like I had wheels.

I returned with a large box of popcorn and a couple Baby Ruths; I'd splurged, spent the whole quarter. I was attentive during the cartoons. Even the *Movietone News* was worth a second look. I concentrated on my popcorn. But when the feature started, I pretty much tuned out, kept puzzling over why Jenny would sit through such a dumb show a second time.

Little did I know.

"Watch now," she said, nudging me a half hour later. "Here's the part you like."

But the golf ball rerun wasn't as funny as the first time. It was almost like I had to force up laughter. Then back to the dancing girls. I went to the bathroom two times.

This feature ended around 6:30, and now I really wanted to head home. "Can we go now?" I itch-bagged.

"Why don't we stay and see it again?" Jenny said, really frantic by then. "Please, Tomás?"

"But it's past suppertime. Ma'll be mad if we don't get home."

"It's okay," she soothed. "Marie told me that you could stay as late as you liked."

"But I'm hungry," I grumped. "I want to go home."

She shoved another quarter into my hand. "Here, go buy yourself some more popcorn, maybe an Eskimo Pie. Or some Coca-Cola. Would that help?"

Reluctantly I trudged up the aisle again. Sure the free treats were great; I knew I'd never fall into such a windfall again. But I was tired and cranky. However, if Ma had told Jenny I could stay out late, why knock it?

I was sleeping when the third showing ended. I'd missed the whole golf ball shtick this time. I wondered why I'd found it funny in the first place. It was around ten o'clock when Jenny gently shook me awake.

"Okay, Tomás," she said, her voice eager all at once, "we can go home now."

It was just as Jenny had said. Ma and Daddy were sitting in the living room with Francisco. They never said a word about the hour. It was almost like the whole thing had been carefully planned. And I'd been stooge number one.

Francisco jumped up from his chair, hurried to Jenny. He hugged and kissed her. She rattled off a gang of questions in Spanish, and he

THAT WONDERFUL MEXICAN BAND

kept smiling and nodding.

Ma placed her hand on my shoulder, smiled down at me, almost as if she was proud of me. "Are you hungry, Thomas? Did you eat something at the show?"

I nodded glumly, truly dragging by then. "Yeah, Ma. Popcorn and ice cream and two candy bars. I think I'll just go to bed."

"Goodnight, Tomás." Jenny said, hugging me. "Thanks for taking me to the movies." Her smile was radiant all of a sudden. Weird.

I muttered a weak "*De nada*," forced a smile, then dragged myself upstairs.

When I got up in the morning, Jenny and Francisco were gone. Ma was humming under her breath as she made breakfast.

"Where's Jenny and Francisco?" I asked. "I thought they were going to spend the night."

"No, they left right after you went to bed. Francisco found a car…they had a long way to go…"

Baby that I was, I never questioned the strange happenings. But I did wonder for a long time why I had to see that crummy movie three times and why Jenny was so gloomy at the theater and then all smiles when we got home.

I was maybe ten when Ma explained the whole thing to me. Jenny's dad had arranged a marriage for her; she was supposed to marry a much older man from Mexico. That's how Mexican families did things in those days, she told me.

But Jenny was in love with Francisco, and even at sixteen she knew what she wanted. And it wasn't some baggy, wrinkled *viejo* from Mexico. So she and Francisco had run away. Hopping a bus from Milwaukee, they'd trusted themselves to the mercy of the only grownup friends they knew. Daddy had come north with Jenny's father; he'd known Jenny as a child. He and Ma had done what they could for the crazy kids.

While Jenny and I were in the movie, Francisco had been out scouting up a used car so they could flee to Detroit, where he had friends. Fearing that Jenny's father would come looking, it was imperative that they both remain out of sight. So off to the movies, *mis amigos*. More anonymous than that you don't get.

"And what became of them?" I asked. "Did they get married?

Were they happy?"

"We don't know," Ma said sourly. "We never heard from them again. They said they'd write, but they never did. Even after we stuck our necks out for them and lied when Jenny's father came looking for her. Not a word. That's gratitude for you."

"Yeah," I agreed. "That wasn't nice at all."

And there it was: Intrigue. Thwarted love. Melodrama. I'd been a hero of sorts, even if it had all gone right over my head. I hadn't even known I was in the script.

And would you believe? To this day, although Turner Classic Movies screens it now and then, I have never watched *Flying Down to Rio* again.

Once was damned well enough, don't you think?

Once?

Get outta here!

CHAPTER FOURTEEN

Turn the Radio On

Those old enough to remember TV in the early fifties still tell their kids how the screen featured arctic snow storms much of the time. Now and then it would clear, and they'd get blurry vision of something or other.

"Oh, look, there's Kukla, Or is it Ollie? Fran, perhaps?"

It was the same with radio during the thirties. A passing car, an electric motor next door, or a speedy sparrow would create obliterating static. When that happened, we'd all scream with frustration. Often the interference went on forever, and we kids went bonkers waiting for the signal to clear. Sometimes it never did. Then Ma would switch off the radio and firmly announce, "Bedtime, kids."

This was especially maddening when we were following a serial like *I Love a Mystery* or *One Man's Family*. Or when a professional boxing match was scheduled. (The Friday night fights were a national mania back then.)

As example, take Joe Louis' second matchup with Max Schmeling—summer 1938—when he regained his world championship crown:

We kids were jumping up and down, screaming at the top of our voices as The Brown Bomber turned Schmeling into puppy chow. Then, abruptly—crashing static. How we howled! Of all times for the radio to quit on us! Daddy kept fiddling with the dial, but there was noise all across the band.

Minutes later, when a neighbor apparently quit brushing his teeth, the signal returned and we heard Clem McCarthy yelling, "He knocked him down...not once, but twice. It's the first time that a world championship ever changed hands in a round...less than a round...it was two minutes and forty seconds of the first round..."

And sure, we jumped up and down excitedly to learn that Joltin' Joe had won, but it just wasn't the same. We'd missed the exact moment when he'd put Hitler's pet boxer away.

Bummer!

Not long after that, Daddy spent a whole weekend jerry-rigging an aerial from the back of the house to a high standard he nailed onto the garage roof. It consisted of two X arms, with strands of bare copper affixed to the end of each arm, then stretched taut across the backyard. A lead was dropped to the foundation, fed up from the basement, and drawn through the living room floor. But even this wasn't foolproof; we'd still lose the station now and then.

What did we listen to during the Dark Ages? We tuned in on *Fibber McGee and Molly, The Fred Allen Show, Edgar Bergen and Charlie McCarthy, The Eddie Cantor Show, The Bob Hope Show, Gang Busters, Ripley's Believe it or Not*—shows like that.

We especially loved *Major Bowes Amateur Hour*. "Around and around she goes...where she stops, nobody knows..." Perhaps Daddy envisioned our band playing on that program some day. Dreams die hard.

We were, in all probability, listening the Sunday night in 1935 when Frank Sinatra began his career as one of the *Hoboken Four*.

That Frank Sinatra? Well, golleeee.

To this day I remember a Ripley show about a whacko Chinese empress who had an immense palace built by slaves, the project taking a lifetime. This nutso was so enamored of Hoffman's *Barcarolle*, she had it played nonstop by court musicians during the construction of the entire project.

Now who, other than a dummy like me, would buy tripe like that?

To this day, whenever I hear those annoying strains, I am reminded of that tinkle-brain queen. And Robert Ripley.

Believe it or not!

Another of my absolute favorites was Warden Lewis E. Lawes' *20,000 Years in Sing Sing*, a show consisting of weekly case studies of prisoners in that infamous pokey. When the good warden offered

THAT WONDERFUL MEXICAN BAND

a book tie-in, I *must* have it. It was a paperback item, and I devoured it.

Partially, anyway.

Would you believe? The book disappeared a week after it arrived; I was hardly into chapter three. Ma, disturbed by my psychotic interest in crime, already envisioning me in prison gray, made it disappear one day. When I questioned her, she claimed total innocence. Billy the Brownie must have spirited it away. And though I searched every corner of the house for weeks after, I never found the forbidden volume.

She tried keeping me from listening to the program as well, but I raised such a howl that she relented. A life of crime was perhaps preferable to enduring my nonstop whinings.

Racial prejudice was blatant on radio at the time. *Amos 'n' Andy* parodied the blacks, and *Abie's Irish Rose* zeroed in on the Jews, exaggerated accents and all. I have vaguest recollection of a particular Saturday afternoon program featuring a Jewish character named Isadore Finkelstein. This half hour consisted mostly of putdowns and stereotypes, all outrageously exaggerated. No way could a show like that be aired today. However, as a kid, I was not in the least offended. Didn't all blacks and Jews talk that way? Didn't they always exhibit intellectual shortfall?

Would I have been so forgiving had there been a *Juan and Juanita* hour?

Radio was the real deal during the Depression. It was free; movies weren't. These programs served to take our minds off an economy gone disastrously awry. Every evening, when the dishes and homework were done, it was time to gather around the Philco. Ours was one of the oversized consoles, mahogany veneer with overdone, scrolled speaker ports. Daddy bought it second hand, and it occupied a prominent place in our cramped living room. Ma and Daddy sat on the davenport, while we kids sprawled on the floor.

This mostly happened during winter. No matter how compelling a summer radio show might be, it was no match for outside fun and games. But when the winds howled and the snow fell—radio time!

Hard to believe, but radio vacuum tubes were sold in the dime stores or at Walgreens. I can still see Daddy testing tube after tube at a do-it-yourself console.

Bring your imagination! Nobody knew what the characters looked like; their physical features coalesced in our kid brains free-style. Yes, photos of Edgar Bergen and Charlie McCarthy, Eddie Cantor, Bob Hope, and the like appeared in newspaper ads and movie magazines. Otherwise their pusses were engraved on cereal bowls and drinking cups. (I still own a blue Shirley Temple mug.) But shows like *Gangbusters, Suspense, Lux Radio Theatre, Death Valley Days,* and *Lights Out* featured network stable actors and actresses who hopped from show to show.

I later learned that sound effects were generated right in the studio. The audio techs positioned themselves close to the mike; they clopped small coconut shells for horses' hooves and brought up authentic horse whinnies (*The Lone Ranger*) when needed. Pistols loaded with blanks stood ready. Thunder sheets simulated storms, BBs in a cup sounded like a rattlesnake. Later on sound recordings replaced these corny effects. Another early radio mainstay was the studio organist who set a mood with a few bars—for suspense, raise the pitch and hold it, or fade in and fade out for scene changes.

No matter. To gullible kids like us it was all the real McCoy.

Ma's daytime soaps included *The Romance of Helen Trent; Ma Perkins; Mary Noble, Backstage Wife; Portia Faces Life;* and *Our Gal Sunday.* ("Can this girl from the little mining town in the West find happiness as the wife of a wealthy and titled Englishman?") I can still hear that hokey lead-in. These shows all featured unknowns as well.

Cast publicity photos were sometimes offered, and when they arrived, our visualizations went out the window. The actor who played Flash Gordon was in his sixties, gray-haired, and fat. What a comedown.

Did we kids suffer because our favorite radio characters were faceless? Hardly. If anything, this constant exercise of our imaginations was beneficial; we were all the better for it. Kids today don't know imagination from a pail of worms.

The canned roar of the trains that opened *Grand Central Station* will forever rumble in my mind. Henry Aldrich and his squeaky "Coming, mother!" echoes there as well. We kids loved *Let's*

Pretend, starring Nila Mack, which involved a loose retelling of fairy stories. (This overgrown kid was still listening as a married man in 1947.) *Mr. First Nighter* featured Don Ameche and aired original three-act dramas.

Soup to nuts.

Then, of course, true Depression fare: Franklin Delano Roosevelt's *Fireside Chats*, which occurred whenever an important issue faced the nation. Blue-collar workers listened faithfully—those who had homes to listen in. He was their hero, a President who'd actually done something about the Depression. I listened off and on, if only to gather grist for my Democratic mill as I hawked papers next to Bob Keller and Ray Baum. Those saps still believed in elephants.

Unlike our windbag pols of today, FDR's chats seldom ran over ten minutes. Most lasted five minutes or less.

Movie crazy as I was, I never missed Walter Winchell, Louella Parsons, and later Hedda Hopper, who kept the U.S. abreast of celebrity scandals. Winchell, with his mile-a-minute delivery—"Good evening, Mr. and Mrs. North and South America and all the ships at sea...let's go to press."—was a Sunday-night must. Frenzied tapping of a telegraph key between newsbreaks added an authentic, suspenseful touch. Louella and Hedda knew every naughty move the Hollywood gang made. Although some of it didn't register —mistresses, infidelity, party debauchery—I became instant kid insider. Hotcha!

Then came such breakthrough news reporters as Gabriel Heatter, Lowell Thomas, and Boake Carter, who interrupted regularly scheduled broadcasts with on-the-spot reports on the Charles Lindberg baby kidnapping in 1935, the Bruno Hauptmann trial, and the gruesome details of the baby's death. Gabriel Heatter stood outside New Jersey State Prison the night of April 3, 1936 to provide minute-by-minute account of Hauptmann's execution in the electric chair.

"Old Smokey" became kid smart-aleck talk for weeks after.

When some mush-head tried to assassinate President Roosevelt in Miami, Florida (February 15, 1933), radio listeners were on the scene thirty minutes later. Then, horrific tragedy: Lakehurst, New Jersey, May 6, 1937, when the German zeppelin *Hindenburg* exploded, killing thirty-five passengers—we were definitely there.

Routine coverage by Chicago newscaster Herb Morrison remains devastating and memorable to this day. Ma wept while listening; I was dumbstruck by the emotion in Morrison's voice ("Oh, the humanity of it all!") as passengers and crew dropped to the ground, and some ran past him, their clothing in flames.

Small wonder Depression radio took such an important place in our lives.

In due course it was only natural that compulsive consumer *número uno* must have his very own radio. This happened on John Street, when, flush with newsboy cash, I bought a little Crosley. Price: $6—an exorbitant sum in my eyes. I could now listen to *my* programs in complete privacy. I became "master of the dial."

I soon learned my little cheapie was no bargain. Stations faded in and out like ships in the fog. Following Daddy's lead, I built and strung an antenna from the back of the house to the barn. Now that's more like it!

The late Sunday afternoon airings of *The Shadow* were special. I hung on every ghostly word—spook stuff was red meat to me. I loved *The Mercury Theatre on the Air*. Commercial free, there was nothing to ruin the scary mood. Ma was tuned in on Halloween in 1938, when Orson Welles terrified the nation with *The War of the Worlds*. I was listening in the background. But Orson didn't scare me—mainly because I was too young. Creatures from outer space? C'mon, get real!

But later on, when we moved to John Street, I became a dedicated *Mercury* fan. Those times I kept the volume low, my ear close to the speaker. *My* thing.

Some of my other can't-be-missed shows were *Mr. District Attorney, Tarzan, Adventures of Frank Merriwell,* and—truly gruesome—*The Hermit's Cave*, which came along even later in my radio-listening career. A tough guy, I could take it.

Or could I?

Yeah, kid, fess up. Some of those nights, after listening to all the rattling bones and graveyard shriekings, I didn't douse the lights until Ma yelled. I dove under the covers like a shot once the world went black.

THAT WONDERFUL MEXICAN BAND

Bad dreams?
You bet.

CHAPTER FIFTEEN

Lost in the Stacks

The Fond du Lac Public Library was located on the corner of Sheboygan and Portage Streets, right across from the Elks Club. It resembled a towered castle—all fieldstone, the result of an Andrew Carnegie bequest. "I'm going to the Library" became ever-reassuring mantra to Ma. She knew I'd be out of her hair—and in safe hands—for at least two hours, possibly three.

Today kids would call it "hanging out." It was much more than that to me; the library became second home. Visiting two, sometimes three times a week, I was either returning books or hurrying to check out new ones. And like the dim-wit kid in Saroyan's *The Human Comedy*, I stood frozen in those musty, gloomy aisles and fervently vowed that I'd one day read every book in the library.

Fat chance.

The bi-weekly visits from the traveling librarian at Washington School were never quite enough; I must crack the motherlode. From fifth grade on, I became a Fond du Lac Public Library mascot. All I needed was a uniform and a large badge reading "LIBRARY BUG."

Mostly I went alone. I needed no early "C'mon, Thomas, let's go home" refrains from my brothers or my buddies. Let the man be!

The librarians knew me by name and greeted me warmly. Sometimes they even let me withdraw more than the three-book limit. The Depression had mangled library budgets too. *Hey, kid, quit taking all our books!*

One librarian, Miss Kraemer, would—unawares—wiggle her ears. Whenever I checked out, I focused on them, not her smiling face, and there they went—waggle, waggle, waggle. It was hard to keep from laughing.

Her pencil had a point on one end, a date stamp at the other. She would scribble my name on the withdrawal card. Down went the stamp, imprinting the due date on the card and then onto the due date sheet pasted inside the back cover. A surefire way to peg a book. If you saw a bunch of dates, you knew it was probably a good read.

The *shush* regime prevailed back then; we all but tiptoed in the library. We whispered to each other as we scanned the shelves. Marian the Librarian was quick to give us the finger—across her lips—when we talked too loud. If a kid persisted, she pointed toward the front door. Out! No hesitation whatsoever.

The library consisted of seven main areas. First, as you entered, you came upon the rotunda that housed the checkout desk. From it extended arms: a reference room where all the encyclopedias, atlases and such were kept. Then the main reading room where newspapers and magazines hung upon a series of racks. A grandfather clock stood in one corner. I can still hear those drowsy chimes!

Next the children's section. Then, directly behind the checkout desk, the main stacks—perhaps twenty of them, the aisles cramped and gloomy. To the right of this area was another reference and study room where exhibits of city interest were often displayed. Now we're back at the main entrance.

The restrooms—medieval dungeons, the water tank tight to the ceiling and the flushings near deafening—were located in the basement. A stairway led to the second floor, where the Fond du Lac Historical Society maintained a museum.

The huge hall was home to wooden Indians, barber poles, old furniture, and display cases crammed with Civil War pistols, rifles, cannon balls, spent Minié balls, military insignia, and uniforms of every description. Bloodthirsty little apes that we were, we hung on these cases, imagining shooting these weapons, drilling Confederates and, yes, wearing those cool forage caps.

The spent slugs, pried from dead bodies (we imagined), sent delighted shivers through us. The World War I stuff, for some unknown reason, never held the same charm. The museum was only open on Saturday afternoons; I visited every chance I had.

But, ah, the children's section! My introduction to regimented library fare. The baby books were to the left. Next came a section for intermediate readers. And to the far right—irresistible lodestone—the fifth-to-seventh-grade shelves, a major beachhead.

Beneath the windows to the east, stood low, lift-door cabinets that housed the stereopticons. Here were stored a half dozen viewers plus a dozen or so trays of black-and-white glossies devoted mostly to exotic lands and peoples—some U.S. landmarks as well.

Review time: A stereopticon consists of a viewing unit with metal eye mask that you snugged to your face. On a wooden arm, ten inches from the eyepiece, was a wire rack to hold each card. You slid it to focus.

There were two photos to a card, each seemingly identical—at least until you looked through the viewer. Instantly they came alive with amazing three-dimensional effect. Magic! You could almost reach out and touch those houses, those fishermen, those African natives. Times being what they were, the bare-breasted African ladies had already been removed by the ever-watchful library staff.

Once we picked out our books, we'd spend a half hour or so—oohing and aahing—with the stereopticons before heading home. I never got through the entire collection. Was I amazed at such technical wizardry? You'd better believe it!

Stereopticons aside, my main thing was the books. Most summer vacations—starting in my ninth year—I read thirty or thirty-five books, some of them classic, some pure trash. Discrimination was not my strong suit.

Early on, I fixed on Grace and Carl Moon's *Chi-Wee* series: *Chi-Wee, Story of An Indian Girl; Chi-Wee and Loki of the Desert; Chi-Wee's White Boots.* Loki was her boy companion; they were always getting into trouble. Those naughty Navahos always made me smile.

Or I might zoom in on Albert Payson Terhune's dog books. Titles like *Lad of Sunnybank, Wolf, Lad: A Dog, A Dog Named Chips*—these were always most satisfying.

William Heyliger wrote fast-moving adventure, and I got hung up on his Boy Scout series: *Don Strong, Patrol Leader, Don Strong of the Wolf Patrol,* and others. He also wrote lots of baseball stuff. *Batter Up!, Captain of the Nine,* I remember well. I wasn't especially keen on *playing* baseball, but I sure liked reading about it.

One of my most endearing finds was *Two Little Savages* by Ernest Thompson Seton, the famous American naturalist. Though I considered it a major work, none of my brothers (or friends) could get into it. It was a long book, written in a wordy, scholarly style that spooked most kids. But I got hooked, and believe it or not, for the following three years I checked *Savages* out every spring—my annual version of sulfur and molasses, I suppose.

In the novel two kids—Yan, a city boy, and Sam, a farm kid—strike a deal with their parents and live in the woods for three weeks. They must hunt their own food, learn to cook it, find clean water, and build a teepee to live in. They learn to make passable bows and arrows, Indian drums, and head pieces; how to track animals; and how to identify every bird in sight. They study herbal medicine with the "Sanger Witch," a crusty female squatter who lives deep in the woods.

Even though I'd be the last boy in the world to want to live in the woods, once I opened the book, I was a goner. I trudged in with Yan and Sam and never emerged until page two-eighty-six. Even better, the book was illustrated with hundreds of Thompson's ink sketches —medicinal plants, birds, Indian trail signs, on and on.

And the ending, when they return to civilization? Sam's father's coarse greeting still rings in my ears: "Boys, your two week holiday, with one week's extension, was up at noon today. In an hour and a half the pigs is fed."

What a comedown!

In the main reading room I pounced upon each new issue of *Boys' Life* and *Open Road for Boys*. The *Open Road* covers were knockouts, featuring thrilling pictures of men and boys in perilous action. *The Saturday Evening Post* and *Liberty* were other favorites. A few times I even cracked *National Geographic*. In that quiet sanctum—a bum sometimes dozing at a far table—the hours passed so quickly that the librarians had to sweep me out.

In those days the adult stacks were off limits to kids under twelve.

What they were protecting us from, I don't know. If there were sexual descriptions, you needed code to find them. Authors sure knew how to camouflage the juicy stuff back then.

And when I was finally allowed to withdraw adult novels, I was sorely disappointed. Most were tediously written, heavy with description and endless reference to family relatives—Aunt Mabel, Uncle Joe, Cousin Angela. My extended family mostly in Mexico, genealogy simply didn't register. Also they were maddeningly long and dealt with stuff no self-respecting kid could ever begin to care about. Where's the action?

All that expectant waiting for what? Maybe when I entered my teens…

Until then, back to the juvenile section. Any new John R. Tunis novels?

On library day—alone or with brothers or buds—there was often a near-mandatory detour. "C'mon, Thomas," David or Bernard would say, "Let's go see Custer again." Immediately we'd veer off to Schmitz's Tavern on the corner of Division and Main. The bar has been a Fond du Lac fixture since Moses lost his sandals.

I drank sodas there many times there with Daddy when he cashed his check—and wet his whistle. One beer, one shot. Fifteen cents.

Even Carry Nation dropped by once, heading a crew of axe-wielding amazons (WCTU), who laid waste to the place. To this day a weather-worn sign near the front door proudly announces:

HISTORIC
SCHMIDT
Sample Room
SCENE OF THE FAMOUS
CARRY NATION
HATCHET SWINGING EPISODE
JULY 18, 1902

The Division Street window, just east of the ladies entrance, was a must-see event. Here stood the famous Budweiser poster, perhaps thirty-by-forty inches, labeled "Custer's Last Fight." Mounted in a fancy frame, the Anheuser-Bush logo beneath the title, it showed the Oglala Sioux overrunning Custer's beleaguered troop at Little Big Horn. On horseback and on foot, they hacked and scalped the palefaces with vengeful glee.

Dead center stood Lt. Col. George Armstrong Custer, his long hair flowing, his saber slashing, dead bluecoats and Indians piled around him. Indian teepees were seen in the distance, and clouds of dust billowed as mounted Indian reinforcements hurried to join in on the happy slaughter.

Talk about exciting! To us boys it signified glory, bravery, and gory folly in equal measure. Small wonder we went out of our way—time and time again—to press our faces to that fly-specked window.

But the city library—and grade school libraries—weren't my only exposure to fine reading. Literary treasures pop up in most unexpected places.

Somewhere along the line, Bob Keller and I hitchhiked to Milwaukee to spend a few days with Aunt Hazel. Here, two blocks away, I stumbled upon my first Goodwill outlet, where I came upon hundreds of used books.

"Look, Bob," I called excitedly, "all these books, only five cents."

Bonanza. To actually *own* books was a driving obsession back then.

A book called *Ragged Dick* caught my eye. Then and there, Horatio Alger Jr. entered my life. His were books about honest, hard-working lads clawing their way to fame and fortune—hey, that was me all over! *Driven from Home, Bound to Rise, Only an Irish Boy*, and *Risen from the Ranks* are titles I still recall. In due course, however, I came to realize that Alger told the same story over and over. Only the names changed.

I later learned that although Alger wrote more than seventy of these pot-boilers, he died almost destitute, apparently oblivious to his own guidelines.

It was also at Goodwill that I picked up my first *Buddy* book.

Buddy on the Farm, Buddy in School, Buddy and the Secret Cave, Buddy at Lost River. There were more than twenty-eight of these, authored by Howard R. Garis all all written so simply written that a third grader could plow through one in a few hours. Pure Pablum. I became addicted. I must have read ten *Buddy* books before I burned out on the plucky little brat.

Upon returning to Fond du Lac, I looked up our own Goodwill. Where I hurried to buy more of each author's books. No taste whatsoever.

Another literary venue was Fond du Lac's dime stores. Here I discovered, early on, Big Little Books. These were chunky, hand-sized volumes, almost two inches thick, which ran two-hundred to two-hundred-fifty pages. Printed by Whitman Publishing in Racine, Wisconsin, most sold for a dime. They featured a photo or cartoon on alternate pages. America's kids were wild about them; all the dime stores carried them.

Most were based on comic-strip standbys. In the movie versions, the storyline was simplified, with endless movie stills to hurry kid *literati* along. How many kids back then became speed readers while drugging out on Big Little Books?

How in the world, I still wonder, could they sell these gems for ten cents? They became choice trading items, and my BLB library was constantly in flux. Some I prized so highly that I never dreamed of trading them. We smuggled them into school and read them on the sly. A Big Little Book could make the classroom rounds for days.

At one time I owned over a hundred-fifty, everything from *Felix the Cat* to *Big Chief Wahoo* to *Alley Oop*. Such movies as *David Copperfield, Union Pacific, The Last Days of Pompeii, The Plainsman,* and *Charley Chan* were adapted as Big Little Books. The ones based on Shirley Temple movies repeatedly sold out. The refrain "Read the book, see the picture" was never more relevant.

And when you got to standbys like Dick Tracy, Buck Rogers, or Li'l Abner, they called for a series with sometimes as many as twenty different titles devoted to each comic strip celeb. Take

Tarzan for example: *Tarzan of the Apes, The Beasts of Tarzan, Tarzan Lord of the Jungle, The Return of Tarzan, The Son of Tarzan*—on and on into the night. The inevitable Tarzan movie editions starred Johnny Weissmuller, Herman Brix, and Buster Crabbe. *Blondie, Dick Tracy, Buck Rogers,* and *Captain Easy* also inspired movies. Some became Saturday matinee serials.

More featured comics? *Don Winslow of the Navy, Betty Boop, Flash Gordon, Little Orphan Annie, Maggie and Jiggs, Tillie the Toiler, Mutt and Jeff, Joe Palooka, Mickey Mouse, Chester Gump, Hairbreadth Harry, The Lone Ranger.*

Overkill? Perhaps, but just to nail down the multitude of titles available. Hundreds upon hundreds.

I bring up distinct image of a large Oxydol box crammed with Big Little Books. The same box I carried to the curb upon returning from service in 1946. Collectors today pay anywhere from ten to fifty dollars for the commons—as much as five-hundred dollars for the rares.

I could cut my wrists.

Today I own only two Big Little Books. One is a movie edition of *Treasure Island*, starring Jackie Cooper and Wallace Beery. The other is *This is the Life*, with Jane Withers as the lead.

Storyline? Famous kid stage-star Jerry Revier escapes from double-dealing guardians and runs away with escaped convict Michael, who, wrongfully accused of theft, is on the lam. They join a traveling medicine show. Jerry has the time of her life, Michael is proven innocent, the kid's guardians are discredited, and Jane and Michael live happily ever after.

Pure hokum? Yes, indeedy. Nevertheless *This is the Life* lives in my heart to this day. I've searched for a possible video for years, all in vain.

With both books, the pages are yellowed, the covers battered, and the spines all but non-existent. Heavy rubber bands hold them together. I turn the pages with loving care and let the happy memories swarm back!

Memories of the movies themselves.

And more importantly, memories of a whacky, slap-happy childhood!

CHAPTER SIXTEEN

God and Company

I was baptized at St. Patrick's Church in Fond du Lac when I was ten weeks old. Coming from Mexico, Daddy was positive that salvation came only via intervention of the Roman Catholic Church. Ma, basically unchurched, went along.

By the time I was five, the Great Depression had revved into high, and the priest at St. Pat's was continually on Daddy's case to make a pledge. Which was impossible; there simply was no money. As result my parents switched to St. Paul's Cathedral (Episcopal) on Fond du Lac's west side.

At St. Paul's there was no pressure whatsoever for a pledge. When they could, Ma or Dad dropped a quarter in the collection plate; we kids gave a penny. Even that piddling amount wasn't always easy to find. I suspect that there were Sundays when my parents skipped church because they couldn't bring up even a quarter. Daddy was too proud to give less.

And, despite the jibes of the neighborhood RC brats, who constantly taunted us with threat of hellfire because we weren't Catholic, I never came to regret leaving the Romans.

Daddy was an early riser—always work to do—so he and Ma attended 7:00 Mass. As a family, we seldom attended church together—Easter and Christmas probably, perhaps a few random Sundays. Because they wanted us in Sunday school, we got rousted out when they got home. Then it was race, race, race to get to church on time.

St Paul's is located on Division and Sophia Streets, a scant block and a half west of Main Street. A small-scale Gothic cathedral, people come from all over the nation to tour it. The stained-glass windows are art treasures, as are the three-quarter-size statues of the twelve Apostles who stand watch on the east and west walls. There is a dramatic rood beam as you approach the altar, upon which the crucified Christ is attended by Mary Magdalene and the Virgin Mother on the one side, with John the Beloved and Mary, wife of Cleophas, on the other.

The high altar is beautifully conceived, with murals on the east and west walls and carved bas-relief panels behind, depicting Christ's Resurrection, plus scenes from the life of St. Paul. As one proceeds up for Holy Communion, the effect is stunning. Thanks for this must go mostly to Bishop Charles Chapman Grafton—the second bishop—who came in 1888. He was a huge benefactor, mover, and shaker in the cathedral's early life.

And yes, there was a closed confessional, dimly lighted, where we knelt before a screen that shielded the priest's face. I think entering that narrow cubicle, adjusting to the gloom, was as frightening to me as my confession itself.

And yet, despite all this grandeur, St. Paul's was situated in a slum area of sorts. Located across from St. Paul's was Pautz Beer and Liquor Depot. Next-door, going east, stood Williams Used Furniture. An alleyway ran between the weathered, clapboard structure and the Fond du Lac River all the way to Forest Avenue. All are gone today.

Insult upon insult, on the corner directly across from the cathedral's main entrance stood an immense three-story residence, which—it was rumored—housed ladies of the night. I never heard any of this until I was in my teens, and had become oh-so very worldly. On Sunday mornings no one, but no one, was ever seen entering or leaving that house. Self-imposed blue laws? Other than the Bishop's Mansion, just across Sophia Street from the church, most of the homes surrounding the church were ramshackle and poorly cared for.

Back then Division Street was paved with red bricks from Main to Brooke. Honest! Riding a bike down Division was a teeth-chattering experience.

A tavern and Zinke Wholesale Foods were located across the river to the east.

Location, location.

The Fond du Lac River bounded the cathedral property to the east, and a high river wall mostly kept the floods at bay. As kids, waiting for church, we scampered up and down the walks or hung out on the bridge—spitting into the water, throwing stones, and watching fishermen when the white bass were running.

St. Paul's was a most prestigious church in the '30s. Many lawyers, bankers, and businessmen attended. It was unspoken writ that the richies mainly took pews on the west side of the cathedral, while we blue-collar slaveys worshipped on the east side. Actual or not, that was where the Ramirez tribe landed; we never dreamed of drifting west. Not in church anyway.

Not much jars my mental screen when I try bringing up early St. Paul's incidents. Flashback to 1933, when I was seven. At that time the Sisters of the Holy Nativity were in charge of the Sunday school kindergarten and grades one to six. The dean or an assistant priest taught the older kids. The Convent of the Holy Nativity was located on East Division—three blocks from the cathedral.

The good Sisters were fully robed back then, heads cowled in black, their faces trapped in sparkling white, perfectly creased wimples. They walked two by two, a silent column of misplaced penguins.

Babies as young as three and four, along the lower grades, met in the Parish Hall. Their parents dropped them off before 10:00 Mass. The older kids, arriving at 9:00, gathered in the cathedral proper. These classes met in random pews, front and back.

Only one nun, Sister Alisha, Mother Superior of the order, lights up my screen. She taught me in sixth grade and also saw to my Confirmation drills.

This class took place every Wednesday afternoon after school in St. Augustine's Chapel. Endless catechism, with meanings of the various sections of the Mass, scripture on the life of Christ, and lives of the saints were main thrust. We learned about the statuary and other art treasures throughout the church. We learned to bow our heads, close our eyes during the Consecration, and strive to envision Christ and his apostles during The Last Supper. We learned to bow as we passed before a cross, when and where to cross ourselves throughout the service, to genuflect as we entered and left our pew, to kneel briefly as the Bishop came down the aisle blessing the congregation.

How come so much ritual lingers? Mainly because Sister Alisha was a demanding teacher. *And* because I honor these graces to this day, even though most have fallen through the grate as result of recent modernization of church liturgy.

Genuflect? What kind of duck is that?

Back then, even although I considered myself a devout, sanctimonious little cheese, I mostly hated these catechism sessions. B-o-o-oring!

On the Saturday before Confirmation, I made my First Confession. A stellar, frightening event to me. I basically went through the motions at the time, pretty much at a loss for naughties to spill.

As for later on—best we don't go there.

St. Augustine's chapel is my favorite spot at St. Paul's. I dearly love the altar there—as well as the beautiful, mosaic-decorated tabernacle containing the consecrated bread and wine and the chapter seats along each side. On sunny days the afternoon sunlight streams through two deeply recessed windows to the west. I never tired of studying the large mural (gone now) on the west wall where a brooding St. Augustine sat in an ornate chair, his eyes fixed on the human skull in his hand.

The altar frontal is a wonder—paint imbedded marble—an arcane art technique lost forever. Here sits the Virgin Mary, the Baby Jesus in her lap. While on both sides, a slew of female saints pay court. One of them, St. Elizabeth of Hungary, holds a bouquet of flowers. I love the story of how she smuggled bread to the poor against the king's stern commands. When his soldiers accosted her during one of these missions, the bread was miraculously transformed into lilies. I puddled up then, and I puddle up now when I tell this story to visitors requesting an impromptu cathedral tour.

On Maundy Thursday the altar area was always filled with dozens of potted hyacinths—annual gift from dedicated parishioner Ed Jewson, a plumber. These were moved to the stairs beneath the rood beam on Easter Sunday and presented to every Sunday school kid at the close of Mass. The aroma of the flowers in St. Augustine's, when I took my turn at the "watch," was overpowering and helped me better envision the Garden of Gethsemane. Childishly transfigured, I was there; I kept watch with Jesus, even though his disciples dozed off.

Slackers!

This remembrance still moves me today. I go to mush when I recount this childhood ritual. Sad to say, the practice ended when Ed died.

Oh yes, Sister Alisha…

She was broad-faced, a trifle ruddy, soft spoken, but stern; we paid attention in class or else. Though her eyes were a watery blue, they could burn holes if she turned them on you. We recited our catechism in a loud, clear voice. No mumbling.

I remember little of her Sunday school sessions. But even as frightening as Sister Alisha seemed, she did, at rare times, crack a wan smile. The class cut-up, I once asked if she wore clothes beneath her robes. Another Sunday: "Do nuns have hair?" Yes, of course.

Later, when I graduated to Sunday school with a priest, she always conferred a quiet "Good morning, Thomas" when we met and favored me with a dour smile. So I must have been a favorite despite my bonehead lapses.

I remember none of the priests who taught me—save one. This was Fr. Ted Dunnigan, age thirty-six, who arrived at St. Paul's fresh out of seminary in 1937. This man changed the world for me. He was homely as sin, a wee-bit paunchy, balding slightly. He had a jagged white scar—fully four-inches-long—on the left side of his face, souvenir of a Chicago gang fight. He used street argot with us, his words clipped, and delivered from the corner of his mouth. Now and then a soft "damn" escaped his lips.

We boys adored him from the start. He'd come to religion late in life and was quite open about his slum background. His lessons were real he-man stuff, often verging on irreverence, but it was abundantly clear that he loved his boys and wanted to instill in them the same love for God that he'd discovered, almost too late, himself. He talked about Jesus and the disciples in plain language—"St. Paul was a gangster. Judas deserved to croak."—almost as if he'd known each personally.

He once took our class on a church tour, stopping before each statue, paying special attention to those disciples who bore the instrument of their martyrdom.

"St. Andrew was crucified on this X-shaped cross; he felt he was unworthy to be crucified as Jesus Christ was. No nails for him, he insisted they tie him upside down onto the cross. He hung there two days and was still preaching when he kicked off."

St. James holds a club, the instrument of his execution.

"This is poor St. Bartholomew," he explained. "See that flaying knife in his hand? They skinned Bart alive."

Pausing before St. Simon, holding a saw almost as tall as himself, he said, "They sawed this baby in half."

And if we didn't know who took the Apostle Judas' place after he betrayed Christ, we were introduced to St. Matthias. He had his head chopped off.

Oh yes, we remembered our saints.

Fr. Dunnigan talked about the social issues of the day, the Depression, the impending war with Germany, President Franklin Delano Roosevelt, the Oakies, and various other topics—all somehow worked into his Sunday school lessons.

One Sunday he spent most of the hour discussing a wonderful movie he'd seen, spinning the entire plot line of *The Grapes of Wrath*. He managed to weave religious insights into the sad plight of the evicted Oakies. "Feed my poor." He urged us to see it. I went that same afternoon.

He was right. If I'd been feeling sorry for myself, this movie showed me how well off the Ramirezes were compared to the Dust Bowl refugees.

Fr. Dunnigan urged us all to become Boy Scouts, to join the choir, to be acolytes. "Do actual service for God. Don't just sit on your cans," he scolded.

He took us out bird watching at dawn every Tuesday, weather permitting. He had a '38 Ford, and five or six kids would cram into it, and off we'd go—to Lakeside Park, to the city dump, to the Ledge, to High Cliff, driving a reckless seventy miles an hour (an incredible speed in those days) when there was distance to be covered. For a gang-banger brought up in a slum, he sure knew his birds!

I will never forget the spring morning right after Sunday school when he asked me to stay after class. "You've been awful quiet lately, Tommy," he said when the others were gone. "No spark, none of your goofy remarks. What's going on?"

And when I tried shrugging off my funk, he said, "Come see me this afternoon. There are things we gotta hash out. How about two o'clock. Can you make it?"

"I'm all right, Father," I protested. It was nothing new. I was just having one of my moody spells. They came and went, not to worry. "I don't want to waste your time. You've got better things to—"

"Two o'clock," he snapped. "My apartment. Be there."

He lived upstairs in the Parish Hall. There was a bedroom, sitting room, and an adjoining office. When I arrived he was at me immediately. "What's going on, Tommy? Problems at home?"

There was nothing I could tell him. Just the blues, a phase I was going through. Part of growing up, I supposed.

Well, we talked for over an hour, and he kept trying to buck me up. Then—I'll never recall how it started—he said, "What d'ya say we organize a boy's club here at St. Paul's? You boys need a meeting place, a place to hang out, a place that's all yours."

Before the afternoon was over, we hammered out a plan. There was an empty room at the end of the hall, a miserable catch-all, full of ten years' worth of the most ungodly junk anyone could imagine. We boys would clean it out, scrub it down, paint the walls. He'd ask the parish members to donate odd furniture, chairs, tables, rugs, lamps, curtains, the whole nine-yards. He'd call a meeting and get ideas from all the other boys.

Father was definitely an expert when it came to leading kids around by the nose.

Then, out of the blue: "Okay, Tommy, you're good with words. You've always got an angle. What should we call the club?"

Well, gulp. Why me? "Why don't we wait until the gang gets

together?"

"No," he insisted. "You're the guy who came up with the idea." (*I did not!*) "You should be the one to name it."

So I went into my deep-thought mode. And finally: "Well, you know the SPCA...Society for the Prevention of Cruelty to Animals? Well, why don't we call our club the SPCB? Only it'll be for the prevention of cruelty to boys."

"Perfect!" Fr. Dunnigan said, laughing hilariously. "That's just the name. I knew you'd come up with something good."

I went out of his apartment that afternoon floating on air. If I'd been nursing a bad case of the blahs when I came in, there was nothing but blue skies by the time I left.

So. SPCB. He suggested it to the gang, told them it was my idea, and that he liked it. A secret name that nobody would ever figure out. (Ha!) So, naturally, they all went for it. By the following Sunday, Bill Smithers, who ran the Parish Press, had printed a big sign for us: SPCB CLUB – MEMBERS ONLY. It went up on the door before we even started cleaning our "club room."

For three Saturdays in a row, ten or twelve of us pitched in, hauling mounds of junk out to the curb, scrubbing the floors and walls. We washed windows that hadn't been touched in years. Fr. Dunnigan agitated among the parishioners, and four gallons of paint and five or six well-used brushes miraculously appeared on the fourth Saturday. What a time we had—a regular Tom Sawyer scene—everyone squabbling for a turn.

Some of the church ladies came in to hang curtains. Others arrived with armloads of books, magazines—*Life* being our favorite. An old radio floated in one day. Every Saturday there were always four or five of us gathered, playing checkers or Peggity, leafing through the magazines, smarting off. I, of course, became the most constant visitor and elected myself as main custodian.

Mr. Clean has entered the building.

I did join the boys' choir. There were roughly a dozen of us. Another assistant, Fr. Davis, was in charge of turning us into well-behaved cherubs. A dedicated musicologist, he transformed our motley crew into a finely tuned instrument. We often sang solo while the adult choir sat on its hands.

However, the main reason I joined—Fr. Dunnigan's admonitions to the contrary—was because choir members earned the princely sum of fifteen cents a week.

Big money.

The boy's choir rehearsed every Thursday afternoon after school. Fr. Davis pounded the Parish Hall piano, and we sang like angels. Any non-angelic capers were cause for the show-off to be docked five or ten cents. We were all paid after Mass, and there were Sundays when I ended up with just a nickel. Being as money-hungry as I was, such missteps were few and far between.

Fr. Davis decided that my boy soprano was worthy of a solo during Christmas Eve Mass that year. Though I quaked in my shoes, I did just fine. *Ave Maria* had never sounded better, Fr. Dunnigan complimented afterward.

There came a time of minor revolution however, this when some ditso lady in the congregation decided we should all wear little pleated collars with our choir robes. Her treat. We'd be miniature Sir Walter Raleighs.

We all swore that we'd die before we marched out with such doofus trappings around our necks. But Fr. Davis prevailed. "Thou shalt wear a collar, or thou shalt not sing. If thou singeth not, thou receiveth not." Meaning fifteen cents. That ended the revolution, but fast. The ladies fluttered about us later, told us how adorable we all looked. *Adorable.* Just what we roughnecks needed.

My choir career ended a year later, when, avarice prevailing, I began selling papers before St. Mary's Church on Sunday mornings. So I wasn't around for choir anymore. Fifteen cents didn't stand a chance against a dollar or a dollar-fifty a Sunday.

Still, devout and guilt-ridden, I made up for Sunday by hitting the 7:00 Mass in St. Michael's chapel on Monday mornings. When this service was disbanded, I served my sentence at the Convent of the Holy Nativity. Holier than that you just don't get.

I often caught Sister Alisha smiling proudly at me as I knelt at the back of the convent chapel. Heaven, here I come!

THAT WONDERFUL MEXICAN BAND

* * *

Once a month at the cathedral, a father-son breakfast was held in the Parish Hall. (What, no father-daughter breakfasts?) The breakfast featured bakery-bought sweet rolls and donuts, big swirls of pastry covered with chocolate, with vanilla frosting, or with gobs of cherries or crushed pineapple in the center—light years of difference between that and our meager cereal breakfasts at home.

The men drank coffee; the boys had big mugs of cocoa. Arriving at church early, I longingly looked in and thought how lucky those kids were and how utterly delicious those rolls must be. It hurt big-time to see my choir friends chow down—while I was on the outside looking in.

Time and time again, I pleaded with Daddy to come for father-and-son. His answer was always the same: "How can I bring my boys to fancy ting like this? We can no give much money for church, can no pay our share."

In retrospect I can see where Daddy was coming from, but at the same time it seemed a cruel injustice to be denied those pig-out feeds.

Enter Fr. Dunnigan. "Hey, Tommy, why doesn't your dad bring you and your brothers to the father-son breakfasts?"

When I explained Daddy's logic to him, he listened intently, a thin, scheming smile on his lips. "We'll see about that," he said as he strode off.

The Sunday before the next monthly sweet-roll bacchanalia, he drew me aside after Sunday school. "You and your brothers come to the breakfast next week, hear? I've got it all arranged."

Sure enough, there we were—decked out in our Sunday best—while Fr. Dunnigan introduced us to a man named Sam Vandervort, who, we later learned, ran an insurance agency.

"Boys," Fr. Dunnigan said, "meet your new father. Sam's agreed to sponsor you. Feel free to attend every one of these breakfasts from now on."

And to Mr. Vandervort: "Right, Sam?"

"Right as rain," the genial man replied, "I'll take good care of these boys."

And he did, every month as long as they held the father-son breakfasts. He sat us down at the table and all but waited on us. He became near-surrogate father. How good those sweet rolls and cocoa tasted! How good it felt to be at table with my cathedral buddies!

Mr. Vandervort was not only a dedicated cathedral goodwill ambassador, he was also deeply involved in the Boy Scout movement. When any of the scouts moved up a rank, he was always sent a small congratulatory gift. He—along with Fr. Dunnigan—was constantly after me to join up.

Boy Scout Troop Number One had been founded at St. Paul's and met every Monday night in the Parish Hall. I was definitely a goof-up in this environment, mainly because I never bothered to truly focus. I was too wound up with my buddies there, instead of preparing for the meetings. There were projects I never got around to, tests I never passed. My head was off in the clouds.

But it was fun of sorts; I was proud of the neckerchief Ma made for me, of the clasp I carved from a meat bone. I thought I looked pretty keen, even though we couldn't afford an authentic Boy Scout shirt, like many of the other boys wore.

Our Scoutmaster, Bill Smithers, threw Charlie Mowbray and me out of the meetings on a regular basis. It's a wonder we even made Tenderfoot. I worked on my First Class Scout badge for two years. But sorry, no cigar. My knots were always wrong, and my special projects were flubs. My merit badges in art and metalworking were my only shining moment.

Also I didn't much care for the rough stuff that followed the meetings. The first night, immediately after the closing ceremony, three of the other scouts dragged me out behind the Parish Hall and proceeded to pound the stuffing out of me. Just like that. No threats, no warnings. Whammo, I was on the ground and suddenly all three of them were on me, punching away.

"Initiation," one kid muttered, laughing in an ugly way.

I was scared, totally bewildered. What had I done to deserve this? Scouts were supposed to be friendly and kind—didn't the Boy Scout Oath say so? Well, I flailed and kicked and screamed and managed to poke one bully in the eye. I dug my teeth into another's arm, and hung on for dear life. He was suddenly not so gung-ho and fell back.

But one guy, a kid named Don Hayward, hung in there, kept pounding away at me. First chance I got, I broke loose and hightailed it for home.

"Did you have fun at your Boy Scout meeting?" Ma asked as I came in.

"Yeah, I had a great time," I answered. It was kid code even back then; you were a sissy if you brought tales home. I hewed to the rule.

But I was back the next Monday night, the fist-fight forgotten. Those kids never bothered me again. That was one test I did pass.

Despite the bullying and such, I did enjoy Boy Scouts. Always the book-worm, I *devoured* the Boy Scout Manual. It was a proud day when I walked into T.E. Ahern—the upscale downtown clothier dispensing official Boy Scout gear—plunked down my fifty cents, and bought my manual. The hours I spent poring over that book! I must have read every page.

Stuff like the meaning of the uniform, of the scout badge, the history of scouting, the scout oath, secret handclasp, first aid, rope knots, and hiking skills. The First Class Scout, Life Scout, and Eagle Scout requirements. Map study, native trees and vegetation, star study, native animals, weather signs, how to measure tree height with a stick—the list goes on and on.

And though I was seldom ready when it came time to pass the required tests, I sure *knew* the manual.

The words of the Boy Scout Oath are burned into my brain forever: "On my honor I will do my best to do my duty to God and my country, and to obey the Scout Law, to help other people at all times, to keep myself physically strong, mentally awake, and morally straight."

Then the Scout Law: "A scout is trustworthy, loyal, helpful, friendly, courteous, kind, obedient, cheerful, thrifty, brave, clean and reverent." So there.

Dear God, that some of these principles still registered with lads today…

Other Boy Scout mischief: Behind St. Paul's Cathedral, fronting on Sophia Street, stood Grafton Hall. Built in 1890 or so, it was a boarding school, highly accredited—grades nine to twelve—for snooty Episcopalian girls from across the nation. A huge L-shaped structure, it stood three stories tall and took up the best part of the cathedral campus. The school averaged one hundred to one hundred twenty-five students a session.

But by 1932, the Depression hitting the wealthy just as hard as it did the blue collars—all things being relative—the school was forced to close. The buildings were locked down. A hired guard walked the grounds nightly for two years before Bishop Grafton—envisioning the day when prosperity (right around the corner, according to do-nothing President Hoover) might return, finally awoke to reality and called off the watch dog. As result, sealed like a tomb and no maintenance whatsoever, the building deteriorated.

Bemused reflection upon those disciplined times: Kids did not vandalize; not a single rock was ever thrown through any of the myriad window panes the huge complex flaunted.

The rambling complex boasted a stadium-sized gym, a dining hall, piles of classrooms, even a beautiful chapel. The girls bunked two to a room and were closely chaperoned.

Though we scouts had been warned to keep away, there were those kid nonconformists who, flashlights in hand, were bound to go exploring. And little Thomas, always a follower, tagged along. After meetings during spring and summer, we'd hide behind the Parish Hall until the Scoutmaster left. Then we'd invade the building through a jimmied window and wander the halls. Things got scary in those gloomy hallways come dusk. Then we'd bail out like Dracula was hot on our trail.

Kid imaginations.

The place *was* a wreck. Musty and damp, mold covering the plaster, cobwebs everywhere, rats scampering—it became irresistible lodestone to thrill-hungry kids. We explored classrooms where desks rotted, school books and student papers dating back to 1931 still inside them. The mattresses were rolled and tied on one end of the bed, the steel slats rusting. Room after room empty, save for two cots, two dressers, two chairs.

We loved running around in the gym, climbing the thick ropes that still hung from the ceiling. We flung half-flat medicine balls at each other, skated dozens of dumbbells across the warped, heaving floor.

THAT WONDERFUL MEXICAN BAND

On the third floor, where the roof leaked, we moved on tiptoe because more than once patches of ceiling collapsed, sending plaster crashing to the floor, barely missing our sorry butts. We'd work our way down long, dark hallways where gilt-framed art still hung. We thought it deliciously spooky.

The saddest part was seeing the big empty kitchen, cooking pans still hanging, cleaning products and canned food still on the shelves. The chapel, once beautiful, had fallen to wrack and ruin. The pews tipped crazily where the floor had partially collapsed; the altar was flung onto its face. A simple wooden cross still hung upon the wall.

The building was finally torn down in the late '60s; a Diocesan center was built. Otherwise one finds a barren field where Grafton Hall once stood.

Then there were those weekends when Troop Number One was trucked off to Camp Shaginappi on Lake Winnebago's east shore. Here we bunked in cabins, cooked out, swam, fished, went on hikes, and passed merit badge tests. One of the Eagle Scouts, Ray Gilmore, was great at telling ghost stories, and we looked forward to those sessions after lights-out. Some of Ray's tales scared the liver out of me.

One, called "The Green Corpse," I carried it home to my brothers, who begged me to tell it again and again. No matter how many times I spun the gruesome tale, the result was always the same. They would jump out of their skins at the surprise ending. Richard would cry.

Otherwise we scouts traveled to the Ledge, where some passed fire-building, cooking, and tent-raising tests. The Ledge—a hundred-foot-high cliff to the east of Fond du Lac—is the western end of the Niagara Escarpment, which meanders all the way from Niagara Falls. We hiked six miles to get there—another scout test—then climbed a wickedly steep hill, where we camped out in pup tents. A good distance from the edge of the cliff itself, to be sure. Sleepwalkers beware. I particularly recall one of those overnights when it rained all night, and I nearly froze to death.

Back to Fr. Dunnigan.

Somewhere along the line, he established a cathedral basketball team and became our coach. There was a big barn of a room upstairs in St. Ambrose Hall—a two-story building located behind the Parish Hall—which had once hosted a dart-throwing league. Fr. Dunnigan saw to it that regulation baskets and backboards were installed. We ran masking tape on the floor and spent an afternoon painting boundary stripes. Certainly not regulation, but good enough for our roughhouse brand of basketball

And where did the money come from? Church coffers were empty. More of Father's finagling no doubt.

Fr. Dunnigan had played basketball in high school and college. Otherwise on Chicago back-alley courts, where anything went. He taught us some wicked moves, many of them illegal. We learned how to execute these without getting called by the referee. Sly trippings and bumpings, elbows to the ribs, covert body checks while the opponent dribbled for a score.

The Fond du Lac YMCA sponsored a league for kids age twelve to fifteen. And sure enough, before we knew it, Father had the St. Paul's Cathedral Hawks on the schedule. We played every Saturday morning.

I was never much of an athlete, mainly because of my short stature and non-aggressive nature. I couldn't get my head around the rules, the traveling calls especially. Mostly I warmed the bench, entering the game only when the score became ridiculously lopsided. These times I gave it my best shot, but I might as well have stayed home. I was expert at cheering however.

We started out the season feebly, losing our first two games by a wide margin. Back at the cathedral, Fr. Dunnigan drilled us mercilessly, and by the third week we were ready to claw. There were eight games in all, and we never lost after that. Granted, there was much grumbling about our shady tactics, but the refs, thanks to Fr. Dunnigan's guiding hand, were seldom able to nail most of our fouls.

Crooked? Not so holy after all? I suppose. Hey, nobody's perfect.

Alas, all good things—there is a last, sad footnote to my church reminisce:

This when we arrived at Mass one Sunday—perhaps a year and a half after Fr. Dunnigan came upon the scene—to find him gone. Just like that, seemingly overnight, he'd flown the coop. The gang was totally dismayed, crushed by this unforeseen turn.

Even worse, we couldn't find out why he'd left. Every adult we asked—the dean, the sisters, our parents—would give us the old fish eye, look away, and stutter and stammer. "Called to another church," was as close as we came to unraveling the mystery.

Hogwash.

Fr. Dunnigan loved St. Paul's. He was happy there. He loved his boys. He was proud of the change he'd made in their lives. A new parish?

Take a hike, Clarence.

But for him to leave without saying goodbye—oh, but didn't that smart? To a boy, we swore eternal allegiance to Fr. Dunnigan and vowed to have absolutely nothing to do with the new priest, a skinny, blond, blue-eyed creep named Fr. Johnson. We'd make his life hell, just wait and see.

Johnny Edkins, who was a head acolyte, went so far as to put a roofing nail on the seat of the Bishop's throne during his next visit as potent sign of our anger at his dismissal of Fr. Dunnigan. The choir boys and acolytes—positioned in pews directly across—held their breaths, waited for Bishop Sturtevant's reaction upon sitting down.

But it was a fizzle. He wore so many robes that the nail never got to the heart—or seat—of the matter. So much for bloody vengeance.

And though the gang, one by one, eventually turned traitor and lined up with Fr. Johnson, I, loyal to the last and busy with my Sunday newspaper route, was barely civil. He got a quick "Good morning, Father" or "Goodbye, Father." That was the extent of it. He tried making up to me for a time, but I would have none of it.

Fr. Johnson left after a year, and a new priest arrived.

I can't even remember his name.

Fr. Dunnigan's departure pretty much ended my near-psychotic relationship with Mother Church. I still attended Mass weekly, I observed all the Holy Days, I did Confession—either at St. Paul's or the Convent—but the old fervor was gone. I no longer gave my whole heart to God. I came to regard the whole mystic sideshow through older, more cynical eyes.

During my late teens, a new priest, Fr. Dudley Rapp, appeared on the scene and took the gang in hand. He introduced the Sunday Night Supper Club, formed basically for St. Paul's teenagers. We took turns throwing late Sunday afternoon feeds, and teenagers of all denominations came swarming. Dinner meetings followed, and afterward there was dancing in the Parish Hall. For a couple years it was *the* place to be in Fond du Lac on Sunday evenings.

Then came the war. And those happy-go-lucky days ended as, one by one, we marched off to enter the Army, Navy, or Marines. A few of the gang never came back.

And here, at long last, definitive answer to a long-festering riddle:

In 1946, upon returning from military service in Germany, I finally learned why Fr. Dunnigan had been so summarily run off.

No, there weren't improprieties with any of his boys.

Think taller.

Think female.

Think angry banker and lawyer husbands.

Thanks for the lesson in humility, Father. None of us—not even you—were ever destined to walk on water.

CHAPTER SEVENTEEN

Tenting Tonight

Then there were the summer church camps.

As much as I loved the Camp Shaginappi weekends with the Boy Scouts, I went bonkers over church camp, where we were away for a full week. What did camp fees amount to back then? Possibly a dollar a day per kid. Which was an impossible sum for Ma and Daddy to bring up. But after Fr. Dunnigan twisted a few arms, some of our bankers and lawyers sponsored camp scholarships, and Bernard, David, and I (Richard was too young) were shipped off along with a half dozen other cathedral *pobres*.

We slept on the ground and covered up with flimsy blankets—no fancy sleeping bags for us. Our first church camp experience took place at Kettle Moraine State Park; the second, at Bugh Lake, near Wautoma; and later, at Lower Lake Nashotah, located near the Nashotah Episcopal Seminary.

At Kettle Moraine we camped along the east shore of Mauthe Lake. I recall swimming, hiking, and some fishing off a pier. We were awakened at 6:30 by a kid who played crummy bugle, and we grabbed towels, wash rags, and soap and ran to the beach. We washed our faces and hands, then brushed our teeth in the same water.

Morning prayer at 7:00 and after that, breakfast. Anyone who's ever camped out knows that living outdoors makes one ravenous. Pancakes, eggs, sausage, and toast never tasted so good. Breakfast done, we tidied up our tents and policed the area. At 9:00 classes began. Sitting on the grass, we tuned in on Bible stuff for an hour.

Other times we sat through boring Johnny-be-good lessons.

Free time, then, to wander in the woods and run with our buddies. We swam at 11:00 AM and at 3:00 PM, when our lifeguard showed up. I considered myself a pretty fair swimmer and rarely missed a splash—another way to get clean. I had to watchdog Bernard and David, so I didn't have the free range the other kids did.

It was at Mauthe Lake that I—and my brothers—first encountered homesickness. Yes, it is real; you *do* feel an unexplainable, crushing sense of sickness and loss. I comforted my brothers as best I could, all the while fighting to conceal my own misery.

"It's okay…it's going to be okay. Just hang in there. Get a good night's sleep now…"

By the second night, those feelings had fled, and we wondered why we'd been such cry babies.

After lunch there were planned activities—hikes, archery, baseball games. Everyone participated or else. The sixteen- and seventeen-year-olds usually supervised these events and made us toe the line. Early on they were like grownups to us, and we snapped to when they barked orders.

There were a dozen pup tents, courtesy of Boy Scout Troop One, two boys to a tent. The rest of the kids slept in large rented tents—boys in one, girls in another. Counting the adults, who had separate tents, our camp population came to perhaps forty or forty-five. When it rained, the mess tent doubled as our chapel; otherwise we held open-air services, standing and kneeling on the ground before a makeshift altar.

The evening campfire was highlight of the day. Again we sat on the ground—the adults had folding chairs—and sang a few hymns, then strayed off into such familiar songs as *I've Been Working on the Railroad; She'll be Coming Around the Mountain; Bill Grogan's Goat; Swing Low, Sweet Chariot,* and so forth.

Next came old saws using refrains like *Ain't Gonna Greet My Lord No More*. Fr. Dunnigan usually started us off and then the older kids took over, leading us through a dozen variations.

For example:

"Oh, you can't get to heaven in Fr. Dunnigan's boat; the darned old thing won't even float."

Or:

"You can't get to heaven in Dick Martin's car; his beat up wreck won't go that far. I ain't gonna greet my Lord no more."

We did rounds to *Row, Row, Row Your Boat* and *Are You Sleeping, Brother John?* The girls loved the "Be kind to your web-footed friends" doggerel. ("For a duck may be somebody's mother.") Sometimes Daley Cornwall, twenty, a veteran camp counselor, sang a few current-day ballads in his beautiful tenor—songs like *Red Sails in the Sunset; In the Chapel in the Moonlight; Stardust; There's a Long, Long Trail A-Winding.* All mush to us boys, but the girls got dreamy-eyed over the way Daley sang.

Eventually the boys were sure to fire up the ghoulish *Hearse Song*. "Did you ever think when the hearse goes by," they brayed, "that you might be the next to die? They wrap you up in a big white sheet and bury you under six-feet deep." Then it really got rank: "Oh, the worms crawl in, the worms crawl out, the worms play pinochle on your snout. Your body turns a nasty green, and pus runs out like whipping cream. Your teeth fall out, your eyes fall in..."

Verse after verse. We'd be rolling on the ground by the end.

But the camp counselors and the girls found it gross.

It was heaven to sit among friends, chatting and laughing in between songs—the fire warm on our faces and a strong sense of community prevailing. For those who might still be a wee bit homesick, the gang became surrogate family.

In between the songfest, the older campers put on brief skits—jokes in motion—and we hooted and howled at the corny endings.

Then about 9:30, the mosquitoes closing in, Fr. Dunnigan would yell, "Time for Compline," and we'd trek up the hill for the day's closing service. After that, last call for the latrines and off to bed. By then we were so beat, we'd drop off within minutes.

One of those first nights at Mauthe Lake, we had a drenching rain. Inside our big tent—proper trenching done—we were snug and safe. Abruptly we were jolted from sleep by a sudden commotion at the tent opening. And what in the world? There stood Keith Halfman—same age as I—an angry expression on his face. His father was a big wheel at Giddings & Lewis, and Keith had arrived at camp with his *own* spanking new tent. He was a big-mouth bully type who loved lording it over us Orphan Annie kids. No way would he bed down with the peasants.

The very same tent Keith now carried in his arms, tent stakes still dangling in the rope loops. Brashly he announced, "There's no way I'm gonna get my new tent all wet."

We howled. Talk about boners. He was the butt of camp humor all that week.

As we got older and attended camps at different sites, the routine was basically the same: religion classes, swimming, hikes, games, boating, ravenous appetites, deep tans, new friends, and—

An extreme sense of sadness when camp was over.

Another session, this one at Bugh Lake, located near Wautoma:

Here a World War I veteran, John Barnes, had built a small chapel with his own hands by way of thanks to God for safe return from battle. Using native stone and wood he sawed himself, he erected a sixty-by-thirty-foot building. He finished it with handhewn pews and kneelers, a simple altar, blue glass windows, and rough board floors.

Arriving for Morning Prayer or Compline at night, we were crowded in like the proverbial sardines. And yet, no problem; we *were* united in Christ.

The chapel's exterior was another John Barnes masterpiece. At one end, where the chimney peaked, the total wall depicted a crucified Christ. Mr. Barnes had made it of vary-colored pieces of stone gathered from the surrounding countryside. We never failed to stop and admire this unique gift of love.

Church camp wasn't all moonlight and roses. There were always those nit-wits who, once all were asleep, enjoyed going down the line pulling tent stakes right and left. Novice campers were always sent to find the "tent stretcher" or the "cot tightener." Some innocents remained clueless as they were sent from one end of camp to the other on the silly fool's errands. I only got switched back twice before I wised up and quit searching.

At Nashotah (in 1942), we had a real mess hall. Here we boys— even some of the bolder girls—slipped away after *Taps* and scooted through the woods to a nearby highway. From there we hiked a mile into Delafield, where we stormed a favorite ice cream shop and ordered the Hog Special. Fifteen cents bought a huge ice cream cup, containing five scoops of ice cream covered with every imaginable combination of toppings.

I was sixteen, a high school junior. The national economy had improved slightly. Daddy was working again, and I had paper route cash. Fifteen cents was no longer the "impossible dream."

By the time we'd downed this monstrosity, we became queasy and were glad to return to camp and hit the sack. Recovery time.

Camp Nashotah was situated on Lower Nashotah Lake. At the west end, a long, narrow channel led to Upper Nashotah Lake. It was great fun to row through this passage and ease into the much larger lake. Also in this run, rowing with extreme stealth, we caught baby turtles sunning themselves on lily pads. We took them home as pets.

It was also a time of sexual awakening, though we didn't recognize it as such. Seemingly overnight, we boys became aware of girls, of a strange excitement and tension when they were near. And when we talked and joked with them—when we *showed off* for them. We even chose to sit with them at campfire, returning to our tents after Compline with our heads spinning.

One buddy, Cal Gould, got very shook up over a cute blond named Gloria Turner. Total simp, he couldn't bring himself to even talk to her. One morning, in dumb effort to impress her, he challenged Doug Martin, one of her alleged boyfriends, to race him across the lake—a fair stretch of a half mile.

Martin gave up halfway, treaded water and rested until he could swim back. Cal made it all the way across and waved proudly to show Gloria how macho he was. Total wasted effort. For, long before Cal hit shore, she'd wandered back to camp with yet another lad—an even more gal-savvy boy named Dean Tolliver.

Actually, I'd known Gloria for a long time—we attended church together after all. Cal wasn't alone in his spooky feelings; I nursed a secret crush too. But it wasn't until the last two days at camp that I dared approach her.

"Can I sit with you tonight at campfire?" I asked.

She smiled warmly. "Sure, Tommy. That would be nice."

We were together Thursday and Friday night. Dumb-head here never knew what hit him. I said nothing even vaguely affectionate. I didn't try to hold her hand. I was dazedly happy to just sit close and sing those nutty songs with her. The day we broke camp and her folks came for her, Gloria approached me at the last minute and asked if I'd call her when I got home. I couldn't believe my ears.

"Sure thing," I said and moved off in some sort of trance.

Another chapter. Turn the page.

But if we boys were noticing girls, someone else was noticing us noticing girls. Biology is biology, hormones will rage, and unpleasant things do happen. Or so wiser heads decided. As for me, innocent of the century, I wouldn't have known a hormone from a houseboat, raging or otherwise.

Early spring of the next year brought sudden, crushing edict from Bishop Sturtevant: There would be no more co-ed camping; henceforth, the sexes would go separately. What a furor that caused!

We tried it that way come July. Sixteen of us—with yet another new priest, Fr. Rapp, supervising—returned to the wilds of Nashotah for a week. Fun, but not really. Girls, we discovered, did make a difference.

The St. Paul's Cathedral campouts ended as of that year.

CHAPTER EIGHTEEN

We Fight Forest Fires

Living in total addiction to my movies and radio programs, I came to outrageously dramatize common, everyday events. Moving about the marsh among the bums, I was reliving *The Grapes of Wrath*. Wandering in Wilson's Woods, I became Spencer Tracy in *Northwest Passage*. Navigating the Fond du Lac River in the leaky *Tar Baby*—Washington crossing the Delaware.

So it was, this sullen summer afternoon in 1936 (I was ten), puttering in the garage, putting finishing touches on a three-shot rubber gun, that I saw David hotfooting it down the driveway, panic on his face.

"Thomas," he said as he burst into the garage, "come quick! Richard set the marsh on fire!"

There were two marshes. One, the main marsh (where the bums hung out) was located two short blocks from our house, across the river and to the south. A smaller patch of marshland—two acres at best—stood on the north side of Johnson Street. This one, because of standing water and open exposure, was bum-proof. Beside this stretch of marsh stood Lueder's Garage and next to it, the house where the Rahns lived. The marsh stretched along Packard Street and was stopped short by a low rise and an eight-foot-high wooden fence built to keep people out of Sam Manus' junkyard.

"Which marsh?"

"The one next to Elaine Rahn's."

"How did he start it?"

"Elaine Rahn and I were roasting some potatoes behind her

garage, and Richard came along and kicked the fire. The wind caught it, and now it's spreading like crazy."

"Why'd he kick the fire?"

"Because we wouldn't give him a potato."

"There's standing water there. No pails? Didn't you throw some on the fire?"

"We tried, but it still got away on us."

"Mr. and Mrs. Rahn? Did you tell them?"

"They're not home. C'mon, Thomas. Quick! Help us put it out before the cops come. Then we'll be in *big* trouble."

Just then Richard limped in.

"I'm sorry, Thomas. I didn't mean to do it...I..."

"You did too," David shot back. "You did it on purpose."

"Never mind," I snapped. "We've got a fire to put out."

And from my movie/radio mental treasury leaped emergency forest ranger protocol; I knew exactly what to do. The answer was right there in the garage, stored in a far corner. Burlap bags, a whole pile of them. Daddy was always bringing stuff home from the tannery. Rubber aprons, leather scraps, geriatric brooms, and from God-knows-where at the tannery, dozens of empty burlap bags.

"Over there in the corner," I ordered. "Daddy's sacks. Grab a couple and let's go."

Two minutes later, running at top speed, we were down the block, closing on the marsh. Black clouds of smoke were climbing just beyond Wadham's bulk station.

"We tried stamping it out with our feet," David said as we ran. "But the wind caught a big clump of grass, and blew it across the water. The marsh went up in a flash."

A man stood on the tracks, apparently enjoying the fire. He should have brought marshmallows.

I waded right into the foot-deep water and soaked my burlap bag. Dragging it out, water sloshing all over me, I rushed toward the east end of the marsh. Here the fire was spreading in wind-blown semi-circle, heading for an even denser stand of grass and brush. David and Richard ran right behind me. Elaine—eternal tomboy—wet a sack and attacked where the fire was closing in on her Dad's garage.

Senior fire fighter than I was, I waved them to spread out. "David, you stay with Elaine. Richard, follow me."

And Dear Lord, but didn't I lapse, full force, into my Lone Ranger mode? Wasn't I suddenly bare-chested, sweating, my eyes burning—my loyal Indian scout, Tonto, beside me—slashing at the flames with wet blankets, just as they did in the famous *Forest Fire* radio episode?

"C'mon, men, we've got a fire to put out," I shouted. *Honest to God, those exact words.* Perhaps my voice even dropped an octave. And didn't I almost sound like the Lone Ranger?

David wasn't kidding about the wind; the underbrush *was* burning something fierce, the flames sweeping in sixty or seventy foot arcs toward the tracks. The flames were almost up to our waists in places. But sawed-offs that we were, that wasn't saying much.

And while, in truth, the fire area wasn't really all that big, it was a big deal to kids like us. The low rumble of the licking flames, the snap and crackle of burning twigs, the whooshing sound of a patch when a wind gust flared it up—all served to magnify a sense of urgent danger. To us, caught up in mental and visual overload, it *was* hell coming topside.

"Faster, men! Work faster." What a phony, cornball reaction! But I couldn't help myself; I was adrift in high drama. This was Yellowstone, totally ablaze.

Skirting the marsh to the east, we hit dry land and hurried inward, swatting and stamping with all our might. We raced back and forth between the fire and the water hole. Our tennies and jeans were soaked and splashed with mud—our faces too, as we caught sideswipe from each other.

You forget how hot fire can be until you stand face-to-face to it. The smoke burned our eyes, made us cough and choke. Richard swatted his head where an errant piece of burning ash settled in his hair.

"Ouch, ouch, ouch!" he yipped.

It was swat and swat the flames, until our bag gave up. Then back to the water hole. Dunk and dunk again.

Richard and I were making headway on the eastern front, herding the fire in from the tracks, and David and Elaine were holding their own to the west. But the fire was still working its way too close to the junk yard fence. It wouldn't take much to set the bone-dry boards ablaze.

Just about then, brother Bernard and his buddy, Augie Harris, happened by. Right away they came running.

"Got any more bags?" Bernard asked.

"Run home..." I said, "...more bags in the corner of the garage, next to Daddy's work table."

He and Augie took off like rockets. Minutes later they were back and dunked their bags into the marsh water.

"Work toward the fence," I shouted. "Don't let the fire get any closer."

The lonesome stranger still stood on the west side of the marsh. Had a Soo Line freight come along just then, he'd have had to jump for his life. Again, no reaction, just a calm, amused smile. He never made a move to help. He watched forest fires every day.

Smile? He was probably busting a gut laughing. Six little runts—one of them a girl, ages six to ten, none standing over five feet—fighting a marsh fire? Hilarious!

Bernard and Augie kept running back and forth behind me from the pond to the fence. Little by little, swatting fiercely, they herded the flames in. Good. The fence was safe.

And on our front, my "C'mon, men" gradually fizzling out. We were breathing easier. The fire was definitely under control. David and Elaine had closed down their sector. Nearer to the water, they'd had double advantage. I had to hand it to Elaine; for a girl she really held up her end of things.

I don't suppose we were at it more than fifteen minutes, but it seemed an hour passed—rampaging imaginations again—before we had the fire licked. Here and there a patch reignited, and we were on it swiftly.

What a mess. Our clothes were filthy and soaking wet, our faces muddy and smoky. We were sweating like mad—summer after all—and we looked like refugees from a fireworks factory explosion.

But what a keen sense of accomplishment and worth we felt. Band of brothers and all that. A true adventure! We'd got the fire out before anyone thought to call the cops or the fire department; we wouldn't be catching any hell after all. A narrow escape.

On second thought, we weren't exactly home free. Once Ma saw us, the fur would fly. We'd cross that bridge when we got to it.

So we just stood there, catching our collective breaths, super proud of ourselves. Richard, who'd caused the whole thing in the first place, said, "Hey, Thomas, that was kinda fun, wasn't it?"

And though I could've swatted him one, I nodded and sent him a curt Lone Ranger reply: "I suppose."

While underneath I had to agree. *We'd had a ball.*

We tramped around the area for another half hour, making sure no hot spots would flare up when we left. But other than thin, grayish skeins of smoke drifting over the whole scene, the fire was definitely out.

Our watching man was nowhere to be seen.

Then we could dally no longer. It was time to head home and face the music.

"*Dios mío!*" Ma said as she answered our timid knock on the back door. "What happened to you boys? Did you fall in the river? How did you get so dirty?"

"Ma," I said, as levelly as possible, "can you bring us a pail of water and a wash cloth so we can clean up a little?"

"Yes. When you tell me what happened. Were you playing in a mud puddle or what?" Her eyes widened. "David, how did you singe your hair?"

It was apparent that our "unexpected heroes" scenario wasn't going to work. Ma hadn't bought it before; she wouldn't bite this time either.

"I'm waiting."

David took his cue: "There was a fire in the marsh over by Rahn's. And we put it out."

"With what, your clothes?"

We held up the filthy burlap bags. "With these," I said. "We got them wet in the marsh and beat out the flames with them."

"Fire in the marsh? How did that happen?"

It was then that we first noticed Richard was nowhere to be seen. He knew he was going to catch it for starting the fire; he was probably two counties away by then.

As best I could, I filled Ma in on the chain of events, finishing with: "We kept the fire from burning the junkyard fence down. Rahn's house too." And lamely: "We saved the fire department a trip." And hopefully: "We were heroes. Sort of…"

"Did it ever occur to you that you might have got badly burned? That's why we have fire departments. Your clothes are ruined. Just look at you."

"By the time they got there," I said, "the fence would've burned down."

"So? It's not your fence."

"Yeah, but who started the fire? Wouldn't they come looking for us?"

"Just wait until your father hears about this. You say Richard's to blame?"

"Yes," David said. "He went and kicked the fire. That's how it started."

She looked around. "And just where is Richard?"

"Probably hiding," I said. "He knows he's gonna get it."

"And how do you know you're not *all* gonna get it?"

"We just put the fire out," I said. "We didn't start it."

We returned to square one. "David and Elaine were cooking some potatoes beside her garage and—"

"Richard kicked the fire," she said, finishing my sentence. "And why did he do such a thing?"

"Ask him. If you can find him."

Ma was momentarily mollified. She disappeared into the house. A minute later she came back and threw a couple of wash cloths and a bar of soap at us.

"All right. Get a pail from the garage, turn on the faucet beside the house, and wash out there. You're not coming into my house like that. Take off your dirty clothes and throw them here by the steps."

"But, Ma," I protested, "In our underwear? People will see us."

"So let them see you. Let them see what a bunch of bad boys you are." She sniffed. "What a bunch of *dumb* boys!"

She stormed back into the house.

So we stripped down to our underwear and dropped our clothes in a pile like Ma said. We went out in public and scrubbed down. Cold as the water was, it still felt good after the heat of the day—and the fire. We cleaned our faces and stuck our heads under the faucet to rinse the soot from our hair; we did our arms, legs, feet as best we could. People walking by slowed down and rolled their eyes at the bizarre scene. We were genteel enough to turn our backs to them.

We were just about done when Richard showed up. "Did you tell Ma?" he asked.

"Sure, we told her," David said. "You don't think we're gonna take all the blame for your dumb stunt, do you?"

"Take off your dirty clothes," I ordered. "Put them by the back porch."

Richard said nothing. He went behind the house, then returned in nothing but his BVDs. He started washing, his woeful expression never changing for a moment.

Ma hadn't thrown us a towel, so we moved out of traffic and sat on the back porch so the sun could dry us off some. But Richard never came to sit with us. Even in his underwear, he was gone again. Probably in the garage.

"Ma," I called, when we were dry, "can we come in? We're all clean now."

She came out and gave us a severe look-over. "All right. Go upstairs, change your underwear, and put on some clean clothes." As we brushed past her, she said, "Where's Richard?"

We dummied up. "I don't know," I said. "He hasn't showed up."

"All right. Upstairs. Git!" She slammed the door behind us.

And wouldn't you know, we'd no sooner got dressed and come back down, than Daddy walked in. He'd been helping out at Charlie Spencer's farm—probably earning a dollar or so—and was done for the day. Ma clued him in on the day's calamity.

His expression turned dark.

Now we're gonna get it, I thought.

"Ricardo? He start fire?" he asked.

"Yeah," we all chorused, desperate stool pigeons. "It was all his fault. All we did was help put it out."

So he went into the same scold as Ma. Didn't we know that we could have been badly burned? What about our ruined clothes? Clothes haven't been seen growing on trees lately, have they? On and on.

Then the doomsday pronouncement: "You all need good spanking."

But, saints be praised, there came immediate reprieve. "Where is Ricardo? *He* one who need spanking."

Again the stone wall.

"We don't know. We haven't seen him." We all breathed a deep sigh of relief. We'd escaped the bullet.

"Outside? Hiding?"

"We don't know," I said with a straight face, daring David and Bernard to cross me. "We haven't seen him."

"He hide in garage, I bet." Daddy started for the back door.

But Richard wasn't in the garage. When Daddy returned and walked through the back bedroom, he found him hiding under the ice box. No easy feat, with only a twelve-inch clearance there. How he'd got into the house without anybody hearing, I don't know.

Dumb move. He should have taken off for California.

"Come out, Ricardo," Daddy ordered.

Richard was already blubbering when he unwedged himself. He knew what came next. He was a pathetic sight, standing there in just his underwear.

As always, Daddy was up for the situation. There was only one way to handle such transgressions. "Come, Ricardo," he said in a soft, rueful voice, beginning to unbuckle his belt, "we go in basement now."

CHAPTER NINETEEN

Meet Miss Stanford

We may have lacked many material things during the Depression, but we weren't short-changed when it came to stellar school teachers. I shall be forever grateful to have been taught by these ill-paid, courageous men and women.

Once I escaped kindergarten, that is.

My teacher of the century was Miss Beth Stanford, and I will never forget her. When I look back at the wonders that transpired in her classroom, I am, again, awed, grateful, and humbled.

But before introducing Miss Stanford, some minor, but relevant digressions. She was not alone; there were others who contributed to my early wealth-of-mind:

Miss Lind came to Washington School on alternate Friday mornings and went from room to room, giving each grade a hurried art lesson. Yes, *Miss* Lind. There were no *Mrs.* teachers back then.

I clearly remember the tight-fitting royal-blue jacket and matching skirt she wore week in and week out, always with a little puff of white silk at the throat. No other clothes? Granted, teachers only earned $900 a year—no one escaping the Great Depression's ugly grasp—but couldn't she have afforded at least *one* different outfit?

I looked forward to her fifty minute visits. Even in fifth grade, I considered myself a pretty fair artist, and I was always one of her favorites.

On this particular Friday was art appreciation. The painting that day—most likely a Winslow Homer—captured two men fishing in a dory off the Grand Banks. Far in the distance, we saw dim outline of the mother ship. Black clouds boiled; a serious storm was brewing. The dory-mates, faces panicky, studied the sky intently.

Miss Lind pointed out composition fundamentals—the dory wasn't front-center; the mother ship stood off to one side. Color, intensity of hues, how the background faded to show depth and distance, the skill with which the artist portrayed the fishermen's fear, the overall feeling aroused in the viewer. On and on, the usual art teacher shtick.

When Miss Lind left, Miss Stanford adapted her session to her own purposes and asked us to write some lines—in our *very own* words, please—to describe the picture.

I was also a hotshot in English. Duck soup. I imagined myself in the tossing boat; I generated mental terror of my own. Then I was off and running, my pencil racing, telling how the fishermen must frantically lift their lines, pull anchor, man the oars, all the while scrambling over a bed of slippery cod. I described the wind tearing at their clothes and how they must row desperately against wind and waves as the storm's full fury descended. Remember *Captains Courageous*? Man, I was there!

Somewhere along in my account, I used the phrase "The race is on!" This is the only wording in the whole essay that I can, with any real accuracy, revive today.

We turned in our papers. Then it was time for arithmetic, and shortly after we headed home for lunch.

When I returned, Miss Stanford told me that Miss Fahey, our principal, wanted to see me. I was instantly alarmed; what had I done now? Miss Stanford sent a sly smile and assured me I had nothing to fear. "She just wants to talk to you. Something good."

"Come in," Miss Fahey called when I knocked on the door frame.

I approached her desk, stood quaking. "Please sit down, Thomas."

Then she smilingly held up a sheet of composition paper—my theme from that morning.

"This is a very excellent story, Thomas. Miss Stanford was so proud of what you wrote that she showed it to me. And I'm proud of you too. The line where you say 'The race is on' is especially effective. I can't help but wonder if you might become an author some day."

Well, gulp. Puffing up time.

What she wanted to do as reward was to take me into each classroom in the building and have me read my story to them.

Gulp again.

In each class Miss Fahey introduced me as a fifth grader from Miss Stanford's room and praised my wonderful writing. They should all listen carefully to my vivid descriptions and learn from my example.

The first time I read I was shaky and unsure of myself. Miss Fahey had to interrupt. "Speak up, Thomas. Enunciate clearly, please."

There were only a hundred words or so; it took but a few minutes to get through it.

When I finished, Miss Fahey said, "Wasn't that remarkable, class? Don't you think Thomas deserves some applause?"

Of course the little simps—who probably hadn't understood a word of it—began clapping. What a rush! Talk about exploding heads!

Then off to the second-grade room. By the time I got to perform for my own classmates, I was an accomplished reader, and I skipped the blushing when Miss Fahey lauded my efforts. I felt truly special when *they* applauded.

However, by then I was plenty sick and tired of "The race is on."

Another eccentric yet well-loved teacher was Miss Korrer, who also appeared every two weeks. For her lessons we were herded into an unused classroom, which a battered piano called home. She taught us the scales, how to read and sing notes, plus musical staff markings.

Ho hum. Old stuff to me, being a skilled member of a prominent Mexican band and all.

There were new songs to learn, old ones to review. But when she got into music appreciation and the classical composers, she turned dead serious. Words from God—listen up! The girls loved these sessions, but we boys did our truculent best to let her know we'd rather be someplace else.

Miss Korrer stood almost six feet, was perhaps fifty, and had a boney build. She wore her skirts longer than most women at the time (well past her knees). In her youth she'd been an opera singer and had known the famous operatic star Madame Schumann-Heink, whom we kids recognized from her annual Christmas Eve radio appearances when she sang *Silent Night* in both German and English. Ma always herded us into the living room to hear that.

Miss Korrer blew this little pitch pipe to get us on keel. Peep, she'd go. *Mmmm*, we'd go. Peep, peep. *Mmmmm, mmmm*, and so on until we were all well tuned.

When Miss Korrer sang along, she all but drowned us out. She was constantly nagging the boys to sing with more enthusiasm and expression, and she'd come at us if we weren't giving one-hundred percent. I recall her grabbing my forelock more than once and calling out, "Higher, Thomas. Sing higher."

None of us were safe when she was around.

"Higher, Tony. Higher, Frank." And yank, yank, yank.

The class wise guys often commented as we headed across the hall, "Watch out, guys, the yanks are coming." Some even called her "Apple core," since "Korrer" was pronounced "core." But certainly not to her face. So much for kid humor.

Most vivid in my mind was her session about Schubert's *Earl King*. She was quick to impress upon us the fact that Franz was only eighteen when he wrote it, shooting the boys a sharp so-there-too look as she did so. In this lieder masterpiece, a man rides on horseback, his dying son in his arms, rushing desperately to reach the doctor in time. (Anyway that's how Miss Korrer told it.)

Beside him rides the phantom Earl King, who symbolizes death. He coaxes the boy to come live with him, describing the joys they'll share. The father argues with him, and the lad cries out, "Father, Father, don't you hear him?" The father whips the horse to a faster pace, hoping to outrace the Earl King. But to no avail, for at the last the child dies in his arms, and the Earl King is triumphant.

High drama, indeed. She definitely had *our* attention.

Then Miss Korrer proceeded to sing *Erlkönig*—in German—giving us a full blast rendition. It was overdone, it was screechy, the piano thundered. And yes, we could hear the horse's hooves, the raging storm as they rode, and most painfully, the father's final sobs.

Dead silence in the room when she finished. We all let out a deep breath.

Man, were we hooked! We begged her to sing it every time she came. Mostly she refused, but two or three times a year she'd give in.

Seated at the piano, eyes closed—the door deliberately closed lest the nearby classes think a murder was underway—she'd go at it again. And, knowing the story by heart, chilled to the bone, we could tell exactly when the father was talking and when the Earl King was coaxing him to surrender his son. And more importantly, when the poor boy died. No matter how many times we heard it, some of the girls got teary-eyed at the end. And though I fought hard to maintain my tough-guy image, I'd invariably find myself with a walnut-sized lump in my throat.

Welcome to Washington school, 1936, and to the classroom of one of my most gifted teachers. A teacher who made me *want* to be in school, a teacher who coaxed the very best out of each and every student at every turn.

Beth Stanford taught combined fifth and sixth grades, so I was lucky enough to have her for two whole years. Despite her dour appearance, she was a Grade-A pussycat. She could be calling you down for some infraction, and yet, even as she scolded, her eyes shone with lively affection.

I have pictures (which she took) of every kid in that class. The sixth graders were Bette Drolshagen, Ruth Ericksen, Tony Axotis, Shirley May Leu, Frank Kurzynske, Richard Schmidt, Betty Bestor, Jeannette Osborn, Melvina Pollack, Helen Baldwin, Nestor Zille, Marjorie Nack, and Freddy Groesbeck.

Freddy was one of the first to enlist when World War II broke out and among the first to die in battle. Only five of us still remain at this writing. But there is no photo of Miss Stanford. She died in 1990. I still visualize her clearly; I'm back in her classroom again.

We didn't fool around—no way—there was always perfect order in her kingdom. Teachers were God back then. If they sent a note home to your parents, you might as well pack your duds and leave home.

Nevertheless, stern disciplinarian or not, we all loved her. Without saying a word, she let us know that she also cared for every last one of us. Only one or two of my later teachers ever came close to matching her skill and compassion. I paid her thank-you, after-school visits while home on furlough during WW2.

I have no idea how long she'd been teaching; she could have been twenty-five, thirty-five years old. Such things didn't register with kids. An adult. That was that. Thin, standing perhaps five-six in her severe black shoes, she seemed always on the go, hurrying to help her pupils. Her ash-blonde hair was styled to a mannish taper at the back. She had slate-blue eyes and a slightly-lined face and was somewhat lantern-jawed.

What was her secret classroom weapon? In a word: innovation. A surprise a minute—we never knew which thunderbolt would strike next.

She and her close friend, Miss Helen Glissendorf (who taught at Lincoln School), took trips every summer. Money being tight, these were mostly stateside, but once they got as far as Mexico. Come September and the start of a new term, there were souvenirs—coloring books, travel pamphlets, maps, trinkets, window stickers, and special prizes we eagerly competed for.

Where she got the money, heaven knows. She certainly wasn't moonlighting; part time jobs were definite no-no with teachers back then. Pure sacrifice.

One vacation trip took them to Georgia and also to Gettysburg Battleground in Pennsylvania. It was my first encounter with Miss Stanford's largesse; each of us received a coloring book. I still bring up image of myself painstakingly crayoning in the gray Spanish moss that hung from trees bordering a long, winding drive that lead to an antebellum plantation home.

More memorable was a fold-out copy of the Gettysburg Cyclorama, which spread eight feet or so across the back bulletin board. Printout of a life-size painting done by some French artist, the panoramic view faithfully captured the complete battlefield action on the day of Pickett's Charge. Mounted on the walls of a circular rotunda, she told us, the viewers stood on a platform that slowly turned so visitors could follow the action.

Miss Stanford left the souvenir up for almost three weeks while the class covered a Civil War unit. While some of the battle scenes were too gory for the girls, we boys were transfixed. We oozled back every chance we got, studying the battle scenes with open-mouthed delight. American history had never been more compelling!

Miss Stanford baited many, many hooks to lure us into learning. Prominent among these was our in-room library—stocked largely with books she'd purchased herself. It was here that I first gloried in the bold adventures of Robin Hood and the pageantry and chivalry of King Arthur's Court. The Howard Pyle and N.C. Wyeth illustrations were burned into my memory forever. Especially the one where a dying Robin prepares to shoot his last arrow. I agonized. Were there ever more thrilling depictions of such bold gallantry?

Kid versions of Homer's *Iliad* and *Odyssey* came next. Can you imagine today's fifth and sixth graders reading stuff like that? Hell, many college students don't even tackle them. And wasn't that Trojan horse the smoothest thing ever? Such delicious trickery. And outrageous stupidity!

Wouldn't the Trojans have suspected a scam upon discovering a gigantic wooden horse in their front yard? C'mon now.

Even after my kindergarten language difficulties, learning to read and spell were never a problem for me. My language skills had simply been sitting there waiting for me to catch up. Tenses, word order, adjectives, and adverbs were never studied; I instinctively knew how to use them. Native talent? Who can say? Otherwise credit goes to Miss Stanford; she whacked final nails into the plank.

Thanks to her, new books never stopped coming. We were addicts. We *must* get back to the library corner or perish. *Treasure Island; Tom Sawyer; Grimms' Fairy Tales; Pinocchio; Land for My Sons; The Arabian Nights; East of the Sun, West of the Moon; Robinson Crusoe; The Trumpeter of Krakow; Dr. Dolittle; The Wizard of Oz*—even some *Elsie Dinsmore* books. Which we boys avoided like the plague. Girl stuff.

Howard Pyle's Book of Pirates was my hands-down favorite. I think I read it five times, helpless to resist the fantastic illustrations. To my kid brain, there had never been anything so dramatic, so beautiful. Those ships, those cruel pirates! Time and time again, I paged through the volume—for the pictures alone. When other boys weren't fighting me for it, that is.

We never got away with anything at the back table either. Now and then Miss Stanford would randomly zone in on us and ask to see the assignment we'd allegedly finished. Woe betide any kid caught fudging; the poor sap's free-time reading was suspended for a whole week.

She only called my bluff once. I never weaseled again.

We won a gold star for every book we read and proudly pasted it on a printed certificate she provided. She would ask one question about the book. If we answered correctly, we got a star.

Big question: Did she know every book by heart? Almost every kid in class had thirty or more stars (I had almost fifty) by school year's end.

Every Thursday afternoon Library Lady arrived at Washington School. The janitors carried box after box of books—each marked for grade level—up to the second-floor activity room that was used by all grades when they needed spread-out space. The same place the school nurse came to weigh and measure us twice a year.

She would dump a box on a long table and then summon the grades in order. Upon entering we turned in last week's books. This done, we charged the table, where we greedily gathered in an armload of books. We could only check out two—agonizing Solomon's choice. We'd already be reading while waiting to check out.

Can you imagine today's kids reading two books—and they weren't baby books either—in a week's time? But we did it and clamored for more.

If all this wasn't enough, Miss Stanford often suspended routine, and read us whole sections from some of the adult books she was reading at the time—John Gunther, Margaret Mitchell, Carl Sandburg. I distinctly remember a reading from *Gone with the Wind* that dealt with the fall of Atlanta, which had us all sitting on the edge of our seats. A John Gunther section from *Inside Germany* described the rise of the Nazi regime. Special sections from *Abraham Lincoln: The Prairie Years* wrung our hearts.

By way of contrast she read a light-hearted section from Admiral

Richard Byrd's Antarctic book, *Alone*, in which he described ice cream making at the South Pole. The ingredients were poured into a sealed container, which was hung onto a rope outside. After the wind whirled the container wildly for a few minutes, it was brought back inside.

And just like that—ice cream!

Our tongues were hanging out.

Another Stanford gimmick: the play books she purchased above and beyond her school-materials allowance. Thin, gray-backed, some almost in tatters, they contained plays for Christmas, Halloween, Thanksgiving, etc. Also others to honor such American heroes as Abraham Lincoln, Benjamin Franklin, Daniel Boone and, of course, George Washington.

Our *Elson's Reader* also contained random plays. We did them all.

Miss Stanford was eminently fair; every kid in class got to play a role in one playbook or another. We half-pint actors stood before the class, book in hand, and read our lines with squeaky-voiced earnestness.

Look, Ma, I'm acting!

There were also plays where we memorized our lines, Dickens's *A Christmas Carol* being a prime example. I was in sixth grade that year, and I got cast as geezer Ebenezer. We did the play in our classroom. The janitors moved extra chairs in, sliding Miss Stanford's desk to one side before each performance. The second-, third-, and fourth-graders came in separately for a special presentation. And finally, just before we little savages were turned loose for Christmas vacation, the parents came.

Perhaps thirty mothers, even some unemployed fathers, showed up on that festive morning. We were spinning with excitement. Tiny Tim was the biggest problem; we'd have needed a midget to do justice to the role. So we borrowed a bright-eyed second grader—one smart enough to memorize "God bless us, every one!"—to sit in on a few rehearsals, and he brought off the not-a-dry-eye-in-the-house role to perfection.

An intelligent boy, a remarkable boy!—as Scrooge would have put it.

Shirley May Leu played a scornful Mrs. Cratchit, and Frank Kurzynske was a benign Bob Cratchit. Especially when he strode in with Tiny Tim on his shoulder. My Scrooge role called for a bathrobe. A bathrobe? What kind of animal was that? The Ramirezes had certainly never heard of such. The call went out, and Dick Schmitz had one to loan. I was a snarly, grumpy Scrooge, bah-humbugging all over the place in a raspy voice. The moms ate it up.

One of our plays dealt with Abe Lincoln and his love of reading. A book he'd borrowed got rain-damaged when he stored it in a crack in his Kentucky log cabin overnight. He worked for days to earn enough to pay its owner for the loss.

In our rendition the audience saw him lying before a jerry-rigged fireplace, happily reading. I didn't win a part in that one, but I still recall my award-winning performance as sound-effects man. Standing in the hallway just outside the door, I crinkled a big wad of cellophane to simulate the sound of a crackling wood-fire.

You had to be there. Miss Stanford thought of everything.

Another time we built a huge medieval castle in the back of the room. Made of cardboard boxes, it stood head high. Twin towers, notched walls, moats, and drawbridge—bright banners flew from the towers. There was even a courtyard with cutout knights, damsels, horses, and men jousting. All were drawn by the class, painted, and cut from poster board.

Every grade in Washington School was invited to come see our castle. Good publicity gimmick for Stanford; every kid visitor would be looking forward to their turn in her classes.

When we hit Mexico in our geography books, Miss Stanford was in her glory, producing souvenir *sombreros, serapes, maracas,* plus another coloring book for each of us. I don't recall a play dealing with *cosas Mexicanas*, but she did teach us two Mexican songs, *La Cucaracha* and *El Rancho Grande*. And since I was the house Mexican, I became a mentor of sorts, teaching the gang proper pronunciations.

Basically *El Rancho Grande* deals with a big Mexican ranch. There is a sweet thing—*rancherita*—who says she'll make her guy some chaps like the ranchers wear. She'll begin with wool—*lana*—and finish with leather—*cuero*. There are more verses, but all have faded over the years.

La Cucaracha was a song supposedly sung by Pancho Villa's brigands during the Mexican Revolution in the early 1900s.

La cucaracha, la cucaracha,
Ya no puede caminar.
Porque no tiene, porque le falta,
Marihuana que fumar.

We learned that *cucaracha* means roach and that *la cucaracha* couldn't walk because it had no marijuana to smoke. Which made absolutely no sense to us. Had Miss Stanford the vaguest idea of what marijuana was? Hell, it was hemp, and it grew on farms all over Wisconsin; the sisal was used to make rope. To us it was just an obnoxious weed. Smoke it? Who dreamed that one up? Ah, innocence!

Another geography unit, this time France: Here she pinned a four-foot-long foldout of the SS Normandie, France's queen of the seas, onto the bulletin board. At the time she was the largest luxury liner ever built, and the cut-away illustration showed exquisite detail of every deck level, from luxury cabins and salons to the holds and engine rooms.

We boys stood enthralled. More amazing, the poster was up for grabs; it became grand prize for whoever turned in the best summary booklet on France at the unit's end.

The SS Normandie haunted my dreams, and I worked my little tail off, determined that the prize would be mine. I *did* win, and I bore it home triumphantly and pinned it onto my bedroom wall.

The Normandie burned and capsized in New York Harbor in 1942 while being refitted as a troop ship. Having worked so hard to win that poster, I took the loss almost personally. Even so, upon returning home from military service in 1946—*when I became a man, I put away childish things*—the beautiful creation was thrown out. What would a souvenir like that be worth today?

Waste, waste.

*   *   *

Public schools made a big fuss over Armistice Day back then. Even in high school, we still stood facing east and observed a minute of silence at 11:00 AM on November 11 to honor our fallen World War I troops.

At Washington School we did it up brown. We observed the routine moment of silence, of course, but went quite a few steps further. At 1:30 PM on that day, the entire school paraded three blocks to the west, to the house where George Bixby, Fond du Lac's last-living Civil War veteran, lived. When we arrived, a relative would lead him—barely able to walk—onto the front porch. He would sit silently in a chair and smile down at us kids while we sang *My Country, 'Tis of Thee*, after which one of the sixth graders would lead us in the Pledge of Allegiance.

What a scene—one-hundred-fifty kids, each with a hand over his or her heart. Another kid would read a patriotic poem. That concluded the ceremony.

We'd march away, Mr. Bixby waving feebly.

Inventive as always, Miss Stanford asked the class, early in November, if anyone owned a drum. Frank Kurzynske raised his hand.

"My Dad's in the American Legion," he offered. "I'll bet he can get us one."

And sure enough, Frank's dad did come across. Not with one drum, but two. And guess who got to play the second one? A proud, proud moment.

So there we went, Frank and I, the snare drum strapped to our shoulders, side by side, drumming the whole school down Arndt Street, the kids marching two by two. We had practiced the cadence out in the schoolyard the day before, so we were pretty good with the brr-umph, boom-boom, brr-umph, boom-boom when the big day arrived.

Talk about thrilled! I all but floated down the road. And going back to school was just as good. Brr-umph, boom-boom, brr-umph, boom-boom. Glorious! Oh, yeah, we knew patriotic back then.

*   *   *

Miss Stanford was big on Mother's Day. We wrote a poem—short, but saccharine—to let Mom know how much we loved her—in ink, using our best Palmer penmanship. Then we made a card and embellished it with a gang of stick-on hearts and flowers she provided. The poem, on a separate square of paper, went inside, glued close to the right edge.

One sunny morning in late April, she lined us up in groups of six on the playground, careful to leave a space between each of us. Then she photographed the group with her Brownie. When developed, she neatly sliced them so she had six tiny photos. The final, elegant touch: a photo of Mom's favorite kid, pasted beside the verse.

Ma was delighted with her card. The sentiments *and* the picture. There I stood in bib overalls, my hair flying—my belt on the outside of all things and holding a prop baseball and glove. I still recall the opening lines of my ditty: "My Mother is like a poem. She's also handy in the home."

Edgar Guest, eat your heart out!

Another of our bi-weekly special instructors was Mr. Gordon Kiesler, who taught physical education. In his mid-thirties, disgustingly trim and tanned, he always walked in looking like he had a steel rod up his back.

His winter thing was in-the-aisle calisthenics. "Stand straight," he'd bark. "Shoulders back. You there, tuck that chin in." Then such basics as "Right hand up, left hand touch your toes. Left hand up, right hand touch your toes. Right, left, right, left. One-two, one-two. Put some muscle into it, people!"

Then came breathing exercises. "Deep breath! Chest out, chin in. Exhale! Deep breath." He should have been a doctor.

Out of all this came my one and only foray into competitive sports. Those times when we did outdoor activities—the girls with a female instructor—he introduced us to soccer. Which I hated. Out-and-out chicken that I was, I dreaded getting my shins kicked.

That fall Mr. Kiesler formed an after-school, city-wide soccer league for fourth-, fifth-, and sixth-graders, and for some perverse reason Miss Stanford chose me to captain the Washington School team. Even though pleased with the dubious honor, I had definite misgivings. Truth of the matter: I was never meant to be a leader.

Our squad was a disaster; I could hardly muster six or eight boys come game day. Practice sessions? Forget it. We had a fifth-grader, Tyler Hatcher, who was a great goalie; the rest of us were flubs. Without him we ended up twenty-zip. I had to plead for hours before game day to get Billy to even show up. The only game we won all fall was the time Jefferson School failed to appear.

Thanks for nothing, Miss Stanford.

And here, finally, crowning accolade—triple-dip surprise—to Beth Stanford's teaching wizardry:

One afternoon in mid-January—Christmas vacation behind us and all suffering minor doldrums—Miss Stanford ordered us all to close our books. She had an important announcement. We were immediately on guard. Who'd messed up now? A stiff smile on her face, she held something behind her back.

"How would you all like to have a puppet show? Right here in the room?"

How would we like to fly?

"Yes, yes!" we all yipped.

She brought out the booklet and held it up for us to see. *Easy-to-Make Marionettes.* She told us how it would work. She'd pass out materials, templates, needle, and thread. "I'll teach you step by step. "But, there's a catch…"

We all groaned.

"You have to keep up your school work. There will be no slacking off while we're getting ready for our show. Nobody goes to the work table until their lessons are done. If you don't study, you don't get to help with the show." Her eyes glowed. "We'll invite the other classes in. Maybe some grades from other schools. We'll put on several performances. If…our show is good, of course."

We waded in that very afternoon. Everyone would build a marionette, but only the best ones would be used in the show.

Miss Stanford had already found an unemployed carpenter father to build the stage and the platform on which the puppet masters would stand as we made our creatures walk, sit, even dance if necessary. It would be delivered in two weeks. Hopefully we'd have some marionettes finished by then so practice could begin.

Those who were good at drawing would work on the back drops. A long, long piece of paper would be mounted on rollers. We'd use tempera paint for the background scenes and roll it for each scene change. There'd be something for everyone to do.

Well. We sat in stunned silence. Was there no end to our teacher's ingenuity?

What would our show be about? we asked.

Naturally it must tie in with our studies. "We've been learning about Marco Polo," she said. "Wouldn't that be a wonderful story to use? We'll call it 'The Adventures of Marco Polo.' We can show him in Italy, then on his way to Cathay. We'll show him in prison. Think of the colorful costumes you girls can make."

Our hearts pounded with excitement. What wonderful fun!

It was a good thing this happened late in the school day. Otherwise precious little schoolwork would've been done. She opened a folder and began passing out mimeographed marionette patterns, scissors, squares of white cloth. The bodies, the arms, the legs would be cut out, sewed, stuffed with cotton batting, joined—she explained—then sewed again. Creases at the elbows and knees so the legs and arms could allow them to move in lifelike fashion.

During the days following she passed out more patterns and some craft knives. The boys carved pieces from the soft pine she brought in; we made marionette heads and shoulders, sets of hands and feet.

The project, of necessity, called for further study and library research on Marco Polo. How did people dress back then? How did they travel? A story line and script had to be written, lines must be learned.

Miss Stanford saw to it that every kid would contribute. Poster paint must be mixed; materials, passed out. Cleanup had to be done. No task was too small.

Eyes sparkling, she passed out patterns, set us to work. Except for hands going up, questions being asked, there wasn't another sound in the room—just the clip-clip of twenty-eight scissors and the crunch-crunch of crisp linen. Everyone was totally absorbed, too busy to chatter.

That night we all walked home on air.

The woman had absolutely no shame; she just reeled us in!

Then, one Monday morning in early February, as we came to school—there stood our beautiful theater. We were thrilled beyond description! Collapsible, made of plywood, and braced with one-by-twos, it stood eight-feet tall, ten-feet wide. Hinged wings swung back to conceal the puppeteers as they worked their magic. A platform, made of two-by-fours, with a single riser, was already bolted in place. The façade and wings were painted a royal blue. The stage opening was placed low enough to give the puppeteers ample working room above it. Curtains, draw strings must be made!

The days, then the weeks passed, and little by little, things fell into place. The control sticks were constructed, the strings were strung. We learned which stick to lift to make the legs move, which one to tilt to activate the arms. It was infuriating at first; lines were always getting tangled. The insolent creatures refused to stand, walk, and gesture properly. Whether we were in the play or not, we all got a chance to make the marionettes prance.

If ever there was incentive to finish our schoolwork—quickly and correctly—Marco was it. However did we survive all that excitement and heady anticipation?

The girls were in their glory as they designed and sewed costumes. They made clothes for Marco, Marco's father Maffeo, his uncle Niccolò, sheiks, Cossacks, silk-robed courtiers, damsels, and Genghis Khan himself.

Carving the heads proved more difficult than expected, and they emerged basically looking like block-heads. Frank Kurzynske, irritated by the floppy legs, came up with the idea of drilling holes in the feet and wedging lead plugs into them. Smaller slivers went into the hands. Now Marco and company looked like they were really walking, not just flopping around like a *Wizard of Oz* scarecrow.

I was put in charge of the scenery. Studying Marco Polo's route to Cathay, we settled on five major backgrounds: Turkey, Iraq, Afghanistan, the Gobi Desert, and, finally, China. My crew fell to with a will; the poster paint flew.

Did I feel slighted because I wouldn't dangle a marionette? No way. I was having too much fun splashing paint.

The prison wall was a masterpiece—all those mortared stones. It was here, after Marco got captured in some silly sea battle between the city-states of Venice and Genoa, that he dictated his story to another prisoner, a scribe. That development called for a panel showing Italian war ships.

And what did *they* look like? More research. History, geography, English, art—our brains were tumbling. We were literally learning by osmosis.

And didn't Dick Schmitz build the cleverest little benches for Marco and the scribe to sit on?

A script was written. A lot of brainstorming. We were all talking at once. A narrator would stand to one side of the theater and describe the travel routes, the wondrous things they saw, and the alien culture Marco Polo and his uncles found in Kublai Khan land. Each puppeteer, occupied with the devilish task of bringing their character to life, couldn't be expected to speak lines as well, could they? So other classmates stood behind them, provided the voices. Tony Axotis was elected to turn the roller for each scene change.

Santa's workshop had nothing on us.

Someone was always in the back of the room practicing with a marionette, the soft tap-tap-tap of their feet on the hardwood floor carrying clearly through our quiet afternoons. Class periods continued on schedule. Order—though occasionally a wee bit off-kilter—was maintained.

How Miss Stanford managed to keep all those plates spinning at the same time—and retain her sanity besides—the Lord only knows.

And finally, in mid-April, our first real show, this for the third and fourth graders. Our classroom was jam-packed. And there stood Melvina Pollack, quaking in her shoes, reading her travelogue. Tony pulled the curtains open, and the show began. Those of us not onstage stood around the edges of the room, holding our collective breaths.

A hit? Or a bomb?

Yes, some lines got mangled. Marco lost his balance a couple times when he tried to sit down, and Tony was a bit late changing scenery here and there. But all in all, it went well. When the first- and second-graders came, they understood very little of it, but the marionettes held them spellbound. They clapped wildly at the end.

The Adventures of Marco Polo was a hit. When other schools got word of our project, they wanted to come see our play. (The girl I would one day marry was one of those guests.) These visitors were equally enthralled by the story—and the amazing marionettes. I'd guess, counting two evening performances for the parents, that we did it at least a dozen times. By then we were consummate pros, each show better than the last.

We felt distinct sense of loss that day in late May when we wrapped the strings and controllers around each marionette and put them into their box for the last time.

Goodbye, Marco. Goodbye, Maffeo and Uncle Niccolò. Goodbye, Genghis Khan.

It had all come and gone so fast.

And then it was June. The school year was drawing to a close. We sixth-graders would soon leave Washington School—willing our legacy to the fifth-graders—moving into the big-time. Roosevelt Junior High, here we come!

Dumb kids. That last afternoon, blind-sided by the impending freedom of summer vacation, we marched up for our report cards, then fidgeted while Miss Stanford bid us goodbye and wished us luck in our new school. Unfeeling jerks, we hustled away without a decent goodbye of our own. Little did we realize how much her teaching genius would help shape our lives in the years to come.

No one paused to offer special thanks. Certainly I didn't think of it. If anything, it was a hasty toss-away. "Bye, Miss Stanford. See you." And out the door.

Ingrate!

How must she have felt as she watched us leave? We were unquestionably one of her best classes.

Was she hurt? Heartsick? Or perhaps relieved?

Did she think, *There the little twerps go. Good riddance!* I doubt that very much.

Regrets to be sure. On both sides. We would never pass this way again. And neither would she.

School was never again as formative, nor as inspiring; it was never filled with so much nonstop excitement, fun, and surprises.

It was never again full of so much unspoken love.

So here, finally, a much belated and grateful thank you, Miss Beth Stanford.

You *were* a winner! You *were* a teacher in a million!

CHAPTER TWENTY

Rotten Apples

I was living on Johnson Street and in the fifth grade when I started running with Marty Carlosi. Though he was a year younger, he had a strange hold on me. I always felt like I was walking on eggshells when he was around. I never quite knew what to expect.

I was never a leader—always content with being second or third in line—so I was easy pickings.

He lived a block to the east on Johnson, halfway between my house and Bob Keller's. His mom dead and his dad a nasty drunk, he had only Annette, his older sister, to look after him. She was in eighth grade, and there were always one or two guys hanging around the house. But only when Mr. Carlosi wasn't home.

There was an older brother too, Angelo, but I seldom saw him. Seventeen, out of school, he was apprenticing at Tobin Tool and Die. Always in trouble.

This family stuff I learned when Marty and I started junking together.

I'd walk past Marty's house on my way to school and so far had never run into him. However, this day in late May, there he was, sitting on his front porch, almost as if waiting for me.

"Goin' to school, kid?" he asked, an insolent smirk on his face.

"Yeah."

"Washington?"

"Yeah."

"Me too. Wait up." He gathered some books from the steps, and came running. "I thought you might be one of those mackerel snappers," he said as he caught up with me, referring to the Catholic kids who attended St. Patrick's Parochial. "What's your name?"

"Tom."

"Call me Marty. Where d'ya live?"

"Down on Johnson, just past the tracks. Right next to Steve's Bakery."

"One of them Mexican kids?"

I bristled. "Something wrong with that?"

"Nope. Just checking. Then you're used to having people call you greaser all the time. Just like they call me dago."

Greaser? That was a new one. "Dago? What's that?"

"An Italian. If it isn't dago, it's wop. I'm used to it. You?"

"Nobody calls me anything. Not greaser, that's for sure."

"Maybe 'cause you don't look Mexican. You're not dark like me."

"My Ma's white."

"And she married a Mexican?"

"Yeah. So what?"

He shrugged. "No skin off my neck." Shortly he added, "At least you got a Mom. Mine died two years ago."

I was supposed to say, "Sorry about that," but I didn't. "Too bad," was all I came up with.

Somewhere along the line I happened to mention junking.

"You do that too?" he said. "Find any neat stuff? I found a real cowboy hat once. My brother stole it."

"Yeah, I find stuff. Nothing special though. A battery one time. I got a half dollar for it from Dick."

"You sell to that Jew crook? You oughta take your stuff down to the Green brothers over on Forest Avenue. They pay better."

Which was news to me; I'd never heard of the Greens. Later I looked them up—they had a small warehouse on the west side of the Soo Line tracks—and they *did* pay better than Dick. Only catch was you had to drag your stuff six blocks to get there.

Marty specialized in cardboard and seldom bothered with much else. "Why don't you and me join up?" he said. "We'll just go for cardboard. Forget that other stuff. It's easier to find…you get a dime a hundred. We can store it in my garage. When we get a pile of it, we'll call Green, and they'll come pick it up."

Which sounded good to me. But I didn't limit myself to cardboard; I still took metal and rags, sometimes even salvageable veggies from behind grocery stores.

Once school let out, I teamed up with Carlosi two or three times a week. I should've been wary. He talked too much, and he talked too fast, like was selling stolen goods. Always an angle. I should've been warned when he insisted on storing our cardboard in his garage. Dummy! I had a garage too, didn't I?

It was Marty who taught me a special trick with fish hooks and locks. This, just after dawn one June morning, when we came upon a locked, roofed, chicken-wire-enclosed shed behind Dallman and Cooper Hardware. The bin was crammed with hundreds of flattened boxes. Apparently they also knew Green Brothers.

"Holy shit," Marty said, "let's get some of that stuff. We'll have two wagonloads in one helluva hurry."

Another thing about Marty: He used lots of swear words.

"Yeah?" I said. "You wanna climb that fence? You gonna cut the wire? That's stealing."

He sneered. "You got something against stealing? And no, I ain't gonna cut no wire. They'd wise up in one helluva hurry if I did that. You ain't never stole anything?"

"Nope," I lied. "It's one of the commandments."

"Commandments? What commandments?"

"In church. The Ten Commandments. 'Thou shalt not steal.' You never heard of them?"

"Nope. I don't go for none of that church shit."

There he went again. "Well, I do," I said, mustering up conviction.

"So? Go ahead, do things the hard way. Me, I'm gonna help myself."

"Without going over the fence?"

"No need. Watch this, stupe."

And just like that he whipped off his cap, and revealed an assortment of odd-sized fish hooks—ranging from perch to walleye size—stashed in the liner. "Here we go, kid," he said. "Take a lesson."

He used first one hook, then another—there must have been

five—inserting each into the lock until he hit the right size.

I watched intently as he jiggled the hook this way and that, drawing it out a fraction of an inch, wiggling it, tilting it, then readjusting the depth.

And moments later: "Ha" he said, as the lock sprang open, "got it!" He grinned proudly. "How about that, Tom? Nifty, huh?"

He lifted the lock, pulled the door open, charged forward, and began dragging out armloads of cardboard, stacking them onto his wagon.

When his load started to tilt, he tied a length of rope around the lot, cinched it tight under the wagon bed. "C'mon, Tom," he urged. "Get in there, load up!"

"They'll call the cops when they see their cardboard's gone."

"Cops, my ass. They won't even miss it. You think they measure the pile every night? Move, damn it. Load up your wagon."

I pitched in. Really, who was would miss a few boxes?

When my stack was loaded and tied, we headed for home. Oops, to Marty's house. Loading the boxes into the garage (almost half full now—one huge pile of cardboard) we were vastly pleased with ourselves. A morning's work, just like that. Without tracking through every alley in town. What a sweet angle!

Later in the day, alone in *my* garage, I dug out some fish-hooks, and practiced Marty's moves on a couple of Daddy's old locks. Inserting the hook-eye, I pushed and twiddled, pulled and twisted, with no success at all. I was just about to give up, when, with a distinct click, the lock suddenly fell open.

Right away I relocked it, and started over. Just what had I been doing when the lock popped? Five minutes later I had the moves down pat. I could open it in thirty seconds flat. I did it again and again, then picked out a different lock, and worked that one until it snapped apart. But it was like Marty had said, the stunt only worked on cheapo locks; I couldn't crack Daddy's better ones.

And man, but wasn't I proud of myself? Where had I been all my life? The things I could do with this new skill.

And wasn't this crazy, a kid like that—a fourth-grader—leading me around by the nose? Wouldn't Ma have had a fit if she knew what Marty and I were up to?

In fact she'd already warned me. "I don't like you hanging around with Marty, Thomas. There's something sneaky about him. I wouldn't trust him for a minute."

I should have listened. Instead I simply decided not to tell Ma when I headed for Marty's house. "I'm going over to Bob Keller's," I'd say. Another of the seven deadlies.

Like I said, Marty cussed a lot and talked dirty; he told me bad things his brother had taught him. About girls and guys. Most of it I didn't understand. Which was okay with me. I was oblivious; I wasn't in the least curious about off-color stuff. So far as I was concerned, he was talking to himself.

He told me his real name was Martino, but he liked Marty better. He was always talking about being an Italian; it seemed to me he worried it to death. I certainly didn't harp on the fact that I was Mexican.

Around the end of July, I quit buddying with Marty.

I arrived at his house one morning, pulling my wagon, ready to go junking. But we didn't go. Instead, I got bush-whacked. Marty was behind his house, practicing Mumblety-peg.

(Remember Mumblety-peg? It's played with jackknives, and you flipped the knife just so—from your knee, from your chin, from the toe of your shoe—winning points when it stuck into the ground.)

"We got cheated," he said, a strained smile on his face.

"What d'ya mean, we got cheated?"

"Go look in the garage."

And when he pulled one of the doors open—surprise! No cardboard. The garage was completely empty, an echoing cave, not a scrap of anything left.

I was stunned. "Where's all our cardboard?"

"Angie stole it. He called Green when I was in school, and they came and got it. Angie kept all the money. Two whole bucks."

I felt like someone had punched me in the gut. All that work, all that lost sleep, all that risk-taking—for what?

"How can he get away with that? Can't you tell your dad? Won't he make Angelo give the money back?" My rage grew. "That was *our* cardboard!"

"No way, Tom. Angelo's my old man's pet. He always takes his side. He believes him before he believes me. He'd laugh in my face."

"Oh, cry," I moaned, "what a rip-off. Half of that money was mine. A whole dollar."

"I suppose we could start collecting cardboard again," Marty said. "This time I'll put a lock on the garage so he can't get at our stuff."

Anger overcame me. It wasn't right. Getting robbed like that, and nothing we could do about it. I actually verged on tears. "Forget it," I snarled. "I won't give him a chance to cheat me again."

I wheeled, grabbed my wagon, and headed for home.

Ma caught on right away that something was wrong. "What is it, Thomas?" she asked. "Why so glum? Tell your mother."

And like a dummy, desperate to unburden myself, I blurted it out: "Marty Carlosi and I had his garage full of cardboard we found in the alleys. We were going to sell it and split the money. But his big brother sold it out from under us. And he won't give us the money. I got cheated out of a whole dollar."

"I thought you told me you weren't running around with Marty anymore."

"I did, but…"

"You went ahead and did it anyway. That's what you get for lying."

But she didn't swat me, or scold, or anything. She put her hand under my chin and lifted my face so I was looking straight into her eyes. "Did it ever dawn on you," she said levelly, dragging out every word, "that maybe *Marty* sold that cardboard? That *he* was the one who cheated you? That his brother had nothing to do with it?"

It was like a truck hit me. Stupid, gullible jerk! That thought had never once crossed my mind. Marty had been lying in his teeth all along. Dummy! When in hell was I gonna grow up? When was I going to quit being everybody's sucker?

Ma turned away and went back to her canning. I stood there fuming for a while, then walked out. I had to be alone. Before I exploded.

I never spoke to Marty again. Gutless wonder that I was, I didn't confront him either. I never let on I was wise to his swindle. Whenever our paths crossed, I simply went the other way. If he called me when I walked past his house, I ignored him. He'd come over and call for me, but Ma always ran him off. I was done with him.

But Marty wasn't quite done with me. He came back to haunt one last time. A few weeks later I was in the kitchen, absently muttering to myself, and Ma just happened to tune in. Some alien word must have jolted her.

"What was that?" she snapped. "What did you just say?"

"Oh," I replied blithely, not stopping to think—as always, no smarts. "Just a poem I learned."

"What poem? Tell me."

Again, totally stupid, I rattled it off: "I've got a girl, way out west; she's got apples on her chest. She's got hair between her legs. That's where the cowboys lay their eggs."

Honest to God. They were just words. I didn't know what they meant. Just a cute rhyme.

The last word wasn't even out of my mouth, when— pow!—I got a hand across the face so hard it almost put me to the wall. I saw stars Galileo had never charted.

Ma's eyes were fierce. *"Where did you learn such a filthy thing?"* she spat. *"Who taught you that?"*

She came at me again. *"Who? Tell me, or I'll swat you again."*

"Marty...Marty Carlosi," I gasped. "What's wrong? Is it bad or something? I didn't know it was wrong. It's just...something...I heard him saying."

"That does it," she said through clenched teeth. "If I ever hear of you running with that filthy animal again, I'll have Daddy whip you so hard you won't stand up for a week. *Do you hear me?"*

Oh, yes, I heard her. And even though it was already a done deal, from then on I made super, super effort to keep from even *seeing* Marty Carlosi.

Dirty, double-dealing rat! It was like a hollow, mocking voice zoomed in from outer space: *Gotcha, dummy!*

I never recited that doggerel again.

But I never forgot it either.

Up till then I'd thought that the well-known chant "Ladies and gentlemen, take my advice, pull down your pants and slide on the ice" was naughty.

Live and learn.

When Marty was dispatched to the Wisconsin State Reformatory in Green Bay a year later—caught stealing a fancy pair of pliers in Sears' hardware department, not his first offense apparently—I secretly rejoiced. And breathed fervent sigh of relief. Moth to the flame. But no burns. Not yet anyway.

Enter Vincent Slater, who lived on Satterlee Street down next to the Fond du Lac River, just west of Sadoff Iron & Metal. I was in sixth grade, he was in seventh, and I ran into him while fishing white bass behind his house one May afternoon.

Once more—eternal innocent—I got sucked in. Why are kids so attracted to wrong numbers?

Vince was a misfit from the word go. His father was away—a polite way of saying prison—and his mother had her hands full bringing up him and his three sisters. She worked part time at Infant Socks and left the babysitting mostly to Vince and Lila, his older sister. Another relief case.

He had a shock of unkempt blond hair and was rangy, thin as a rail, taller than I. He always seemed to be leaning to one side when he walked.

We got to talking, and before I knew it, we were buddies. He took me down the bank a hundred feet or so, behind some other slumlord houses, to where a small spit of land jutted into the river. And where I'd just been soaking a minnow, waiting for the bobber to go under (I'd only caught three all afternoon), he taught me some new wrinkles.

"Here," he said, pulling up my line, "let's move that bobber down, the bait should be only a couple feet in the water. Got a little sinker? Put it closer to the hook, so your minnow stays down."

Then he swung the line out into the river as far as it would go. But instead of just letting the bobber float, he moved the tip of the fish pole to the right, then to the left with painfully slow movements. And whammo! Down it went. Up came a beautiful white bass, scales flashing in the sun.

Vince unhooked the fish, threw it onto the bank. He put on a new minnow and handed the pole to me. "Now you try it."

Same thing. I eased the bobber over the surface—slow, slow, barely three feet—and bam, down it went again. In the matter of a half hour, I had a dozen fish on my stringer. Was that the beginning of a beautiful friendship, or what?

Strangely enough, rebel that he was, Vince liked to read, so we talked about books. He collected stamps. A homer! He loaned me some of his comic books. He was as crazy about Prince Valiant as I was.

It was the same as with Marty Carlosi. Though I sensed that Vince was trouble, I wasn't smart enough to figure out just why I felt edgy running with him.

But Vince wasn't really all that keen on fishing. He was the kind of kid who just couldn't sit still; he had to be constantly drifting all over Fond du Lac. We snuck into movies and spent time at the library, and—oddly enough—he dragged me through every bank in town. Banks? Was he already casing out his future?

It didn't take long before I discovered another Vince specialty. This on one lazy, July afternoon, both of us aimlessly wandering through the dime stores. As we left Grant's five-and-dime on Sheboygan and Main, Vince sent me an evil grin and drew me into a cubby hole between Penney's and The Big Shoe Store.

"Look at this, Tom." Digging into his pocket, he showed me a beautiful jackknife, a fountain pen, and a snazzy key chain.

I gasped. "Vince, you stole those things!"

"Sure." He smirked and then fished out a small magnifying glass from another pocket. "It's easy as pie." He winked. "Once you know how. And…" He winked again. "…if you've got the guts."

I became instant Oliver to his Fagin as he led me back down to Kresge's and told me to watch for nosey clerks. Sure enough, he approached a counter of lipsticks and with one deft move, slid one into his pocket.

"For my sister," he said upon emerging from the store.

Then he reached into another pocket and handed me a glassine packet containing stamps—Tanganyika triangles, how could I forget?—and said, "Here, these are for you, Tom. I'll bet you never even saw me boost 'em."

I hadn't. And how in blazes had he done that? Hell, I hadn't even seen him detour to the stamp area. Talk about your magic fingers!

"Now I wanna see you do it, Tom. They've got stamps down at Grant's too."

"I...I don't think...I want to...."

"Don't be such a baby. Sure you do. C'mon. Just watch me and do what I do. Don't turn sissy on me."

Well, I certainly didn't want him thinking I was some kind of pansy. Reluctantly, my heart racing, I followed him into Grant's. And when we got to the stamp section—

"Don't touch anything," he said. "Just look stuff over, pretend you're gonna buy something. Those stamps there. Which do you like?"

"The Russian commemoratives."

"And I like that Spain set. Now watch."

His hand flew up to the rack with lightning speed; the see-through envelope was unclipped. A quick swish, and up his shirt sleeve it went. Another quick looksee. He hissed a swift command. "You now!"

Like I was mesmerized, my hand shot up, grabbed *my* envelope. Up my sleeve it went.

"Don't look around," Vince said, moving out. "Smile, look at me. Walk slow, real slow."

He kept talking to me all the way out of the store. "See, nobody's looking. We're just a couple kids killing time."

I didn't draw another breath until we hit First Street and rounded the corner by Fitzsimmon's Shoe Store. "Wow," I said, "that was scary."

"What'd I tell you? Nothing to it. What'd you get?"

I held out the Russian commemoratives, feeling smug as hell.

We did other stamp safaris off and on, and I also stole a pocket knife and a fountain pen, just like Vince's. He even showed me how to stuff Big Little Books under my belt and pull my sweatshirt down over them. Once I even went by myself—sort of testing things.

Another time I almost got caught. A store manager dragged me into a back room and made me go through my pockets and roll back my sleeves. My lucky day. I hadn't lifted anything yet. I laid pretty low for a few weeks after that.

There was another kid we ran with now and then, Dick Sherman. He was in seventh grade, same as Vince. A mousey kid, dark hair, pasty complexion. A total leaner. He also thought Vince was aces, and he did almost anything for him.

Even to the point of stealing money from his Dad.

Frank Sherman ran a tavern on the corner of Follett and Main, a scant two blocks east of Washington School. During the Depression even taverns didn't do all that well. Even so, they had to have change, and this was what Vince zeroed in on. I never found out what Vince held over Dick's head, but he sure worked it into the ground.

"If you don't do it, Dick," he kept repeating, "I'll tell...I will...and you'll be sorry."

It was sick the way he badgered Dick that afternoon. Standing outside the tavern—it was around 4:30; we'd met after school—he just wouldn't give up.

"Go on," he said, "get in there. Just wander around behind the bar like you always do. When your dad's busy, sneak into the cash drawer and grab us some change."

Us? I wanted no part of this. It was just plain wrong, plain mean. By rights I should've checked out. I was suddenly seeing Vince in an entirely new light, and I didn't like it. Even so, I didn't clear out. I was curious (in a twisted way) to see how things would turn out.

Well, he kept after Dick nonstop until he finally opened the side door and eased inside. We waited and waited. Five minutes. Ten minutes.

"I'll bet his old man caught him," Vince said. "He's catching hell. Get ready to scram if he comes out after us."

Just about then the side door opened, and out slid Dick, a panicky look on his face. He was hunched over—like he expected his old man to come storming out after him. He said nothing but just kept running, back toward Washington School.

Vince caught up with him at Macy, grabbed his arm, and wheeled him around. "What'd you get, Dick? Lemme see..."

He forced his hand open.

"Man, oh man," he gasped. "You hit it big, Dicky boy. Quarters!"

And not just random quarters, but a wrapped roll—*ten whole dollars*.

"Holy, oh, Christ!" Vince said. "Man, the fun we're gonna have with that."

Just like that Vince formulated a plan; he knew exactly what came next. We kept moving until we reached Division Street, pulling Dick along roughly, a crooked smile creasing Vince's face. Here we turned left and stopped mid-block, right in front of Hounsell Sporting Goods—always one of our favorite gawking spots.

Hounsell's display window was crowded with mounted wildlife—a deer, an antelope, geese, ducks, fish, even a standing bear—and we usually hung out there for ten minutes at a time. Rifles and pistols of every description were scattered on the floor before the wildlife.

Vince Slater promptly shoved Dick Sherman toward the window. Pointing to a Daisy air rifle—the Buck Jones 107, a compass and sundial imbedded in the stock—he said, "Buy me that one, Dick."

Dick seemed to shrink from Vince's touch. Just like that? *Buy me that gun?* I'd have to save for months to amass that ungodly amount of cash.

"Gee, Vince," he protested weakly, "I don't think I…"

Vince dug his fingers into his shoulder. "Dick," he threatened, "what did I tell you?"

Even I felt menaced.

"But, Vince…"

He gave Dick a hard shove. "March."

Inside we went.

Mr. Hounsell looked down at us questioningly. "Boys?"

"We want…" Vince started. He pointed to Dick. "He wants to buy a BB gun. That Buck Jones special in the window."

He smiled dubiously. "Do you boys have that much money? It costs two-ninety-five, you know."

Vince grinned. "Yes, he's got the money. Don't you, Dick?" He gave him a push.

"Yeah, I can pay." Dick reached into his pocket, drew out a handful of quarters.

Mr. Hounsell slid twelve quarters across the counter, dropped them into the cash register. He gave Dick a nickel change. He reached under the counter, brought out a long, slender box, and began wrapping it in heavy brown paper. "You'll need BBs," he said. "They cost a dime a tube." Wordlessly Dick slid another quarter forward.

"You don't need to wrap it," Vince said.

"Yes, I do," Mr. Hounsell said, regarding Vince severely, almost as if he knew he'd just accepted stolen money. "It's the law."

He watched us suspiciously as we left. Or was it just my own sense of guilt backing up on me?

Once outside, Vince insisted that we backtrack to Macy, where we ducked into an alley behind Grant's. He unwrapped the package, drew the rifle out of the box, and fed a dozen copper BBs into the barrel. He cranked the rifle and began plinking away at a brick wall.

"Let me try it," Dick whined. "I paid for it, didn't I?

Vince smiled indulgently and passed the rifle over. When Dick had fired off six shots, he said, "Let Tom try it now."

Rotten as I felt about how all this was developing, I took the rifle, and shot a few rounds. I was thrilled. My first time with a BB gun.

Vince slid the rifle back into the box, rewrapped it, and licked the sealing strip to hold it in place. "Now let's get back to Main Street. We'll get us some candy at Kresge's. All that money…wow!"

We pushed through Sears' basement, went upstairs, and went out to Main. A quick right and we trooped into Grant's, where we headed straight for the candy section.

It was like Dick had completely given up. Anything Vince wanted, he meekly surrendered the necessary quarters. We walked out with six Baby Ruths and a pound of candy kisses. There went forty cents.

We sat on the curb and ate candy, Vince stuffing it into his face as fast as he could. You'd think he'd never had sweets before. Craziest thing: It didn't even taste good to me. It seemed I had to force it down. I thought to crash out, head for home. I didn't like the way this was turning out at all.

Next we went down to The Sport Shop on First and Main, where Vince saw a nice catcher's mitt he liked. There went three more quarters. Back to Penney's, upstairs to the boy's department, where we each got a dandy Buck Rogers fleece sweater—twenty-five cents each. Vince put his on right away. The street lights were already on, and dusk was closing in; it *was* getting cool.

Vince was promoting a movie at the Garrick Theater. It was here that I finally got my guts up and checked out. If I wasn't home pretty soon, Ma would get on me good. "Tell her that teacher kept you after school," Vince protested. "Sissy. Mama's boy."

I ignored him; I wheeled around and ran south towards Johnson Street. Vince was still yelling after me. When I got home, I eased in quietly and went directly to my room. I stashed the sweater under the bed. I didn't need Ma giving me the third degree.

Later I heard through the grapevine that Dick had gotten a terrible whipping from his Dad. I saw Vince only one last time; I avoided him like the plague from that night on.

"Last time" was just before Christmas when I went over to his house to say goodbye. Even though we weren't chumming anymore, I still felt some idiotic sense of loyalty. He'd been a friend once. He was going to be gone for a long time; in all likelihood I'd never see him again.

And where was Vince going? Right. Green Bay Reformatory. He'd got caught trying to steal a car. He'd be gone for two years. Did I feel a chill?

It was awkward. He came to the door and asked me in. His mom was crying in the kitchen; the sheriff would pick him up in the morning. I fumbled out what words I could. Stuff like, "Sorry, Vince. I wish you weren't leaving. We had some good times together. See you when you get home."

Lame, very lame.

I got out of there as fast as I could. Vince patted me on the shoulder as I left. I looked back one last time. Talk about sick-looking cookies. Too late the dawn.

As of that moment I was definitely cured. Never again would I revert to five-finger-discounting. If I wanted it, I'd pay for it. No exceptions.

No free lunch? Amen. Double amen.

*   *   *

Or so I thought until Fred Garvey slouched into my life.

The Garveys lived next door to us when we lived on John Street. I was thirteen; he was fifteen. Fred was product of a dead father and a slattern mother named Florence, who'd simply dropped too many kids to keep track of. Free-ranging for the most part, most of them were born for trouble. There were three girls ranging in age from seven to fourteen and four boys, ages nine to fifteen. The family totally dependent on relief. Their wagonloads of surplus goodies made ours look like small change indeed.

Fred was a brawny kid with a ruddy complexion, a boxer's shoulders, a mop of dark brown hair, and a shambling sailor's gait. He stood five-eight to my five-one and was in tenth grade. When he bothered to go to school, that is. Living next door as we did, it was inevitable that we'd buddy up.

He came and went as he pleased. More than once I waited on the Garvey stairs as Fred cussed out his mother, daring her to interfere with his evening plans. I was just a squirt in his eyes, but he seemed to like me and occasionally included me in his roughneck plans. Our sketchy friendship lasted less than two months as best I recall.

And yes, he already had a record; he checked in with a juvenile officer every two weeks. We didn't do all that much talking. I was basically a tagalong. I suppose I was drawn to him because he was older; it was perhaps *my* turn to be a little brother. Boys tend to lock on like that. Look at how my brothers shadowed me.

Those times we were out, we mostly wandered Main Street, looking in store windows. Now and then we snuck into the movies. Mingling with the intermission smokers as they went back in was his main stunt. Filching candy kisses and marshmallow peanuts at the dime store or liberating apples, oranges, and peaches as we walked past sidewalk grocery store displays became another quaint pastime.

Fred was a scrapper—always looking for a fight. Some afternoons and evenings we'd join three other buddies of his, all high school kids. Mostly we'd wander around, talking smart. Jack LaShay, a thin, weasel-faced blond, perhaps seventeen, called the shots. Lots of times we just hung around downtown, eyeing the girls, whistling, and making remarks. Which I shrugged off; I wasn't much interested in girls as yet.

One night we got word that Jack LaShay had been challenged by the Scott Street Gang. A rumble was in the cards. Only we didn't use that word back then; gang fight was good enough. It was like something out of *West Side Story*. We were settling some kind of score or other. I had no idea over what.

I had no stomach for it and told him to count me out. But Fred wasn't listening.

"We need you, Tom," he coaxed. "You won't have to get into it at all. You just stand there and watch us murder those Scott Street creeps. You'll be our lookout. You see any police cars, any flashing lights, you sound the signal."

And yet again—eternal nagging question: What in hell was a thirteen-year-old kid doing out at that time of night, running with a bunch of hoods? How did I square this with Ma? What excuses did I make when I missed curfew, and how did I buy permission in the first place?

But, honest to God, that's just what happened. I remember it vividly.

It was a sultry August night, around 8:30 and just turning dark, when the two gangs met at the corner of Doty and Sibley. As best as I can recall, there were perhaps fifteen kids there, ranging in age from thirteen to eighteen. The street lights had just come on, and the four corners took on semblance of a boxing arena.

No chains, no baseball bats, no brass knuckles. Just bare fists, bad language, taunts, insults, and shovings. Until finally someone pushed too hard or called one name too many. Then everything hit the fan. I hunkered down on a nearby lawn, deliberately keeping to the shadows. I was breathing hard, shaking like I had malaria.

They all charged at each other right in the middle of the intersection, kicking, slugging, pulling hair, grabbing each other around the neck. Bodies flew every which way. The language was triple X, and the insults and yelps of pain carried clearly all over the neighborhood.

Fred stood right in the middle of things—he and Jack LaShay, back-to-back—punching away for all they were worth. There was blood on Fred's face, and his shirt was torn, but he didn't back down for a second. Cursing and laughing, he was having the time of his life. Weasel or not, Jack was giving as good as he got, bloodying noses, blackening eyes right and left.

And sure enough, didn't the police come running? Three blocks to the south, I saw flashing red lights. Two cars. Driven by a strong sense of duty and loyalty, somehow overcoming my sissy fear, I darted into the melee.

"The cops!" I yelled. "The cops are coming!"

Fred glanced past me and took up the cry. "The police! C'mon, Jack. Come on, Frenchy. Get the others. Let's scram outta here."

And just like that the gangs separated. They ran like scared rats—down the street, between houses, seeking any available cover. Fred and Jack led our bunch west to Military Road and on down to Brooke Street, to where the Moore and Galloway Lumber Company warehouses stood. Supple's Marsh spread out right behind them.

Ideal cover. The cops would never find us there.

Crouched in the grass and brush, water up to our knees, sweating, gasping for breath, we watched the squad cars move back and forth along Military, then Brooke, spotlights working, going as far as the Scott Street Bridge before circling back. But not once did either squad stop to risk foot patrol.

Adventure? Narrow escape? Excitement? Believe it. And even though I'd had no part in the kid bloodshed, I still felt like I'd been one of the warriors. Later, when the coast was clear, we walked home leisurely, talking a mile a minute. Ma never noticed my wet jeans and tennies as I ducked into my room.

One night Fred invited me to go to the show. An Edward G. Robinson he wanted to see. Me too, only I didn't have a dime to my name.

"Screw it," he said. "We're meeting Jack LaShay. He'll take care of it."

"Did he rob a bank or something?"

"Never mind. You'll see."

We joined Jack and two other hoods at the Retlaw Theater fire door on Sheboygan Street—the same door my brothers and I had barged into a year back. Right away I got strong whiff of trouble.

Jack's gimmick? Shock and awe.

He produced a steel tire iron, the kind mechanics used to pry tires off wheel rims back then. There was nothing shy about his technique. He simply wedged the steel into the lip of the door and began yanking. Noise? No qualms. Jack simply laid into it, taking no pains whatsoever to muffle his assault.

I was already running in place.

And how come Jack was so cocky?

In those days the Thorpe brothers hired high-school boys to take tickets; they served as ushers, swept up after closing, and cleaned the rest rooms. Hey, kid jobs were hard to find back then. Mostly only three people ran the theater, one of them the ticket booth lady, who cleared out right after nine. Basically scared of their own shadow, these panty waists weren't about to face down hoodlums like Jack LaShay. And Jack knew it.

If the customers reported someone trying to force the fire doors, the stupes basically messed their shorts and chose to do nothing. Sure, they could have called the cops, but that would be blatant sign that they couldn't handle their job. Who, in his right mind, wanted to get his face smashed in when he tried ejecting Jack LaShay's gang?

And if Jack didn't get them that night, he'd come looking for them later.

So he kept prying, swearing, never letting up for a minute. If it took force, if it was noisy, so what?

Fact of the matter: Jack was *begging* for trouble; he *wanted* a fight. But I sure's hell wasn't. I already saw myself facing a juvenile officer come morning. Twice I told Fred I was going home. And twice he twisted my arm and threatened me.

"Stay, Tom. Don't be such a wimp. Piece of cake. Nobody's going to bother us."

I stayed.

When Jack pried the door open perhaps six inches, it was no trick at all for him to squeeze a hand inside and trip the locking bar. Click-bang—the door virtually floated open. Immediately we barged into the curtained cubbyhole.

Did we slither in around the curtain and furtively take the first empty seat? No way. Jack ripped it aside and led us in, bold as brass, taking some seats halfway down in front. We put our feet up on the seat ahead and prepared to watch Eddy G. do his thing.

Maybe *they* enjoyed the movie, but I sure didn't. I was as jumpy as hell and spent more time watching for the police than taking in the movie. Were a thousand dollars riding on it, I couldn't have told you a single thing about the plot. Edward G. Robinson in *what*? Next question.

The guys laughed all the way home, delighted by the way the ushers had looked the other way when we sauntered out.

After that scary episode, it was definitely checkout time for little Tommy. More of this kind of fun I didn't need. Fred Garvey—same as with Vince Slater—became history. Whenever he stopped by, I made excuses. After a while, he didn't bother knocking any more.

Which was just fine by me.

One night several months later, there was a big commotion outside, and we looked out to see a police squad car pull up in front of the Garvey house. Two cops banged on the door. My brothers and I watched them haul Fred away.

He appeared before a judge and was placed under house arrest. I never found out exactly what Fred had done, but rumor had it that he and Jack LaShay had broken into a gas station one night and stolen a hundred bucks.

As with Vince Slater, I felt obliged to say goodbye to Fred the morning they hauled him off to Green Bay. I was waiting in the yard when the officers marched him down the steps and out to the car. His mom and all his brothers and sisters stood on the porch, bleak looks on their faces.

Fred, tough guy to the last, he put on a Cagney smirk that didn't quite make it. "Hey, Tom, nice of you to come see me off."

"Yeah, Fred," I stammered. "Sorry to see you go…sorry you got…" I swallowed the word "caught." I couldn't focus; no appropriate words came up. Waving weakly, I said, "Bye, Fred."

They shoved him into the back of the car, slammed the door, and he was gone.

I brooded for days after Fred left. Three friends in the clink, just like that.

Was someone sending a direct delivery?

There but for the Grace of God…?

Yeah, tell me about it.

CHAPTER TWENTY-ONE

Never a Dull Moment

As I grew up, there wasn't a moment that I wasn't busy. Daddy was the same way. The few times I saw him relax were when he sat in the living room, struggling mightily to decipher *The Reporter* before supper. Otherwise he was in the basement, out in the shed, out in the yard, always doing something. Driven.

Genes. I was doomed.

My head swam constantly with must-dos and wanna-dos. There were chores; there were Ma's errands; there was junking, there was school; and there were friends. I had a dozen different hobbies. The ill-fated *Tar Baby* was one of those wanna-dos. And that one—you may recall—came to no good end.

It seemed that every moment of my life I was up and running before I was up and running. Always an early riser, I'd wake before seven, my brain buzzing, ticking off the things I *wanted* to do as opposed to things I *had* to do. Ma wanted me to cut the grass—I wanted to go to the library. It was my turn to take Molly the goat to the pasture; I wanted to go fishing. I must weed the garden; I *wanted* to—

I was absolutely compulsive about collecting. I'd cut pictures from magazines and newspapers—beautiful landscapes, funny cartoons, newspaper articles—I *must* capture and preserve everything. I became a time capsule before time capsules were invented.

Breathtaking beauty, humor, and tragedy were everywhere; they *must* be catalogued. Movie stars, natch. America's Presidents, its heroes, yes. I was captivated by Grant Wood. Dear God, that I would someday paint like that! Aircraft, animals, the latest cars—they all cried out, "Paste me, paste me."

I used loose-leaf notebooks at first, but these were too restricting. So many newspaper double-pages to save. And where did I get the idea of using wallpaper sample books? Probably from dragging one home from the alleys one fine morning. A real treasure. Surely—Daddy's constant refrain—I could find some use for it.

It was bound in hard covers, the wallpaper manufacturer's name embossed up front. The monstrosity was at least six inches thick, its pages three feet wide by two feet high. Oh, Lord, the vistas that opened, the jumbo photos I could paste. And didn't they look slick mounted on that thick, patterned paper?

When my first album filled up almost overnight, I decided on a full-frontal attack. Daddy was a steady customer at Badger Paint, wasn't he? Thus I timidly approached the owner, Mr. Otto Bernhardt, and asked if he would save the old catalogs for me when replaced by the new ones, instead of just pitching them. Which plan he happily agreed to.

Within a year two jam-packed catalogs lay under my bed; another two stood at ready. I was one happy camper!

And as always, my ongoing addiction to radio serials and to the endless premiums the sponsors offered, trifles I simply must have or die. Send a box-top plus three cents postage. Then the waiting, dying by inches every time the mailman passed by without delivering my Orphan Annie decoder ring, my Tom Mix square-shooter revolver, or my Jack Armstrong Hike-O-Meter.

Which radio frenzy led me to Captain Tim. And stamp collecting.

Captain Tim's Stamp Club, sponsored by Ivory Soap, aired at 4:45 Monday, Wednesday, and Friday afternoons. Captain Tim spun fascinating tales of stamp lore. As example, the "Flying Jenny," where the mail plane got printed upside down, making the stamp worth a fortune. Or the German print-overs with a first-class stamp costing five-thousand *pfennings* one day, ten-thousand *pfennings* the next—all result of Germany's rampaging inflation during *their* depression. Here comes Adolph!

I received a pin and certificate upon joining. The pin was a miniature postage stamp, perforated edges and all. Silver edging with a red center, from which Captain Tim smiled out at me. MEMBER CAPTAIN TIM'S was emblazoned on the top, with IVORY STAMP CLUB below. I wore it with button-busting pride, right next to my Orphan Annie decoder pin. An official member. Keen!

Captain Tim taught us how to mount stamps, proper care when soaking them from envelopes, why we should specialize, how to order approvals, on and on. If Franklin Delano Roosevelt and J. Edgar Hoover were stamp collectors, why not me? I searched for every old letter in the house and at Grandma Eva's as well. Letters from Daddy's family in Mexico became treasures. I haunted the post office. Hanging upside down in those tall waste baskets, I sifted discarded mail by the armful, rescuing stamps right and left.

I even used some of my sacred movie money (the sky is falling!) to buy bulging packets of five-hundred mixed stamps—contents unknown, duplicates galore—priced twenty-five cents.

Further absenting myself from cinema felicity, I'd scan sheets of approvals sent by various stamp companies and agonize over which stamps I wanted—or, more importantly, which I could afford. They were priced anywhere from two cents to ten cents each. Occasionally I even lifted some, replacing the filched items with dupes from *my* collection. Never a lot, maybe two or three a time—I didn't want to do prison time for stealing a few crummy stamps. Harris never noticed my petty larceny.

One day Captain Tim announced a contest with rare stamp prizes. Just send an Ivory soap label and tell—in fifty words or less—why you like Ivory soap.

For two nights I sat at the kitchen table, pencil in hand, trying to come up with an angle. Soap? It was good for washing your face, what else? Miss Lind taught soap carving in fifth grade, and I created a fairly decent approximation of a polar bear. But otherwise, what's with soap?

Finally, totally frustrated, I called to Ma where she was washing dishes, "Hey, Ma, I'm not getting anywhere with my letter. Do you have any ideas? Please, Ma?"

She smiled, thought for a few moments, and then said, "Well, Thomas, you like the way Ivory soap floats when you take a bath. Why don't you write something about it being like a little boat?"

Bingo! Just the spark I needed. I went into think mode for five minutes. When I finally broke from my trance, I was ready. The words tumbling out, I wrote about a little fairy boat, afloat on a sea of bubbles, some bubbles even resembling graceful swans.

I may throw up!

Ten minutes later—only fifty words, after all—I showed my entry to Ma. She smiled proudly as she read it. "That sounds wonderful, Thomas. Send it in. Copy it in your very best handwriting."

Well, I was in a stew for a month, waiting on my you-won-the-contest-kid letter. When it didn't show up, I decided I'd fizzled and shrugged it off.

Six weeks later, however, I came home from school to find Ma waiting at the door, an excited smile on her face. "Thomas, there's a package for you. On the table."

I was on it in a flash. Yes, from Captain Tim, and yes, I had won a prize. Not just any award, but *second prize*! Even more exciting: They would read my entry on the radio!

And what was in the package? Well, a magnifying glass, tweezers, an authentic Captain Tim stamp album, and eight non-perforated souvenir sheets, all 1933 Chicago World's Fair commemoratives. I floated on air for weeks and showed off my prizes to everyone within hailing distance. I took the package to school to wow Miss Stanford and my classmates. I told everybody when to tune in on Captain Tim.

The following week, when Wednesday rolled around, the whole family plus some neighborhood kids gathered around the radio. Sure enough, Captain Tim read the first-, second- and third-prize entries and clearly announced each winner's name and home town. I was a national celebrity! My cap didn't fit for days.

The stamps probably weren't worth all that much, but I kept them in their tissue wrappers for about a month. Gradually my glow faded, and the pristine plate blocks lost cloud-nine status. What good, really, were they? Despite Captain Tim's cautionary words about their value, I began snipping stamps from the sheets one by one, using them to mail in more box tops—to Orphan Annie, to Jack Armstrong, to Captain Midnight. Within months all were gone, my moment of glory nothing but a memory.

Later on I learned that, in its heyday, Captain Tim's Stamp Club boasted over two million kid members. Granted, perhaps only a few thousand kids entered his contest, but even so, the odds of my entry winning were staggering. A fluke?

Or did the raggedy-ass lad have talent, after all?

My model airplane craze hit when I was in fifth grade—thanks to buddy Frank Kurzynske. He brought one of his models to school and told the class how he built it. Later Miss Stanford allowed him to demonstrate in our second-floor hallway. He twisted the propeller until I was sure the rubber band would break, then set it on the floor and let it go. The model soared to the ceiling, leveled off, and slammed into the wall at the far end of the hall. One wing fell off as it came down.

Even as disastrously as that introduction had ended, I was sold; I would build airplane models just like Frank's. I bought my first model kit at Valin's Camera and Hobby Shop on S. Main: *The Spirit of St. Louis*, raw replica of the plane Charles Lindbergh flew across the Atlantic in 1927.

The kit, made by a company called Comet, cost ten cents. It was jammed into an oblong box—something like a spaghetti container—and contained plans, tissue, a propeller and nose piece, wheels, wire hooks, a long rubber band, balsa sticks, and former sheets. Airplane glue cost five cents. (Stick-tissue model kits are still available today. They start at $10, and go up from there. Time marches on.)

I built the models in my second-floor bedroom, working at a battered card table.

Here was solitude. Here was extreme concentration. Here was sublime escape from my nosey brothers. All went south when Señor Esteban arrived to hi-jack my room.

Thin, balsa sticks were cut, pinned onto a pattern and glued as you went along. Skinned off with a razor blade, the two sides were joined with formers cut from a printed balsa sheet, this to give them authentic shape. Wings were made the same way. Just follow the kid-simple directions.

The propeller was affixed with a preformed piece of wire, and a long rubber band was stretched inside the body and attached at the rear. You wound the propeller with one finger, tightening the rubber band. Upon releasing the propeller, the model actually skidded across the floor.

Next came the tissue, silver-gray in this instance. It was stretched over the skeleton and glued. Once the fuselage and wings were covered, you wet the tissue. As it dried, it shrank. It became taut and smooth and gave the model additional strength—and didn't it actually resemble shiny aluminum?

Final touches were the cockpit detail—even tiny dashboard printouts—and insignia and numbers on the wings, all included in the kit.

My first model left much to be desired. The wings were a bit crooked, the wheels cockeyed, the tissue sagged in spots. Even so, dumpy as it looked, to my eyes it was beautiful beyond compare; I was filled with a sense of supreme accomplishment.

Sad to say, none of my models ever flew. They would take off, rise perhaps a foot off the floor, then drop. Even when I hand launched them, they made straight for the ground. I became resigned to failure on that score. Wilbur Wright I was not.

Once, over-zealous in winding the rubber band—I'd make this one fly or else!—the entire fuselage collapsed. Bad language. Tears. I never did that again. How many models I built before my airplane craze faded, I don't recall. There were a dozen hanging from the ceiling by the time Señor Esteban showed up. My burnout seemingly happened overnight. One day I was gung-ho, the next I was totally indifferent.

Then there were the Sunday funnies. Early on, our Sunday paper came second-hand from a kind neighbor. Later Daddy, working off and on, we could afford (ten cents) the Sunday edition of the *Fond du Lac Commonwealth Reporter*.

Always up early, I had first crack at the funnies. In summer I'd read them on the front porch. In the evening, right after supper, we'd all gather in the living room, where, clustered around Ma, she'd read them aloud. A ritual; we clamored for it.

Bringing up Father, Tilly the Toiler, The Gumps, Hairbreadth Harry, The Katzenjammer Kids, Tarzan, Fritzi Ritz—these were just a few of the funnies we liked at the time. My favorite of favorites was *Prince Valiant*. He made my heart race. I doted on the adventurous story line and the fabulous art. Hal Foster made Val so handsome and Aleta so beautiful!

But it wasn't enough just to read and admire Prince Valiant. Again I must gather, I must preserve. Awkward as it was—the panels varied in size—I'd cut them out and make little booklets of them. Monday afternoon, right after school, I'd hurry down to the Valley Coal Company (one block west) and request use of their stapler. The manager would smilingly oblige and probably thought me more than a bit addled as I banged my dumb cartoons together on the office counter.

His name was Art Howard, and he *did* owe me. We bought our coal there, didn't we? When we weren't taking our dawn-patrol business elsewhere, that is.

Other comic strips demanded similar rescue. These panels mostly of a size, they were easier to collate. *Blondie, Dick Tracy,* and *Terry and the Pirates* all lent themselves nicely to my devices. More trips to Valley Coal, more stapling. My own comic book factory. By the time I outgrew this compulsion, I had an apple box three-quarters full of these minis. Whatever happened to them? Who knows?

As I say, your compulsive collector.

A half-page, build-it-yourself creation appeared weekly in the comics section. Picture an underwater scene with coral reefs, exotic fish, plus an underwater diver scattered helter-skelter on the page. Or a Grand Canyon panorama with bluff after bluff receding into the distance, a mule and rider on a canyon path. I pasted the half page onto shirt backing, and when it dried I scissored out the various pieces.

The largest panel served as background. To this I curved and pasted a front panel (all included) to form the stage front. Behind this I positioned and pasted the small pieces—fish, the coral reefs, the diver—onto a stage floor. Final touch: A white, Christmas-tree bulb was placed behind the largest figure to bring the panorama to life.

I found these constructions breathtakingly beautiful, and I did up a dozen or so. One, a cave with stalactites and stalagmites woven into it, was my masterpiece. These I arranged around my bedroom. Ma threw them out while cleaning my room prior to Señor Esteban's arrival. I was furious!

Back to my radio programs: *Dick Daring*—when I was seven or eight—became my very first radio serial. In the '30s, most radio programs lasted only fifteen minutes; others, a half hour. They started at 4:30 PM, when kids first got home from school, and ran, one after another, until 6:00.

I remember sending for a Dick Daring jigsaw puzzle for one Quaker Oats box top. I assembled it over and over, studied it feverishly. A tiny city beneath a city—Dick's control center. Council rooms, mystery caves—stalactites and all—where he housed his special planes and speedy cars; all came to life. The gun rooms with secret passages and elevators to move Dick's vehicles into the real world. I was thrilled to actually see what had previously only existed in my imagination.

I recently Googled "Dick Daring," and what do you know—there it was, a picture of that same jigsaw puzzle in full living color! After the first few moments of reminisce, I came to wonder how I'd ever been mesmerized by such flimflam.

The Depression alive and well—we were still living on relief—one might wonder: Wither all these box tops, coins, and postage stamps?

Early on, things were truly tight, and it took a lot of nagging to get Ma to even consider store-bought dry breakfast cereal. Oatmeal, and relief farina were our standbys. But as the Depression slowly faded, a few extra bucks became available. And Ma could, on rare occasions, splurge for Wheaties, Grape Nuts, and Post Toasties. Especially with number-one son being eternal pain in the neck.

"Ma, please? Just this once. Tom Mix is offering a secret compass. I want it so bad...I won't get lost when I run errands for you downtown. Please, Ma?"

Natter, natter, natter.

For a time Pure Oil sponsored a program featuring aviation pioneer Jimmy Mattern, this during my airplane-goofy period. Pure

Oil (at Court and Main) gave away three books he wrote in the *Cloud Country* series: *Wings of Youth, Hawaii to Hollywood,* and *Lost in Siberia.* I was Johnny on the spot when each book came out. They were hardbound, paperback sized, fifty or so pages long, and profusely illustrated. I must have read each a dozen times.

Arm & Hammer baking soda offered sets of bird cards, free—just send in the coupon. They were a tad smaller than today's credit cards and contained gorgeous, full-color pictures of cardinals, orioles, and eagles, with bird info on the back. I had three packs and used them to bone up for Fr. Dunnigan's dawn, bird-watching excursions.

Arm & Hammer also issued wildflower cards, which never rang my chimes. And, believe it or not, another set showing different kinds of cows. Cows? C'mon!

Cigarette cards were common back then, but Daddy always rolled his own, so the only ones I had were discards found on the street. These featured baseball players, golf players, military uniforms, movie stars, even classical composers. Somebody must have collected them; they'd been around since the early 1900s.

Another collecting mania: matchbook covers. I had a boxful. I intended to mount them in an album but never got around to it. Poor deluded kids, we were thrilled silly to find some touting out-of-state businesses. It took so little to amaze us back then

I still possess a Tom Mix secret spinner. A chrome disk, mounted in a small collar, with a tab to hold. On the base: "Ralston Straight Shooters." The disk faces are embossed with haphazard squiggles. Upon spinning the disk, the squiggles magically became "GOOD LUCK."

And didn't that boggle my baby brain!

Another Tom Mix prize was a set of six-by-eight-inch photographs of Tom Mix and Tony, The Wonder Horse. They were printed on glossy paper—a weird magenta color—and caught Tom and Tony racing through gullies and canyons, chasing bad guys, six guns blazing. Treasured then—now lost forever.

Practically every radio show touted these must-have premiums. Jack Armstrong offered a dragon's eye ring, Buck Rogers offered the ring of Saturn, and The Shadow offered a luminous ring that glowed in the dark. Tom Mix had a sliding whistle ring, a horseshoe-nail ring, a flashlight, a miniature revolver.

We kids gobbled the junk up and were mostly disappointed when the item arrived. Few of the prizes ever lived up to the radio hype.

My Orphan Annie decoder badge was such a rip-off. Every day, at program's end, the announcer provided a series of numbers to enter into the decoder. I'd copy the numbers, eagerly twist the dial, only to discover that the crucial message simply gave a vague five-word clue to the next day's installment, hardly worth the bother. Even worse, the secret message sometimes read, "BE SURE TO DRINK OVALTINE." Rats!

Annie's theme song still resonates: "Who's that little chatter box, the one with pretty auburn locks, who can she be? It's little Orphan Annie…" Gloryosky, Zero!

Another favorite, *The Shadow* aired Sunday at 4:30 PM. Sponsored by Blue Coal (whatever that was), it ran a half hour. All over school come Monday morning, you'd hear the refrain: "Who knows what evil lurks in the minds of men?" And we'd all come back in our best imitation of that menacing laugh and intone: "The Shadow knows."

The Shadow followed me right into my mid-teens, when I peddled papers at Fond du Lac News. Every month brought a new *Shadow Magazine*, and every month I'd plunk down my dime. Some I'd read, but mostly they just piled up in the corner of my bedroom. Compulsive even then, I'd vow to someday read them.

We were druggies before our time, strung out on *The Shadow*.

Intertwined with all these wanna-dos were just as many gotta-dos.

Brother David's many sicknesses have already been mentioned. Harking back to his Mexican childhood, Daddy believed goat's milk was a surefire cure for any health problem. Worked in Mexico! So one day a battered farm truck pulled into the yard, and Charlie Spencer, a farmer friend who worked with Daddy at the tannery, commenced unloading a goat. She was reddish brown, long-haired, and shaggy as could be.

We all stood around open-mouthed. What's with the goat? I recalled the pig Daddy and his Mexican cronies had slaughtered. Oh, no! What would goat taste like?

Ma came out of the house about then. "José?" she asked, just as mystified as we were, "*qué pasa?*"

That's how it was with Daddy. Totally impetuous, never explaining anything to anyone, not even Ma. His wild ideas were never discussed; they just happened.

He explained the benefits of goat's milk to her. "David be healthy now. Goat milk good for rickets."

Ma was understandably dubious. "Where will we keep it?"

"In garage. Down at end. Nothing there, Mama." And to us boys: "Take goat next door. In grass. Let her eat."

She had a rope around her neck, and while Daddy talked business with Mr. Spencer, we led her to the vacant lot and stationed her amidst a lush growth of clover. The goat followed docilely, like she'd lived on Johnson Street forever. Moments later she was up to her ears in green stuff, chomping up a storm.

I don't recall who named her, Ma probably. But she became Molly—placid, single-minded, without a care in the world. We broke open the bale of hay Mr. Spencer had brought along and spread it in the shed's back corner. He even threw in a sack of oats. When we led Molly into the shed, she settled in nicely and munched the armloads of grass we gathered. We filled a galvanized pail with water, and she dipped right in.

After supper Daddy said, "Come, boys. We go milk goat."

Another pail, this one from the kitchen. Daddy drew up a little box, reached under Molly, and began pulling on her teats, the sound of the projected milk drumming on the bottom and sides, and then—the pail filling—just squirt, squirt, squirt.

As he worked, Daddy launched into another boy-in-Mexico tale; he told how he'd been put in charge of a small herd of sheep and goats when he was my age, taking the herd up into the hills around Irapuato and watching over them all day.

Did I learn how to milk Molly? Probably, but I can't be sure. Even thinking about it, I get a sense of being afraid I'd hurt Molly while milking her. Had Daddy reassured me that goats needed milking, that it would pain Molly more if she wasn't milked on schedule. Morning? Night? Blanko. Some things sink in, some don't.

Ironic turnabout: Rickets or not, David simply refused to drink Molly's milk. Threaten and coax as Ma and Daddy would, he'd have none of it. So the milk got shifted onto Bernard, Richard, and me. I can't honestly describe the taste. Sweet or on the bitter side? Naturally I preferred cow's milk, but when it came out of the ice box, it was okay.

I think.

Molly was most tractable and was easily led to her pasture across the driveway. We tried tying her to a concrete block and leaving her to graze, but invariably she'd tangle the rope and commence to bleat up a storm.

"Thomas, Bernard," Ma would order, "go untangle Molly."

In due course the vacant lot passed completely in and out of Molly, and we were forced to seek new graze. A virgin field across the tracks became Molly's new domain. For a couple hours every morning and afternoon, we'd take turns easing Molly across the Chicago & Northwestern tracks, then down a small incline into a vast heaven of grass, alfalfa, and clover. One block east stood the Giddings & Lewis factory. They made industrial machinery. Today Fives Giddings & Lewis occupies the entire expanse.

Molly was in goat heaven.

One lonely tree provided shepherd shade. Every now and then, we'd herd Molly back within watching distance. She loved to wander. So much grass; so little time.

Bernard and I usually brought along a library book, and time passed quickly enough. Other than an occasional passing train, it was peaceful. On hot days it was pleasant in the shade. We perched atop the railroad right of way, sunned ourselves on cool days. I remember it as a time when, for a brief space, I wasn't so infernally busy, when I actually enjoyed being idle. I became Peter to Shirley Temple's Heidi. Later Molly settled into the grass beside me and chewed her cud. It was pleasant to have her close, to listen to her soft, squishy munchings.

Along about 11:30 I'd head home for lunch. David or Bernard would take Molly in the afternoon.

But, all in all, an exercise in futility. If David wasn't drinking goat's milk, what was the point in keeping Molly? Late one afternoon in mid-August, Mr. Spencer drove up again; Molly was going back to the farm. As much of a nuisance as she'd been, we all gathered to pat her shaggy head one last time.

Definitely a bittersweet moment.

Every summer morning at 11:45, Ma would send one of us to the tannery, a long block beyond Molly's chomping grounds, with Daddy's lunch bucket in tow; he dearly loved a hot noon meal. We'd meet at the corner of Rees and Doty. He always had a soft, loving smile on his face.

"My big boy," he'd say and give me a quick hug.

If it was raining, we'd shelter in a shed full of empty barrels and fifty-gallon drums next to the long brick building. But when it was clear, we'd sit with our backs to the wall and take the sun. Daddy especially—still in knee boots, a thick rubber apron around his waist—would soak up the rays gratefully after the cold wetness of the beam house and the wet hides he swung there.

Daddy told stories of his boyhood in Mexico, most of which I'd heard before. I liked hearing the Pancho Villa tales, how he tried to save Mexico, about how Daddy had held the great man's horse when he stopped in Daddy's village.

He also talked about his early adventures in America. Many of these new to me. A friend who stole his money, the mine explosion, how he met Ma. I felt so sorry for Daddy; his life had been so hard. Looking back, I wonder if many boys today get that close to their father.

Some of the stories were current. And cruel. There was a gang of Germans, fellow workers, who constantly taunted and threatened. "Dirty (blank, blank) Mexican" was the least of the insults. All the Mexican workers became victims. Prejudice was a given back then. Daddy, being a small man, couldn't retaliate; he bore the insults stolidly. But anger and hurt existed just the same.

Then, when the starting whistle sliced the air, Daddy slammed his lunch box shut and handed it to me. He'd head one way; I'd head another. Another day in the salt mines.

Once school started, the noon missions ended, and Daddy carried his lunch bucket when he left home in the morning.

Where I got the idea to start a museum I'll never know. Definite brain sizzle waking me early one summer dawn, I deemed it a neat way to make some money. Molly's shed had long been empty, so why not put it to good use? A row of shelves on one wall would be perfect for displaying stuff. Extra shelves could be added if necessary.

But what stuff? What in the world was I thinking? Did any of us have anything customers would pay to see? A museum? Ridiculous.

The longer I thought about it, the more the idea hammered. Those bird nests of David's. A good start. Maybe he'd even know which birds had lived there. I had all kinds of metal samples—aluminum, brass, copper, steel, zinc—even a fake, dead gold watch I'd found in the alleys. And, yes, of course! I could hang some of my airplane models from the garage ceiling, just like in my room. There was that goofy statue of Daddy's, some Mayan God or something. And...and...

My brain spun like a gerbil wheel.

Back then it seemed that each new day was forty hours long; the parade of projects capable of filling those hours, endless. So. A museum. How much time would that take? Maybe we could open tomorrow.

Well, not quite.

I suggested the museum to my brothers, and again, eternal Pied Piper, they bought my pipe dream. Now *they* scratched their heads for objects to display.

"What about some of your stamps?" Bernard asked. "The ones you won in that contest?"

"They're gone. I used 'em up." Then I brightened. "Good idea, Bernard. I've got other valuable stamps."

David suggested coins. We had a Mexican peso Daddy had gotten somewhere. Anything else?

So, for the next couple days we scrounged the neighborhood non-stop. Among the things we came up were a ham-sized chunk of bituminous from Valley Coal—and a piece of coke for contrast—a couple hornet nests, some baseball cards, some fused green glass we found among the driveway cinders, my *Normandie* poster, a couple fishing lures, a fish skeleton we found down by the river.

People would love to see Snowball, my pet rabbit.

A pointed example of our addled time continuum:

David found a dead snapping turtle under the railroad bridge. A turtle shell! Just the thing! Big drawback. The shell was still occupied by the rotting turtle. We gingerly carried it to the east end of the garage, where we halfway buried it. The teeming maggots would clean it out in no time at all. A week or so later, it was ready. We took a hose to it, and set it in the sun to dry. It turned hard as a rock.

In between we cleaned the garage, swept the walls, polished the window, washed the shelves, and covered them with newspaper. I made little cards from shirt liners and carefully lettered: HORNET'S NEST, BRASS, COPPER, GOLD, BLUEBIRD NEST, MEXICAN COIN, SNAPPING TURTLE SHELL, RABBIT—a wealth of educational detail.

Every day we came up with a new treasure. By the time we went public, at least fifty items were on display.

Ma regarded our excited hustle with amused silence. She could have given us the big hee-haw and told us our venture was doomed from the start. But, no, as with so many of our harebrained schemes, she simply stood aside and let us find out for ourselves. A growing process? Experience is the best teacher and all that rot?

During our collecting, I'd made a wall sign—plus a modest sandwich board—to alert the world of our grand opening. The cardboard was cut from a couple Rinso boxes. MUSEUM, they read, 204 W. JOHNSON. AMAZING THINGS TO SEE. COME ONE, COME ALL. PRICE TWO CENTS.

I toiled for two afternoons, first drawing pencil lines, then using black crayon—no magic markers then—to produce each. Using scrap leather from Daddy's garage trove, I fashioned shoulder straps. The second sign was tacked onto the house, just to the left of the front door.

Then came the big day.

It was early August by then; we must make our fortune fast,

before school started. We took turns carrying the sandwich board, each walking for an hour at a time. We paraded up and down Johnson from Brooke to Packard Street, back and forth, back and forth. Later, as our efforts drew not a single customer, we enlarged our route, first going as far as Doty Street, then all the way to Main Street. Passing traffic couldn't read the puny lettering, and those who could mostly smirked at our pathetic ad.

Tally: Three or four neighborhood kids we cajoled into parting with two cents. Ma and Daddy indulgently paid admission as well. We cornered the milk man, the ice man, Dick the junk man, Steve the baker, and they embarrassedly let us guide them through our hall of wonders. No other adults showed up.

Some neighborhood toughs stormed our porch one night and tore our sign down. No matter; we still had our sandwich board.

After the third day of fruitless parading, Bernard, David, and Richard signed off.

"No one wants to see our dumb museum anyway," Bernard scoffed. "It was a dippy idea to start with."

Stubborn me, I continued walking. Then I just went out afternoons (when everybody was up, I reasoned), and by sheer dint of whining, I found a few more dumb kids willing to part with two cents. Then I just walked every other day.

And, finally, not at all.

The gullibility, the innocence! The shattered dreams. Kids—they believe, they delude themselves, and they think they can do anything! I felt so whipped the day I tore the sandwich board to pieces, and crammed it into the garbage can. I went out to the shed, and began taking down our exhibits. Most of those went into the garbage also.

Our total take for the month's work was a measly thirty-eight cents. Split four ways, it wasn't worth spitting on.

Good thing school was starting soon.

CHAPTER TWENTY-TWO

Montello Again

It was a lazy August day, and Bob Keller and I were sitting on my front steps counting cars. I had Fords; he had Chevys. Whoever got the most in a half hour was the winner. Sound exciting? Not really. Especially when there just weren't that many cars back then. You were lucky to see forty or fifty an hour. Even a few horse-drawn wagons passed here and there.

"Let's go fishing," Bob said.

"Sounds good," I replied. "Where? The river? Stinky Point?"

Stinky Point was a favorite fishing spot. Here the Fond du Lac River emptied into Lake Winnebago. The city sewage plant was located a quarter-mile away—thus the sullied name.

"No, bonehead. Let's hitchhike to Montello. The bluegills should be biting good over there about now. Bluegills love hot weather."

"Yeah, just like last time," I said ruefully, memory of *The Tar Baby* still rankling.

Bob frowned. "No, nothing like that, Tom. Just our fishing stuff. Only forty miles...we'll be there in an hour or so. We'll only stay a couple nights."

Pied Piper time. "And where'll we sleep?"

"In my new pup tent. I'm dying to try it out. On a real camping trip, I mean."

"You've got a tent?"

"Yeah, got it for my birthday. I told you before. Don't you ever listen?"

Truth was that Bob *hadn't* told me. I'd certainly have remembered something as important as that.

So I asked Ma, and she said okay. That's the way things were back then. No qualms. I was big enough. I'd hitchhiked before. Camping out? Sounds like fun.

Go for it, son.

"Tomorrow all right?" Bob asked. "I'll come by around nine o'clock."

That afternoon I checked my fishing equipment and dug some worms. As for my owning a real casting rod then—in a pig's eye. If I hadn't found this wreck of a collapsible, bamboo pole in the alleys during one of my junking expeditions, I'd have been stuck fishing with a tree branch.

Bob's mother jinxed our plans with a forgotten doctor visit; he had to baby sit his kid brother. We didn't hit the road until 1:30 that afternoon.

We hoofed it all the way down Johnson to Hickory Street, where we took our stand. Back in the '30s, west-side Fond du Lac ended at Hickory; to the west stood nothing but open country. Old man Eaton had built a half-dozen little cabins right behind his store to bunk any tourists unlucky enough to overnight in Fond du Lac.

Right away we ran into problems. Our duffle, the pup tent, blankets, cooking stuff, jackets, fishing gear, and a hatchet were small enough—no *Tar Baby* to scare drivers off. But just the same, we had a hard time getting a ride. Again, no streams of cars like today. Another half hour and our thumbs would've been sun burned.

When a car did stop, shortly after 3:00, the driver leaned out and said, "Where you heading, boys?"

"Montello," Bob said. "Gonna do some fishing."

"I can take you as far as Green Lake. That okay?"

"Sure is," we both agreed.

"Okay, throw your stuff in back and hop in."

He didn't have to tell us twice.

"Can't recall hearing anything about hot fishing spots in Montello," the driver said as we got underway. "Where you gonna fish?"

"There's a little creek there," Bob said. "It comes down from the quarry. My Dad took me there once. It runs along the east side of the main drag. There's a little park and everything. We caught bluegills right off the bank."

"Well," the man said, "if you say so. Live and learn, I guess."

We were in Green Lake by 4:00, and again, serious setback. The man dropped us off at the road leading into the village, where we were stalled for the next two hours, car after car blithely ignoring our frantic thumb-wavings. The sun was getting low.

"Guess we'd better find a place to camp," Bob said. We backtracked into Green Lake. I swear, Bob must have been born under a shamrock. We'd walked perhaps two blocks, Green Lake glistening blindingly on our left, when:

"HATTIE'S SHERWOOD FOREST — CAMPING," announced a three-by-four sign nailed to a tree. We almost walked by it.

"There's a place," Bob yipped. "We'll set up right here."

It was a beautiful spot, covered with trees of every description. A few trailers were parked at the north end but no tenters. We picked a spot a distance from the cabin—the camp owner's place most likely. Nice and quiet. Nobody to bother us.

Bob dropped his knapsack, whipped open a flap, and produced a hatchet. Next he unrolled the tent and shook out a gang of wooden stakes.

"Spread her out," Bob ordered, flipping back a corner.

The tent was made of tan-colored canvas and had an enclosed back end to keep the weather off our heads as we slept.

"Here we go. Hand me those pegs, Tom. Wow, the first night in my new tent."

It was dirt simple. Once one side was tacked down, Bob crawled inside, jimmied the two uprights into place.

"You pound the stakes on the other side while I hold these poles in place. Pull the canvas tight as you can." As I hammered the stakes down, slanting them for solid purchase, he said, "Good work, buddy. We're in business. Now, let's spread our sleeping bags."

There was no floor in the tent, so Bob, ever experienced, showed me how to run my hands on the ground to feel for any rocks, acorns, or twigs that might dig into us while we slept. We threw out a few stones and some pine cones. Bob spread his sleeping bag on the right side. No sleeping bag for me; a couple mangy blankets had to do.

"Now, just in case it rains," he said, "we gotta dig a trench along the edges of the tent."

Out came the trusty hatchet, and he began cutting up the lush, green grass. He dug a trench wide enough to float toy boats—definite overkill. When he threw the hatchet to me, I dug a trench even deeper than his. Finished, I fell back on my heels with a proud sigh. Those troughs would handle typhoon runoff.

We threw the rest of our duffle into the tent. "There," Bob said proudly, "snug as a bug in a rug."

By then it was almost 7:00, and our growling stomachs told us it was time for supper.

"Let's go into the village and find something to eat," he said.

Thinking there might be a concession stand available, we went to the little house, and knocked on the door. But nobody appeared. We shrugged and walked a couple blocks to the east until we came upon a small grocery store. Our funds were minimal to say the least; according to Bob, we'd mostly eat fried bluegills. I had two dimes. Bob, ever affluent, had four quarters.

Supper that night consisted of a bag of potato chips and a Baby Ruth—total outlay: ten cents each.

Around 7:30 we headed back. Bob got the bright idea of fishing for a while. "Fish always bite best around sunset," he said. The old fishing sage.

We fished off of a boat landing area. Bob used a casting rod, and made great show of flinging a medium-sized Daredevil this way and that. I rigged up my line with a worm, attached a small bobber, then threw it out as far as I could. And while Bob had no luck whatsoever with his fancy rig, I had bites by the dozen. All baby bluegills, no keepers.

A half hour later, we called it a day.

Back at the park, we prepared for bed. "It would be keen to have a campfire," Bob said. "Lots of little branches laying around. But I didn't bring any matches. Did you?"

I shook my head. Some campers we were.

After a brief trip into the woods, we undressed, threw our clothes into the alcove. My wadded up jeans became my pillow. "Wish I'd thought to bring a flashlight," Bob groused. "Can't see a blasted thing."

Yeah, I thought. Why not bring the kitchen stove too?

It was a hot night, and we slept in our underwear. (I didn't even know what pajamas were in those days.) Some mosquito friends had already joined us, but the screening at the doorway kept extra friends and relatives out. We spent five minutes swatting them before their dive-bomber whines stopped. Alone at last.

The ground was hard; it took me awhile to get comfortable. But five minutes later, the day's adventures taking their toll, I conked out. It was like somebody hit me in the head with a rock.

Next thing I knew Bob was shaking me. It was morning, bright and sunny.

"C'mon, Tom, wake up. It's past eight. Time to hit the road."

I couldn't believe that I'd slept that hard. I shagged into my clothes quickly.

Bob was already pulling stakes. "All that work," he said, regarding the trenches we'd dug, "and not one drop of rain."

"What about breakfast?" I said. "Do we go back to the village?"

"Skip breakfast. We'll eat when we get to Montello. We'll be there by nine."

We were so busy packing up that we never noticed the woman who suddenly materialized behind us.

"Well," she said, "did you boys sleep well?"

We whirled around. She was a fat, stubby, mean-faced lady, her hair a wild bird's nest, her clothes baggy and wrinkled. "You never checked in last night. You boys got a dollar? That's what I charge for an overnight."

Bob's face fell. "Nobody was around to tell us we had to pay. We went up to the cabin, and nobody was there. A dollar?" he said. "Just for camping?"

"Yeah, kid. A dollar. You got it?"

We both had money. But not a dollar. Bob, always quick on the draw, wasn't about to part with his cash. "No…no, we don't have a dollar."

"No money?" She laughed harshly. "You think I'm running some kind of a charity here?"

"Nope," Bob said, summoning up minor bravado. "I told you. We don't have any money." He turned to me. "Do you have any money,

Tom?"

I fell into his game immediately. "No, Bob, I don't have a cent."

"No money? How're you supposed to eat?"

"We're going to Montello," Bob said. "We're gonna catch some fish. We'll eat those."

"Just fish?" She laughed. "Now I've heard everything."

"Yes, fish," I chimed in.

"You two don't have *anything*?" she said, mile-wide disbelief on her face.

"No, not a cent," Bob insisted.

"I don't know what you kids are thinking, coming out with no money." She looked at the trench we'd dug around the tent. "And then to go and ruin my property like this. That *was* a nice lawn. Did you have to dig a damned canal?"

"We're sorry…very," Bob said.

"All right, then. I'll let you kids off this time. But you put back those clods of grass, make the place look a little like you found it. I'm standing here watching you."

Bob and I fell to quickly replacing the sod as best we could, sweeping loose dirt into the cracks with our hands. We tamped the patches down with our feet. It looked a little bit better but was a far cry from its original state.

"All right?" Bob said meekly.

"No, it's not all right. But I suppose that's the best you can do." She turned away, started walking to the cabin. "Now get off my property. Before I call the cops. And don't ever let me see your ugly faces around here again."

We packed hurriedly, neither of us saying a word.

The woman stood near her cabin, watching us.

As Bob and I slung our stuff onto our shoulders and started walking down the road toward Highway 23, he turned to me.

"That old bag really expected us to pay a whole dollar to camp for one damn night? What a dreamer." And then, his eternal closer: "Wouldn't that just frost you?"

*   *   *

If we thought we were home free, we were badly mistaken. For as we kept hailing cars and trucks, nobody was stopping. It seemed we'd be stuck in Green Lake until we were twenty.

Finally, an hour later, a car stopped, but this guy only took us as far as Princeton. We were still fifteen miles from Montello. By then we were both so hungry, we could've eaten our shoes. Tennies. Stinky. Not good.

"Okay," Bob finally decided, "we start walking. Someone's sure to pick us up soon."

We hiked on for perhaps two miles before stopping to rest. It was a hot, muggy day, and we were sweating like mad. As we sat down, Bob said, "Hey, Tom, look behind you...that field there. Potatoes. C'mon, let's get some."

We dug into the ground with our fingers and brought up some half-grown excuses for potatoes. Each taking five or six, we went back to our gear and sat on the tent. I got out my jack-knife, began peeling. When I'd skinned three, I handed the knife to Bob. And then, the potato filmed and yucky with dirt, I began eating.

Some breakfast. It wasn't corn flakes, that's for sure, but we *were* hungry!

I peeled one more and ate it. That was enough. My stomach was beginning to rebel. Raw spuds—not what it was used to at this hour. So bear up, I scolded, quit your whimpering. Like Ma always says, beggars can't be choosers.

Around ten o'clock we finally got a ride in a farmer's truck. A half hour later we entered beautiful downtown Montello.

It wasn't any more than a jog in the road, the quarry on the left, with Highway 23 running straight ahead, and the main drag a sharp right.

"Well, boys," the wizened farmer said, slowing, "where do you want to go in Montello? I'm fixin' to go right in, down Main Street."

"Yeah, fine," Bob said. "There's this park on the right side with a little creek running through it."

"Yup," the man said. "Know right where it is."

It was just as Bob had described. The fast-rushing creek, a small park situated alongside. Three tables. Even a little fire-pit. It was green, heavy with shade—just what we needed after the searing heat of the day.

We unloaded our stuff from the back of the truck and waved as the man drove off. "Thanks for the ride, mister."

Back then no more than five hundred people lived in Montello. The quarry had been a main source of employment but was mostly shut down now. The main drag boasted a movie theater on the west corner and then about eight business places—grocery stores, hardware, a farm implement dealer. That was about it.

To the east stood a craggy prominence dead-ending Main street, possibly a hundred feet high, rust-red and covered with trees.

"Granite," Bob explained. As if he really knew. "There's a big quarry back there. Later on we'll go take a look."

I stood beside the stream—a mill race actually—that rushed down from the quarry and wondered how Bob expected to catch fish in raging water like that. When I asked, he said, "Just wait. You'll see. But right now we gotta find something to eat. Them potatoes ain't setting right with me."

We dumped our gear on a picnic table and wandered down the street to a grocery store. There was no such thing as MacDonald's back then. Fast food was science fiction in the '30s. We were inside for maybe ten minutes, pondering our purchases, and when we came out, we had a super breakfast. Lunch too. We each bought a pack of Twinkies and a bottle of chocolate milk. Twinkies a nickel, and milk a nickel. Now I was flat broke.

Bob asked the clerk if she had any free matches. She smilingly handed over a pack.

"We're camping in the park," I said, "we're gonna be frying ourselves some fish later on."

Another smile, very dubious.

We sat at a picnic table and made our Twinkies and milk last as long as possible. The road was deserted, and the Montello business area pretty much ended up across from where we sat. We could see a residential area to the south; there couldn't have been more than fifty houses in the whole town. We figured the stores counted on farm trade to survive. And the rickey-tick theater? More hayshakers.

It was noon by then. "Okay," Bob said, "let's set up the tent. And then we can get some fishing done."

And right there, alongside the creek, not more than fifteen feet from Main Street—not seeking permission nor seeing any signs announcing park rules—we made camp. We were the only people in the park. Seasoned campers now, we had the tent up in ten minutes flat. We spread our bedding and haphazardly pitched our other stuff inside. Fishing first; we could tidy up later.

One important omission: Still smarting from "Hattie's" scolding, we skipped the rain trench. Precious good it had done us last night. It didn't look much like rain. Why not take a chance?

We went maybe sixty feet to the creek and baited up with worms. Still skeptical about catching fish in the mile-a-minute current, I asked, "How we gonna fish in that?"

"Just watch," Bob said. "Live and learn."

He put on a bobber and a medium-sized sinker, then walked to the bank. But instead of just dropping the bait, he flung it far to his right, and let it float back toward us. And whammo, just like that, his bobber went down, and began zigzagging back upstream.

"Yow!" he yipped, setting the hook. A minute later, after a feisty tussle, he pulled in a bluegill—a hand-sized beauty. "Keeper," he said, laughing.

Back to the tent for the forgotten stringer...

I followed his lead, swinging my bamboo rod to the right, dropping my bobber upstream. Down it came, and before I could even set my feet, the bobber disappeared. I laughed with delight, then horsed in another bluegill, this one even bigger than Bob's.

Up came the stringer; on went the fish.

The bait barely hit the water, and the fish slammed it, took our bobbers down. They they kept coming in like crazy, one right after another. Bluegills are real scrappers; I was having the time of my life.

"How many fish can you eat?" Bob asked, a wide grin on his face.

"Maybe five or six."

"Same here. We'll keep a dozen, then. No sense in taking fish we won't use. We sure can't keep 'em alive till we head home."

An hour later, keeping only the biggest, we'd caught and released over forty bluegills and crappies. The traffic never let up; we could've fished all afternoon. It almost became like work.

Bob finally called a halt. "Enough," he said, laughing as he threaded a final bluegill on the stringer. "My arm's getting tired. There's our supper."

I moved to lift the stringer, but Bob stopped me. "Leave 'em. They'll stay cool in the water. We'll clean 'em later. Let's go do some exploring."

We dropped our fishing equipment beside our tent, and without the least trace of concern that our gear might walk off, headed out.

We backtracked on Main Street to where it bumped into the quarry. There we stopped and stared up at a looming granite palisade. How would we climb that? Easy. There was a rugged path there, and we began fighting our way upward.

Grabbing small bushes and random rocks, we pulled ourselves up the trail. When we reached the top, puffing and sweating, we looked down into the quarry. It was a breathtaking sight—a minor Grand Canyon—bluffs stretching as far as we could see. A placid, dark green lake nestled at the bottom. Piles of cut rock cluttered the landscape; roads meandered like snakes. *Fan-tastic*, I thought. The view was well worth all the effort and then some.

We sat on a rock, and caught our breaths as we admired the scenery. "I never saw anything so beautiful," I said.

"Yeah," Bob agreed, "it's really something. But nothing like the Wisconsin Dells. Now that's real scenery."

It was pure Bob. Why did he always have to put a spike in things? Was there *anyplace* his Dad hadn't taken him?

"Maybe we could climb down there and swim? I'm all sweaty and dirty."

"Tomorrow. We'll really need a scrub down by then."

After ten minutes of gawking, we headed down. We were hungry again. "Let's get some candy bars," Bob said.

"I'm outta money."

"My treat."

Again we sat at the table beside our tent. We made the Powerhouse bars last as long as we could.

It was now three o'clock; Bob was still keen on exploring.

"There's a big lake…Buffalo Lake…down that way." He pointed west. "And a big dam where the lake narrows down before it joins the Wisconsin River. Let's go take a look."

We walked west for a mile until we reached the dam. It was perhaps three hundred feet long with thin sheets of water—a miniature waterfall—washing over it. A lone fisherman stood in waders out in the river, casting a lure, bringing in a fish now and then. We couldn't see what he was catching.

"Bigger than bluegills, anyway," I muttered.

We took off our shoes and socks and waded into the cold water. Refreshing. The bottom all sand, we were able to go out quite a way. When we stood still, we saw baby bluegills darting at our feet. A few even nipped our ankles.

"Maybe we should come down here," I said. "We might catch some really big ones." Eternal quest, the bane of my life. *Bigger fish.* Would I ever be satisfied?

"Tomorrow," Bob said. "We just might give it a shot." He pointed downstream. "Let's walk downriver a ways."

When we came to muddy water, we scrambled out. Rinsing our feet, we put our shoes and socks back on.

A half mile further, walking the bank, we came upon a wooden boat—a twelve-footer, no oars—chained to a tree. We paused to look it over. I climbed in, worked my way to the stern. I leaned over the edge to check for fish. But there was a drop-off; I couldn't see a thing.

"Man," I said, "if we could just go out to the middle...the fish we'd catch. Big ones..."

"What are you gonna do, Tom?" Bob said. "Steal it?"

"Nope. But maybe we could...*borrow* it...for a while. We could find some poles...something to use for oars. There's even an anchor here."

Bob sneered. "And what do you intend to do about that lock and chain?"

"Oh," I said, turning on my "velly clevah" voice, "I've got ways."

"Oh? What ways?"

I scrambled back, jumped out of the boat, and studied the lock and chain. For some unknown reason, I hadn't left my Prince Albert can—full of fishhooks—back at camp.

"Like this," I said, drawing the can from my back pocket and sorting through a tangle of hooks. I tried one, then another, until I found a walleye hook just the right size. Turning the hook in my hand, I inserted the eye shaft into the keyhole and carefully began pushing it back and forth, twisting it slowly.

I fussed with the lock for perhaps two minutes before I got the right angle. And then, turning it skillfully, exerting just the right amount of pressure—bingo! The lock clicked, fell open.

"Holy cow," Bob marveled, "where'd you learn how to do that?"

"Marty Carlosi taught me."

"Marty Carlosi? He's in Green Bay, in reform school..."

"Well, before he got sent away. It's a cheap lock. This fish hook thing won't work on good locks." I smiled smugly. "Well, do we have a boat or not?"

"That's stealing," Bob said, beginning to sound like a broken record.

"No, it's borrowing. How're they gonna know we even used their boat? We'll come back tomorrow with our fishing stuff, we'll scout up some poles, and push out into the middle, and—"

I was cut off in mid-sentence when we heard a car door slam at the top of the river bank. Wow! We hadn't even known there was a road up there.

"Quick," Bob said, "run! If they catch us fooling with their boat, they'll kill us."

I flung the hook into the river and shoved Prince Albert back into my pocket. We shot out of there like a rocket, heading downriver.

Reaching a little bend, we ducked behind a stand of bushes. Sure enough, there came two men—loaded down with oars, rods and reels, and bait pails—approaching the boat. One reached down, examined the open lock. Then he turned slowly, looked up and down the river bank. He scratched his head. We were too far away to hear what they were saying, but obviously they were plenty puzzled.

"Oh God," Bob gasped, breathing hard. "Another minute, and they woulda caught us. Talk about close calls. We gotta get out of here."

We climbed the bank, then hid in a corn field, eyeing the Ford pickup for five minutes in case the guys came back. When they didn't, we edged down the road, dodging behind trees. When we heard the squeak of the oars, we crossed the road, looked down and saw the boat gliding away. We opened up and ran like our pants were on fire.

We got back to camp by 4:30, all sweaty and pooped. We checked to see if anybody had bothered our stuff. No way. We hadn't seen a soul in the park all day. But it wasn't downtime just yet. We were both hungry again.

Time for a fish fry.

We took our knives and scalers down to the creek and pulled up the stringer of fish. Using a big flat rock for a table, we cleaned the dozen bluegills. The guts and heads were dumped into the creek; we watched them wash away. When the fish were rinsed and we washed the blood and scales off our hands, we wrapped them in a newspaper I'd scrounged from the trash barrel and carried them up to camp.

A previous camper had been kind enough to leave a batch of dry wood. Our lucky day. We got a decent fire going in the barbeque pit. Bob dug out an eight-inch fry pan, opened the jar of lard he'd brought along, and got the grease popping. We dumped in three bluegills and watched them sizzle to a golden brown.

Bob produced some paper plates, and we piled the fish on them while cooking the next batch. A random pedestrian passed on the road or on the sidewalk across the street and smiled amusedly at us. Kids!

"Here," Bob said, digging a dime out of his pocket, "run over to the store and get us a couple Cokes."

It was around six before we sat down to eat. We were famished. A bite of bluegill, a sip of coke. We ate with our fingers, wiping the grease on our jeans. Bob had even thought to bring some salt along. The fish tasted fabulous.

Is this living, I thought, or is this living?

But there's a limit to how many fish hungry ten-year-olds can eat. I got five down and Bob, six, before we'd had it. One dejected fish went into the trash can.

"Was that worth all the trouble of getting to Montello?" Bob asked. "Are we having fun yet?"

"Sure thing," I answered with gusto. "I'm sure glad we came."

We sat by the fire talking until it started getting dark. Bob had popped for two more cokes. Still determined that we'd go back to the river again tomorrow and "borrow" that boat, I pushed my program.

"We'll decide tomorrow," Bob said, putting me off. "Sounds pretty risky to me."

They rolled up the sidewalks early in Montello, and we were basically alone in the park. An occasional car, a random walker went by, but that was it. And yet we weren't in the least afraid. Little by little the day's excitement took its toll. We caught ourselves doing more yawning than talking.

"Time to call it a day," Bob said.

There was an outhouse down at the end of the park. We nixed that and took our last call down by the creek. By nine o'clock we were in the tent. I don't think I was down five minutes before I was out for the night.

Or so I thought.

For, sometime around one o'clock in the morning, the wind came up, thunder boomed, and lightning crackled. But it didn't register right away; we were that far gone.

Then it began to rain. I mean, it came down in torrents; we heard it lashing first one one side of the tent, then the other. Even so we were safe, and none of it filtered into the tent. At least not at first. We went back to sleep. But only briefly.

"Uh-oh," I heard Bob say. He began shaking me. "Tom, there's water all over the place. It's coming into the tent like mad. Damn, why didn't we dig a trench?"

What to do? It was certainly altogether too late to get out the hatchet. For what? The trench would've overflowed anyway. And there we'd be, sitting like ninnies up to our pockets in water.

"Grab your blanket," Bob—always decisive—ordered. "We'll go across the street to that store. There's a little cubby-hole there behind the screen door. That should give us *some* shelter. We'll wait there until the rain quits."

I didn't need to be told twice. We pulled on our pants and dashed across the road, our bare feet splashing in runoff at least six inches deep. And just as Bob had said: a tight space approximately five feet by four, just big enough for two drowned ten-year-olds. And—blessed be the saints—perfectly dry, with no trace of rain blowing through the screen.

We promptly settled in, Bob shaking out his sleeping bag, me wringing out my blanket as best I could. Shivering, we stretched out full length and adjusted for wiggle room.

Even though my blanket was mostly wet, it was cover of sorts, and the heat of my body warmed it slightly. By then, I was so tired and disgusted, I didn't care. Somehow, hard concrete, wet blankets, and all, we dozed off.

How long we slept, I don't know. But all of a sudden, I lurched up in alarm—a glaring light shining in my eyes. We both came awake and found ourselves staring into the business end of a powerful flashlight.

"What's goin' on here?" a gruff male voice challenged. A night watchman? Why in blue blazes did a hole-in-the-wall village like Montello need a night watchman?

"What are you kids up to?" He lowered the flashlight, and we could see him better—a dark silhouette draped in a gleaming black rubber raincoat and a matching wide-brimmed hat, rain streaming from both.

"We were camping," Bob babbled, "across the street. And it was raining so hard, we got soaked. We had to find someplace to get out of the storm."

"Is it all right, mister," I asked, "if we stay here? We'll get drowned out there."

"Please…" Bob said, some beg in his voice too. "Is it all right if we stay here?"

The man chuckled. "I guess, lads. Looks to me like you're doin' just fine." As he backed off the steps, he called back, "But don't be around when Mrs. Temple comes along to open up. She'll have a fit, probably call the sheriff."

"Yes, sir," Bob said. "We'll be gone long before that."

"Nice guy," I said. "I thought he'd shove us out in the rain again."

"Yeah, nice guy," Bob snapped. "Now how about we try getting some sleep?"

Minutes later, we oozed back into dreamland. Toward the end I almost got warm. We never woke up until the first light of dawn silvered the dew-slicked screen. The rain had diminished to a drizzle by then. No sign of the sun. It wasn't going to be a nice day at all. So much for all our happy plans.

With our covers over our heads, we re-crossed the street and stood before our campsite, gloomily examining the mess the storm had made of our tent. Bob crawled inside. "Some of our clothes are still dry."

We dressed, pulled on our jackets. Bob stood outside the tent, a grim expression on his face.

"What d'ya say, Tom? Do we stay and hope that things will dry out?"

"No way in hell," I shot back. "Let's go home."

Wet tent, wet blankets, wet everything. Yuck! What a mess! Ten minutes later we were packed and heading back toward the quarry. Had the road been dry, we'd have left drip tracks all the way down the main drag.

We stood beside the road, looking like drowned rats, our gear in a big pile beside us. We waved our thumbs desperately at every vehicle that passed. For once the camping gods were watching. A man in a blue Oldsmobile stopped.

"Get in, kids. I'm heading for Fond du Lac. Where you want to go?"

"Fond du Lac!" we both shouted.

He came out and opened the trunk. "Go ahead, stow your stuff in there. A little rain won't hurt this old wreck."

Bob sat in front. I was happy to be in back, where I could burrow in.

"Looks like you fell in the creek," the man, bald, probably in his fifties, said with an amused smile.

"Almost," Bob said. "We were camping in the park. I never saw so much rain in my life. We hid out in the front of a grocery store."

He told him the whole story. The man chuckled all the way to Fond du Lac, like our predicament was the funniest thing he'd ever heard. An hour later he drew up right in front of my house. It was just eight o'clock. He helped me unload my gear. Ma was standing on the porch, a puzzled look on her face.

The guy offered to drop Bob off at his house, a couple blocks east on Johnson.

"Bye, Tom," Bob said at the last, trying to put a bright edge on things. "Wasn't it fun catching all those bluegills?"

"Sure was." I forced a grin.

"Let's go back again before school starts. We'll really slaughter 'em next time, won't we?"

"I'll think about it," I said, starting up the steps. *But not very hard, Bob. Not hard at all.*

Truth of the matter: Bob and I never went to Montello again. Not that summer or any other.

CHAPTER TWENTY-THREE

The Midas Touch

There were always ads in the back pages of *Boys' Life, The Open Road for Boys*, even my comic books. One, especially, caught my eye:

BOYS, EARN PRIZES, EXTRA CASH: SELL LANCASTER SEEDS TO YOUR FRIENDS AND NEIGHBORS.

Typical, garden-variety dummy, I went for it.
And where was my information packet? I'd sent their coupon two weeks ago. Didn't those creeps know their number-one champion seed seller was standing by?
Visions of binoculars, air rifles, baseball gloves danced in my head.
It was March, and Wisconsin's growing season would soon be upon us. The successful kid merchant plans ahead. When their letter finally arrived, Ma and I went over the list of seeds I'd order. Total trust: I'd pay for my seeds after they were sold. I ordered fifty packets—carrots, tomatoes, radishes, string beans, cucumbers, plus some flower seeds.
Ma made a carrier from a two-quart grape basket; she sewed a cloth liner (with flaps) to keep my seeds dry. Daddy was enthusiastic; his little boy would become a big time seed merchant. Suit salesman extraordinaire, he taught me secrets of the trade, concentrating on how to best approach my customers.
I was to introduce myself and then tell my customer what compa-

ny I represented. I should put my foot in the door and ask, "May I come in?" Once inside, I'd hold up sample seed packets—visual display a must—then commence my spiel. Ma bought four packets to get me off on the right foot.

The next day after school, I hit the streets, aglow with happy expectations.

Wedge my foot in the door, present a sales pitch? Dream on. Instead I got a harsh "What do you want, kid?" And slam went the door. Those polite enough to listen were unmoved by my sterling sales lingo. None ever let me inside. I was out for two hours that first night and sold only two packets.

Not looking good at all.

I quickly ditched Daddy's approach. "Would you like to buy some seeds, ma'am?" became my drastically revised sales pitch. My feet remained on the porch. No? Thank you. And off I'd go.

I did persevere, however, and after six weeks of sheer stubbornness, I managed to sell out. What prize did I earn? Nothing registers. Certainly nothing worth all the grief and time involved. I received letters from Lancaster, Pennsylvania for weeks after, wanting me to reorder. No way.

Ma didn't raise her boy to be a seed merchant.

Next up was my entry into the exotic perfume business. Some enterprising housewife concocted these magic potions in her kitchen, then suckered kids like me into selling them door-to-door. She provided a small box lined with vials—lavender, lilac, and rose—perhaps two ounces in each, the man-killer scents trapped with a tiny cork.

A housewife? In her kitchen? Times *were* tough.

I'd knock on the door and hold up a vial. "Would you like to buy some perfume? Only ten cents." I'd remove the cork, and waft it past the would-be customer's nose.

"Even in poverty vanity prevails." An original proverb? Believe it or not, I sold out my whole ten bottles the first morning. My cut was two cents per bottle. All that travail for twenty cents? When I paid off the lady, I politely declined her kind offer to refill the box.

Kid Chanel has left the building.

Next came the punchboard caper. A dime a punch—win an

electric razor. My incentive? A second electric razor, just in time for Christmas. Daddy would be so pleased. A hundred times ten comes to ten dollars. Some razors those had to be! I think I sold fifty chances before I gave up. Daddy took the punchboard to work with him and sold the rest.

The razor was noisy, it overheated, and it didn't shave worth a darn.

My next clarion call: "Boys wanted for weeding." I walked all the way from Johnson Street to the end of Fourth Street—two miles easily—where Mr. Lallier had a truck garden. The rows were a good two blocks long. Fifteen cents a row. It took me all day to weed two rows. I got my three dimes around 4:00 PM and never went back.

Talk about exploitation! Mr. Lallier must have been a Republican.

Then came the time I answered a farmer's ad. "Boy wanted for light farm work. Temporary."

Living on Doty Street then, barely thirteen, I'd supplement my paper route income. I used Keller's phone. What kind of work? Threshing, a dollar a day, noon meal included.

That sounded fair to me. The farmer—call him Mr. Schneider—lived three miles out. Fourth Street again. I rode out after pitching my *Tribs*, arriving around 9:00 AM. Field work couldn't commence until the world dried off a bit.

Mr. Schneider was a roly-poly German ("Cherman"). He spoke with a funny accent, but we got along okay.

"You're a bit small," he joshed. "But you'll do. Nobody else eefen botter to answer mine ad."

He sent me out with a hired hand named Otto. I rode on the wagon; he drove the horse. Otto and I worked on each side of the wagon, pitching wheat. When the load got higher than our pitchfork handles, we headed back and fed them into the combine bundle by bundle. Bringing in the sheaves? I now understood that hymn.

Noon hour was a revelation. The three crews were assembled; I met some other kid hay-shakers. Then there was the lunch. Lunch? It was a food festival. I was stunned; I'd never seen such a feed. Meat at noon even.

Another field hand treat: a quarter barrel of beer resting in a tub of ice. The men gathered, put down beer right and left.

"Go, Tommy," Mr. Schneider urged. "You work hard. Take a glass. But just vun. I von't tell your mudder."

I sipped my beer cautiously, tuning in on all the good-natured chatter. The brew got to me fast, and I found myself smiling, loving my fellow man a lot more than minutes before. I chatted with the other boys, all of us respectfully standing apart from the men. Good thing we ate when we did. Talk about woozy!

After eating—the crews sat at a long table under a shade tree—my buzz faded. The food: sausages, chops, homemade bread, potato salad, corn, iced tea, cakes, and pies. I ate until I ached. The men sat against a shed after; some dozed. By 1:30, we were back in the fields. When 7:00 rolled around, I was truly dragging. I rode my bike home in a fog and ate leftovers. I was in bed by nine.

I worked there for three days and enjoyed it a lot; I was actually sorry when Mr. Schneider said he didn't need me any more. Six whole dollars!

Then there was my dawn patrol—the paper route.

I did my *Citizen Kane* number until I was fifteen, when I started setting pins at The Alhambra Bowling Alley, located on South Macy Street.

But there was one more "Old MacDonald" venture in my life, this when we first moved to Tompkins Street. Daddy was the proud owner of a car by then.

Out of the blue Daddy announced that we'd be working the sugar beets next week. Sugar beets? To use his favorite phrase: "What next?" He'd signed on for five acres with a farmer named Henry Walden. We'd all pitch in, Thomas right on down to Richard. Ma became straw boss.

Mr. Walden seeded in late April. By June, school out, we were on the land, located a mere two miles west on Forest Avenue. It was all fields and woods there back then. Daddy drove us out in the Buick around 6:30 AM, then went on to the tannery. He'd return around 4:30 and pitch in for a while himself.

There were three stages: blocking and thinning, then weeding, and finally, in the fall, harvesting.

The planting was done with a horse-drawn seeder, and three weeks later, you had a solid line of sugar beet seedlings, the rows seemingly stretching all the way to Milwaukee. Our initial chore was blocking. Each kid wielding a hoe (tools courtesy Mr. Walden), we chopped away a hoe-width of seedlings and brushed them aside, leaving one thin clump of baby beets.

Next came the thinning. On our knees, we worked our way down a thousand rows, weeding each clump, leaving just one plant. A quick press to firmly anchor it, and down the line we went. We usually started together, talking and joking, Ma scolding when we poked. That made the time pass and helped us ignore the blazing sun.

Little by little, Ma and I, working faster, ran ahead of the crew. Then Ma outstripped me. Bernard came behind me, David behind him, while poor Richard—always lollygagging, stopping to play with bugs—brought up the rear. Martha sat or slept under a shade tree.

It was hard, deadly boring. We'd work from seven till noon, then break for lunch. There was cold Kool-Aid, pinto bean burritos, an apple for dessert. Our kid appetites being what they were, even this simple fare became a feast. All too quickly we were back on our knees.

When Daddy showed up, he'd pitch in. He always wanted to work until 6:00. But by 5:00 we kids were beat, and Ma would firmly call: "*Basta, José. Vamos a casa!*" Daddy would grumble, but we'd gather our tools and head for the car.

This went on for a week. After that, back to our summer fun and games.

In mid-July, came the second stage. Manning our hoes again, we chopped out the weeds that overran the beet plants—now sturdy and fat, the leaves three feet high. Another week shot.

In mid-October came the harvesting—six days this time. Daddy kept us out of school. And how did he get away with that? Don't ask.

The day before we started topping, Mr. Walden ran a cultivator down each row, the blades digging deep and laying the beets on their sides, the heads all facing one way. We were issued chopping knives—a machete-type tool perhaps two feet long—with a sharp, four-inch tooth on the end.

Down the rows we went (pure stoop labor, which, apparently, was why God invented Mexicans), slamming the barb into each sugar beet. We'd lift with one hand, grasp the sugar beet root with the other, and slash. Off went the leafy top. Each beet landed in a pile, ahead and behind us.

Some of those beets weighed as much as three pounds. Our wrists (and backs) took a real beating. It was cruel work, and we'd stop to rest often. Poor Richard, only nine then, couldn't begin to keep up. At the end we were all (even Ma) moving in semi-trance. How many tons of sugar beets we hooked and chopped, I won't even try to guess.

Daddy never contracted for the sugar beets again. How much the *family* earned that ghastly summer and fall is beyond recall. But, a real mind-sticker, Daddy gave me—the oldest and hardest working son—fifty dollars. I imagine Bernard, David, and Richard received correspondingly lower amounts.

I became instant John D. Rockefeller. Off to the bank, full speed.

A real laugher: the morning I bussed dishes at Lion's Café.

Yes, *the morning*. I kept forgetting to slide my tray forward onto the table as I cleared away, and down the whole thing would crash. Not just once, but three times. Dumb, dumb! I must have smashed twenty dollars worth of crockery before I opted for a different line of work. As I carried my last tray into the kitchen, I simply dropped my apron, grabbed my jacket, and kept on walking.

The pin setting—age fifteen—came next. We earned five cents a line. It was during this time that the Disney movie spectacular *Fantasia* enchanted me beyond reason, and I drove my pit-mates nuts as I whistled and dee-daahed Tchaikovsky's *Waltz of the Flowers* nonstop.

I also did the archetypical soda jerk bit while in high school, this at Lalis' Drugs on Sixth and Main. (I became most popular with the girls.)

More? I worked at the fairgrounds stands for one night—the Fond du Lac Panthers baseball team in town—picking up empty soda bottles. A dime a rack. I earned perhaps thirty cents before I told them to pick up their own bottles.

I did deliveries and cleaned up at Marcoe Meat Market—right next to the old firehouse near Main and Johnson—for a gang of Saturdays. I pedaled a bike all over town delivering call-in orders. Between trips I worked in the back room, scrubbing greasy kettles, trays, pans. I earned a dollar a Saturday. Add an occasional tip, and I was rolling in money.

For a time I worked for Haentze Floral weekends and holidays, running the pretty buds up to the houses. Then, for perhaps five Saturdays, somewhere along the line, I labored at Fond du Lac Canvas Products, on E. McWilliams. There was a war on; the military needed sports equipment. My slot? Stuffing baseball bases with cotton batting for a quarter an hour. Now and then I was put to filling punching bags, tamping down fill until my arms were ready to fall off.

For two summers before I was drafted, I hired out at the Rosendale Cannery, where they processed peas in summer and corn in the fall. Bosom buddy Dick Hecker and I hitchhiked back and forth daily. We worked the "end of the line." Here the cans came down a conveyor belt from the canning room and then went into a steel basket—five feet in diameter, three feet deep—before being swung into the air and shunted to the steam cooker.

Dick worked one side; I, the other. We had a ten minute break every fifty minutes. Otherwise the silver stream came at us nonstop.

Some days we worked eighteen hours straight; we saw the sun go down and saw it come up the next morning. My knuckles remain deformed to this day from flinging six cans at a crack. Off the conveyer apron they came in unending stream, and then *slam*—in exact line, circle within circle, and layer upon layer—into the cooker basket they went.

I earned thirty-seven cents an hour. Some of my bi-weekly checks came to the ungodly sum of seventeen dollars.

Croesus? Midas?

My middle name!

CHAPTER TWENTY-FOUR

Last Farewell to Johnson Street

Miscellaneous kid events that got left standing in the hall:

Ma had a church friend named Mrs. Baldwin, who used to visit on Thursday afternoons. She always came with the same treat—cottage cheese—which we boys hated. How about some ice cream, lady? She was tiny and thin with white hair, and she was quick to praise each of us. She lived on Algoma Street near St. Agnes Hospital.

Fresh in my mind was the fact that, a year or so back, for reasons unknown, her husband had hung himself in the basement. Ma always warned us before Mrs. Baldwin's visits: We must never, never mention the tragedy.

Now and then Ma would bundle us all up, put Martha into her buggy, and off we'd go to spend an afternoon at Mrs. Baldwin's. We enjoyed those trips, because when *we* called, there were cookies—no cottage cheese.

One of those afternoons, nosey Thomas, age seven, weary of female chatter, decided to find something fun to do. He'd sneak down into the basement, where Mr. Baldwin had reportedly done himself in. When Ma wasn't looking, I drifted off. I stealthily opened the door. I flipped the light switch. I started down the stairs.

I'd taken no more than four steps when I came—almost eye-to-eye—upon a pair of khaki-colored boots, hanging (feet down) from a nail in the rafters. I freaked out. *Mr. Baldwin's ghost!* Shrieking at the top of my lungs, I thundered back up the stairs and into the living room.

"Someone's down in the basement!" I screamed. "Mr. Baldwin!

He's hanging down there!"

Poor Ma. She turned ten shades of red. Then her mouth tightened into that thin, hard line I knew so well. I'd done it again. Though Mrs. Baldwin pooh-poohed my gaffe, Ma was embarrassed to tears and apologized over and over. Our visit was cut very short.

Upon arriving at home, she took the razor strap to me herself.

After my kindergarten trauma, nothing much registers until fourth grade. I was eight and a half when the school year commenced; it was my first year at Washington School, and Miss Monica Baker was my teacher.

She was cute-pudgy, short, with close-cropped, reddish hair—almost resembling a kid herself. I remember her laughing a lot. After Christmas vacation, she appeared with a leg cast and crutches.

"I fell while skiing," she explained. We thought it quite funny as she went clump, clump, clumping around the room.

I remember that, occasionally, I forgot where I was—all school kids do it at one time or another—and called Miss Baker "Ma." Everyone poked fun, but she smilingly reassured, "That's all right, Tom. You can call me Ma. I don't mind."

Another time as she walked down the aisle, I—a totally out-to-lunch move—reached out and yanked the bow on the back of her smock. The kids gasped at my audacity. Would I catch it now! But Miss Baker simply smiled, and slowly retied the bow. She sent me a gentle smile and walked on. I *was* teacher's pet.

This was never more evident than on Valentine's Day when all the kids—prior to opening bell—scurried about the room passing out valentines. There were, sad to say, no everybody-gets-a-valentine-or-nobody-gets-a-valentine guidelines back then. More than a quart low on common sense, I waited patiently for some to land on my desk. This, even though I hadn't brought any myself.

Upon calling the class to order, Miss Baker found me slumped over my desk, blubbering away. "Tom," she asked. "Whatever is wrong?"

I looked up, tears running down my face. "I didn't get any valentines."

She sent a reproachful look around the room, then hurried to her desk, where she picked up the biggest of *her* valentines. She put it on my desk. "There. Now you have a valentine." Another annoyed glance at the class.

And did I bring valentines that afternoon? Nope. Even so, upon returning from lunch, I found five on my desk. My aching heart was somewhat soothed.

Scandalous revelation about Miss Baker surfaced later that year. Rumor had it that a parent had seen her in a restaurant—smoking of all things! Horrors!

Another Valentine's Day tragedy: The following year, in fifth grade, I was ready. I'd taken a hard-earned dime downtown and bought sheets of red paper, along with a half dozen paper doilies. The night before, I sat up late cutting out Valentine hearts. I embellished them with paper lace and printed "Be my Valentine" with a crayon. These I passed out at school with great display. I was finally in the game!

Nobody was all that much impressed.

I made an extra one for Dorothy Radtke, who lived next door. My first mild crush? She was skipping rope with girlfriends when I marched up and proudly presented it.

"Happy Valentine's day," I said.

Dorothy paused, unfolded it, and gave my masterpiece a quick, scornful look. "Who wants that dumb thing?' she said and threw it onto the ground. It landed in a puddle where snow had melted. Again—big sissy—I verged on tears. I quickly turned away and left. Not even a nasty comeback. Guess who went home with a broken heart that day?

A long block to the west of our Johnson Street address, directly across the Soo Line tracks, ran a rutted, north-south unpaved road—Packard Street. One solitary, dilapidated wreck of a house stood there, halfway between the river and Johnson Street.

A crippled World War I veteran named Harold Bascomb lived there. On rare occasions we'd see him laboriously rolling his wheel chair down the road, heading downtown. If we were out, we'd run to help push him up the steep incline there and across the tracks.

But mostly he stayed home. He sat on the porch in summer, and we could hear him muttering to himself, his dog, Prince, barking whenever we passed by.

Every day around 3:30, winter or summer, rain or shine, we'd see Bascom's German shepherd coming down Johnson, a two-pound lard pail hanging from his mouth. He stood at the Tip Top Tap's back door until the bartender appeared. He took the pail—there were coins in the bottom—and filled it with cold beer. He'd replace the cover, then hold it so the dog could take the handle between his teeth. Prince would then head for home.

It was like clockwork; you could almost tell time by the dog's appearance.

But sadly Prince died, and Mr. Bascomb was left to his own devices. That summer he called to Bernard as he passed one morning, and offered him a penny a day if he'd take over Prince's job. He jumped at the offer. Bernard later informed that fifteen cents was in the pail. His job ended sooner than expected, as that winter Mr. Bascom was found dead in his house.

The Johnson Street garage was the home of so many disasters. First *The Tar Baby*. Next our futile experience with Molly the goat. Then our sad-sack museum. But one final tragedy awaited.

In 1936 (I was ten) we had a bitterly cold winter. Snowball, my rabbit, consigned to the garage, had a nice warm box and plenty of hay to shelter in. In the summer she grazed in the grass around the garage and in the nearby field. In winter I fed her oats.

Daddy, in some ways, was almost as suspicious as Ma. So the garage must be locked down every night, no matter what. Why, I don't know; there as nothing there worth stealing. Arriving home from school, I'd hurry to water and feed Snowball, then lock up for the night.

Snowball was totally white except for a black patch at her nose, and she had the thickest fur coat imaginable. Always gentle, always happy to see me, she was the sweetest pet.

There were times, when, busy with my endless projects, I'd forget to feed her until after supper. Ma, trying to teach me some responsibility, didn't nag. She'd remind me once, and that was it.

But as the nights grew colder, Daddy's padlock began freezing up, and the key refused to turn. Then, furious at the stubborn lock, I'd scream with rage. There was a window there, the glass long gone. So I'd grab the frame, shinny up the door, and wriggle myself through the opening. Dropping down inside, I'd go to Snowball's cage, bring out her bowl, and fill it from a nearby bag of oats.

When I'd put her bowl down, Snowball would scurry out of her hutch, nose my hand, then eat hungrily. I'd pet her and ask how she was doing. A pail of water handy, I'd break the ice on top and fill her water bowl. Then, up the door, and out the window I'd go.

Well, we had a bad blizzard in early December, and the temperature dropped below zero. Selfish, rotten brat that I was, I couldn't bear the thought of fighting through the drifts and squeezing through that window to feed Snowball. So I didn't. She'd survive one night without food, I reasoned.

The next morning I was late for school and forgot to feed her as I'd planned. When I got home that afternoon, I went directly to the garage. Through the window I went.

"Here, Snowball," I said, lifting the top of her cage and filling her bowl. "Here's your supper."

But she didn't scurry out.

"Snowball," I called again, shaking her bowl to coax her, "supper time."

When she still didn't appear, my heart suddenly lurched. *Oh no.* I reached inside her box and felt around for her. What I found was a dead rabbit, frozen stiff—no give to her at all when I pulled her body through the opening.

Dear God, how I sobbed, how I lashed myself for being so lazy as to let my poor bunny die. I cursed Daddy for having such a dumb lock; I cursed Ma for not making me go out and feed Snowball. But mostly I cursed myself.

The food, oh-so close—but no lazy master to bring it to her.

That happened so many, many years ago. To this day there are times when vagrant association triggers memory of Snowball. Once more I'm back in that garage, holding her frozen body in my arms.

Though I try excusing myself with *Tom, she was just an animal*, the guilt remains. No matter that so many more tragic things have happened in my life since, I am still filled with crushing regret.

I'm sorry, Snowball!

There were three dogs in my childhood. I already mentioned Snoopy. Penny, the bull terrier, whom someone stole, and Billyboots were both Johnson Street pets.

Billyboots, was named after the comic strip. One summer evening, while skating, Billyboots running alongside, the dumb mutt happened to run across Johnson Street. Without thinking, I called him back. And wouldn't you know, even though cars were few and far between those days, didn't one come along just then. It hit and ran over poor Billyboots. The car never stopped.

I skated to the middle of the road, gathered his bloody body in my arms, and carried him home, sobbing all the way. He died before I reached home. I blamed myself. Why, oh why, hadn't I looked for traffic before calling him?

The next day I buried him beside the house and spent the best part of that afternoon chipping his name—ruining one of Daddy's chisels in the bargain—into a jagged piece of concrete I salvaged from Osborn's junk pile. Sad excuse for a marker.

One Saturday afternoon—when I was ten—I herded my brothers and sister down to Remington Drugs on the corner of Arndt and Main. Ma had somehow acquired coupons offering ice cream sodas for five cents. Where she scraped up the quarter, God only knows. We sat on padded stools (I held Martha's glass for her) and sucked the exquisite concoctions down. An unforgettable first. We felt like royalty!

Other tidbits:

- I remember using salt, sometimes baking soda to brush my teeth. Later on came Dr. Lyon's tooth powder. I can still see the odd-shaped, turquoise blue can.

- Soap powders came with a dish inside the box. Ma had a whole set of them.

- When people died during the thirties, a black wreath was hung on the front door, and the casket was often viewed in the deceased's parlor. I got dragged to several of those spooky wakes. In Mexican homes the women sat along the wall reciting the Rosary by the hour. The men gathered in the kitchen and drank beer.

- We kids all came down with—and merrily passed on—measles, chicken pox, and the mumps at one time or another. We all stayed home from school until cleared by the health officer. To warn others, he stapled a bright red, twelve-by-fourteen-inch placard beside the front door: WARNING, MEASLES or WARNING, SMALL POX, whatever.

As children we were told that there are no such things as ghosts. And yet I still remember nightmares where I'd wake up shouting at phantoms who lurked in the corners of my bedroom. Relative to this, another terror—age eight to ten—I experienced on Johnson Street:

We had a steep, enclosed stairway, fifteen steps or so, that led to our bedrooms. No problem going up those stairs. Coming down was quite another matter.

Definitely driven by an overactive imagination, I descended those stairs at fifty miles an hour, many times nearly falling. I swore that the moment I started down, a demon, the boogie man—I never actually saw anything up there—would suddenly appear at the head of the stairs and start throwing daggers, one after another, into my back. My skin would crawl, my hair would bristle, especially at night when the stairway was shrouded in darkness. And I'd scramble down the stairs in a pure frenzy.

That thing, it would get me this time!

At the bottom, safe in the kitchen, I'd scold myself for being such a dummy—and experience the same terror the very next time I came down those stairs.

"Whatever gets into you boys?" Ma would scold. "You'd think

you'd seen a ghost or something. You're going to break your fool necks one of these days."

We kept our silly hallucinations to ourselves; we'd die before admitting our fright to her. To this day my brothers admit that they'd felt that same spooky panic. And we wonder how we could've been such idiots.

Over the years, I've asked other we-lived-through-the-Depression friends if they'd had ghosts at the top of *their* stairs. Surprisingly enough, some admitted that they had.

Silly juvenile terrors? Or was it simply part and parcel of an unspoken, underlying fear that haunted us all as we fought our way through the Depression?

CHAPTER TWENTY-FIVE

We Move to Doty Street

When I entered the fifth grade—age ten, 1936—the national economy was inching forward. Daddy was called in at the tannery more often. Things were seemingly looking up for the Ramirez tribe.

We weren't exactly rolling in dough, however. Thirty hours a week at thirty-five cents came to $10.50; forty hours, which seldom happened, came to the staggering sum of $14. And because it was relatively steady—all the difference in the world. Our weekly allowance jumped to a dime. Call me moneybags.

It was May when Daddy announced we were moving. We'd be leaving our $8-a-month shack for a better one—rent $12. The Doty Street house had stood empty for two months, and Mr. Balsam, the owner, had been forced to drop the price. A bargain Daddy couldn't resist.

Though I hated leaving my Johnson Street stomping grounds, site of so many exciting adventures, my regrets quickly faded. The house at 192 S. Doty Street was newer, bigger, and much classier than our old address.

But then—get real—it didn't take much to improve on that dump.

"Look, Bernard!" I yelled during our first visit, mounting the stairs and swinging open the bathroom door. "David and Richard, come quick! Holy cow, a bathtub!"

We all stood goggle-eyed, looking into the spacious bathroom, stunned by the sight of a gorgeous white tub.

"I can't believe it," David said, his voice almost reverent. "A real bathtub!" And turning quickly: "I get the first bath."

"Like hell, you do," Bernard snapped.

David yelled down to Ma, where she was unpacking boxes, "Ma, can we take a bath? Right away? Now?"

Ma had a fit. "Don't you dare mess up that bathroom! Saturday night. That's when you get baths. Get down here! There's work to be done!"

Dear God, what a glowing prospect! We could scrub and soak for hours. No more galvanized wash tubs. No more seconds on water. And best of all—endless hot water.

Not only our first bathroom, but our first dining room too. No more eating in the kitchen. The large living room was almost scary. Ditto the bedrooms and kitchen. There was a spacious, white-washed basement, a pantry even. A sundeck off the second floor gave Ma a place to hang short loads of laundry.

Another plus: a bay window in the dining room that opened on a beautiful view of—oops—the house next door. Never mind, the window seat with storage beneath became Shangri-La to me. The many hours I basked there, happily reading myself off to Sherwood Forest, Robinson Crusoe Island, and Camelot were golden.

We boys constantly fought over the spot (especially in winter, when the sun shone in), until Ma assigned turns. But I, the family's most rabid reader, occupied it most of the time.

It was the first move I clearly remember, mainly because my brothers and I were hands-on this time. Daddy had borrowed a push-cart from somewhere, and it was up to Bernard and me—David and Richard's help minimal—to shove that contraption up over the tracks, then east down Johnson to Doty. It had a six-by-six platform with fourteen-inch rails; the wheels were four feet in diameter. The load must be balanced just right, or it would tip and spill, no matter how fiercely Bernard and I fought the handles.

The air turned gunmetal blue those times.

The big stuff—furniture, ice box, stove, tables, and such—were loaded onto Luiz Landero's pickup truck. Even so, it took days to haul the boxes upon boxes of dishes, bedding, clothing—even our neglected band instruments—the two long blocks to Doty. Also to be moved was a huge amount of junk from our basement and backyard sheds.

The Doty Street house's main drawback? No garage. Thus, back at Johnson a mini-mountain of Daddy's salvaged treasures grew daily curbside, waiting for trash pickup. I can still see Daddy poking through the discard, a woebegone expression on his face.

Not only was 192 S. Doty a bigger and better house, but the neighborhood was a bit upper crust as well, and I'm sure the neighbors weren't overjoyed when the pushcart Mexicans showed up.

Again, almost as if it had followed us, a large vacant lot stood directly to the north of our rental. Seven other houses stretched between us and Arndt Street. And there, just across Arndt, loomed a huge, double-storied, red brick monstrosity—Washington School. We'd never be late again.

Now we lived a half mile from the Fond du Lac River. No *Tar Babies* to be built, no hobo jungles to roam, no forest fires to put out. Different ground rules. We played softball next door with new kid friends; occasional marble tourneys took place. Bob Keller lived kitty-corner from our place now. He and I were again thick as thieves.

Down the block Kenny Colquist raised pigeons. So naturally I must have pigeons as well. After much wheedling, Ma agreed to let me buy a pair—thirty-five cents. The male, all white except for a black speckled breast resembling a splash of war medals, became General. His mate, solid gray with an iridescent green head, I named Maude. I'd thought to erect my pigeon coop on the sundeck, but our landlord nixed that idea. No one would pound any nails into his property!

So, this warm summer day, I was preparing to pound some poles into the lawn behind the house, close to Ben DuFrane's garage. Here I'd erect a platform for my pigeon coop. Mr. DuFrane happened out, watched as I worked. And surprise, surprise, a few moments later he said, "Hey, Tom, why don't you just nail that thing onto my garage?"

I was stunned. I couldn't believe my ears. Mr. DuFrane had been a friendly enough neighbor from the start and often took time to talk and joke with us kids. But to let me pound nails into his garage? Was I hearing right?

"Are...are...you sure, Mr. DuFrane?"

"Yes, Tom, I am. No harm if we're careful."

As it turned out, not only did he allow me to mutilate his garage, but he helped do it.

"Here, Tom," he said, "I think if we nail two of these long two-by-fours horizontally onto the wall, they'll bear the coop nicely."

He did the measuring and nailed the first piece lengthwise, careful to match each nail to the garage stud behind. Then, yours truly holding it, he nailed the second piece three feet lower.

"Now," he said, "when you attach the coop, use the nail heads for guides. That way we'll only have one set of holes in the garage."

Yeah, sure.

He went into the garage and returned with a box of sixteen-penny nails. "Use these, Tom. They'll pass through the clapboard and get to the studs behind." Then, with an abrupt "Good luck, Tom," he was gone.

Well. I stood there for a while, my mouth hanging open. Talk about nice guys! I've never forgotten that generous accommodation.

I spent the rest of the afternoon building the coop. It was roughly a yard deep, six feet long, and forty inches high. There was a strutting area, then a box at one end with a small doorway, where the birds would live. I even built a shelf inside for the pigeons to perch (and later nest) upon. I hinged the top so I could reach in to clean it.

Bernard and David held the coop while I nailed it to the stringers. When it was solid, I stapled chicken wire onto the front and top. I installed a flight door and then tacked black roofing paper to the top of their hutch to keep out the rain and snow.

Finally I spread a heavy layer of newspapers inside the hutch and dumped in a bunch of straw. A layer of sawdust was spread onto the floor of the outside exercise area. It was late afternoon before I finished.

Then it was time for the pigeons to move in. I dug into their holding box, grabbed General, holding him tight lest he escape. Lifting the cote's hinged roof, I eased him in. Then it was Maude's turn. They scrambled around inside briefly, cooing up a storm. Shortly they strutted out to look over their yard. Next they made for the bowls of water and pigeon feed I'd set out.

Home sweet home.

I watched them for a good half hour, vastly proud of my carpentry, already in love with Maud and General. Then Ma called me for supper.

I kept them caged for six weeks so they wouldn't fly back to their former home. Come the day of their first flight, I was all pins and needles. But Kenny was right, the long captivity stuck, and they soared and circled, then rested on the roof of our house, and atop Mr. DuFrane's garage. A half hour later, their recon complete, they circled down, landed on their perches, and strutted back into their cage. *Yes!* I secured the door. Enough exercise for one day. Talk about proud! My shirt had never felt tighter.

A few months later there were two eggs. Then two squabs. I was a father!

When we weren't playing ball on the vacant lot or flying kites and such, the big thing was marbles. Ted Flitcroft and I were out there often, drawing circles, dropping marbles for position.

Glassies were the real prize; these I acquired by saving Eskimo Pie wrappers and trading them in at Verifine Dairy. Teddy always wanted to play "keepers," but I usually dragged my feet. With megs maybe, but not my glassies. Megs were made of hard ceramic, smaller than glassies, and they had little brown freckles on them like pinto beans. They were much cheaper than glassies, which came ten to a bag for a quarter, if you bought them.

Both of us used steelies for shooters; they really sent the opponent's marbles flying. Afterward you gathered your marbles and went home.

If Teddy harped enough, I'd relent and show him I could be a sport—even though it meant "goodbye marbles." I'd usually skimp, and put out five or six. A guy can collect Eskimo Pie wrappers only so fast.

We played marbles only in the spring. Good thing. I'd have been in hock to Verifine until I was eighteen.

*   *   *

We moved to Doty Street in early summer, and before we knew it, winter rolled around—snow up to our ears. God knows why it hadn't dawned on us before, but—out of the blue—we discovered the joys of shoveling walks.

We had a big snow one Sunday afternoon before Christmas, and the four of us were outside, shoveling our walk. Down the street we could hear the distant scrape-scrape-scrape as other people cleaned theirs.

It was around 3:30—the day thinking about getting dark—when the brainstorm hit.

"Hey, guys," I said, "why don't we go around the neighborhood and see if we can earn some money shoveling snow?"

Lights went on all over the world. David ran in to tell Ma our plans, and off we went. We knocked on six doors. "Shovel your walk, mister? Shovel your walk, ma'am?"

Times being what they were, most people did their own shoveling. When the seventh person, an elderly man, said, "Sure, how much?" we hadn't the slightest idea of what to charge.

"You want both the walk and the driveway done?"

"Well, of course."

"How about fifteen cents?" I held my breath, waited for him to laugh. An outrageous price. Who'd pay that much?

It wasn't. "Sounds good to me," he said. "Go to it. Be sure to sweep the porch and steps too."

Well. That was easy. We all charged in—sheer frenzy—snow flying like crazy. We finished in twenty minutes flat. The quickest fifteen cents we'd ever earned. The man came out, and checked our work. He gave me a quarter.

"Keep the change," he said.

"Thank you, mister," we all chimed, immediately reassessing our price range. Down the block we went.

Well. Before we were done, we'd cleaned five walks, our prices ranging from twenty to fifty cents. We were excited; we worked like junior lunatics. All that snow. And so few of us.

Again: Why hadn't we thought of this before?

We came home around seven—very late for supper—and Ma was fit to be tied. Cold as it was, we were dripping with sweat, our undershirts soaked. When she learned we'd earned a dollar-fifty, her temper faded. What industrious little boys she had.

After that we prayed for snowstorms and were disappointed when they fizzled.

But the charm gradually wore off. Now and then, easy money or not, I couldn't muster the gang; only David and I ventured into the storm. And still later—just me. Then it *did* become hard labor. In due course I discovered a few old ladies—too infirm to shovel or sweep—who contracted me for every snowfall, some at ten cents, fifteen cents, seldom more. By February I'd amassed the amazing sum of seven dollars. I could finally afford that longed-for bike— second-hand—at Badger Paint.

"You bargain," Daddy had instructed—to jawbone Mr. Bernhardt down from six to five. I felt like Rockefeller as I counted out the change. Because I didn't know how to ride a bike, I walked it home.

The bike was blue and had twenty-six-inch wheels. Its gawky, upright frame was much too high for shorty here. I dropped the seat and handlebars to their lowest setting. There was no chain guard, so I tied my jeans with string. Later I acquired bicycle clips.

The very first afternoon the streets and walks were clear of snow and ice, I went out to master the balky beast. Launching myself from the porch steps—none of that kid-brother running alongside stuff for me—I hung onto the handle bars for dear life, jittering the front wheel frantically to keep my balance.

I went fifteen feet down the sidewalk before keeling over. So intent on steering that I forgot to pedal, I found myself bracing with my right leg, my left laying across the bike frame—gee-hawed to a thirty-degree angle—more down than up.

Then and there I learned why girls learn to ride bikes easier than boys.

Back to the porch. Concentrating on pedaling *and* steering, I got twenty feet down the walk this time. Again the two-legged straddle, the bike sliding sideways. Brother Bernard sat on the steps laughing his butt off.

Again and again, I re-launched from the porch steps, losing my balance every time. Perhaps a half hour later, after twenty failed attempts, I got the thrill of my life. I finally managed to steer and pedal—and stay upright—all at the same time. I got halfway down the block before I lost it. No steps available, I walked my bike into the street and used the curb for liftoff.

Had the city intentionally built curbs for novice bicyclists like me? Ingenious!

All the way down to Arndt Street this time. And—instead of keeling over—I balanced my right foot on the curb when I faltered.

I turned right at Arndt Street, and, still curb launching, I was off again. I got all the way down to Macy this time. A whole block, wow! At Macy another right—and wobble, wobble—I made to Johnson Street. West on Johnson. I was really sailing. Another right onto Doty, and I was home. Success!

Now was that all so hard?

I went around the block five times with hardly a tip over. By that time I was higher than a kite. To this day I remember it as one of the most exciting days of my life. To be able to ride like the wind—to cover block after block in minutes flat. A thrill beyond description. I felt like Superman—faster than *two* speeding bullets.

If I had been entranced with roller skating, this was a thousand times better, a thousand times more exciting.

I rode to the city's eastern outskirts—DeNevue Creek. Then I rode to its western boundary, Hickory Street. Open country as far as the eye could see on each end of town. Even then, tired, sweating, out of breath, I couldn't bring myself to stop. Ma had to almost shoot me off my bike to get me in for supper.

Then, in mid February, when I got my first paper route, my wild stallion suddenly became beast of burden. I spent a whole dollar-twenty-five on a spanking new bike basket. My junior merchant career was enjoined.

Another unexpected neighborhood discovery:

A month or so after we first moved in, we learned that our Doty Street neighborhood wasn't as upscale as we'd thought. This when we learned about the Hartley's—mother and daughter—who lived north of us, just beyond our vacant lot.

Many nights around dusk, both dolled up in flashy clothes, silk stockings, and high heels, they headed out and moved through the downtown bars. Sooner or later, one of the women, then the other, would be seen driving up—or strolling home—a client in tow. They'd disappear into the house for an hour or so, and then these guys would sidle out, scurry down the street, or hop into their car. Otherwise—I suspect—regulars phoned for appointments.

And though I was too young to understand this shady traffic then, Ma caught on immediately. She'd watch from the window as they passed—swaying shamelessly in their seductive finery—all the while grinding her teeth.

"They do bad things over there," she'd fume. When I asked what kind of bad stuff—an angry glare. "Never you mind, Thomas."

Back under the bushel I went.

In January of that same winter, here came Bob. "Hey, Tom, let's build an ice boat." Him and his eternal, world-beater confidence. An idea a minute. I swear, he should've worked for Thomas Edison.

Eternal bookworm, to me winter was definitely not a time to build anything. An ice boat? I'll come visit you at the loony bin.

"No way," I said. "Are you nuts or something?"

But Bob, professional dream merchant, prevailed, and there we were in his garage—doing what? Why, building an ice-boat, of course.

Just like when I built *The Tar Baby*, Bob had been to the library. Yep. *Ice-Boats Any Boy Can Build*. All the nuts aren't in Brazil.

Bob's garage wasn't heated, so we worked in our sheepskin jackets, caps, and earmuffs. The lumber, two-by-fours mostly, we scrounged from his garage and the alleys. An old clothes pole—six feet high—became the mast, and pieces of canvas left from a kid sandbox canopy were magically reborn as a sail.

We used five-foot lengths of aluminum counter trim to transform other two-by-fours into sled runners. We drilled a hole in the main staging, where the operator would lie, and ran a bolt through it. To this we attached the back crosspiece—a runner on each end. A rope to each end would steer our craft once underway. If we ever got underway.

If I'd been cold in Bob's garage, it was Florida compared to the day we pulled our jerry-rigged monstrosity two miles north to Lake Winnebago. We put down the sail, lashed *The Golden Eagle* (Bob's name for our bundle of slats) onto his American Flyer, and off we went.

I'm sure that the few hardy souls who saw us, our sad excuse for an ice boat in tow, must have sent amused, pitying smiles. No matter; we'd been smiled at before.

Sail boats, by their very nature, need wind. And wind in mid-January just happens to be cold. Icy cold. Polar bear cold. And there I stood, in my sheepskin jacket, long johns under my jeans, galoshes on my feet, braced against those Antarctic blasts, shivering my teeth loose. Someone light a fire!

Dubious from the first, I became even more disenchanted when we carried our craft down into the Big Hole and set it up. The lighthouse served as windbreak of sorts. Even so—bone-chilling cold! Words can't begin to describe my misery.

"We gotta go farther out," Bob said, "so we can catch the wind better."

Out onto the lake we went. Yeah, we caught the wind. My spine instantly shrunk four inches. It took us forever to get the sail right; it kept blowing down. Finally we got it up—"Needs more work," Bob kept repeating—and prepared to turn the sail to the wind. There was snow on the lake, but there were clear patches big enough for a trial run.

The wind roared even harder. If ever *The Golden Eagle* was going to fly, this was the day.

Dream on!

The mast kept breaking loose, and we spent more time up-righting it than anything else. By then my teeth were chattering like the castanets in Chabrier's *España*. I danced in place to keep my feet from freezing to the ice.

When the mast collapsed for the fifth time, I'd had it. "I'm going home, Bob. I can't stand any more of this cold."

He pleaded with me to stay—he'd get the mast right this time—but I turned my back and started walking toward the lighthouse. Bob saw I meant business and followed, dragging the crippled *Golden*

Eagle as best he could.

And—dummy of the year—didn't I go out with Bob again the following Saturday morning? He'd built some braces to keep the sail upright; the *Eagle* would fly this time. Same story. The mast stayed up okay, but he was no sooner underway than the wind tipped the whole thing over.

After three more upsets, I actually lay on top of him—our combined weight would surely keep the runners down. In a pig's eye. We tipped over three more times before I once more headed back to civilization.

Not once did we get *Eagle* to skate—not even as much as ten feet—across the ice.

Talk about disgusted.

Bob tried to get me to go out again the following Saturday. I peeked out the back door and told him I was grounded for the entire winter. Before he could utter wheedle number one, I firmly closed the door and returned to my cozy window seat to read. A new Horatio Alger awaited.

No regatta that day.

My continuing friendship with Bob Keller introduced me to the birds and the bees, whether I was interested or not. Though he was only in seventh grade, he already had a crush on a girl—Eleanor Bentley—who lived down on W. Arndt Street, right next to Sherm's Bar and Grill. A nervous Don Juan, he needed a backup and pestered nonstop until I broke down and agreed to tag along.

Those summer evenings we'd ride our bikes over there, and I'd sit off to one side, while he and Eleanor yakked on the steps. She *was* a cute little kid, I must admit. But their chatter—dumb, so dumb—bored me out of my skull. They talked about the stupidest things: school, the weather, movies and radio shows they liked. Then they'd giggle like ninnies.

If I volunteered a comment, it was mostly derogatory. Never any action—no hugging, no hand holding, not even sitting close. As for kisses, I should live so long. If this was woo-wooing, it was all lost on me.

When do we go home, Bob?

After an hour or so of such nonsense, he'd bid Eleanor an awkward goodnight, and we'd pedal off. Bob would regale me with blather about her beauty and her supreme intelligence all the way home. Give it a rest, buddy.

As I said, sexual awakening. In due course, Bob Keller introduced innocent, little Tomás to the birds and the bees. He told dirty jokes, which, for the most part, he was obliged to explain. The things kids learned at St. Patrick's Parochial!

In the course of all Bob's wicked explanations, I learned, in very explicit terms, what men and women do when they get married—some even when they don't get married. Imagining Daddy doing such with Ma, I was aghast. In my total naiveté, I was overcome with overpowering pity for womankind. That they had to submit, to endure such grotesque attentions was beyond comprehension.

I vowed that I'd never inflict such indignities upon my wife! Better still, I'd skip marriage altogether.

And the Hartley ladies did this nightly to earn a living? Give me a break!

I suppose, all in all, it was for the best. Some education—even faulty education—is better than none at all. One thing for certain, neither Ma nor Daddy ever took us aside for that vital "how babies are made" session. Everything we learned, distorted or not, we picked up on the street. No wonder so many warped grownups wander the American landscape today.

We lived on Doty Street for about eighteen months. And while it didn't turn out as dizzy as life on Johnson Street, it *was* the time of Beth Stanford, a plus of monumental proportions.

I was growing up.

But this was merely calm before the storm. Little did we dream that our next move would plunge the Ramirez family back into the Dark Ages again.

CHAPTER TWENTY-SIX

Get Your Papers Here

I was twelve when I applied for my Social Security card. For most of my life I stowed it in my wallet, and it became creased and faded. Now, almost too late, we are told to keep it in a secure place—a safe deposit box would be nice. I passed on bank security, but have it safely stored just the same.

Or "jesty same" as Daddy would've put it.

I recently had cause to dig out the card. When I did, I couldn't help but smile. That kid signature—Tom Ramirez—done in pitiful, childish scrawl.

There oughta be a law.

This jogged memory of a terrifying rite of passage. No more kid admissions for me; movie tickets would now jump from ten to twenty-five cents! I must find a more prolific cash cow—the random pennies earned from my downtown alley trollings simply wouldn't cut it any more.

God must have been listening. For suddenly, out of the blue, came distinct *Hallelujah* chorus. "Newsboys wanted," the *Fond du Lac Commonwealth Reporter* ad read. "Must be twelve years of age. Apply, Fond du Lac News, 33 W. Forest Avenue."

I was on it like a flash. Fond du Lac News I knew; it was located a few doors west of the Fond du Lac Police Station, right next to the Fond du Lac River. A set of railroad tracks ran alongside the building.

"You gotta have a Social Security card," Bill Bredlaw, my boss-to-be informed. "Go down to the post office and apply."

And so it began. It would seem that, from childhood on, I was destined to be a man of letters.

I was sorely disappointed when Mr. Bredlaw informed me that he wasn't offering a *Reporter* route, but a *Chicago Tribune* one instead. Forty customers, a penny a paper. That sounded good. But wait—the hours. The bundle of *Tribs* was dropped off at the Chicago and Northwestern depot by 5:00 AM daily.

The worst thing about the *Chicago Tribune* was its size. Where the Reporter usually ran a puny thirty pages or so, the *Trib* was a back breaker, the smallest edition going at least sixty. Throw in advertising flyers, and there were days when each paper weighed a full pound.

Try rolling these and jamming them into your paper bag.

So every morning, there was Daddy, standing beside my bed. "Come, Tomás," he'd say softly, shaking me, "is time go to work."

Daddy was always proud to see his boys earning *dinero*.

It was agony, those bitterly cold mornings, to drag out of bed, dress warmly, and ride my bike to the depot. There, on the brick walkway, next to the outdoor waiting room, my bundle waited. Some mornings, however, the train late, I'd be stalled a half hour or so.

Thump! The bundle would be thrown from the moving mail car and land on the bricks. I'd charge out and drag it in. I'd slide my clipper under the wire. Click! The bundle fell open. I'd discard the wrapper and wire in a nearby trash box.

Now came the time-consuming part—rolling the papers, and fitting them into my *Chicago Tribune* paper sack. Impossible some mornings. No *Trib* pitching today. Now I was obliged to dismount from my bike, climb the steps, and place each copy on the porch. I'd anchor them beneath a doormat or a brick left for just that purpose. For special customers, rolled or not, I put their paper inside the storm door.

The rolling finished, I'd carry the sack out to my bike and jam it into the metal basket as best as I could—a real hassle on "big paper" mornings. Then I'd head off for the east side (only five west side customers), where all the richies lived.

When the weather was good, I'd finish in an hour and be home in time to change clothes, wash up, and eat breakfast, and I'd still get to school—Roosevelt Junior High—on time. I mustn't be late; too many tardy checks, and my work permit would be pulled.

If it was tough sailing for me, it was equally painful for Mr. Bredlaw; he simply couldn't keep *Tribune* carriers. Nobody wanted the grief that went with that particular route, and most kids usually quit after a month, some in a few weeks even.

Even worse, I was beginning my newsboy career in mid-winter; the weather became my worst enemy. Even though I was an expert bicyclist by then, the ice and snow were constant threat. More than once I skidded, lost control, and ended up in a snow bank, my papers scattered all over the tundra.

I distinctly remember more than one freezing morning that I delivered papers with a blizzard roaring at my back. Most of the walks unshoveled, the roads near impassible, I walked my bike the entire route, and this took two and three hours.

I'd be soaking wet and frozen to the bone upon arriving home, hours late for school. Where Ma would decide that I should stay home. An excuse note—"Thomas was very sick and vomiting"— must be written. Heaven forbid that Miss Ahearn, the school truant officer, should come knocking upon our door.

It happened once too often, and the assistant principal got wise to Ma's game—why was I always sick during blizzards?—and called to chew out Mr. Bredlaw.

"Damn it, Rammy," he'd scold, "you gotta move faster. You're the best carrier (the only *Trib* carrier) I've got. I don't wanna lose you. If you can't get done in time, deliver the rest after school or during the noon hour. If the customers complain, I'll cover for you."

Though I didn't let on, by now I'd talked to past carriers and knew I had him at my kid mercy. He'd give me all the leeway I needed and then some.

There were other major kinks in the operation, these being my fussy, fat-cat *Trib* customers. *The poor, they shall always be with us?* Goes for the rich too; a more insufferable bunch of jerks never existed. If, just once, the paper landed in the bushes, Mr. Bredlaw would get a nasty phone call. From his ear to mine.

Some of those cranks, the women especially, wanted special

privileges galore. The paper should be placed on the right side of the door, I should open the storm door and the inner door, and then put the paper in the vestibule. I should fold it in the shape of a star and set fire to it on the lawn. On and on. And wouldn't you know, these were the dips who never tipped? Not so much as a nickel.

One prize pain, a lady who lived way out on the south end of Park Avenue, complained constantly because I wasn't tucking the paper under her pillow every morning. The same woman who wouldn't know a tip if it ran over her.

And when Mr. Bredlaw cornered me, I finally played my ace card and told him if she wasn't going to tip for extra service, then I'd be damned if I'd give her any. Bill—we were buddies by then—was reluctant to tell Mrs. Rich Bitch she had to offer at least a token tip.

Instead he'd alibi: "Tommy is a very independent, nasty boy, ma'am; I can't do a thing with him. Would you like to have us discontinue delivery?"

This, of course, would mean a trip downtown for her, and eventually Mrs. Whiney Pants learned to keep her yap shut. She'd have to go out on the porch—bend over, of all things—and actually pick up her paper, just like every other tightwad on my route.

A nickel or a dime—rarely more—was about the extent of tipping frenzy in 1938. I remember one wealthy customer, Duke West, who owned a dairy firm located on W. Johnson and Main, who, in lieu of a monthly tip, always hinted at a big Christmas payout.

Dreaming of a buck or two at least, I catered to him—I even sat beside his bed and read the paper to him some mornings. So, came the holidays, I appeared at the plant, and was ushered into his office, face aglow. He beamingly rose and said, "Merry Christmas, Tom."

And proudly dropped three dimes and a nickel into my palm. Disappointed? I could have wept.

No more bedside service for him. Another call to Mr. Bredlaw. A broken record: "I'm very sorry, sir. Tommy is incorrigible. Would like to cancel home delivery?"

End of story.

Another canker sore: Quite often when I collected—a maddeningly onerous monthly chore in the first place—people refused to answer the door, or when they did, they'd offer lame excuses: "Mr.

Prentiss didn't leave me any money. Can you come again next week?"

Or next year maybe?

Plenty of times, knowing it was collection day, some simply ignored my knockings. I'd peer into the window and see movement inside. The wife would look up, stare me in the eye, and just continue with her dusting or vacuuming. Eventually they paid up, but it was an infuriating chore dogging the deadbeats.

Yes, there were kind customers who tipped generously, who thanked and complimented me. Some gave me cookies, homemade candy, once even a pair of new leather gloves. These precious few restored my faith in mankind.

One summer morning around 6:00, during my last remaining weeks with the *Chicago Tribune*, a crazy thing happened. It was a customer who lived on the southwest corner of Amory and East Merrill, kitty-corner from Roosevelt Junior High. Here the paper got flipped onto a side porch. I was blithely wheeling along, slinging papers, when I flubbed and threw the thick Friday edition harder than usual.

Crash! The sound of splintering glass stopped me cold. And how in hell had I done that? I'd been tossing the Caddell's paper for months and had never missed before.

My heart sank. *There goes this month's profit.* I got off my bike, dropped the kickstand, and walked to the steps. I resignedly waited for one of the Caddells to storm out.

But, would you believe, no commotion? Nobody appeared. How, I wondered, could anyone have slept through all that racket?

There. Did I just hear movement inside? Nope. Nothing.

A brilliant idea surfaced. Very quietly I climbed the steps, paused again, fully expecting Mr. or Mrs. Caddell to appear at any moment. But again, only total silence.

So I tiptoed to the window and looked inside. Even in the dawn gloom, I could see the paper lying on the kitchen floor, two feet from the sill. Another quick look. Ever so carefully I reached over the jagged spears of glass and plucked it out. Backing off, I shook the paper vigorously, making sure no shards of glass were caught in the folds. Then—clever, clever boy—I replaced the paper at the farthest corner of the porch—no incriminating glass shards in sight.

Moments later, I was on my bike, whizzing down Rees Street. At month's end, collecting at the Caddells', I was ready for a big shootout. But no, not a word. An accident. Some kid flinging stones? I'd gotten off scot-free.

Finally I could endure the *Chicago Tribune* torment no longer and announced, at summer's end, that I was quitting. Bill Bredlaw pleaded long and hard for me to stay—where would he find another carrier as expert and dependable as I?

"C'mon, Rammy, please stay." Real melodrama. "Your customers love you. They're always calling to tell me what a good carrier you are." (Lie.) "Stick it out a little longer, won't you?"

But I stood my ground; I'd run the route for another week—no longer—to break in my replacement. That would be the end of it.

To this day I still have dreams—nightmares—in which I'm on my bike, delivering the *Trib* again. Only now I'm lost, and for the life of me, I can't remember where my customers live. I frantically race back and forth across town looking for the right house. In other dreams I'm teaching the new kid the route.

Memories. No wonder they write songs.

But I wasn't done with the newspaper racket just yet. Two weeks later Mr. Bredlaw dropped by—no phone, of course—at my John Street address. Would I consider selling the *Fond du Lac Commonwealth Reporter* on a downtown street corner? Another kid was quitting, and he desperately needed a real "go-getter" like me. Ahem.

He was in luck, because, already missing the *Trib* money, I was still jobless. Bagging potatoes at the Piggly Wiggly (located kitty-corner from the Fond du Lac Public Library) on Saturdays for a measly twenty cents a morning was definitely not the road to fame and fortune.

Yes, I was interested.

I set up shop on the corner of Forest and Main in front of Walgreens. I received thirty papers an afternoon, Monday through

Saturday, and earned a penny per. Most nights I'd earn twenty or twenty-five cents. Other nights I might sell out. I also had a few regulars who stopped on their way home from work, plus a half-dozen nearby home deliveries.

I'd stand on my corner loosing an occasional yell: "*Fond du Lac Commonwealth Reporter*...get your paper here! *Fond du Lac Commonwealth Reporter*..."

It was boring some nights, but when Ray Baum or Bob Keller stopped by to sell their extras of *The Milwaukee Journal*, there was someone to talk to, and time passed quickly. I'd start around 4:00 and call it quits around 5:30. Sometimes I'd walk the length of Main hawking papers, ducking into every tavern along the way, going from stool to stool with a breezy "Paper, mister?"

One of my first nights—eternal eager beaver—I stayed out past 9:00, cruising through the taverns time and time again, totally convinced I must sell out or else. When I inadvertently mentioned this to Bill, he had kittens.

"Damn it, Rammy, how many times do I have to tell you? We got new child labor laws now. I'll lose my license if one of those snoops finds you working that late. Don't let me catch you doing that again."

Another advantage of working my corner was that I could pretty much gauge the pulse of the city. I knew what movies were showing, what stores were closing; I saw all the signs advertising upcoming medicine shows and where the sales were.

When they set up the incredibly beautiful Colleen Moore Dollhouse exhibit (admission: ten cents) in an empty downtown store, I came close to being their very first customer. Another big plus: I knew which bars set out a free lunch, and I learned just how to filch summer sausage, cheese, and rye bread without the bartender rousting me.

Quite often I ran into some girls from school and got all puffed up when some said hi. Some even stopped to chat.

Also, wandering the streets, I couldn't help to notice the panhandlers, the drunks, the bums, the cripples on the sidewalks trying to sell pencils—constant reminders of the tough times the nation was living through.

The cheese became even more binding when Bill cornered me one afternoon, and said, "Hey, Rammy, how'd you like to peddle the Sunday *Tribune?*"

"A *Tribune* route? Keep it."

"No route. You camp out in front of St. Mary's Church."

I agreed to try it. Again I was rising at 5:00 AM, but this time picking up my papers at Fond du Lac News, not the depot. By 6:30 I was stationed in front of St. Mary's Church, located on Merrill and Marquette, waiting for 6:00 Mass to let out. Beside me stood *Fond du Lac Reporter*, *Milwaukee Journal*, and *Appleton Post-Crescent* carriers.

Far to my right a kid chanted nonstop, "Fr. Coughlin's paper, Fr. Coughlin's paper..." Though I was unaware at the time, it was an anti-Semite yellow sheet. But there were those who bought it regularly. Christians? Go figure.

St. Mary's had Masses on Sunday at six, seven, nine, eleven, and twelve o'clock, and I must be on hand fifteen minutes before each Mass ended, come hell or high water. Business was brisk, and on a good Sunday, I'd sell perhaps fifty papers. At three cents per—a cool buck-fifty. Prosperity was right around the corner.

But it wasn't all church trade. Between Masses I'd bicycle all around the area delivering papers to church customers who'd rather have their *Trib* home-delivered. This was ideal because they'd hand me the twenty cents at the door or leave it under the door mat—no Saturday collecting.

Otherwise I'd station myself on the corner of Johnson and Main and walk beside the cars at a traffic light. "*Tribune*, Mr.? *Tribune*, Mrs.?" Some Sundays, business slow at St. Mary's, I'd stay out on the street until almost 2:00 PM trying to sell my last paper. Bill didn't like returns. Afterward I'd check in, then head home.

A long morning but a profitable one. I'd get home ravenous.

A happy memory: Every Sunday between the seven and nine o'clock Masses, my home deliveries done, I'd treat myself to a hamburger—five cents—at Happy's Restaurant, located on the corner of Main and Merrill.

And treat it was. The burgers at Happy's were super delicious, bigger than those most restaurants offered, and slathered with fried onions. I can see them now. Slap on some mustard, shake a little salt—yum! And, man, but didn't I feel like Mr. Big Cheese as I chomped my sandwich down? A glass of chocolate milk—three cents—and I was set for the morning.

I'd sit on a stool at the long counter and wish some of my school friends would walk in just then and see the poor Mexican kid eating in a restaurant. Wouldn't that be a kick! Ma and Daddy had never taken us kids out to eat.

A second burger? Beyond the pale. Times were tough, sonny.

Often, when it was raining or, heaven forbid, snowing, we paper boys would gather in the church basement between Masses, sit on our paper bags, and swap lies. Now and then we'd pitch pennies. The penny landing closest to the wall won. That kid took all the pennies.

Once a priest—call him Fr. Jones—caught us by surprise in our kid casino. We were so busy sliding pennies, we never saw him walk in.

"Well, boys," he said, a stern look on his face, "gambling? In God's church?"

Oh, we'd catch it now!

But no, Fr. Jones dug into his pocket and hauled out a few coppers. Then he squatted down and pitched pennies with us. Falling back on childhood skills, he won three games before he quit. Then he strode off, robes swishing.

"Keep the noise down, boys," he called back, "people are praying."

Summer in front of St. Mary's was the best. The sun just coming up, the air cool before six o'clock Mass let out, the hymns carrying, it was good to be alive. I made good newsboy friends, kids I ran with for years after. Many of the parishioners were friendly and kind; some stopped to pass the time of day. Others asked, "I have a friend who'd like the paper delivered. Could you arrange to do that?"

Could I? Do cows moo? Do pigs oink?

There was one guy, Red Harrigan, older, who sold *The Milwaukee Journal*. Yeah, I remember Red. More sexual awakening. At the time, I was a late bloomer; sex was an unknown to me. Where do babies come from? How would I know? Why should I care?

I recall Red pulling at my sleeve one Sunday morning, then pointing east, where a woman was walking toward us.

"Oh, honey," he muttered softly, "go home and put on a slip."

I looked up to see a tall, pretty lady, the sun shining behind her, the dark shadow of her thighs plainly visible through her skirts. Later on I noticed women with dresses so sheer that you caught glimpse of shadowy bare flesh, stocking tops, dark garters. Red was always on top of this.

"How about that, Tom?" Red said. "That turn you on?"

It really didn't. I was embarrassed instead. I knew I shouldn't be looking at stuff like that. I felt sorry for these women, unwittingly becoming sport to snotty little kids.

If I thought about sex at all, I wondered why such things excited Red. Sometimes it did make me feel funny inside. Why, I'd ponder, did shadowy legs become fascinating? Were the woman in a bathing suit or summer shorts, would we bother to look? Hardly. My church teachings still mattered. A hint of things forbidden? I suppose.

Besides my newspaper shtick, I eventually came to sell magazines. Bill provided a different paper sack, this one made to accommodate *The Saturday Evening Post, Collier's, Liberty, Cosmopolitan,* and *Ladies' Home Journal*. The *Post, Collier's, and Liberty* sold for a nickel; the others, a dime.

I'd pound the cement downtown, hitting barbershops and beauty parlors, but mostly I'd walk the streets on Fond du Lac's east side—Division, Park Avenue, Sheboygan—and sell door-to-door. I seldom worked the west side, which was mostly blue-collar. The Depression. No spare change there.

Within a month or so, I found a few kind women—even men—who took pity on the sad-eyed waif behind the overloaded magazine bag and became regular customers. Hard to make money with magazines. A penny a sale—can you believe? Two cents on the dime mags. Bill kept telling me Andrew Carnegie got started that way, and now he was a millionaire.

So began a long-standing love affair with these mags. I still read some of them in my twenties. The cover art was incredible, and here

I was first exposed to J.C. Leyendecker, Maxfield Parrish, and Norman Rockwell.

I'd study those covers long and hard. Oh, that I'd ever be able to paint like that! The way Norman Rockwell did kids, parents, pets, and especially holiday scenes hit me where I lived. Maxfield Parrish's scenery was stunning. Leyendecker's fantastic detail deserved second, third—tenth—looks.

I was there, June, 1938, when Action Comics Number One first came out, and Superman zoomed out of the cosmos. Later came Captain Marvel, Spider-Man, and Wonder Woman. At Fond du Lac News, at Walgreens, I'd sit on the floor and pore over these nonstop. I owned dozens of the first Supermans and Captain Marvels, all in mint condition. These early issues bring six-figure prices today. How many of them did I unthinkingly throw away? Especially upon my return from service in 1946.

Idiot! *Zo zoon oldt, und zo late schmardt!*

When I hit high school and commenced to set pins at The Alhambra Bowling Alley—located on Macy between Second and Court Streets—I became ashamed to have my classmates see me peddling papers on Main Street or at St. Mary's Church. Kid stuff. Enough, already.

I finally bid Bill Bredlaw and Fond du Lac News sad adieu. But Bill wasn't left completely in the lurch. Brother Bernard and later David eagerly took up where I left off. Bill had new "Rammys" to pester.

At The Alhambra I earned fifty and sixty cents a night. Working three and four nights a week, and sometimes on weekends, I'd wind up with three-fifty, even four dollars a week. A junior Rockefeller.

Did this new wealth go to my head? Did I squander my hard-earned cash?

No way. I now owned a bank book. I proudly marched into The National Exchange every Monday during noon-hour and salted most of my earnings away. A kid miser, I delighted in studying the steadily growing balances. Anticipating the day when I'd become an artist, a writer, or both, I knew I'd need funds for college or art school—Ma and Daddy wouldn't be able to help.

So entrenched did these goals become that I finally broke down—

believe it or not—and actually *withdrew* funds. The world comes to an end in thirty minutes! I bought oil paints, brushes, and canvas boards. Following a wrenching tussle with my conscience, I next splurged on a Royal portable typewriter. Then a desk—all from the Montgomery Ward catalog. The typewriter cost thirty-five dollars; the desk, twenty.

Pulitzer Prize and Caldecott Medal judges, please stand by!

New winner coming through!

CHAPTER TWENTY-SEVEN

The Bedbug Wars

We were moving again.

This time from Doty Street to John Street. Which was a real downer. Back to the slums.

Once more the trusty pushcart stood at the front door, concrete blocks bracing each end. With Ma supervising, we lugged stuff out of the house and packed it with precise care.

"No, Bernard," she scolded, "Don't put that box there. There's still room at the back. Yes, squeeze it in by the chair."

It was the *Chicken Wagon Family* all over again.

We felt no chagrin, no embarrassment whatsoever at doing our own hauling. Been there, done that. Everybody owned a pushcart, didn't they?

I was twelve then, in my first year at Roosevelt Junior High.

Daddy had decided that he was tired of paying rent and abiding by a nit-picking landlord's rules. One day he simply announced, "I buy house. We move in month."

And that was that. Daddy had decreed. The stone tablet.

And how come, in light of his on-again, off-again work history? Answer: The owner, Francisco Morales, anxious to move back to Mexico, was selling at a give-away price. Our lucky day? Hardly.

Houses went for two and three thousand dollars at the time—third- and fourth-class ones, anyway. The John Street property was certainly that—maybe even fifth-class. Think one thousand dollars. Even so, how had Daddy and Ma raised that kind of *dinero*?

Simple. They hadn't.

A mortgage. Two hundred dollars down and eight dollars a month at Fond du Lac Building and Loan.

A mortgage? What part of Africa did that animal come from?

Goodbye to our beautiful, *clean* bathtub. Goodbye to a dining room and to that window seat where I'd spent so many happy hours reading and sunning myself. Goodbye to our short walk to school.

Day by day, on weekends and after school, we piled our pathetic possessions into the pushcart and rolled them over to our new/old house.

We headed south on Doty, wheeled past Fred Reuping Leather, and over the bridge. Then it was down a long slope—Bernard and I hanging on for dear life—to Division Street. Here we took a right for two short blocks (red brick paving again) and, finally, another right onto John Street, to the middle of the block.

There stood 23 John Street, a board-certified hovel if there ever was one. We unloaded our stuff onto a tiny, glassed-in porch or into the living room, where it awaited further positioning by Ma and Daddy—Ma mostly. By mid April we were completely moved in, even the pigeons.

It quickly became apparent that Señora Morales had been a dedicated slob. Mexico deserved her. Ma went over every day for weeks beforehand to scrub floors and walls, to paint walls and trim, to clean the filmed-over windows. The floors were made of softwood planking and hadn't been scrubbed or waxed in years.

Whatever faults Ma possessed, tolerance of dirt wasn't one of them. No matter how broken down the house, it would sparkle! She was the original White Tornado.

Even more disgusting—if such was humanly possible—the bedrooms were infested with bedbugs. Ma used bug killers, kerosene—everything she could think of—to destroy the man-eating pests. I can still see her hovering over my bare mattress, a vengeful frown on her face, teeth clenched, as she probed the cording and tufting with her fingers, exposing the obscene bugs in the crevices and killing them one-by-one between blood-stained thumbnails.

There were hundreds. All of us were covered with tiny scabs, ugly souvenirs of their nocturnal picnics.

"Filthy, filthy animals," she seethed as she worked. "No, you little devil, you don't get away on me." Then the dull crunch as she dispatched another to bedbug heaven. If ever there was a holy crusade, Ma was in the vanguard.

Little by little the battle was won. But our bedding smelled of kerosene and lye soap long after the bedbug wars ended. Even so Ma never relented; she remained on eternal vigil lest they infiltrate anew.

The house was somewhat larger than our Johnson and Doty Street addresses. The porch opened into a big living room. To the right, as you entered, was a small bedroom with a heavy curtain serving as a door, which I immediately laid claim to.

The bathroom—the bathtub dingy and stained—was next to my room and was accessed through the living room. Directly across was Ma and Daddy's bedroom, definitely bigger. There were two rooms on the second floor, one small (Martha) and the other big enough to accommodate my three brothers.

A doorway adjacent to the biffy opened to a kitchen-dining area that was easily twenty-five feet long by twenty feet wide. Apparent afterthought by some screwy builder, it was grossly oversized compared to the rest of the house. A long sink took up a third of the west wall; floor-to-ceiling cupboards occupied the rest.

There was a closet-like landing and stoop at the kitchen's far end. An outside door gave way to a small, four-by-five platform and two steps. It was here that we often found a stray hobo taking advantage of Ma's soft heart. A skimpy basement, graced with a cistern and laundry tubs, lay directly beneath the kitchen. A narrow concrete walk, partially overgrown with weeds, ran along the side of the house.

The backyard was huge. Ragged, unpainted fencing partially enclosed the eighty-by-two-hundred-foot lot. But it wasn't all free range. At the very back to the east stood a two-story barn, its doors wide enough to accommodate a farm tractor. To the left, a long, open shed ran the length of the fence from the barn almost to the house. The wild games of hide-and-seek we kids could have in these!

In a far corner of the shed, we found three oak barrels and a lot of copper tubing, obvious remains of a one-time still. Dollar signs immediately flashed before my eyes! Junkyard, here I come!

It was here that I built a new pigeon coop. My birds seemed perfectly happy in their new setting. However, dummy me, I released them too soon, and they all flew back to Doty Street. When we went over we found them nesting—and pooping from—an exposed beam in the roof peak. Had there been no sundeck, we'd never have recovered them.

We went over around 10:00 at night when they were sleeping. The new renters had carried a step ladder up during the day, and for two nights—we only caught two the first night—we crept up after them. Into a burlap sack—flapping and chirring—they went. The next night we got General and Maude. I caged them for two whole months this time, and the confinement took; they homed perfectly.

But by then my interest in pigeons had faded, and I sold all four to David for seventy-five cents. He was overjoyed. As for me, I had the fun of watching my babies fly without caring for them or having to buy feed.

Back to the house: On the left, as you faced the street, lived the Morgan family and on the right, the Garveys. Always regarding ourselves as impoverished, we were amazed to discover that we'd suddenly been elevated to rank of landed gentry by comparison to these dysfunctional misfits.

In due course we learned that Marvin Garvey, father of five kids, was in prison, leaving his family to live on relief. Mrs. Garvey must have learned domestic skills at Señora Morales' knee, for their house was an absolute mess.

But it was a palace compared to the Morgan hovel.

Yes, Virginia, there is such a thing as a pecking order.

The father, Aaron, a onetime carpenter, was alive and kicking and daily robbing the welfare system blind. The wife, Clara—honest to God, a mail-order bride—was the most useless piece of female anatomy on God's green earth. That two such grotesques managed to find each other strains belief.

However, one thing they did do well: there were seven kids, all younger than I. David and Richard played with them on occasion, but Bernard and I, older, barely acknowledged their existence.

I never ventured inside their house, but according to David and

Richard, their living conditions were atrocious. There were no beds, only bare, grossly stained mattresses on the floor where the kids slept. The furniture—all thrift-store rejects—was filthy and ragged, and you must wade through dirty clothes, garbage, and piles of empty relief boxes to get from one room to another.

In warm weather Mrs. Morgan lounged on the front porch rail—or in a rusted lawn chair—by the hour, staring blankly into space. Face dirty, teeth missing, hair greasy and straight, her clothes a shambles, she read movie magazines nonstop. Credit where credit is due: She *could* read. When we walked past the house, she stared at us with dazed, manic intensity but never uttered a word. She took particular delight in watching the Northern Trucking semis roll up and down John Street. Heaven forbid that she should ever go indoors to clean the house.

Whether she and her husband ever left home, went to church, shopped, or perhaps attended a movie, I don't recall. Pity anyone who sat anywhere near them. As best as we could, tell no one in the family ever washed; all smelled like walking outhouses.

Refuse and garbage littered the entire yard, some even drifting out into the street. To them garbage cans were lawn ornaments. On one side of a falling-down, backyard garage stood a mountain of tin cans which, over the years, had come to fill—almost to the eaves—the entire space between it and the fence. Come a flood, they would have inundated the entire neighborhood.

Often some of the Morgan kids appeared at meal times and peered through the screen door as we ate. "Ooo, hot cereal," they marveled, their expressions hang-dog. "We never get that."

At first Ma tried to be kind and offered them treats, but they became such nuisances that she finally had to drive them away.

"Git," she'd yell if she saw them coming up the drive. "Go back home!" If their brain-dead parents ever noted these rebuffs—and Ma could really yell—they blithely ignored them.

Aaron Morgan was, intentionally it would seem, an unemployed carpenter. He was always home, either loafing on the porch with Ella Cinders or working in his cluttered garage workshop. He spent hours out there with a fancy jigsaw rig, creating incredibly beautiful, cut-out corner shelves featuring flowers, deer, horses, butterflies—all sawed from quarter-inch plywood. True works of art.

He'd sand, stain, varnish, and then sell them. Sears Roebuck allotted a small corner of a back display window to these catch-alls, prices clearly marked—none over five-dollars. How many sold, I don't know, but some revenue was generated. The entire world wasn't poverty stricken.

Mr. Morgan, like his wife, seemingly hadn't bathed in months, and to be close to him—bad breath, body odor, filthy clothes—was insufferable. I doubt that he ever brushed his teeth; they were gapped, brownish yellow, and black at the gums—nothing halfway about him. He often volunteered to help Daddy with some of his projects (while similar effort was desperately needed at home), and it was his habit to dawdle if dinner time was near.

"My, that stew sure smells good," he'd slyly wheedle, time and again embarrassing Ma into inviting him to eat with us.

He was a self-proclaimed Communist, always spouting off about the wonders of Soviet Russia. I once made the mistake of asking him for help with a social studies report I was doing on Russia. A prime source right next door—could anything be easier?

Big mistake. He came over two nights in a row and stretched the process beyond all reasonable limits. Communism was the wonder of the ages. All men were created equal, and the State saw to it that every Russian citizen was employed, fed, and cared for.

Had Aaron Morgan been transplanted to a commune, Stalin and company would have stood him before a firing squad the very first day.

Sitting that close to him was misery. Angle myself as I might, there was no way to escape his rank odor. Not only did he chew tobacco, but he smoked a foul-smelling pipe as well. Ma would mutter under her breath—using words the clergy do not know—as she cleaned up after him where he'd knocked his pipe against the chair leg before lighting up again.

"Filthy pig," was the mildest of her names for him—and Mrs. Morgan.

But apparently he knew his stuff; I got an A on the paper. When he asked about the report, and I showed him my grade, he got so puffed up it was silly.

"See, Tom," he gloated, "whenever you want to know something, always go to an expert." I had a devil of a time getting him out of the yard after. He kept asking if there were other school reports he might help with.

This, when his shack of a house was falling down around his ears, when his own kids desperately needed help and supervision, and when his bone-lazy wife needed a good kick in her back porch.

I never sought his expert assistance again.

Another sad, telling remembrance: When Charley Morgan, age ten, was diagnosed with TB, the county nurse got him admitted to an Oshkosh sanitarium. Charley was gone for seven months, and when he came home he was actually fat, his face and teeth shone, and his hair was combed. Dressed in pressed, clean clothes, he resembled something out of a kid fashion ad. Sitting on the porch amongst his grimy parents and siblings, he almost glowed.

A month later you'd never know he'd been away. Once more he was filthy, teeth stained, face smudged, his welcome-home rags in tatters. He was gaunt, hollow cheeked, and slumped like an old man.

And yet we were the dirty Mexicans who'd sullied their neighborhood?

To the south, the Garvey house was another disgrace. Nevertheless, it was a dozen times cleaner than the Morgan pigpen. Yes, there were dirty dishes in the sink, un-ironed clothes piled on chairs, beds unmade, and floors unswept, but there was feeble show that Florence Garvey was at least trying. But failing just the same.

Of the five kids I remember Fred and Craig best of all. And, oh yes—Lamonica.

Fred was two years older than I, and we exchanged offhanded greetings now and then. He ran with an older bunch, hoods mostly, and I kept my distance. At least early on.

Lamonica (whacko names not exactly a modern-day trend), on the other hand, was quite another matter. She was thirteen and sexually precocious.

Her brothers teased her, calling her "Harmonica" at every turn. Sometimes it would bug her, and she'd chase them around the yard.

She was their second Mom; many evenings Mrs. Garvey would be away, and Lamonica was left in charge. I always thought she was kind of nice and never got into that nickname thing.

Craig was a year younger than I, a blond, willowy kid, with brilliant blue eyes. Today he'd probably be called effeminate, perhaps even gay, but that term didn't exist back then. Not so far as I knew, anyway.

Craig's big thing was basement theater. Gaga about movies and radio, he vowed he'd be a film star one day. His eyes would glaze over as he shared his dreams; it was like you weren't even there. He usually conscripted his younger brothers—Preston, ten, his main victim—for supporting roles.

Craig's movie interests meshed completely with mine, and by rights we should have been brothers under the skin. But there was always something about him that bothered; I was content to sit in on his shows now and then, and that was it.

He'd actually built a small stage in the basement—pullback curtains and all—and put on plays there, always free, Saturday afternoon after Saturday afternoon. He'd scour the neighborhood, pleading for customers. But, desperate as he might be, never the Morgan kids.

When there was no new play, he beguiled his kid audiences with sock puppets, monologues, even one-man dramas where he played all the roles, hopping back and forth like a demented Barrymore. It got really pathetic at times.

The show would go on, whether there were a dozen kids or two.

Craig *was* talented. For all I know, he might have ended up in Hollywood. I remember being much impressed those times I sat in. He once ran away from home—a box of stage curtains in tow—and the police picked him up hitchhiking out on Highway 175. Yep, he was Hollywood bound, but he was working the wrong side of the road.

California, here I don't come!

The Garvey basement was a mess, but the corner he used for his theatricals was always slick and clean; he swept it weekly. He even rigged up some hooded workshop lights overhead.

Lamonica had a dusky complexion, and her dark, curly hair hung halfway down her back. She was on the stumpy side, with mannish shoulders, and was sort of a tomboy. She wasn't what you'd really call beautiful but pretty enough, and eventually I came to notice her—and the nice bumps in her blouses and sweaters.

She was always friendly, and I'd occasionally walk her home from Roosevelt Junior High. She was fun to talk to. Talk *at* was more like it, because I, immersed in my "busies" and nonstop reading, pretty much monopolized the conversation. No small talk for me.

Which she seemed to enjoy, and she often waited for me after school. She told me that she loved talking to me; she thought I was smart. Not smart enough, apparently, for I never suspected there was more than talk on her mind.

Our walks were mostly hit and miss, and when I began my newspaper career, our encounters, of necessity, ended.

Anyway, it was after one of brother Craig's theatricals that this incredible, absolutely zany thing occurred. I was sitting next to Kenny and another of the Garvey kids when she came in. Without a word, she lifted Kenny to the seat next and planked herself beside me. Craig always set up wooden boxes plus some battered lawn chairs for his audiences. There were eight other kids present—my three brothers, four Garveys, and Peter Wiley from over on Military Road.

Craig's one-man play was coming to a close when I felt her lightly slide her hand into mine. She left it there a moment, then slowly drew it away. I shrugged it off as an accident. Some accident.

Because, somehow or other, after the show, this goofy thing took place. I honestly don't know exactly how it started. Very ancient history. Did Lamonica stand up and say, "Does anyone here want a kiss?" or did she just lean over and kiss me? My best guess would be the latter.

If that's what happened, it was just a quick peck, and she quickly withdrew. Right away the other kids jumped on it and set up a howl.

"Lamonica kissed Tom! Lamonica kissed Tom!" Kenny Garvey chanted. "Kiss me too."

And right away the boys lined up, Craig first in line.

Laughing, she gave him a quick kiss. "Next?"

My brothers and I were up for it and eagerly took our turn. If ever the term "it was like kissing my brother" came home to roost, this was certainly it.

I think we all got in line four times.

By then I'd figured it out. She didn't want to kiss her brothers. Or my brothers. She wanted to kiss me. As long as we were making a silly game of it, she would play along. Every time I hit the front of the line, she sent me a really happy and loving smile, and each kiss lasted longer than the one before. Her final lip-lock was a real scorcher. She put her arms around my neck and ground her mouth into mine really hard. The kiss made my head swim. Then, with a last, saucy smile, her eyes flashing, she whirled, and dashed up the cellar stairs.

"That's enough of this crap," she called back. "I've got better things to do."

We were all laughing, but not really. We shuffled around self-consciously, avoiding each other's eyes.

"Boy," Craig said, for want of something better, "Lamonica must really like you."

I stood like a dope, a sheepish smile on my face. "Just playing games," I mumbled. "Nothing serious. C'mon, David, Richard, Bernard, let's go home."

I walked out of there in some sort of trance. I was filled with the strangest of feelings—a sense of disquiet intermixed with an eerie yearning—sensations the like of which I'd never felt before. And what had just happened?

Lamonica was the first girl I'd ever kissed.

There was nasty comedown after, however, this during supper when Richard, who always ran his mouth before engaging his brain, let the cat out of the bag.

"We were over in Garveys' basement this afternoon, and Lamonica let us kiss her."

"What?" Ma snapped, her eyes fierce. "What are you talking about?"

I glared at him. *Richard, I am going to kill you. Why can't you learn to keep your blabber-mouth shut?*

And before we could shut him up, it all came out.

Ma was fit to be tied. Daddy too. They both stared at me, like it was all my fault. *There they go with that big brother stuff again.*

"It wasn't anything, Ma. We were just fooling around," I mumbled, trying to come up with some fast words.

Before we were done, Ma had wormed every last detail out of me—hell, there wasn't really that much to tell—and then she really laid into us. Result: We were confined to quarters for a whole week. We weren't ever to play with the Garvey kids again. No whipping, thank God, but being grounded—a new wrinkle for us—was no bushel of roses either.

A couple weeks later, memory of our basement orgy fading, Ma's edict fell into oblivion, and David, Richard, and Bernard were over at Garveys' again. But I stayed away. The thought of bumping into Lamonica again made me feel all antsy inside.

But I wasn't quite quits with her. Memory of our clinches, of her hot, wet lips haunted me. Anyway for a week or so. Then, like Ma, I got over it.

But apparently Lamonica didn't.

Remember my mention of laying hard claim on the downstairs bedroom just off of the living room? The room was small, perhaps ten by ten, with two windows, one opening onto the screen porch and the other to the south, facing the Morgans. On hot summer nights I opened both windows. A narrow sidewalk led from the back steps to the front walk, and pausing there you could look right into my bedroom.

Because of my paper route and getting up at 5:00 AM to pick up my papers at the depot, I tried to be in bed no later than 9:30 PM. The lad needed his rest.

Well, there I was, this Thursday night in late July, cutting Zs like there was no tomorrow, when abruptly I became aware of noise outside. Someone calling my name? No, not calling. More like whispering.

"Tom, oh, Tom, wake up in there. *Tom!*"

I sat up and checked my clock. What the hell? It was after eleven. Everyone else in the house was fast asleep. My head clearing, I glanced to the side window and saw a dark shadow there, not more than three feet from my head.

Lamonica Garvey.

"Wha...what's going on out there?"

"It's me...Lamonica," she said, keeping her voice low. "I came over to say hello." She backed off, and now another girl was looking in at me. "I brought Evelyn along. Can you come out for a little while? We wanna talk to you."

The other girl was Evelyn Costello. I knew her from school; she lived over on Doty Street, right next to the river. She was a scrawny blond, a bit taller than Lamonica and had a rep. She smoked already and ran wild most nights.

"Hey," I protested, "I'm trying to get some sleep here."

Evelyn laughed. "You can sleep when you're old, kid."

"C'mon out, Tom," Lamonica urged. "We just want to talk a little. Evelyn thinks you're cute."

"Don't get me into this, girl. You're the one who wanted to call him out. C'mon, Tom, get dressed. Let's take a little walk." She snickered softly. "Your lucky day."

"Don't talk so loud. My ma'll hear you."

"Oh, a mama's boy, huh?" Evelyn mocked. "Not the way Lamonica tells it. From what I hear, you're some kisser."

Looking back, I suppose I should have thrown caution to the winds and crept out to see what might develop. But, sap that I was, I wasn't thinking straight; I had no idea of what these girls were up to. More kissing? That might be nice. But then what?

"Hey, it wasn't just me. She was kissing everybody. My brothers ...*her* brothers."

"Yeah?" Evelyn giggled. "You never told me about that, hon."

Lamonica cut her off. "It's not important. We were just playing a game."

"Okay," I interrupted. "Let's forget the whole thing. Why don't you girls just broom off and let me get some sleep? Before you wake the whole neighborhood."

"C'mon out, Tom," Lamonica pleaded. "We won't do anything. We just wanna talk." There was a long pause. "So we...I...can get to know you better."

Evelyn laughed harshly. "Yeah, that's one way of putting it."

"Oh, shut up," Lamonica snapped, her voice raising a few

decibels.

Ma was sure to hear. She'd come storming in at any minute now.

"Go away," I said. "I gotta get some sleep. I ain't coming out. I don't want to have anything to do with you."

"Oh, Tom," Lamonica coaxed, "you know that's not true. We...you and me...we get along so good together. I love talking to you."

Was someone moving out in the living room?

I jumped up and ever so slowly eased the window down. "You poop," I heard Lamonica say at the last, "you're no fun at all."

I caught fleeting glimpse of them as they streaked up the walk.

I lay in silence, holding my breath, expecting Ma to appear at any moment. But nothing happened. Just my imagination working overtime.

I plumped up my pillow and fought my way back to sleep.

But that wasn't the end of it. Three nights later they were back. But this time I was prepared. And when Lamonica put her face close to the screen and said, "Tommy, can you sneak out? We wanna..."

I sat up carefully and grabbed the full glass of water I'd placed on the window sill. With one quick move, I swooshed the whole ten ounces through the screen, right into her face.

"No, I ain't coming out," I hissed. "Go away, damn it! And stay away!"

Lamonica yelped, and ducked back. "You rotten little turd," she gasped, dashing water from her eyes. Again they took flight, Evelyn hooting all the way.

I laughed softly too, pleased with myself. I replayed the sound of Lamonica's surprised gasp in my mind. *She had that one coming.*

I listened for any trace of noise in the living room. Had the commotion awakened Ma? Apparently not.

I fell back onto my pillow and smiled smugly into the darkness. *Boy, did she get a soaking!*

Love finds Andy Hardy?

Nope. Not yet.

Andy wasn't quite ready. He still had some growing up to do.

CHAPTER TWENTY-EIGHT

The Great Watermelon Raid

The watermelon caper happened when we lived on John Street—1938 or so—still close to the Chicago and Northwestern tracks, but this time on the east side of the tracks.

A mini tangle of switching track was situated to the northwest, roughly a block away; passing trains woke us. There were only three houses on our street—Morgans to the south of us, Garveys to the north. Next to Garveys stood the Northern Trucking garages and warehouse. Their drivers used our street for a parking lot; a line of semi-trailers often plugged it up. They mostly loaded and switched at night, and Ma was in a constant stew about the nonstop yelling and cursing.

My room fronted on the street, so in summer, my windows open, I got the worst of it. When the racket became too much for Ma, she'd get up, shag into her robe, and go out to give the drivers a nasty what-for.

Beyond Northern Trucking stood Cohodas-Manis Produce; their warehouse sprawled halfway to the banks of the Fond du Lac River.

Anyway, this hot, sultry, June afternoon, brothers Richard and David were in the process of stirring up a hornets' nest.

They'd been down at the produce warehouse earlier in the afternoon to watch a crew unload watermelons. Cohodas-Manis had a private track. Boxcars of produce rolled right up to their loading dock.

Watermelons, watermelons, stacked from floor to ceiling! They'd never seen so many watermelons in one place before. Trolley after trolley rolled into the warehouse to await local delivery. A six-man crew was unloading melons, sweating, straining, and complaining up a storm.

As expected, melons got dropped. The shattered husks were kicked aside in the straw—red, succulent, tempting as all hell to hungry kids. Watermelon was a rare treat; Ma could seldom afford one. So, his mouth watering, Richard slowly climbed the stairs to the loading platform.

"Say, mister," he addressed the foreman, his voice timid and polite, "would you mind if we took one of those broken melons?"

The man looked Richard up and down for a few seconds, his expression disdainful. Then, finally: "Yes, I would mind if you took one of those broken melons," he mocked. "They can damn well rot before I give any of 'em to you dirty Mexicans. Now get the hell out of here!"

And before Richard could move, he wheeled, and viciously kicked Richard in the pants. "Git!" he snarled. "Before I call the cops on you thieving spicks."

Foreman and crew hooted riotously as Richard fled down the stairs, his eyes filled with hurt and surprise.

He was only eight at the time, short, pudgy, mostly afraid of his shadow, so he and David didn't pause to call names but ran down the tracks like their shoes were on fire. However, the insults, the unnecessary kick, had set Richard off. Halting at the corner of the Northern Trucking warehouse, he looked back, fire in his eyes.

"I'm gonna get even with those dirty crooks," he said, "just wait and see."

And get even he did.

They waited until after supper when everyone had clocked out, the warehouse doors locked, the loading dock deserted. Then he, David, and another recruit—Wally Forstner, who was bigger, a year older, a bit on the slow side—stole back to the boxcar and checked out the tin seal, the only thing standing between them and those beautiful melons.

If Richard was aware that it was a Federal offense for unauthorized persons to break that seal, it didn't matter. He was storming; he simply didn't care.

Back then we kids were afraid of cops, we minded out parents, we respected and feared our teachers, and we never addressed adults by their first names. So it was quite a departure for Richard to strike out like this.

He used a pair of Daddy's tin snips. Click! The tin band snapped and fell to the ground between the dock and the tracks. Together, grunting and straining, they pulled the boxcar door open, already salivating at the sight of hundreds and hundreds of watermelons— the car still half full.

I was sitting in my room, fooling with my stamp collection, when I glanced up to see Richard scooting past my window, a huge watermelon in his arms, a foot-wide smile on his face.

I quickly got up, ran through the living room and kitchen to the back door, arriving just in time to see him ducking down the basement stairs. Down I went, hot on his trail. It was around 6:30 PM, the sun still up, and yet, even as gloomy as it was in the basement, I could see what was going on down there.

What was going on down there was that Richard was carefully lowering the watermelon—long and striped, the way watermelons used to be—to the floor. Where it joined two other melons already resting there.

"What's up, Richard? What's with the watermelons?"

But before he could answer, here came David with another one. Down on the floor it went—number four. He was grinning like a ninny too.

"What's happening?" I repeated. "Where'd you get those watermelons?"

"Down at Cohodas-Manis," Richard said. He laughed like he'd just told the world's funniest joke. "They're giving watermelons away!" A wicked wink. "Only they don't know it yet!" Then he wheeled and headed back up the stairs. "C'mon, Thomas, help us get some more!"

And where were Ma and Daddy while all this was going on? They'd taken off for some church function, leaving us kids to our own devices.

And evil ones at that. As things quickly developed.

Like I said, Richard was just a little bit of a kid and on the shy side. He wasn't normally given to loony bravado. What in blazes was going on?

As I broke out the front door, I put the screws to Richard and David. En route, I was briefed on Richard's run-in with the Cohodas-Manis foreman. Then it was my turn to get mad; I wanted to get even too! The dirty so-and-so!

When we reached the boxcar, we found four other kids, some of Wally Forstner's buddies from over on Military Road, happily filching melons. Wally stood in the car, passing them out as fast as he could. Down the steps his pals went, smiling victoriously, scuttling across back yards full speed. When they came back, they brought along more little ruffians. Before we finished there were at least twenty kids carrying off melons.

"Take some to my house too, hear?" Wally called. "Don't go ripping me off."

I quickly appraised the situation, then climbed up into the car to help Wally distribute melons to the poor. "Move it," I warned, "before somebody calls the cops."

But strangely enough, none of the adults in the neighborhood made slightest motion to stop us, to alert the police; we seemingly had free rein.

The houses on Military were a bit closer to Cohodas-Manis than ours. So we three brothers got the worst of it, ferrying melon after melon past the Northern Trucking warehouse and two hundred yards to our basement. Up the stairs to the loading dock, grab a melon, down the steps, dash down the street to our place. The basement was filling up fast. We were sweating up a storm.

The night dispatcher at Northern hadn't shown up yet, or else he was sleeping in the office; no other employees were around to alert the police.

By this time eight or so of the Garvey and the Morgan kids had come running to get in on the watermelon bonanza.

Climbing into the boxcar and watching each kid climb the steps for a melon before scampering back for home, I had a mini-brainstorm. I grabbed one boy while he was mounting the steps and held him in place. Then I cut off another and guided him to the bottom of the steps. The next arrival was manhandled into line. A melon was passed down to the first kid, midway down the stairs, then to the one waiting on the ground. That solved the stairway bottleneck.

Still too much wasted effort; there had to be a better way.

Then it hit me broadside. Why hadn't I thought of this before? I hopped to the bottom of the stairs, waved some other kids up.

"Hey, guys," I called, "make a chain…let's pass these melons hand to hand."

Being older and bigger—hell, I was all of twelve—I became the boss. Sure enough, the little rats caught on right away and began forming a line that stretched diagonally to the northeast, right to Jed Harvey's back yard. Each kid stood about four feet apart, on the alert, waiting for the next melon. I waved Jack Martin up, put him to work with Wally. Both began pushing out melons hand over fist.

The watermelon relay worked like a whiz. By then I was first in line, halfway down the stairs, handing melons to kid number two, actually lofting the smaller ones. Two handed off to three, three handed off to four, and so on down the line.

"Pile 'em in Jed's yard," I yelled. "Yeah, like that. You can sort 'em out, all take your share later."

And sure, in all the commotion, melons hit the ground, split into pieces, and got kicked aside. But nobody bothered to pick any up. Melons were falling from the sky! Forget it!

What a sight! Maybe thirty kids by then, all working in tandem, the melons zipping down the stairs, across the tracks, down into the yard like clockwork. The pile in Red's yard grew until it contained at least seventy melons. Little rug rats were standing around, some even climbing up on the pile.

"That's enough for over there," I yelled. "Move the line toward Sal Binnotto's house."

The general had spoken. Instantly the line fragmented, veered to the right, and reformed in diagonal flow, heading southeast. The melon express rolled on.

We were all sweating like crazy by then, the melons pouring out in a steady stream, some actually slipping in our wet hands. More broken husks. The melons were heavy—in the eighteen to twenty pound range—and awkward to handle. Some were almost as big as the kids passing them along. Hey, this was getting to be like work!

Shortly the line began breaking down. We were waiting longer to pass off. Even my arms were giving out. Time to call it a day.

I could see a small mountain of melons on Sal's lawn. Some parents came out of the houses and stood watching in small clusters, but none made move to interfere. Their seeming acceptance of our wholesale thievery made us even bolder.

"How many?" I called when David came dragging up from John Street for yet another melon.

"About twenty," he said.

"That's enough," I muttered. "We've been at it for a half hour now. The cops are bound to show up any minute now." I grabbed a last melon, headed for home. Pausing, I called back: "I'm outta here, gang. You're on your own. You kids better hide those melons fast...make yourselves scarce."

Again, an older, wiser voice. The line collapsed just like that. Wally and Jack jumped out of the boxcar and strained to close the door. Another kid lent a hand, and it finally slid shut with a dull clang.

The last time I looked, I saw gangs of kids gathered around both piles of melons, running every which way to get them out of sight, even parents helping now. Melons were going into the back doors of almost every house on the block. Kids were ramming across yards, racing down Military Street, scurrying like a horde of manic ants.

Madhouse!

When I got home I counted twenty-four watermelons—fat, green torpedoes—all neatly lined up the length of the basement. And, good Lord, how were we ever going to eat that many melons?

"What're we gonna tell Ma and Daddy?" Richard said "Will the police come looking for us?"

Kinda late to worry about that.

"Tell 'em the truth," I said. "They won't say anything. Tell 'em how the guy kicked you and called you nasty names. They'll be on your side, just watch."

Richard's eyes glittered, his smile verging on evil. "I sure wish I could be around when that ape foreman opens that boxcar tomorrow. He'll have kittens."

"Yeah, and so will Mr. Manis and Mr. Cohodas," David said.

Even so, we didn't say a word when Ma and Daddy returned from church. I became super busy with my stamps. David and Richard were at the kitchen table, deeply involved in a game of Chinese Checkers. Bernard had been running with some of his Johnson Street buddies—he'd missed all the fun.

Ma sent us a quizzical look, almost as if she sensed trouble, but said nothing. Did she suspect something, or was it just the guilt in our hearts?

Shortly it was bedtime, and off we went like quiet, little mice. Not a word about our crazy escapade.

It took me a long time to get to sleep that night.

Next morning, around eight o'clock, Ma went to the basement for something and almost tripped over the melons.

She came running upstairs, her face stricken. "Thomas," she said. "Where did all those watermelons come from?"

I bristled. Why me? Was I responsible for everything that went wrong around the house? Being number-one son had its drawbacks now and then.

It was just as I'd predicted. I told her how the Cohodas-Manis roughneck had kicked Richard and called him names. I told her how he and David simply snipped off the lock and stole their melons—a way to get even. How almost every other basement in the neighborhood was bulging with watermelons as well.

She went silent. I could almost read her mind. Somebody kicking one of her kids? Her face hardened.

"If that's how it happened, Thomas," she said, sighing, "I guess it's all right. They had it coming, didn't they? Just don't say anything to anybody. But there are an awful lot of melons down there. What will we do with them?"

Was there an echo?

Around 10:00 AM there came a knocking on the door, and a couple policemen, dressed in summer tans, stood waiting for Ma to open up.

"You kids," Ma snapped. "Get out of sight. I don't want a peep out of any of you. Let me take care of this."

Did she know anything about kids in the neighborhood breaking into a box car down the street and making off with a couple hundred watermelons?

Ma remained calm, put on her surprised face. Somebody stealing watermelons? How terrible! "No, Officer, I don't know anything about it." Ma should've been on the stage—what an actress!

"It was family night at the cathedral last night," she added. "First a Bible lesson and then a Laurel and Hardy movie. It was a very funny movie. My children enjoyed it a lot."

She was great! How did she manage to keep a straight face?

"Are the boys here?" the boss cop said. "I'd like to ask them some questions."

"No," Ma said, thinking fast, "they're swimming at Taylor Park. They like to go early, before it gets too crowded."

Muttering to themselves, the policemen went on down the street. They seemed almost relieved; no reason to probe further here, their expressions said.

We watched them knock on the Morgans' door. Old Man Morgan, unshaven, bare-footed, smelly—he hadn't brushed his teeth in months—wearing just an undershirt and trousers, came onto the porch. He and the police jawed for perhaps five minutes. Probably Morgan was trying to get them to join the Communist Party.

Again the cops went down the street, shaking their heads.

Apparently the flatfoots never found out a thing. The whole neighborhood had shut down like a coffin. They weren't about to get search warrants for every house on the block. In poverty there is solidarity, I suppose. Anyway we never heard anything further from the law—or the big suits at Cohodas-Manis either. They probably stuck it to their insurance company. And hiked the figures to boot.

If you ask me, the police didn't really try all that hard; they were just going through the motions. That's the way things were in those days. They could see our crummy neighborhood and how poor we were. Kids gotta eat, right? And watermelons are nutritious, aren't they?

And that was that. We ate watermelon until the seeds bubbled out of our ears. Toward the end there, we hoped we'd never see another watermelon as long as we lived.

The big question remains.

How come?

Why had every parent in the neighborhood clammed up, covered for their kids? They knew it was wrong. Their kids were thieves, no two ways about it.

And yet?

I suppose they justified their kids' crimes with that one ominous word. The same word that allowed Ma and Daddy to fib as well.

Times were tough, remember?

It was the Depression.

CHAPTER TWENTY-NINE

Fr. Johnson and the Tamales

As many Mexican restaurants as I've visited in my lifetime, I have never—and I mean *never*—had a tamale I liked as well as those Ma used to make. They were superb: not too wet, not too dry, just the right thickness of *masa*, the filling spicy, but not too spicy.

Many Mexican families make tamales just before Christmas; others, at random times during the year. At our house the big event took place between Christmas and New Years Day.

In case you're not familiar with tamales, they are made by spreading *masa* dough, made of corn meal, on dried corn husks that have been pre-soaked to make them pliable, and then layering in specially seasoned, shredded beef and pork. The husks are then rolled up, resembling a clumsy, oversized cigar. The ends are tucked in, and the finished tamale is placed upright in a kettle along with as many other tamales as will fit. They are then steamed for thirty to forty minutes until the *masa* is firm. At which time they come out hot and delicious.

Oh, what I wouldn't give to taste one again.

These days you can go to a Mexican store and buy the *masa* flour and the corn husks outright. Or you can buy the *masa* pre-mixed and ready to spread. But back then Ma ground the corn by hand, made the dough herself. The husks were carefully salvaged from the summer corn and then strung up in the back entryway to dry.

According to movies, television shows, and novels featuring the Mexican culture, making tamales is traditional family-fun time. Everyone pitches in, spreading the *masa*, scooping in the meat, rolling the tamales up, and a warm and loving atmosphere prevails, everyone chatting and laughing. Afterward everybody lays into the fresh tamales—always best just off the stove—until they can't eat any more.

Yeah, that's how it goes in the movies and in books. But it wasn't at all like that at *Casa* Ramirez.

In the first place, we boys didn't like being cooped up in kitchen for a whole day; we wanted to be outside, playing, roaming the neighborhood, and doing kid stuff. God didn't mean for livewires like us—macho piglets or not—to do sissy-boy chores.

As much as I loved eating those tamales, to me it was an interminable chore—and bore—mainly because Ma was so maddeningly particular every step of the way. Then here came Daddy criticizing our tamale technique nonstop. "Who gonna want eat tamale like that?" was his constant refrain.

In later years, come February, we would drive 225 miles to brother David's house in Portage, Indiana and join all his kids and grandkids for an all-day session on the tamale assembly line. However, sister-in-law Elaine's tamales, good as they were, still fell a tad short of those that Ma used to make. On average we turned out sixty, seventy dozen, and each family took home their fair share. It made for a very long day. And here, at last, came the warm, happy, close-knit family scene: We joked and laughed and teased and, at day's end, ate tamales until they dribbled out of our ears.

As kids, the eating part was fine and dandy. But that tamale factory routine was for the birds.

This particular year, Christmas fell in mid-week, and on the following Sunday I got the brainstorm to invite my good friend Chuck Mowbray to dinner after church on Sunday—while there were still a few tamales left. He'd finally get to see how good Mexican food could be. I asked Ma, and she said it was fine by her.

Trouble was, I was thirteen then, already a kid merchant, and I worked Sunday mornings, delivering papers. First on my regular *Chicago Tribune* route, and then, in between, I sold papers in front of St. Mary's following each of their four Masses. I was running every minute. Usually I wouldn't return home until after 12:30.

Thus, the night before, I asked Bernard and David to corner

Chuck at church (no phone, of course) and invite him to dinner (lunch.) Can do, they assured me.

Little did I suspect the calamity that was about to befall me—and the entire Ramirez clan.

Many a slip, and all that.

When I came wheeling home that Sunday, anxious to welcome my good buddy, I was brought up short. We lived on John Street then, three blocks from St. Paul's Cathedral on Division Street, an easy walk. And then, who should I see, entering our front door, but Fr. Henry Johnson, our new Canon.

I was thunderstruck and instantly braked my bike, did a wheelie, and broke for the corner, hoping he hadn't spotted me. Hiding behind a billboard there, I kept peeking out, trying to figure out what was going on. Where was Chuck? And why Fr. Johnson?

Qué pasa?

I hated Fr. Johnson with a passion. New at St. Paul's, he'd come to take Fr. Dunnigan's place. I wanted nothing to do with him! Poor guy. It really wasn't his fault.

But of course, I wouldn't even cut him even that much slack.

Secondly I was overcome with false pride. And what was this terrible man—priest or no priest—doing in our shack of a house? In a *Mexican* house? In our crummy, rundown neighborhood? Would he go back and laughingly tell Dean Carter about our pathetic lifestyle?

Tamales, indeed! I was suddenly ashamed of Daddy with his broken accent, of Ma and her plain housedresses, and of Richard, who was always running his mouth, saying the craziest things, embarrassing us time and time again.

I was ashamed of being so damned poor!

What must Fr. Johnson be thinking of our chicken coop? He must be laughing up his sleeve at our pretense. Eating in the kitchen, of all things. Can you imagine—inviting a priest to a dump like this?

Becoming more furious by the minute, practically sputtering, I took off again, rode my bike ten blocks down Military Road before heading back. And when I hit our corner, I saw David standing out in front of the house, looking around. Seeing me, he came running.

"What's going on?" I asked. "Why is Fr. Johnson at our house?"

"Oh, that dumb Richard invited him. That's who he thought we were talking about last night."

"The stupid jerk! And what happened to Chuck? Is he here too?"

"No, he didn't come to church today. So we couldn't ask him."

"And Richard asked Fr. Johnson instead?"

"No, he really thought that's who you wanted to invite. Aren't you coming in? Ma's holding dinner for you."

"No," I stormed. "I'm not coming in. Not until he's gone." And as I turned my bike around, headed off: "And don't you dare tell anybody you saw me out here."

Another hour of aimless riding. Surely Fr. Johnson must be gone by now. This time when I hit the corner, there was my little sister, Martha, age seven, standing out front. I waved her down the street.

"Why didn't you come home, Thomas?" she asked. "We were waiting for you. We had a wonderful dinner. Ma's really mad at you."

"I don't want to come home while Fr. Johnson is there," I snapped. "And don't tell anyone you saw me out here either, do you hear?"

Little did I guess the meaning of her shy, consenting smile.

I waited for twenty minutes more, well concealed behind the billboard, until, finally, I saw Fr. Johnson at the door, saying goodbye to Ma and Daddy. As he walked to the corner, his head was down, he appeared lost in thought. I shrank further into the bushes. But he was totally preoccupied and never looked up.

When I finally went home and entered the house, there were Ma and Daddy sitting on our threadbare couch, hurt and anger in their eyes—while my brothers and sister stood off to one side, now-you're-gonna-get-it expressions on their faces.

What had happened was that Martha had immediately gone into the house and loudly announced: "I saw Thomas out there, and he said he won't come home because Fr. Johnson's here."

I later learned that Fr. Johnson had paled, gone silent. Up to that time, he'd been talking freely and enjoying his visit. He'd told Ma several times how much he'd enjoyed the tamales. After Martha's announcement, he talked less and less, and the long pauses became painfully awkward.

Ma and Daddy had been stunned, embarrassed, and they made what apologies they could, but it didn't help. Shortly he'd risen, thanked them again, and departed.

"Why did you do it, Thomas?" Ma said, a bleak look on her face. "He was waiting especially to see you. I told him about your paper route and explained that something had probably gone wrong and..." She paused. "You should have seen him. He was so hurt."

I was pretty sick myself. I felt all drained inside, at a total loss for words. But I couldn't answer her question directly—I couldn't tell her I was ashamed of my parents, of my brothers and sister, of my shabby house.

"I don't like Fr. Johnson," I said, almost shouting. "I hate him. I don't want to have anything to do with him. I want Fr. Dunnigan back."

I don't know why, but I think Ma understood my kid pain at that moment; she knew how much I'd loved Fr. Dunnigan. For a time she went silent. That look in her eyes made me feel like the lowest of crawly creatures. I had to turn away.

"You come with me...to basement," Daddy said gruffly. "I teach you to make shame you Mama like that."

But Ma waved him off. "No, José, leave him alone," she said. "I think he's sorry for what he did."

After things had calmed down a bit, Ma told me I had to go down to the church, to the Parish Hall, where Fr. Johnson's upstairs apartment was located. I was to ring the bell, and when he answered, I was to apologize for being such a rude boy. I was to tell him this wasn't the way my parents had brought me up.

I headed out reluctantly, my feet feeling like they were encased in lead. I had never been so ashamed. The closer I got to the church, the more slowly I walked. My heart was pounding by the time I reached the front door of his apartment. I put my hand up to ring the bell.

But no matter how much I wanted to obey Ma, I simply couldn't make myself push the button. Instead I turned away, ran east across the bridge all the way up to Main Street. After a while, calming down somewhat, I retraced my steps and passed the church on the opposite side of Division Street.

I moped around for another twenty minutes before I finally

returned home. It was almost 5:00 by then.

"Did you tell him?" Ma insisted. "Now, don't lie to me."

"Yes, I told him....I told him I was sorry. He was nice about it. He said he understood. He said he forgave me." And then, finally, that wee-small-voice cutting in: "He said I should just give him a chance."

Ma let it drop at that. It was lucky she didn't press me further. For I'd certainly have blubbered all over the place.

"Come, Thomas," she said, "You must be starved. I'll fix you something to eat.

I *was* hungry—I was *famished*. It had been almost eight hours since I'd eaten. And yet, as I forced down two of the remaining tamales, I tasted nothing. I might as well have been eating sand.

CHAPTER THIRTY

Digging to China

I was living on John Street when Johnson Smith & Company entered my life. Instant addiction. I became a junk junkie almost overnight.

Johnson Smith was a major novelty house based in Detroit. I found their ads on the back of my comic books, all describing an endless variety of dirt-cheap gadgets. "Surprise your friends with our unique joy buzzer!" "Learn how to throw your voice!" "Try our amazing rubber nails!"

Rubber cigars, whoopee cushions, magic tricks, gag auto-engine bombs, nose flutes—page after page of the most useless gadgetry known to mankind.

To me, of course (Mr. Dimwit here, may I help you?), these became instant must-haves. I pored over their catalogs. I read every line of the super-fine print from cover to cover.

I want it, I want it!

I was thirteen, in eighth grade, and was earning modest but steady money with my newsboy ventures. This new found world of trash was well within my means. I was evolving into a solid American citizen, backbone of the nation—a consumer!

A few other Johnson Smith standouts: a magic money maker. Insert a blank sheet of paper, and a dollar bill comes out. (Was the U.S. Treasury aware?) A Baltimore printing press, $8.00. Honest to God, a real—albeit small—printing press plus ink, type, type trays, etc. A player roll harmonica—insert the player roll, turn the handle and blow—for $2.50. Player rolls (fifteen cents) came extra.

Wedding rings—ridiculous even by Depression standards—were

fifty cents. Oh, you lucky lady!

Saucy water glasses, which, when filled, revealed nude babes cost fifteen cents. A See-O-Scope—look over fences, around corners—twenty-five cents. Another quarter special: "Live chameleons, watch them change color." I didn't order, but couldn't help but wonder how the poor things survived the U.S. mails, especially in winter.

My first buy was an electric telegraph set for fifteen cents. "Send messages to your friends!" Yeah, if they're in the same room. However, I did learn Morse code, one of the few Boy Scout tests I managed to pass. I later ordered a "Made by Navaho artists, genuine sterling silver ring," a coiled rattlesnake on its face. Fifty cents. And yes, it *was* real silver! I wore it proudly for years.

Then the educational items: *Five Minute Harmonica Course, From Dancehall to White Slavery, The Book of Great Secrets: One Thousand Ways of Getting Rich, The Mystery of Love Making*. The sex manuals (most ten to fifteen cents) definitely intrigued. After my torrid fling with Lamonica Garvey, I sensed that this was definitely information every young boy—this young boy especially—must have. But how to sneak it past Ma?

As always, one thing leads to another, and eventually, among the how-to manuals, *The Beginner's Photography Book* caught my eye. I'd recently splurged on an Agfa camera ($2.95) and was tired of paying for developing and printing. Why not develop my own snaps?

The mail brought Johnson Smith's *Boys Photo Developing Kit* ($2.00). I was now proud owner of developing and rinsing trays, a photo light and screen, printing paper, a red bulb, and various bottles of chemicals.

I set up shop in the kitchen. When the supper dishes were done, the family gathered around the radio—my time to learn photo developing first hand. I'd turn on my red light—regular light would turn my film black—and go to work.

I taped a large KEEP OUT sign to the door. I might as well have put up one reading LEGIONAIRES WELCOME for all the good it did. My kid brothers never stopped barging in. Interrupted during a crucial step, I'd scream and throw them out with my bare hands. Then, muttering all kinds of censored words, back to work.

I was pretty much a flop when it came to developing. In the first place my Agfa took mini-film, tiny rolls selling for a dime at Ford Hopkins, made especially for tiny elves. A strip of twelve photos was barely twelve inches long and less than an inch wide; I needed tweezers.

Time and time again I ended up with nothing but a strip of black celluloid. Later on—never say die—I could make out the dimmest of images. When I printed these, exposing sensitive scraps of photo paper to the light box, they emerged semi-dark. *Who is that? Martha? David? Our dog Snoopy?*

I trucked down to Valin's hobby shop one afternoon—film processing kept his doors open—and asked Mr. Valin how to improve my technique. He sent me a sly smile and said, "Now, Tom, if I told you that, I'd be out of business in a big hurry, wouldn't I?"

Eventually, after much trial and error, I learned how to make my photos come out clear enough so that I could actually recognize my subjects. Several of these are still found in one of my early photo albums.

Revolting turnabout: By the time I finally perfected my photo lab skills, wouldn't you know, I simply lost interest. A couple months later, my photo equipment cluttering my bedroom, I threw it all into a box and stored it in our backyard barn. When we moved from John Street, the whole mess went to the curb.

Goodbye, Ansel Adams.

And if it wasn't enough that I had schoolwork, a paper route, house chores, and my many hobbies—didn't Daddy pull a double-whammy on his boys?

Previously mentioned: Our John Street shack was jerry-built, the oversized kitchen definitely an afterthought. It had simply been pasted onto the original structure. And where there was no basement under the main house, there *was* one beneath the kitchen. Ample enough. Or so I thought. Ma did her washing down there; it boasted nice storage shelves for her canning. At the west end was an opening leading to the furnace room (and the coal bin), both part of the original structure.

Rube Goldberg had nothing on these bonehead builders.

As usual with Daddy, there were no discussions, no family meetings. With him things simply happened. What he wanted was a bigger basement. He needed a downstairs workshop. Call in a contractor.

In a pig's eye. He had a contractor—himself. His four sons would become his work crew.

We would dig that new basement room ourselves.

Simple as pie. Or so he told us.

A few logistics are definitely in order. The original house had been built on a concrete slab. Beneath that concrete lay a thousand yards of good old red clay. And we were about to dig out a chunk of it, a few truckloads at a time.

"Be easy," Daddy told us. "My big, strong boys help."

Every afternoon after school and on weekends, we would haul out shredded concrete blocks, then red clay, in galvanized pails. Onto a growing backyard pile it went.

Was there danger? Could the concrete slab break off, cave in on us as we dug?

Certainly. But Daddy was oblivious.

He started the very next weekend. With a pick-axe and a sledge hammer, working in a cramped space, he began knocking out the concrete block wall behind the furnace. Deadly dark, he rigged up an extension cord, and we worked by light from a single bare bulb. There wasn't room enough to swing a cat, but by dint of sheer determination, Daddy prevailed.

And would you believe? Nary a sign of Mr. Morgan…

It took one entire weekend to break down the designated span of wall. Then he attacked the stone-hard clay behind. The task, at first, was exhausting; only Daddy was strong enough to handle it. Mostly we boys stood waiting, filling our pails when Daddy took a break. By late Sunday afternoon—using a narrow-blade shovel and an ice fishing chisel—he began digging under the house itself.

Ma was dead-set against the whole project from the start. She feared for our safety.

"I put bracing and jack pole when we dig," Daddy reassured. "Nothing fall on boys."

Ma went away muttering.

Had Daddy applied for a building permit at the courthouse? No way. The building inspector would have looked at Daddy's sketches and died of a laughing fit. We were definitely flying solo here.

We dug and lugged clay most of the summer. When Daddy got home from the tannery around four o'clock, he'd go directly to the basement and start digging. After supper, he went at it again.

Chunk, chunk, chunk—we could hear his shovel and chisel upstairs. Daddy would come up around 8:30, all sweaty and dirty; it would take him a half hour to clean up. Then off to bed.

Say whatever you want about Daddy, he was a worker.

The next day our work would be waiting; his after-supper diggings saw to that. Later, when Daddy cleared enough space, number-one son dug with him. We'd chip our way to China side by side. I learned deep compassion for coal miners.

Finally, by early September, the room—ten by twelve—was chewed out; jack poles, planks, and beams were strategically placed. We started hauling concrete blocks into the basement, and Daddy, learning as he went, began building the walls. We kids took turns bringing blocks, mixing, and carrying mortar.

By mid-October, sluicing concrete through the coal chute window, two Mexican friends helping, the floor got poured. A week later, Daddy had shored up the ceiling with more planks and finished the wiring. His new work room was ready.

I had nightmares for months after. The hard, deadly boring work I could cope with. But the endless hours working in that cramped, damp darkness, the menace of those clay walls and the concrete slab overhead, haunted me every minute. Claustrophobic? You bet! When Daddy's workshop was finished, I religiously avoided it—a first for me. The place totally creeped me out.

Otherwise things went on as normal on John Street. I kept busy with my paper route, with my stamps, and with my radio programs. Johnson & Smith catalogs showed up in my mail box regularly, demanding immediate attention. This was the time of Fr. Dunnigan and my heavy involvement with the church. It was the time of the SPCB club, of the church basketball team, of Boy Scouts and the church choir. Busy, busy.

Bad vibes as well: Fred Garvey randomly drifted into the picture.

Who can say? Maybe the weeks and months I dug and sweated in Daddy's hellhole served as buffer; it kept me from running with Fred as much as I might have. Had it, in the end, perhaps saved me from ending up in reform school as well?

Idle hands and all that? Devil's playmate?

As for Lamonica, she came whispering at my window one more time. I merely shooed her off—no water-in-the-face that night. Her ardor faded. I saw her occasionally in the halls at junior high; she was always hanging on this boy and that. She never bothered to speak.

So much for burning passion.

CHAPTER THIRTY-ONE

Do You Want to be a Teddy?

Every Monday morning all one thousand-plus Roosevelt Junior High students gathered in the auditorium, each kid in his assigned seat—ninth graders in front, eighth behind, and seventh graders in the balcony. Using a standup microphone, Principal "Woody" Woodworth rattled off a bunch of announcements—upcoming events, new rulings, class changes—in a dry, precise monotone. We all sat in respectful silence, waiting for the inevitable lecture about school discipline.

"Just last Friday I saw some of our students who were..."

B-o-r-i-n-g!

After that Miss Halfpap and Miss Hanuska took over—Hanuska hammering the piano full force, Halfpap directing—and for the next fifteen to twenty minutes, we did community singing. Yes, community singing! The words were beamed onto a big screen, and we all joined in. We took it all in stride. Didn't every school in America belt it out on Monday mornings?

In seventh grade I sat in the balcony. During eighth and ninth grades, I sat in the lighting booth, where I helped man the slide projector. Never one for volunteering or joining anything, I have no recall of how I landed that job. But there I was, along with Tom Schuessler, slapping slides, joking, and singing along.

Seventy years later I can still sing the opening lines of such numbers as *On the Mall, The Lost Chord, Stout-Hearted Men,* and *Do You Want to be a Teddy?*

"Do you want to be a Teddy? Just come along with me. By the

bright, shining light, by the light of the moo-oo-oon..."

"Teddy," of course, being Theodore Roosevelt, our school namesake. The song was a takeoff on a University of Wisconsin rouser (*Do you want to be a Badger?*) it had an irresistible tune, and we kids raised the roof.

A few weeks before Christmas came "Up on the housetop, click, click, click...down through the chimney comes old St. Nick..."

Bill Grogan's Goat always brought down the house.

We sang patriotic songs such as *God Bless America; My Country, 'Tis of Thee*; and *The Battle Hymn of the Republic*. Still blank slates, our hearts brimming with kid patriotism, we went bonkers with the "Glory! Glory! Hallelujah!" refrain.

How would such dumb stuff sit with today's middle schoolers?

Welcome to Roosevelt Junior High. I was twelve, newly hatched from the grade-school egg.

Those opening weeks were hell; I was frightened and confused. *May I please come back, Miss Stanford?* New faces—*many* new faces—jumping from class to class, different teachers at every turn. It was a scary transition. But eventually I mastered the routine, and things slid back into focus again.

Roll room 135 (Abbe Sullivan) was where most of my junior high friendships began. Strange how transfers to a new school result in shedding old friends and taking on new ones. Never fails.

Much of what happened during seventh, eighth, and ninth grades whizzed by me, little of it registering. Recently entered into the world of commerce—newsboy magnate—nothing they were selling at RJS seemed important. The news must go through.

But there were *some* golden moments.

Previously mentioned was my half-year in band, where I was a star tuba player. Then the slide projector thing. After that, pretty much zilcho. I could have easily won a place on the *Roosevelt News* or *Review* staff, but—my inferiority complex alive and well—I never thought to try.

As with Miss Stanford, there were never to be forgotten instructors, mostly in the arts. Very special teachers like Miss Hazel

Epstein and Miss Vivian Gamble drew me out, despite my stubborn resistance.

Who in God's name teaches the classics in junior and high school these days? With Miss Gamble, we read (and understood) *The Rime of the Ancient Mariner, Sohrab and Rustum, The Gold-Bug, The Man Without a Country, Tales From The Alhambra, Ivanhoe* (how I loved the gallantry!), and *A Midsummer's Night Dream.* These just for starters. And while they may have been a tedious bore to most of my classmates, I was in hog heaven.

Water, water, every where,
And all the boards did shrink;
Water, water everywhere,
Nor any drop to drink.

And from elsewhere in *Rime*:

To Mary Queen the praise be given!
She sent the gentle sleep from Heaven
That slid into my soul.

I still remember stuff like that?

Miss Gamble was slim and had long dark hair and a ghostly white complexion. I nursed a silent crush; to me she was one of the most beautiful teachers ever. One morning she read Poe's *Annabel Lee* to the class. I sat enchanted by her hauntingly expressive voice. She put so much of herself into the reading—this for a bunch of eighth-grade numb-heads? Dedication indeed.

Later in life the opening verses became surefire heart-melter when I promoted various girlfriends. "*I* was a child and *she* was a child, in this kingdom by the sea..." Dear God! Who says boys aren't sensitive?

In Miss Epstein's class, we learned poems by heart—and delivered them before the class with feeling! I still recite Richard Le Gallienne's *I Meant to Do My Work Today* to this day.

Epstein was very emotional and wept easily. On Armistice Day at eleven o'clock sharp—the class facing east, standing silent for a long minute to honor our fallen troops—I glanced over to see tears streaming down her face. Not a strong disciplinarian, she also wept when we goons misbehaved, and some took advantage. However, this house ape settled down, but fast, whenever the water works started.

Another poem I learned—a real choker—was Eugene Fields' *Little Boy Blue*. It was written, Miss Epstein informed, by a Chicago columnist on the anniversary of his little boy's death. I asked for a different poem; I didn't want to blubber in front of the class. I remember every word of it to this day, but I'll be damned if I can get past the second verse.

> Time was when the little toy dog was new,
> And the soldier was passing fair;
> And that was the time when our Little Boy Blue
> Kissed them and put them there.

Go ahead, break my heart.

Art was also my big noise at Roosevelt, and I had two splendid art teachers, Jean Tack and Ernestine Wagner. I mostly got A's. Except one semester.

One morning during second hour, in Miss Wagner's class, she happened by while Milton Dietz and I were whispering. She accused us of talking dirty. Out in the hallway, she kept accusing, and we kept denying. She went into her classroom and emerged with a note.

"Take this to the office," she ordered.

Well, when assistant principal Ed Schultz read the note, he took us into his office and commenced chewing us out. Again and again we denied we'd done anything wrong (we honestly hadn't; Miss Wagner had misheard), but Schultz kept at it.

Milton, who was a slight, sawed-off kid and timid as hell, was slouching against the wall. Abruptly Schultz reached over and slapped him, hard, right across the face.

"Stand up straight when I'm talking to you," he snarled.

Well! We certainly stood up straight. Our story never sailed, and we drew a week's worth of detention. Big serious. Money out of my pocket. I was an hour late every day taking my downtown stand to sell *The Reporter*.

Such administrative behavior wouldn't pass today. But Milton never said a word to his father. Nor I to mine. In those days if you mentioned school discipline, you got whacked twice as hard at home. Daddy was real handy with that.

Were Mr. Schultz alive today, he'd certainly think twice before swatting Milton. At seventeen Milton enlisted in the Marines and fought twenty-six days on Iwo Jima, surviving without a scratch. He now stands over six feet and weighs in at two-twenty. Whenever we meet these days, we laughingly recall that sad/funny incident.

I sat behind a genius-type gal named Fern Pygall in Miss Ford's science class—red hair, done in Shirley Temple curls, freckles on top of freckles. As a prank, I'd pick leaves from a plant on the window sill, roll them into little green worms, and drop them on the back of her neck to make her scream.

What a ruckus! (To be continued.)

While most boys back then loved manual arts—woodworking, electricity, metal arts, drafting—most of it pretty much sailed over my head. I remember my woodworking semester with Mr. C.V. Liner best.

Liner was in his fifties but looked and acted like he was eighty. Grouchy with a capital G. And particular? Nothing was ever good enough for him. We made broom racks, book stands, and letter holders. We'd bring a nickel or a dime, and Liner would issue a piece of pine, oak, or maple. Before we could begin the project, we must square the piece. Using a plane and a square, we trimmed every edge to exactly ninety degrees.

Well, hell, didn't that stock come from the lumber yard already squared? That wasn't good enough for Mr. Liner—square it again, dummy. But then if he was particular, so was I. By the time I finished, my piece shrank by fifty percent. Some wimpy broom rack that was. Whisk brooms maybe.

We also learned to stain and apply varnish. I got a C. I'd have gladly taken an F to see that old geezer—just once—crack a smile.

Apparently all I could build were boats that barely floated.

Evil, extracurricular activity transpired behind Liner's back. Some precocious weasel—I never found out who—kept passing around badly typed, X-rated stories. Why Liner never caught us reading them, I'll never know. He sure caught us at everything else. Sensing that they were naughty—little prig—I usually passed them on unopened. I'd already done birds and bees with Bob Keller. I was sure I knew it all.

How wrong I was. One afternoon, surrendering to temptation, I unfolded and read one. Had Liner been watching he'd certainly have seen smoke roiling from my ears. Then and there my world tipped precariously. Even worse was a flip-book that later was passed along. Holy smoke! Did men and women actually do things like that?

Woodworking wasn't a total loss after all.

In metal working I made a flour scoop; in electricity I learned how to do three-way wiring. In drafting—it was art, after all—I drew compliments galore from Mr. Atwood. This skill featured prominently in later years.

The Depression still with us—especially for the Ramirez family—there were privations. One of these involved the annual ninth grade trip to the State Capitol in Madison. There was a fee—$4 for the bus plus money for a restaurant stop—but Ma couldn't afford it. No need for embarrassment; a couple dozen other kids couldn't raise the money either. We urchins spent the day in study hall, basically marking time.

Hard to believe, but it wasn't until ninth grade that I discovered I was going blind. It was in Mr. Hlinak's algebra class (I just wasn't getting algebra—never did) that the seals were finally lifted.

Revelation: I simply couldn't see the blackboard. How hard is that to figure out?

Not until the school nurse did her annual eye exam—first line STUPID, second line BONEHEAD—did I come awake. I actually had to be told: "Thomas, you need glasses."

Meet Mr. Four-Eyes.

No plastic glasses back then, and how many times I dropped and broke mine, I don't care to think about. Poor Ma and Daddy. Here money was scarcer than dancing pigs, and clumsy Thomas kept running up optometrist bills.

And last, but not least—stirring RJS finale—my first real date:

Her name was Helen Markert. She was a tiny thing, and I found her most pretty. A ninth grader by then, I died inch-by-agonizing-inch before mustering enough courage to ask her out. I almost keeled over when she said yes.

That Friday evening I brushed my teeth, scrubbed my face twice, and combed my hair five times, applying generous daubs of Rose Hair Oil, before setting out. A frigid January night, I wore my best winter jacket (J.C. Penney, $1.98). Living on Tompkins Street then, I walked at least two miles to Helen's house on W. Arndt Street. We trekked another mile to the Retlaw Theater without giving it a second thought.

If you went anywhere during the Depression, you walked. Unless you knew how to fly.

The name of the movie? Does it matter? I was at *a* movie—with *a* girl. *An event!* (My disastrous *Rio* matinee with Jenny at age seven doesn't count.) Halfway through the show, I sprang for a bag of popcorn, and our hands brushed as we dipped in. Talk about thrills up and down your spine! Later I got my guts together and reached over and took her hand. And when she didn't pull away—sheer electricity!

And hell, hadn't I splurged—twenty-five cents for her ticket, a dime for popcorn? Didn't I deserve better payback? Ten minutes later, I put my arm around her. Well, not quite. What I did was put my arm on the back of her seat. Then I timidly lowered my hand onto her right shoulder.

Was that a Casanova move or what?

Helen never said a word; nor did she shrug my hand away. So we sat until the movie ended, my arm numb as stone by then. Bliss!

We stopped at Stateson's Restaurant afterward, where I blew forty more cents on two hot-fudge sundaes. How grownup can you get? Then I walked her home.

I flirted with the utterly outrageous idea of laying a quick kiss on her before she went in. After all, an experienced kisser like me (memory of Lamonica's basement lip-lock session still alive), I could certainly bring it off. But, nope, no nerve. If Helen was expecting such, she never let on. Did she linger a bit before going in?

"Thank you, Tom," she said at the last. "I had a really nice time."

Here was my opening—grab it, dummy! So what did I do? I took her hand and gave it a weak, clumsy shake. "Goodnight, Helen. I had fun too."

Then I headed down the steps with more haste than absolutely necessary. Whew!

My feet hardly touched the ground as I walked home. It seemed I covered the distance in minutes. I was surprised, as I broke from my trance, to find myself standing at my front door.

I never dated Helen again. In fact it was early October of my sophomore year before I asked another girl out.

But after that?

Gangway!

CHAPTER THIRTY-TWO

Wisdom at the Ironing Board

Ma was a stickler for routine. Monday was wash day. On Tuesday we ironed. She seldom varied the program. I can see her now, with her water-filled pop bottle, the cap perforated with an ice pick, sprinkling before pressing. And the sound of her electric iron—flat irons ancient history at this time—as it hissed, then swished back and forth over a shirt or pillow case.

So many mornings, sitting nearby, we made quiet conversation. Sometimes she talked about mundane subjects—household happenings, school, nasty people on our party line. On rare occasions she lapsed into tales of her childhood in Oklahoma—how she came to marry Daddy and about their life before I arrived upon the scene. Those times my ears were out on strings.

Some very sad details spilled out.

In 1970 Daddy sent me a cassette on which he'd recorded *La Historia de mi Vida* (The Story of my Life). Imagine, a lifetime captured in one hour! So his history is in place.

Not so for Ma. It seemed, at times, that she was deliberately secretive about her past. But now and then...

"C'mon, Ma," I protested as she finished a very dubious yarn. "You and Daddy lived in a boxcar for two weeks? You're making that up."

"No, Thomas, it's true. Every word."

"But didn't someone come and chase you guys off?"

"Nobody knew we were there. We were traveling with Luiz Landeros and his wife, Verana. In the Oklahoma City rail yards...

there were hundreds of boxcars standing idle. Nobody bothered us. Nobody ever walked back in there."

Ever the neat-nik, I asked, "Weren't the cars dirty?"

"We picked the cleanest one and swept it out with pieces of cardboard."

"You slept on the floor? In a boxcar?"

She smiled. "Better than sleeping on the ground. Our money was running out, and your father and Mr. Landeros kept looking for work. So we just moved in."

"Was it winter? Didn't you freeze?"

"It was spring, but still, it got pretty cold at night. Even with the doors shut."

"Didn't you have blankets?"

"Yes, but not that many. After all, we couldn't carry everything."

"How did you carry your stuff?"

"We lugged it in a big canvas bag with a drawstring on top. We threw it over our shoulders...Verana and me too...and hiked along the road. We were going past the railyards late one afternoon and saw those cars. We just got lost in there. We could have lived in there for months, I suppose."

"How did you eat? Did you go to a restaurant?"

She laughed softly. "Hardly. Daddy and Luiz would bring home groceries, and we'd start a fire on the ground, get out our pans, and cook right there."

"Where'd you get the wood?"

"No problem...there was scrap wood all over the yards."

"And water?"

"The men found a faucet in the yards somewhere. They brought water back in glass jugs."

"Sounds terrible. Didn't you get tired of sitting around all day, waiting for Daddy?"

"Yes, it was really boring...nobody but Verana to talk to." A rueful smile. "She wasn't very bright. Then the men heard about work in Chandler, and we were off again."

Jobs kept closing down, and they were always on the run. Things were tough everywhere. Especially since Daddy didn't know much English. Ma helped where she could. Hard to believe; she was nothing but a kid herself.

The boarding house romance, her marriage at age thirteen, the death of her first child, my arrival—these are in place. What else to tell?

She was born in Guthrie, Oklahoma on March 6, 1908. Her mother was Jessie Eva Moreno. Daddy boarded with them for a time, and that was how they met. Grandma's marriage history was tangled because my mother's maiden name was Marie West. Grandma's first, or second husband? A third? I, totally delinquent when it came to genealogy, never bothered to nail any of this down.

There was a kid sister, Hazel, who eventually married a man named d Kirkland. A half-sister? A Moreno? A West? Something else? Occasionally I'd visit her downtown apartment—she lived just down the hall from Grandma Eva. Cowboy music was her thing. Her radio played Red Foley, Gene Autry, Lulu Belle, and Scotty all day long.

I sometimes hung out with my cousins, Caroline, Bryan, and Daniel. We were never all that close. A shame really. They and Grandma Eva were my *only* relatives. (The dozens in Mexico didn't count.)

Ma wasn't that close either. Aunt Hazel and hubby spent Saturday nights in taverns; Ma, ever the prude, frowned on drinking. But this was only the top layer. There was lots of other baggage.

Most galling was the fact that kid sister Hazel was the pampered, praised, and loved child in the family. "She could get away with anything, and my mother wouldn't scold," Ma once informed during one of our ironing seminars. "She always got the new dresses...I had a neighbor girl's hand-me-downs."

Here her voice fell. "I did all the work. I took care of both of them. And I was just a little girl myself. Your grandma wasn't right in the head even then. So I was really taking care of two babies... mother *and* Hazel. When your father came to stay with us, he must have seen how things were, and he took pity on me."

She shrugged. "Who knows, maybe that's why he married me in the first place."

There was more: "I think your grandma was glad when Daddy took me away." Now the hurt and pain really broke through, and I could barely make out the muffled, chewed-out words. "She pawned me off on your dad. Good riddance of bad rubbish, so far as she was concerned." Then, grimacing, she fell silent.

I didn't have much to say after that. I seldom saw Ma cry, so I was thrown for a loop. It sure soured me on Aunt Hazel.

Shortly she recovered her composure. She dragged up one of my shirts and arranged it on the ironing board. The iron hissed and raced across the fabric. Ma was killing demons.

There was an affinity, no mistake. Oldest son and all that. She told me things that she never told the others. I know because my sibs were surprised, decades later, Ma gone, when I spilled some of these confidences.

Hazel's husband, John, was a loud-mouthed, arrogant truck driver. When I was eleven, he took me for a ride on his motorcycle, and we sped to Oshkosh at eighty miles an hour. He took great delight in weaving back and forth across the highway. The cycle tilted at a forty-degree angle at times, the concrete three feet from my head.

I have never ridden on a motorcycle again.

Uncle John was once dragged before a judge for short-wiring the electric current to their apartment, and he paid a hefty fine. A smoker (chewing tobacco *también*), he once told me he could make smoke come out of his eyes.

"Watch close, Tommy," he said. "Don't look away for a second."

Then, as I stared at his eyes, he took a puff and drew the smoke in. I stared with super intensity but saw no smoke. Just then the lighted tip of his cigarette closed on the back of my hand, and I jerked, yipping in pain.

"Well, darn it, Tommy," he said, laughing. "You looked away. You missed it."

During one of their John Street visits, employing my fish-hook technology, I tried starting his '36 Ford sedan. But the hook shaft got stuck in the ignition, and try as I might, I couldn't dislodge it. He used some very bad language when I told him what I'd done. He worked a pair of pliers for five minutes before he wiggled the fool thing out.

Oh yeah, I remember Uncle Johnny.

But not a whole lot about Aunt Hazel. Except that she was always seemed to be putting on airs when she was around Ma, always criticizing and whining about something. Had I been Ma, I would've slugged her.

Eventually I learned that Ma was actually twelve when she married Daddy; she turned thirteen three months later. And where was she married? The ceremony—most likely barren and perfunctory—took place in the Guthrie courthouse.

She and Daddy picked cotton on their wedding day—under a searing sun—earning a dollar between them. After that they became wanderers, going from work site to work site in a mule-drawn covered wagon. She fretted over the fact that they couldn't call anywhere home, not even for a little while. When they did manage to settle in for a time and acquire a few meager household essentials, they were forced to sell them off for a pittance as they hurried off to yet another job site.

Ma apparently had no say in these decisions; Daddy was boss. She just tagged along.

Her education was sketchy. I think she'd finished sixth grade when school doors closed on her forever. Even so, she spoke and wrote English correctly throughout her life—no trace of hillbilly twang whatsoever. Everyone should speak two languages as well as she did. Those letters of hers that I still retain reveal a clear and concise sense of the language. Spelling, tenses, and mechanics are, for the most part, all there. To this day I marvel over her language skills.

Daddy worked in different coal mines, but oil was coming in, and mine after mine closed. At one company—Daddy working as a scab, of course—they hid in an outlying woods one long, terrifying night, watching union miners burn their camp to the ground. They lost everything. She was carrying her first child, John, at the time. He died three months later.

During another listen-in, Ma told of the time Daddy sold homemade ice cream on the streets of Tulsa.

"Your father was so shy back then," she explained, "he was afraid of his shadow."

I found that hard to believe. "And where did you get the ice cream?" I asked.

"We made it in a little ice cream churn. Just like the one we have now…you know how that goes." She smiled softly as she told the story. Happy-sad memories.

"Did you make lots of money?"

Ma laughed. "No. We hardly cleared expenses. Daddy pushed his little cart around the streets all day and come home with little or nothing. The people would cheat him when they paid…he was so bad at making change…and he never stood up to any of them. He'd come home so angry and discouraged. Poor man."

Daddy heard about work in Minnesota—sugar beets—and they drifted north. Once more they sold everything—except for her proudest possession, a sewing machine—and drove north with Mexican friends. They worked side by side in the fields, thinning and weeding in the summer, topping in the fall.

Next Daddy heard about railroad work in Wisconsin.

Fond du Lac, here we come!

Here, at first, they shared a house with two other Mexican families. Ma's voice turned bitter as she gave me fleeting glimpse into what life was like for a white woman married to a Mexican man. Double-barreled torment. For not only did the whites scorn her, but the Mexican women did likewise.

Later, when my sibs and I were born—David and I, fair; Bernard, Richard, and Martha, dark—we were openly taunted as *bolillos*. Half-breeds. The multitude of crosses Ma stoically bore!

But there was one small recompense. Close proximity to the Mexican wives conferred a unique schooling, for when she and Daddy moved out, she spoke fluent Spanish. Graduation day!

Yes, she was strict and unrelenting with us kids, and punishment came swiftly when we crossed her. If she sometimes went overboard with her discipline, it could most likely be blamed on the hardness of the times she'd lived through, on the hurts and deprivations she'd suffered. She had to take it out on somebody, didn't she? Lucky us!

Today, with some adult perspective, I understand how it all happened and can empathize with Ma over the bad shuffle life dealt her. Back then most women lived in the background; they had minimal status and existed as mere shadows of their real potential. Ma, a child herself when she married, was never able to exorcize this mindset.

At the mercy of her addled mother and her sister, she'd simply exchanged one form of tyranny for another. In Mexico, observing his mother's subservient role at *his* father's hands, Daddy's macho standards were carved in granite; this was the way marriages should go. She simply fell in line.

Ma was never one to put on airs or to try impressing anyone with her instinctive language talents. She was not a vain, showy, or pretentious person. During the time we grew up, she had, at best, two or three good dresses, all extremely modest and understated. Sears Roebuck chic. She'd have a stroke to see how young women dress today.

Her daily uniform consisted of plain cotton housedresses—easy to put on, easy to wear, and easy to launder. Otherwise she wore jeans and a blouse. She sometimes donned cotton or rayon stockings—silk only on Sundays. Mostly she emerged from her bedroom mornings wearing half-socks with her clunky, brown half-heeled shoes. An apron—a coat sweater in winter—completed the ensemble.

On Sunday she dolled up for church in long-sleeved, dark gowns (always with a tightly buttoned collar), hose, and black semi-pumps. The minute she was home, she quickly changed back into her shapeless housedresses.

There were times when I was ashamed of how she dressed; other kid's moms always seemed so much more stylish. Once I ventured to point out this concern to her. And why couldn't she put herself out once in a while? Her quick retort: "This dress covers me, doesn't it? That's all it has to do."

End of fashion critique.

Was Ma pretty? I suppose all kids think their moms are beautiful. But I never saw her that way. She was basically plain; nobody—except Daddy—ever gave her a second look. Her perpetual frown put people off, and her smiles seemed forced. They came and went quickly.

I have a photo of her taken on Division Street before I was born, in which her brown hair washes down over her shoulders. Later she wore it in a bun. Even later it was cut short, and I often saw her in curlers. (Vain hussy.) When prettying up, she powdered her face and touched a dab of rouge to her cheeks, but she never wore lipstick. She seemingly took great pains not to draw attention to herself.

I *was* her favorite child. Good and bad came with that status, to be sure. However I seldom received preferred treatment at her hands. She was just as cross with me when I messed up as with my brothers —I got my share of basement ballroom. Nevertheless, a bond existed between us that her other children never shared.

I was ten or eleven before most of these confidences took hold, and they continued until I finished high school and was whisked away by Uncle Sam. Many were shrugged off, but the more telling ones remain to this day.

The open discrimination did its ugly work, and Ma, though ruler of her household domain, was always self-conscious in public. Perhaps this explains how I came to be envoy—her number-one intercessor and errand runner.

I remember on Johnson Street, as early as age nine—our finances at low ebb—being sent to Molagaines Grocery Store—a block east on Johnson Street—to plead with owner Pete Molagaines for extended credit. And later to proudly pay up when Daddy somehow managed to scrounge up spare cash.

I did most of Ma's downtown shopping as well, even buying her personal items at the Ford Hopkins drug store. At the time I didn't understand the male clerk's sly smile when I handed over Ma's slip.

One summer morning I was sent to do some banking at the National Exchange Bank, located on First and Main back then. Here I turned over Ma's permission slip and a check (yes, I wonder too) and was given twenty-five dollars in exchange.

When I got home, Ma counted the bills and immediately began screaming. Ten dollars was missing! It might as well have been a thousand. "Thomas, Thomas," she wailed, "how could you be so careless?"

It must have slid from my pocket at the bank while stashing the cash. Calamity! The end of the world!

Not a word, not a moment's hesitation. I burst from the house and raced back—down Johnson to Macy, Macy to First Street, then east to Main, and into the bank itself—my heart jammed into my throat every step of the way. *Stupid, stupid*, I raged. *How could I have done such a dumb thing?*

If only some honest person had found the money and had turned it over to an equally honest cashier...

It was a distance of almost two miles, and when I charged in—gasping, shaking, sweaty—and raced to the window I'd just left: There on the floor—half-folded, pushed back against the floor molding, next to a discarded envelope—lay the ten-dollar bill.

Dear God, how? I thought. I couldn't believe what I was seeing.

I knelt, grabbed it, and was out of the bank before anyone noticed me. Ma wept when I placed the crisp currency in her hand. She couldn't believe my story either. How come? Had anyone seen the bill during that frantic forty minutes, it would have been finders keepers. It was a Depression byword.

And yes, to be sure. I was man of the house that day!

Part of the self-consciousness and prejudice-driven shame pervading those early years of Ma's life in Fond du Lac were not-so-subtly transferred onto her kids. I remember, even as late as high school, Ma would say—overcome by an extreme down moment—not just to me, but to my brothers as well: "Why do you try so hard? Why do you even bother? You'll never amount to anything. You'll never be anything but dirty Mexicans."

You tell me. With a load like that—?

And yet, despite this heavy onus, when I excelled in school she was greatly pleased. She quietly rejoiced with me over each successful picture I drew. And later, in high school, when I was writing eight- and ten-page themes for English teachers who'd gladly have settled for three, she was visibly proud.

Even so, she never foresaw college for any of us. Her boys would work in a factory, just like their father, and bring home a steady paycheck; her daughter would clerk in a department store. That must certainly be our lot.

* * *

Starting in my sixteenth year, a spell of moodiness descended, especially during autumn. When the leaves fell, and the world turned sere, I was overcome by a deep sense of sadness and loss.

Add to this my discovery of classical music (thanks, *Fantasia*) and Richard Strauss, Peter Tchaikovsky, and Sergei Prokofiev, whose dirge-like sonorities intensified those bleak moments. A particular line in Gershwin's *An American in Paris* always hit me like a stab to the heart. Often I tried describing these feelings in my school compositions. What emerged were "What is life all about, anyway?" whinings.

How Tessie O'Brien, my favorite English teacher, must have smiled at this adolescent angst. Nevertheless she always gave me A's.

Ma, because of Grandma Eva's loopiness, was understandably alert to any signs of mental instability in her kids. She couldn't help but notice my moods and fret. Genes again.

During those late Sunday afternoon broadcasts of the New York Philharmonic—Arturo Toscanini conducting—I'd lay on the floor before the radio, my face anguished, glorying in every plaintive note. Ma would send me a cross look (she hated classical; Bing Crosby was her noise) and say, "Why don't you turn that junk off, Thomas? It's so boring."

I'd send her a condescending "Oh, Ma, if you only knew" look and crawl deeper into my moody thoughts.

"What is it, Thomas?" she'd ask. "Why such a long face? Are you happy being sad? Is all this moping doing you any good?"

It was a phase. All teenagers are thus afflicted, I supposed. (Hormones?) Therefore I'd patiently indulge Ma and tell her why the music moved me. I'd try to explain how the season's passing, how falling leaves, how the bare trees hacked me.

To which Ma would invariably reply, "You just think too much, Thomas."

Yeah. That had to be it. Try turning that off.

And though I—and my sibs—don't ever recall hearing Ma use the *I love you* words with us, I'm sure love was there. Perhaps her

THAT WONDERFUL MEXICAN BAND

mother had never used those words with her; thus she was fresh out.

Try smiling and being benevolent when you have only potatoes—and no meat—to feed your kids.

But there were other times when she demonstrated her love and concern in unmistakable ways. Like when we gathered to listen as she read the funnies on Sunday nights, like when we played Old Maid and Peggity at the kitchen table, like when we laughed at *Fibber McGee and Molly* together.

There was the time she read *Mary Poppins* to us. We always listened to *The Happy Prince* and *The Littlest Angel* phonograph records on Christmas Eve. Then came the popcorn nights, the nights we roasted pumpkin seeds, the times we made saltwater taffy together—what a mess!—and then that one wonderful time she came outside and had a snowball fight with us.

No cause for complaint. The L-word wasn't really necessary. We knew it was there. Considering the times, we understood that she did the best she could for all of us.

God love you, Ma.

I know we did.

CHAPTER THIRTY-THREE

In My Merry Oldsmobile

During the Depression only bankers, lawyers, merchants, and the like could afford an automobile. It was 1940 before Daddy even dared think of owning one. Imagine, walking to work all those years through rain, snow, bitter cold. When he did break down, it was for a beat-up 1930 Buick he bought for the stunning sum of $38.

It was a beast, no mistake. Back then sedans ran two tons, were sixteen feet long, and had monstrous wheels. Most were six-cylinder and boasted 65-HP engines. There were three shifting positions, a choke, manual brakes and steering, and a floor button you tapped with your foot to dim the headlights. Daddy's Buick was a dark blue, four-door model; all five of us kids could easily crowd into the back seat.

Of course the heap didn't run. The seller, probably an enterprising Mexican friend, actually dragged it into our driveway with a battered pickup. He and Daddy pushed it into the garage, headlights facing out. Where, ever resourceful, Daddy would overhaul the engine, fix the brakes, and patch the tires—whatever it took to breathe life into the moribund wreck.

Automobile repair books were available at the library, weren't they? Hadn't he built a twelve-string guitar by reading a book? Couldn't he resurrect this dead engine the same way? I can still see Daddy and Ma sitting at the kitchen table night after night, poring over the diagrams, photographs, and text, Ma explaining and Daddy pondering words he could barely read.

In poverty there is unity I suppose, and all else failing, Daddy gained expertise from more mechanically gifted friends.

We were living at 361 Tompkins Street then, and guess who got drafted as mechanic's assistant? How many nights after school, how many Saturdays and Sundays I spent in that gloomy garage, holding a light, handing tools to Daddy as he worked under the car—helping him grind valves, holding down the clutch, and tightening tire lugs—I won't even try to recall.

Those times my kid brothers exhibited more smarts than I, and though they did help on rare occasions, most of the time, whenever the wheels started spinning in Daddy's eyes, they ducked out. But good old, dependable, ever-responsible, number-one son was always a half-step behind and got stuck time and time again.

Even Ma wasn't above conscription. Many were the times she held a wrench while I pushed a pedal and Daddy fought a new fan belt or brake arm or muffler into place.

His patience, determination, and optimism were boundless. If it took a lifetime, that Buick would rise again! It took almost three months before he got it started. A historic moment indeed, as we kids helped push the monster from the garage and Daddy hopped in, set the clutch, and turned the key.

All of us held our breath.

Time and time again the engine actually turned over, sputtered, and popped—but just as quickly died.

Back to the garage.

I don't recall ever hearing Daddy swear. Maybe he did, under his breath and in *Español*, but I wasn't aware of it. His favorite expression when frustrated or angry was "For the love of Mike." Otherwise: "What next?"

But he didn't say "For the love of Mike." Instead it came out a garbled "For da lova Meek." No matter how many times we corrected him, it didn't sink in. "Mike" always came out "Meek."

Finally, one day, it happened. It was a hot July afternoon, and once more the Buick emerged from the garage. Once more Daddy hopped into the seat, and made all the necessary adjustments. Once more we all stopped breathing.

Then he turned the key. The engine cranked over once, twice. And then: VAROOM! The engine roared, and the car shook violently. In deadly earnest this time: VAROOM, VAROOM! But now, when Daddy lifted his foot off the gas pedal, instead of dying, the engine kept running. He sat there for perhaps three minutes, his face tense, just listening to those six cylinders chatter. Not the smoothest timing in the world, but that baby meant business.

It was really something to see Daddy's reaction. Proud? Happy? You'd think he'd just won the Irish Sweepstakes. If ever a face reflected pure bliss, it was his.

Shortly the smile faded, and his expression turned grim as he shifted from neutral into first. Up came his foot, and the car jerked forward and moved to the end of the driveway, almost onto the street, where Daddy braked. Then re-shifting, checking traffic, he headed out. Second gear now. He turned left, heading for Superior Street.

Where he'd learned to drive, I don't know. From one of his Mexican cronies, perhaps? But what the hell, he smoothly shifted into third, then picked up speed, sailing due west. We kids were cheering, jumping up and down with excitement as he turned left onto Superior and went out of sight.

Four minutes later we saw him rolling south on Hickory, driving —we thought—like a professional. He'd gone north on Superior, then turned left on Western Avenue until he hit Hickory. Now he was coming back down Tompkins Street. By this time Ma was out on the lawn with us. Daddy braked in front of the house, leaned out the window, and called, "Come, Mama, come boys, come Martha. We go take ride."

We didn't need to be asked twice. We flung ourselves into the back seat, while Ma got in front next to Daddy, her smile an exact replica of his. Proud as proud can be. Her José had finally done it. Had she ever doubted him?

Daddy took us around the block three times, all of us laughing and squealing and hopping up and down in the back seat. We felt like royalty.

Then we were home, and this time Daddy drove the car *into* the garage; no more backing in for him. But as we clambered out, Daddy was already muttering, "Engine no sound just right. I have work on distributor. Timing no good."

Up came the hood doors, and in went his head. More mechanical magic.

That next Sunday we took a shake-down cruise. Ma had prepared a picnic lunch—real bologna and Miracle Whip sandwiches, cookies, even some bottles of pop—and at 11:30 sharp, we moved out. We could have just driven to Lakeside Park and picnicked there, but no, Daddy had grander plans. He headed toward Lake DeNevue, and—as simple as that—we would find an empty field out there someplace, picnic under a convenient shade tree, and have ourselves a wonderful time.

Once out of town, we'd barely gone two miles when we all noticed an acrid smell. We were getting over-warm in the back seat. Then smoke began seeping through the floorboards. "José!" Ma yelled. "*Ten cuidado!* Something's wrong!"

Daddy quickly pulled over onto the shoulder, and we all piled out to see what boo-boo he'd pulled now. The back wheels were smoking something awful. Daddy took one look, then hurried back to the driver's seat and looked in. Total exasperation twisting his face, he reached into the car and yanked something. And when he came back:

"José," Ma called, "what is it?"

"*Qué estupido*," he muttered. "I forget take off hand brake." He was furious with himself. And then, as sure as clockwork: "For the love of Meek! What next?"

Once the handbrake was released, and the car started again, we went on our not-so-merry way. Eventually we found a perfect field, shade tree and all, and had a lovely picnic. But Daddy didn't enjoy it at all; he was in a foul mood throughout. We pretended not to notice.

When we got home, he dropped all of us off at the front door and then carefully edged the Buick back into the garage. It took him two weeks to get new brake do-jiggies—brake shoes, pads, rotors, whatever—installed. Not an easy job. Ask his number-one assistant.

He drove that Buick for two years. Once behind the wheel, he was king of the world. But the driving was never smooth. There was always something going wrong with it. It seemed Daddy lived in that garage. And when he wasn't fixing, he was out there washing and waxing, making his pretty baby gleam like a gold tooth.

Somewhere along the line, he even went down to the court house and bought a driver's license.

Years later I heard a mildly racist joke and was immediately transported back to my mechanic-apprentice days: A southern California sheriff talks to his deputy and says, "I just love Sunday mornings." When the deputy asks why, the sheriff replies: "Because it's so peaceful. All the blacks are in jail, all the Poles are in church, and all the Mexicans are out in their driveways, trying to start their 'Chebby.'"

It was Daddy all over again.

That vintage Buick lasted until 1944, the year I went off to the army, when he bought a used 1937 Studebaker. And later, in 1947, prosperity truly steaming around the bend, he broke down and bought a spanking new Oldsmobile 98 sedan. His all-American dream had finally come to pass!

Another memory fragment: "Won't you come away, Lucille, in my merry Oldsmobile…"

Ah yes, Daddy. I remember it well.

CHAPTER THIRTY-FOUR

Girls, Girls, Girls

My adjustments to Goodrich High School were considerably less traumatic than those I faced at Roosevelt Junior High. I was used to high traffic by then. And while it didn't affect my studies all that much, I was growing up. Girls now loomed large on my juvenile screen.

But I was hardly what you'd call a Lothario. No backseat conquests—so common in today's high school parking lots—for this kid. I was thrilled merely to hold their sweaty little hands. A kiss? That would instantly call for an air walk.

That's how boy/girl went in those prehistoric times. Ninety-eight percent of us remained virgins throughout our teens; high school pregnancy was a specter of monstrous proportions.

When I consider the near-paralyzing self-consciousness I suffered, I wonder that I ever dated in the first place. (In class I feared leaving my seat to sharpen my pencil; I seldom raised my hand when a teacher asked questions.) And yet, as the sweet things became increasingly irresistible, I somehow summoned up the necessary bravado. Little did I dream how badly some *wanted* me to ask them out.

Was the poor boy brain-damaged?

One of my earliest "flames" was Brenda DeTroye. A senior, our paths crossed during after-school art class sessions. She was rail thin and had long, straight ash-blond hair that swung enticingly across boney shoulders. Crystal blue eyes, a tiny mouth, an exquisitely thin nose, a ghostlike pallor—picture a benign, blond Cruella—all served to set off her exotic (to me) beauty.

She was basically a loner and considered "strange." Probably because she outshone her classmates in the brains department.

Mostly she ran with Jeremy Dallman, a senior class nerd. They had Cokes together and often hung out at the downtown library. A wannabe writer, he was addicted to August Derleth.

Brenda was into such heavy authors as Aldous Huxley, W.H. Auden, T.S. Eliot, Evelyn Waugh, and Christopher Isherwood, who were, to me, aliens from Planet Xylophone. Even so, I hung on her every word as she talked *so intelligently* about these birds. She looked down her nose at my reading tastes. Why she deigned to hang out with me, I'll never know. Probably because I stood in awe, something few others did.

Brenda lived in a shabby house on Sophia Street, a half block south of St. Paul's Cathedral. Her father dead, her mother working at Model Laundry by day and waitressing by night, the place was clean, dimly lit, and sparsely furnished. No pictures on the walls. The parlor was cold those winter evenings we huddled on her threadbare couch.

We held hands. We eventually hugged when I arrived and departed. A kiss? Beyond the pale. Was she frustrated and puzzled by my feckless approach? Perhaps.

When Brenda graduated, I was back on my own. I never saw her again.

Remember Gloria from church camp? I did call later that summer, and we dated sporadically (she already had many boyfriends—her parents forbade her to go steady). Everything was very casual. When she arrived at Goodrich High School, fall of 1942, I was a junior, already involved.

Pre-Gloria, I saw a half dozen or so different girls, mostly one-timers and movie dates mainly. With friend Norm Jacky, I attended dance classes at Bragg School. (I'll never forget instructor Cleo Smith and his "Attention, class!" castanets.) Norm applied himself. I didn't. Upon mastering the square step, my brain (and feet) locked up. No matter: I adapted that basic step to almost any tempo, from foxtrot to waltz.

Now an accredited dancer, I began hitting the YMCA after-game hops. I'd swing away with various cuties and walk none home. Ever the tightwad. We danced to jukebox or disc jockey music (occasionally a kid band)—ballads like Glen Miller's *Serenade in Blue* and *Moonlight Becomes You,* Harry James' *I Had the Craziest Dream,* Dick Haymes' *You'll Never Know.* Mostly slow, dreamy stuff. My oddball improvisations on the square step proved more than adequate.

Another gal and I hit all the Community Concerts together—free passes, no other students interested—but otherwise went no further with our coulda-shoulda romance.

A telling example of what boy/girl was like back then: I dated this goodie-goodie named Kelly Anderson a few times before drifting on. On our second date, I tried kissing her goodnight. She pulled away.

Her actual words: "If I let you kiss me, you'll think I like you."

"Well," I said, amusedly pondering her silly logic, "*do* you like me?"

A long pause. "Yes, Tom, I...I...think I do."

"Well then..." I tilted her chin and planted a long, hard one on her.

No words of protest; no pull away.

Seconds? Thirds? But definitely.

Kid innocence? That's the way things went back then.

One day during my junior year, upon opening my locker, a folded letter fell out. It was from a girl named Ione. In essence: Did I remember her, and could we get together sometime soon? Big riddle. Who the hell was Ione?

An hour later, she clicked in.

Flashback to June, 1940. Dick Hecker and I are walking to Roosevelt to attend a choral concert when—typical Marx Brothers—he hits the curb and starts hitchhiking. Even loopier, a car immediately stops. A couple and their daughter are also concert bound. They know Dick from the neighborhood. Hop in, boys.

It's one of those wild, effervescent nights—end of our junior high years and all—and we climb in back with the daughter. She's a year behind at RJH, a total nonentity. I start kidding with her, and before we cover three blocks, I take her hand—spur-of-the-moment zaniness—and hold it the rest of the way. She smiles self-consciously but makes no move to pull away.

Upon reaching Roosevelt, Dick and I say thanks and quickly lose ourselves in the crowd. I never give her a second thought.

Oh, *that* Ione!

Well. For the next few days, there were more notes, now with SWAK—"sealed with a kiss," dope—printed on the back flap. She included her locker number, and would I write back?

After all, a natural born writer, why not? Wrong move. When can we get together, she kept asking. Ione was fairly good-looking—thin, with long, dark hair, a longish nose, nothing much in her sweater—but no knockout like Gloria.

We were living on Tompkins Street then. Tompkins is located two miles from Johnson and Chestnut, which was where Ione lived. One night she and a girlfriend appeared outside my house and commenced to call me out. I stayed put. The second night, when Ma asked what was going on, I explained and told her to chase them off. Which she quickly did.

"You girls go home. You shouldn't be out this late."

They didn't come back again.

The letter barrage continued. Couldn't we go to a movie together? Her treat—she had baby-sitting cash. Failing in this, wouldn't I walk her home from school?

Flattered, I gave in two weeks later. She tried holding my hand, but I shook her off. We stopped a block from her house; she didn't want her parents to know she had a "boyfriend." How about a goodbye kiss? No way. Well then, would I walk her home again? I told her no, that I already had a girlfriend—maybe two. Ione actually teared up.

Fini, I thought.

But no, the notes kept coming. Many times she'd wait at my locker. Seeing her I'd veer off. But one late April day she finally cornered me.

"I'm babysitting tonight," she said. "Why don't you come by?" She shoved a scribbled address at me. "Please, Tom?"

I'd think about it. Aside from my brushes with Lamonica, I had no experience with overly aggressive gals. I was curious. What, exactly, did Ione have on her speedy, little mind?

I showed up at the house around 8:30. She dragged me inside so fast my shoes got left on the porch. Kisses flew. The baby was asleep, the radio played softly, only one dim lamp burned—most romantic. Tonight, I concluded, I'll definitely learn birds and bees first hand. Wrong again. She loved the kissing and hugging, but whenever my hands wandered, she shut me down fast.

"No, honey," she said, "I'm Catholic. I can't do those things until I'm married. Please…don't!"

So, more hugs and kisses, some idle chatter. I was getting bored. Suddenly—noise out in the driveway.

"They're home early!" Ione hissed. "Quick, the back door!"

I was out of there like a shot. I hit the back stoop, promptly lost my balance, and landed on my face in the grass. Whammo! There went my glasses. Half blind, holding them in place, I fled into the night. I had a sore wrist for weeks after.

That ended our romance. I never answered any more of her notes; I avoided her at every turn. Ione finally got the message. She sent me dirty looks in the halls.

Along came Faye, who carpooled in from a farm twelve miles west of town. I was smitten. To me she was the most beautiful creature on God's green earth. Faye was in my Spanish class; we chatted often in study hall. When I asked her for a date, she agreed—somewhat indifferently, I thought. It meant an overnight with a townie friend. I later learned it was her very first boy/girl; she was as nervous as I.

Again, the big scrub down, the long walk to her friend's house. I made no moves in the theater, but after, walking her back, I tried holding her hand. She jerked away; she definitely wasn't having any of that.

I hung tough, decided to wait her out. She stayed in town several more Friday nights, and we got cozier with each date. A month later she invited me to her home one Saturday afternoon. I would hitchhike out, stay for dinner, and she would bake lemon meringue pie, my favorite.

After dinner Ma and Pa left us alone in the parlor. Our first kisses were heaven—light years different from those Ione extorted. Granted, she was a beginner and needed coaching, but she was eager to learn. I was thrilled, I trembled, I sighed. Faye was the real deal. It *had* to be love.

She invited me to the Sadie Hawkins Day dance and (observing Daisy Mae protocol) came to pick me up. Ma liked her—especially her hillbilly costume, her painted-on freckles, and corn cob pipe. She pinned a carrot corsage on my hillbilly shirt. We had a marvelous time. We whirled, we clung; she followed me beautifully. It almost broke my heart to kiss her goodbye just before her girlfriend bore her away.

Here's where it gets sticky.

Back to Gloria. Our early hookup had been easy. We dated often. Extra bonus: She was a cheap date. Her father, the editor of the *Fond du Lac Commonwealth Reporter*, had a courtesy pass to both downtown theaters. Gloria and I hit at least one free movie a week. Upon returning home, we'd sit on her front porch. Just talking at first, but as time passed, trying some tentative lip locks.

As I said, off and on. Another guy, a flashy senior named Jim Morris, came between us; they managed a covert "going steady" arrangement. (Don't tell Ma.) I was crushed—for a few weeks anyway. It was about this time that Ione got beamed down. Next came Faye. Too much, too soon.

Crazy, unexpected turn: I happened upon Gloria in the halls one noon hour in early May. It was definitely one of those "What could I do but laugh and go?" days. I had a raging case of spring fever.

Acting on sheer impulse, I said, "Hey, Gloria, what do you say we skip? It's too beautiful an afternoon to waste in school."

She darted her head around—was Jim Morris nearby? Then, sending me a blazing smile, she put her hand in mine, and away we went.

We walked west to a branch of the Fond du Lac River (mostly woods back there then) and hiked south along the bank for a few blocks. We spent the afternoon talking—hugging, kissing here and there, nothing more. I distinctly remember sitting with my back against a tree, Gloria lying in my arms. The air warm, flowers blooming, birds singing, we spent an idyllic afternoon together.

There was talk of getting back together again—perhaps after Jim left for service.

We returned just as classes were letting out; our truancy had gone unnoticed.

Or so we thought. No good deed goes unpunished. When I saw Faye in Spanish class the next day, I fielded some furious looks. She confronted me after, and gave me a real going over. Nothing I said would convince her that my matinee with Gloria was an impulsive caper, *nada más*.

I tried getting back into her good graces for days. I stopped her in the hallway. I sent notes. The same painful reply: *Adiós, muchacho*. Go skip school with Gloria.

Not only had I lost Faye, but I lost my straight A's in Spanish as well. She'd been letting me copy her conjugations, irregular verbs, and figures of speech. Can you believe? With my super grounding in *Español*, I resorted to cheating!

Grammar had always been bugaboo with me—in English as well as Spanish. I spoke and wrote the language perfectly, so why bother? But ask me the difference between an adverb and an adjective, and I was a goner. At year's end I emerged with a B.

Pure benevolence on teacher Gerta Benowitz's part. The fact that I could *read Español* perfectly (she often had me read aloud so the class could hear how chili-pepper lingo should really sound) was what saved my lazy neck.

By June I'd gotten over Faye—and with Jim Morris now in the navy—Gloria and I were fast track again. Movie time! Together at least two nights a week (frequent after-school Coke dates at Kramer Drug also), we hit an occasional dance, we double-dated, we roller-skated at the Armory, we swam at Lake DeNevue. A couple times she even cycled over to my house.

In summer we held woo-woo seminars on her porch swing—otherwise in her parlor. Her parents went to bed early. Dad would call down at ten, and after a few more hasty kisses, I'd walk home.

One night, during an especially passionate clinch, I actually broke one Gloria's ribs. Her mother gave me a real scolding. It remained a three-cornered secret; her father never found out.

We were still temperamental kids. When we weren't romancing, we were fighting. For some ungodly reason Gloria had an inferiority complex almost as bad as mine. She wept often. Nobody liked her. We were constantly bucking each other up.

We broke up repeatedly, sometimes for weeks, sometimes a few days—hours even. Sure, we were both miserable, but what the hell? It all goes under the name of growing up.

Gloria had long blond hair, which hung halfway over her face *a la* movie star Veronica Lake. I was gaga over Veronica, so ours was an easy tie-in. I saw all Veronica's films, I read every magazine article about her, I constantly clipped photos. One, then two—here we go again—scrap books got filled. *Sullivan's Travels* and *I Married a Witch* were special favorites. I catch them now and then on Turner Classics. Gloria was thrilled that I thought she looked like Veronica Lake.

Though I strongly suspected that brothers Bernard and David were doing more than just kissing their girlfriends, I still moved in reverent trance where my ladies were concerned. So I never went overboard with Faye or Gloria. If I'd almost copped a feel with Ione, so what? That didn't count. And yes, Gloria and I *did* get "fiendish" (my term) now and then. Who wouldn't, considering the long hours we spent necking. As for me, every time I got dangerously close, I imagined cold showers.

The saucy song says it best: "We stopped, and always just in time."

And so the days, the weeks, the months passed, and during my senior year I saw Gloria pretty much exclusively. We were certain that upon my return from service—heaven forbid that I'd be among the fallen—we would marry.

However, as things so often happen…

Many a slip twixt the cup and the lip.

CHAPTER THIRTY-FIVE

Remember Pearl Harbor

On December 7, 1941, the Japanese bombed Pearl Harbor, and the United States went to war. The world changed forever.

Newly installed at Goodrich High School, age fifteen and in tenth grade, I was, of course, stunned by the news. But then—in typical me-first mindset—I gradually became mostly oblivious. Life is so daily—especially *my* life. Would the good old U.S.A. win the war? Natch. How long would it take?

Was there chance that I'd get drafted?

Serious considerations to be sure. But not for long. There was a new school, new awareness. More importantly, it was time to ponder my future career path.

Daddy was working fulltime now, and we were no longer living hand to mouth. Granted, his wages at the tannery weren't anything special (fifty cents an hour?), but there was a check every two weeks. The effects of FDR's lend-lease programs prior to 1941, the surge of war contracts after—some of this fallout was bound to revive Fred Reuping Leather. People always need shoes. And now, all those army boots...

Thus, so far as we—and the nation—were concerned, the Depression was tip-toeing out. Daddy had sold the John Street shambles to some unsuspecting boob, and in late1940 we moved again. This time to a seven-room, two-story brick house at 361 Tompkins Street. Daddy paid $5,000 for it. Granted, a hefty mortgage, but to us, Paul Bunyan strides.

Added indication of our new prosperity: no pushcart enterprise.

This time Daddy hired a big truck, and we moved our stuff in one fell swoop.

Galloway-West Milk Company stood to the east of our new place—and again, believe it or not—a huge, empty lot spread to the west. The Fond du Lac River ran roughly four hundred feet from our backyard. There was a spacious lawn. A long stand of lilacs and peony bushes flanked the house on one side; a cherry tree grew on the other. And on insufferably hot, summer nights, a large sleeping porch to retreat to.

The garage was big enough for Daddy's tinkerings—plus a car if we had one—with an adjoining shed. Here one of Ma's wildest dreams came true: Daddy turned it into a chicken coop. Fresh eggs, chicken on Sunday!

Wonder of wonders, for the first time in our lives we had a phone. But there were drawbacks. It was a three-party line, and we often fought with our co-share neighbors. If there was an emergency, we could beg for calling time. I'll always remember Ma sparring with some of those creeps. And of course there were always interruptions and "listen ins" when we were on the phone.

To kids today, with myriad electronic toys and a new breakthrough every minute, this must seem so Middle Ages.

Again, as at RJH, my art and English classes were main focus, the rest was mere ho-hum. I had the O'Brien sisters—Kitty and Tessie—for eleventh and twelfth grade English. The more memorable of my heavy lit exposures: *Beowulf* and *The Canterbury Tales*. Ah yes, "Whan that Aprille with his shoures soote…"

Spare me!

At the other end of the scale, Miss Mary Ann Lackner worked spectacular art magic. In one my earliest sessions, she asked the class to draw (shading of cylindrical objects) a wooden, ten-pound, cheese tub. When she saw how I'd lopsidedly contorted it, giving it original perspective, she was impressed. Her encouragement throughout those three years convinced me that I'd one day attend art school.

Added assurance came in late 1943 when I won an honorable mention in *Scholastic Magazine*'s national art awards. It was a proud day when Lackner drove a few of her prize students to Milwaukee to view the Wisconsin regionals at Gimbels. A blue ribbon, a gold crested certificate! (But no money...damn!) My watercolor of a factory—one of my brawny guys in the foreground—looked terrific. At least I thought so.

If I'd had my first teacher crush on Miss Gamble, it was nothing compared to the one I had for Miss Lackner. She was a gorgeous woman—her figure perhaps a wee bit opulent—but to me, *muy fantástico*. Beauty *is* in the eye of the beholder.

Lackner reserved numerous art history texts in the school library; we must outline them from Renaissance to modern day. Ugh, and double ugh. However it was a valid approach because it stuck, and I can, to this day, still name Renaissance greats (Giotto, Raphael, da Vinci), impressionists (Cézanne, Degas, Monet), post-impressionists (van Gogh, Seurat), cubists (Picasso), on and on. I yell out artists' names in seconds flat when I watch *Jeopardy*.

Something that wouldn't go today: Miss Lackner and I became friends. She even visited my parents to practice her *Español*. I was often invited to her Forest Avenue apartment; otherwise I simply dropped in. Sometimes, buddies Norm Jacky or Dick Hecker along, we chatted until midnight. If my classmates were gossiping, I—original naïf—was blissfully unaware.

Though commonplace today, thought of teacher/pupil intimacy never entered. Absolutely inconceivable! Her roomie, Virginia Christopherson, who taught Spanish, was usually around and was equally warm and friendly. Mostly she tried jacking up my self-confidence: "Stand up straight, Tom. You *are* special. Believe in yourself," she harped.

Once I even took Christopherson to the movies. Another time I rode her home from school on my bike frame, her hair blowing in my face. Times *were* different.

It was always a respectful Miss L. and Miss C. I never overstepped myself.

In May, 1944 Miss Lackner threw a farewell picnic for Norm, Bob Khunz and me—all service bound—at Lakeside Park. And *if* there was slightest possibility of impropriety here, I attributed our closeness (whacko stretch indeed) to the fact that all the "big boys" were in service. These shady ladies could toy with our adolescent emotions all they wanted.

In spring I brought bouquets of peonies from Ma's bushes. We'd talk about art, about school, schoolmates, and teachers, and she kept pushing Michigan's Cranbrook Academy of the Arts at me.

I was reading adult novels now. I even joined a book club, ordering such books as *Kings Row*, *How Green Was My Valley*, *Three Comrades*, *For Whom the Bell Tolls*, and Saroyan's *The Human Comedy*. I've never forgotten the transfiguring torrent of words in Thomas Wolfe's *Of Time and the River*. His prose set off major mind-blitz. Later in life I read all his novels.

As example of my kid naiveté, Parris Mitchell, chief protagonist in *Kings Row*, is told by a female playmate that babies are delivered via the female belly button. To me, pure gospel. My birds and bees definitely needed finetuning.

Phantom remembrance of ninth grade algebra still haunting, I passed on the hard math. In general mathematics I learned to figure postal rates and how to balance a checkbook. Good boy! U.S. history with William Sizer was the only other class that stands out.

In those days girls wore skirts to school; slacks were *verboten*. When the dress code was modified in '43 to allow girls in slacks, Dave Herbert, eternal class cutup, arrived one morning—his idea of faux protest—wearing a skirt.

He got sent home.

Back then high school dudes often wore jackets, buttoned shirts, and ties to school. Eric Preston, the class nerd, wore a suit and tie every day of the week. I had two sport jackets and various ties, which I wore now and then. Once I even borrowed Bill Solberg's zoot suit. I felt so smart parading down the halls in it. Considering my infernal inferiority complex—I chose to call attention to myself? Where was my head?

Another house-ape move: As one of my electives, I chose typing, taught by Miss Hayward. But for only one semester. That idiotic lapse haunted the rest of my life.

An author who can't type?

So I wrote. I smeared oil paints onto canvas boards. I zoned in on classical music. And I more or less muddled through with my other academics.

THAT WONDERFUL MEXICAN BAND

Dick Hecker and I were pretty thick during high school. He was big on boxing; he knew every boxer by name, weight, and ranking. He fought in the Golden Gloves. Two days a week, we jogged two miles to Esterbrook Cemetery and back. Dick had a droll sense of humor and kept me in stitches much of the time. I loved his Mom and Dad.

We hitchhiked often, our longest jaunt being Chicago, where we visited an uncle of his for two days and got an all-day auto tour of the city. I remember driving past a factory where they built military tanks; we saw them being tested in a vast field. A huge thrill for hick town kids. I went downtown and took in an original cast presentation of *Porgy and Bess*. Ticket: $1.35 for a mezzanine seat. Dick spent the afternoon watching the plug-uglies spar at Trafton's gym.

Big turmoil upon returning home. We'd been spotted hitchhiking on a school day. Monday morning we faced the music with assistant-principal Art Filbey. Ma got called in. I loved her; she defended my cultural escape belligerently. Filbey never knew what hit him. We got detention just the same.

Never a dull moment. I set pins, I worked at Lalis Drug. I painted, I wrote, I listened to my dolorous music, I did my homework. And I dreamed. The three years at Goodrich High School passed in swift flow.

Oh yes, somewhere along in there I received my draft notice. The war *had* waited for me.

One of Miss Lackner's favorite artists was Diego Rivera, the famed Mexican muralist. She ecstatically described her visit to Mexico City's National Palace, where she'd stood transfixed before his most famous mural. It became a compelling dream—I'd also one day stand before one of his magnificent walls. Which had definite bearing on my last high school endeavor.

The city fathers opened the Teen Canteen in May 1944 (just east of the Lion Café on First Street), and Miss Lackner thought it would be wonderful if I painted a mural there. She was positive I could handle it. Dippo me, I went for it.

I spent every weekend of my last month at home there. Sometimes Gloria would sit with me while I painted (oils) on a four-by-eight sheet of Masonite.

The theme: "We Are the Future."

Skyscrapers, suspension bridges, a Mount Rushmore spinoff comprised the background. Grown men and women stood along the bottom edge—construction workers, engineers, nurses, teachers, soldiers, lumberjacks, and artists (of course)—you name it, I painted it.

It turned out well, I suppose. Artists—even wannabes—are rarely satisfied with their work. Miss Lackner was pleased; the canteen clientele seemed impressed. But six months later, the Teen Canteen closed (unbeknownst to me—in Texas at the time) due to lack of interest, and the mural came down. It got stored in the basement at Grafton Hall. There was a flood; the mural got ruined. A few years after returning from service, I rescued it—peeling and faded—and nailed it up in my Ashland Avenue garage. Eventually I tore it down, sawed it into pieces and burned it.

Masonite blazes nicely.

Fast forward to graduation day, 1944, when that "little red-headed girl" reentered my life.

Fern Pygall and I had sat next to each other in roll room for three whole years. We kidded, we discussed our current flames, I pulled her ribbons. She even typed some of my early stories for me. No sparks; we were just warm friends.

On the morning of Thursday, June 8, our graduation ceremony rehearsal was held in the gym. It took an hour or so for the senior class to nail it before being excused. Somewhere along the line, Miss Christopherson informed me there was a graduation gift (John Marquand's *The Late George Apley*) waiting on her desk; I should go get it.

It was as I headed out of the gym—I using the boy's door and Fern emerging from the girl's—that we met in the hallway. Totally deserted, would you believe? Both of us moony because our high school days were over, lamenting the fact that most of the boys would soon leave for service, we were both vulnerable.

I'll never know why, but I simply took her hand and said, "I'm going up to Christopherson's to get something she left for me.

Wanna come along?"

She didn't say yes; she didn't say no. Robot-like, we slowly climbed the three flights. I never dropped her hand. We said absolutely nothing. We didn't even look at each other. Talk about trances.

The third-floor hallway was deserted also. I opened the door—Room 335, I still remember—and we walked in. Then, just like that, no more than twenty seconds later, still without a word, I took her in my arms and kissed her—long and hard.

How tiny she is, I marveled.

There was an embarrassed silence when we broke, both of us more bewildered than anything else. What comments did she make? Did I make? Forever lost.

Despite my experience with girls, it was most certainly not my style to just up and kiss one, out of the blue. It usually took at least a couple dates. And where did I get off mugging the smartest girl in the senior class? (Fern would be announced class valedictorian that evening.)

Fate? *Que será, será?* Who knows?

As best as I can recall, we said absolutely nothing about the clinch. Some things just happen. Our brains spinning, we rambled on, neither of us hearing what the other said. Oh, a book. How did Miss C. know I liked John Marquand? It won the Pulitzer Prize? May I borrow it?

Make up whatever you want. The stunning kiss was foremost.

So we babbled. We left the room and wandered to the end of the empty hallway, where we perched on a window sill and looked down on the brilliant summer day. It was almost noon. Did I dare touch her? Did I dare kiss her again? Well, yes, I did. Not once, but three times. Each time she seemed more pliant than before.

Fern had a date with her boyfriend that evening, right after graduation. I was supposed to see Gloria; she had a graduation gift also. We'd cancel out. We'd meet after the ceremony and let things take their course.

I called Gloria to break our date. What excuse? God only knows. Fern did the same with Howie. I don't know about her, but I was numb the rest of the day. I have faintest recollection of the graduation ceremony. Afterward Fern and I regrouped in our roll room. We joined Ma and Daddy in the parking lot, and she came home with us. Then I took Daddy's old clunker, and off we went.

We drove to The Ledge—about six miles out—and parked in a well-known lover's lane. A late rain had begun; we had the place to ourselves. We must have talked and kissed and hugged—*such a tiny mouth, such an exotic scent, such lovely long hair*—for an hour or more, rain drops drumming on the roof. And then, making no further plans, making no promises—strange turn indeed—it was time to drive her home. A few final kisses and goodbye.

Gloria was foremost in my life again. But not permanently. Two months later she sent me my "Dear John."

Twelve days after graduation (June 20, 1944), I boarded a train that took me, along with hundreds of other Fox River Valley lads, to Camp Sheridan, just outside Chicago. From there, on to Camp Hood, Texas. You're in the army now, bub!

For the first time in my life—a fulltime job. A buck private, $21 a month.

And now, at long last—absolutely, positively—The Depression was finally over.

AFTERWORD

All but one of the homes described in this memoir are gone today, turned into parking lots. Honest to God! The Johnson Street residence still stands—overpowered by a huge, sixty-foot-high overpass. Though it's still called Johnson Street, the four-lane highway is the new Johnson Street and the new Highway 23. It runs due west, past an endless sprawl of fast food palaces, super markets, building supply stores, malls of every sort—commerce seemingly growing by the hour—and crowds into areas where once only farms existed.

The place has seen changes: An addition to the back of the house now usurps our backyard playground; a smaller, two car garage has replaced our long shed. The front porch is enclosed. There is even a badly pitted concrete drive. I keep promising that I'll knock on the door one day and ask if I might look inside for old time's sake, but I never get to it.

Steve's Bakery and the Tip Top Tap are gone. A house stands where we had our kid skating rink. So many changes.

The hobo jungle where we so happily roved, the site of Larry Manske's dip net, and the spot where we first launched *The Tar Baby* is completely overgrown with huge willows and oaks. Old Man Bascom's falling-down house is gone; an auto repair garage sits there. The Valley Coal Company yards—no coal piles—now harbor derelict semi-trailers.

Most wrenching of all: Time has cruelly shrunk our childhood kingdom. Everything seems so pitifully small now.

Following a futile labor strike at the tannery during the '50s, my parents moved to California, where they opened a small ice cream shop. It survived a year before it went under. One more of Daddy's dreams down the drain.

My mother died in Monte Sereno, California in 1980; she was seventy-one. I spoke to her on the phone the day she passed away. Busy with my insufferable dailies, I lost track. I hadn't realized that her death was that imminent. Her words were garbled and made no sense at all.

"I can't talk anymore, Ma," I said, my eyes hot with tears. "I've got to go now."

Brother Richard, who sat watch with Daddy at her bedside when she died, called later to tell me she'd brightened upon hearing my voice.

Sad excuse for a last loving goodbye.

Fern and I flew to California to attend the funeral. I wept again when they played a medley of her favorite hymns.

So many questions, Ma. If you'd only been around while I worked on this sad/happy memoir.

Daddy never got over losing Ma. He often cried when talking about her. Living with brother Bernard in Evans, Georgia by then, he suffered a stroke and was placed in a nursing home. He was mostly aware and pleaded to return to California: "I want to be with my people" was his constant mantra. (We weren't his people?)

One afternoon in 1992, he fell asleep and returned to his beloved *México* forever. He was ninety-three. In writing this memoir, my love for him—and Ma—found new depths.

Longed-for appreciation always seems to come too late.

As I sort through my memories of Daddy, this poignant episode flares up: One afternoon, after returning from service, he and I were puttering in our Tompkins Street basement, and he abruptly began to sob. Out of the blue, he put his arms around me and said, "Tomás, my big boy. You do not hate me, you please forgive you father."

"Daddy," I said, puzzled at the outburst, "why should I hate you? What's to forgive?"

"I spank you…my boys…all time. I was mean father. I want you forgive me."

We stood hugging for long moments, my own tears spilling by then.

And now, altogether too late: Daddy, I never blamed you. You did what you thought was right. You followed in your father's footsteps, as I followed in yours. The particulars of those basement whippings have mostly faded from my mind. I remember that it happened, but none of the hurt resides in my heart today. I forgave, I forgot so many years ago.

During one of our several visits with Ma and Daddy in California, she asked if I remembered a time when buddy Louie Williams and I separated brother Bernard from his jeans and ran off with them. Why had I been so cruel?

I took a deep breath and patiently reminded her of the countless times I was encumbered with the care of my siblings. I explained why, this time—a last-straw solution—we'd been forced to deal severely with the stubborn tagalong. She fell silent, changed the subject. Had it finally registered that I'd been surrogate parent in more ways than she cared to acknowledge?

At this writing, only my sister, one of my brothers, and I are still alive—Martha in Florida, Bernard in Georgia, and I in Wisconsin. Richard passed away in 2011, and David followed in 2016. A family reunion was held in Ocala, Florida in 1970. Thank God for that last gathering of the clan.

Daddy's work ethic has served us well. None of his children have ever been jobless. We've done well in our careers; we all live most comfortably today.

I *did* marry the "little red-headed girl." Fern Pygall corresponded faithfully during my two years in service. She finally accepted the fact that she was doomed; she *would* marry the village idiot. She marched resignedly to the gallows on September 20, 1947. We recently celebrated our sixty-ninth wedding anniversary. Two children, Gregg, a heavy equipment operator, and daughter Vianne, a PhD/housewife and earth mother—came of the marriage.

Chilling thought: How differently might our lives have turned out had Fern and I not chanced into that deserted hallway—at just that exact moment—back in 1944?

Life certainly throws some wicked curves.

I continue to suffer from "Depression hangover." Though relatively well-fixed financially and living in a spacious, nicely appointed country home, I am still close with a buck. I rigorously bargain shop; I hit the Saturday rummage sales. Invariably—

throwback to boyhood junking adventures—I study curbside trash as I drive past. Fern complains, but to no avail. Old habits die hard.

And, like Daddy, I am eternally busy. There never seem to be enough hours in the day. The old saw about becoming your parents definitely applies. I write, I paint, I frame, I mow, I blow snow, I correspond, I keep up our photo albums, I repair, I—

I'm sure you get the idea.

My movie mania has, of course, subsided. How to keep abreast, when hundreds of movies are available on TV 24/7? An occasional vintage film reminds me of my misspent youth; I still choke up bigtime at the close of *Captains Courageous*. I've seen The *Wizard of Oz* so many times I can recite the dialogue line for line.

The names of yesterday's bit players—John Litel, Alan Mowbray, Eugene Pallette, Fay Bainter, William Demarest, even Margaret Hamilton before she morphed into the Wicked Witch of the West—come to mind in a flash. While today's Hollywood cash cows barely register. The movie giants—Bogart, Tracy, Hepburn, Gable, Davis, Fonda, Wayne et al.—will live in my heart forever.

Career-wise, I taught school—middle grades in Campbellsport and Fond du Lac—for eight rewarding years; the rest of my life was spent freelancing. I authored hundreds of short stories, articles, and novels. I was a writer/editor at a Chicago tabloid for three years and a *National Enquirer* stringer for twenty-two. Though I never had a bestseller (nor even a hardcover), I am content with my publishing history.

We can't all be John Grisham, Stephen King, or Sandra Brown.

The Depression has left its mark to be sure. It was a tragic, threadbare time and yet crammed with so many adventures, so many whacky dreams—*and* with so much love. I can't help but mourn and wonder: How does life slip away so fast?

During random visits with my sibs in all corners of the U.S., we often talked about our childhood, and the stories flew. David would remember things I've forgotten; Bernard corrected me on certain episodes; and Richard had a different slant on the same event. The fire in the marsh, the bums, the alleys, the circus, the fishing—all would come tumbling out.

Martha, a baby at the time, regrets that so many of these whacko escapades passed her by. But how she loves hearing about them!

We share regret that we never lived up to Daddy's grandiose expectations and that our pathetic band fizzled. We all agree it was a most impossible dream from the start; he'd expected altogether too much from his kids—and himself. But did we really need those severe wakeup calls from nasty neighbors?

In the end it doesn't matter. What *does* matter is that the band existed for a brief time and that we lived though those perilous times and emerged unscathed—a united, loving family. The band became the glue that held us all together. Even remembrance of those times serves to build loving cohesion.

It seems only yesterday that I abandoned *The Tar Baby* beside a distant highway. Only yesterday that I flourished in Miss Stanford's sixth-grade class. And only yesterday that I nervously kept my first date with Helen Markert, that I left home to attend a war.

The kaleidoscope swirls and tumbles; the memories swarm. Señor Esteban. The Retlaw Theater amateur hour. The watermelon caper. What a rush! But again, what a wicked kick in the heart!

No trace of regret or bitterness comes with this memoir. Only an overwhelming warmth and an abiding respect for parents who did the best they could in such tragic times. Mostly I remember the sense of community, the sense of family. I remember total essence of love.

Many years back I taped Ma and Daddy as they sang *Las Quatros Milpas* together. I play it but not all that often—too much emotion. It's almost like having them back again. The electronic revisit hits me hard. It hammers home crushing realization of how valiantly they fought—babes against the storm—to create a decent world for their wayward brood.

And, dear God, but didn't they succeed!

THOMAS P. RAMIREZ was born of a Latino father and Caucasian mother on Feb. 5, 1926, in Fond du Lac, Wisconsin, where he and his wife live today. Following the Great Depression and service in World War II, he graduated from Oshkosh State Teacher's College and taught intermediate grades in Campbellsport and Fond du Lac.

In addition to this memoir, Thomas has written dozens of short stories for *Boy's Life*, *American Heritage*, as well as others and has authored more than 150 paperbacks, spanning such genres as mystery, military, and erotica. A freelance journalist, he also penned hundreds of articles for major tabloids, including *The National Enquirer*. Much of his writing has been published under pen names.

Visit allied-authors.org to view his complete bibliography.

Made in the USA
Columbia, SC
11 July 2017